The Big Book of
Bread Machine
Recipes

Donna Rathmell German

Bristol Publishing Enterprises, Inc.
San Leandro, California
www.bristolcookbooks.com

Printed in the United States of America
ISBN 1-55867-238-9

Cover design: Shanti Nelson

This collection is a compilation of the following books:

THE BREAD MACHINE COOKBOOK
Donna Rathmell German
©1991 Bristol Publishing Enterprises, Inc.
ISBN 1-55867-025-4

THE BREAD MACHINE COOKBOOK II
Donna Rathmell German
©1991 Bristol Publishing Enterprises, Inc.
ISBN 1-55867-037-8

THE BREAD MACHINE COOKBOOK III
Donna Rathmell German
©1992 Bristol Publishing Enterprises, Inc.
ISBN 1-55867-048-3

THE BREAD MACHINE COOKBOOK V
Favorite Recipes from 100 Kitchens
Donna Rathmell German
©1994 Bristol Publishing Enterprises, Inc.
ISBN 1-55867-093-9

THE BREAD MACHINE COOKBOOK VI
Hand-Shaped Breads from the Dough Cycle
Donna Rathmell German
©1995 Bristol Publishing Enterprises, Inc.
ISBN 1-55867-121-8

Table of Contents

The Bread Machine Cookbook I

Introduction

Shortly after purchasing an automated bread machine in 1989, I became frustrated by the lack of bread machine recipes. When other owners were queried, although excited about the machines, nearly everyone was dissatisfied with the available recipes. While initially developed only for the machines on the market at that time, these recipes have been tested and continue to be tested on all makes and models of all machines on the market today.

When this book was first published in 1991, there were no other cookbooks available for bread machines nor were there any manufacturer "help" lines available for individuals to turn to. People turned to me for answers to their bread machine baking questions or to share their hints and ideas. The Hints and Troubleshooting chapter is the direct result of many of these contacts.

I urge you to read the information in the chapters which precede the recipes themselves. Many of your questions will be answered before you begin baking bread, and many problems that you may have had will be avoided. The techniques you learn in these pages will help you to produce a perfect loaf every time.

Join the millions of bread machine owners who are finding delight and satisfaction in producing an endless variety of delicious loaves in their own kitchens!

About Bread Machines

The recipes in all of my books are continuously tested and updated as new bread machines are introduced. Because there are so many machine makes and models, I do not describe each. It is important for you to become familiar with the owner's manual and/or the recipe book that came with your machine. There are a few pieces of information which you must determine about your particular machine in order to know how to make any recipe.

Ingredient Order

Manufacturers indicate the order in which the ingredients should be put into the pan. In 9 out of 10 machines, you start with the liquid; in the other 10%, you begin with yeast and then flour. For example, DAK, Welbilt and Citizen machines call for yeast and flour first, so the liquid will not leak through the hole in the bottom of the pan. For such machines, reverse the order of ingredients in my recipes, beginning with yeast. The really important point is that the liquid ingredients are kept away from the yeast until the machine starts.

Recipe Size for Your Machine

You must determine the size of your machine. Machines are sold as 1 lb., 1½ lb. and 2 lb. machines. This may be somewhat confusing, because the weight of a loaf will vary depending on the ingredients used. If your machine manual does not specify the size of the machine given by weight of loaf, it is easily determined by looking at the amount of flour in the recipes that come with the machine.

In general, 1 lb. machines use 2 to 2¼ cups of bread flour or 2 to 2¾ total cups of combined flours such as bread flour, whole wheat, rye, oats, corn, etc.). For whole grain flours, 2½ to 3 cups may be used. If you have a 1 lb. machine, you will be using the Small recipe, depending on the ingredients and flour equivalents.

A 1½ lb. machine uses 3 cups of bread flour or 3½ to 4 total cups of combined flours such as bread flour, whole wheat, rye, oats, corn, etc. Up to 5 cups of whole grain flours may be used in most 1½ lb. machines without fear of overflows. Most 1½ lb. machines will take the Medium recipe depending on the ingredients and flour equivalents.

A full 2 lb. machine can use up to 4 cups of bread flour, although I find that 3½ cups usually results in a nice loaf of bread at or just over the lip of the pan. A total of 4 or 5 cups of combination flours (bread with whole wheat, oats, rye, corn, etc.) may easily be used and up to 6 cups of whole grain flours. Some machines are being introduced as 2 lb. machines, but the size of the pan is the same as the 1½ lb. pan, and therefore must use Medium size recipes. It is necessary to keep an eye on the dough to prevent overflows. A full 2 lb. machine will use the Large recipe.

After years of working with all machine makes and models, I can assure you that there are some variables and individual preferences in the sizes of recipes used. For example, one friend with a 1 lb. machine (2 cups of flour, generally) makes Medium recipes, which would seem too large for her machine. My father, however, has a large machine and consistently uses recipes with just 2 cups of flour; in the identical machine I use 3½ cups of flour with success.

Unlike any other bread machine cookbook on the market, I give you three different sizes for each recipe. If a recipe is too large, next time use a smaller size. With the exception of National/Panasonic 65 model machines, all machines can make a smaller size recipe.

A few words about pushing the maximum flour capacity of your bread machine:

If at any time it sounds like the machine is struggling with a large amount of flour, add a tablespoon or two of water (or more if necessary) to soften the dough. If the machine is struggling, it could cause damage to the motor.

The sides of the machine may require scraping to help get all ingredients to the kneading paddle. Once the dough has formed a ball it will do just fine and may be left. If it has taken the machine a long time to knead the ingredients into a ball, you can stop the machine and start it over from the beginning, giving the dough a little longer knead.

One of the main concerns about using too much flour is overflowing the sides of the pan. Usually you will end up with a mushroom — the dough may cook onto the lid of the pan or may not cook properly at the top. The real mess, however, is when the dough spills down the sides of the pan into the inside of the machine and onto the heating elements. Cleanup is a messy, time-consuming chore (I've done it often in testing). It is difficult to remove all dough from the heating elements, but it burns off the next time the machine is used.

It is wise to check the dough during the second rise. If it looks too high, use a bamboo skewer (or something similar) and pierce deep into the dough to deflate it. Do not use metal objects which could scratch the pan. If you have absolutely used the wrong size recipe and it is starting to overflow, remove a portion of the dough. This enables you to at least salvage something!

Bread Machine Features

Cycles

Initially, all recipes were tested using only the basic white cycles. Later testing has indicated that the DAK and Welbilt ABM 100 machines perform more consistently on the sweet cycle.

The same cycle may have many names. A sweet cycle may be called sweet, mix or fruit and nut. Most machines now have whole wheat cycles, but any machine can make whole wheat bread on the regular (basic, white) cycle.

You may have a specific cycle with a "beep" for adding raisins, a beep on all cycles or no beep at all. In any case, add ingredients at the beginning of the second kneading, or during the rest between kneadings. If you have only one kneading, add extra ingredients as soon as dough has formed a ball, about 5 to 10 minutes into the kneading.

Basic white bread cycles may have one or two main kneadings depending on the machine. Some machines have only a basic cycle which is used for all breads.

Sweet cycles should be used with recipes containing 2 tbs. or more sugar and/or fat (butter, margarine or oil). These cycles may have a longer rising time. The baking temperature is lower than the basic cycles for the higher sugar content of the breads.

French bread cycles may or may not have a longer rising time but all have a higher baking temperature to crisp the crust.

Raisin cycles have a beep to indicate when to add raisins, nuts or other similar ingredients. Generally the beep is about 5 minutes before the end of the kneading. The cycles may have a lower baking temperature (like the sweet cycle).

Whole grain cycles generally have longer kneadings and longer risings.

Dough cycles include the initial kneading of the dough and one rise, after which time the dough is removed from the machine, shaped, allowed to rise and baked in a conventional oven. This is the cycle used for bagels, rolls, pizza crust, etc. For best results, DAK, Welbilt ABM 100 and Citizen machines should be stopped after the first rise and before the second kneading.

Other Features

Timers enable the user to place ingredients in the machine and to tell the machine when to have the bread ready, whether at 6:00 in the evening or 7:00 in the morning. Most timers have a 12- or 13-hour limit. With the exception of the Seiko 211 and the Welbilt ABM 600, all machines have a timer feature. Recipes containing ingredients that could spoil if unrefrigerated (eggs, milk, cheese, etc.) should not be used with the timer.

Preheating periods are found on only a few machines. Basically the machine heats all ingredients to the proper temperature prior to starting the kneading period.

Crust controls are usually buttons pushed when you start your machine, such as basic white, light setting. Some machines such as the DAK/Welbilt 100 machines have a control knob. The controls shorten or lengthen the baking time by about 5 minutes.

Power outage protection prevents a short (usually 10 minutes or less) loss of electricity from stopping the entire machine process. If this is not included with your machine and you have a loss of electricity, simply remove the dough and finish baking the bread conventionally.

Viewing windows are a nice feature if you like to frequently check the process of your bread. It is always a good idea to check the dough about 5 minutes into the initial kneading to make sure that all is going well. If you don't have a viewing window, simply open the lid long enough to check the dough. Don't leave the machine open for long periods of time.

Cooling/warming periods. Many machines have periods to either start cooling the bread or to keep it warm until it is removed from the machine. This is to prevent the bread from becoming soggy and wet if not removed as soon as the baking is completed.

Bread Ingredients

Yeast

A living plant, yeast eats sugar and produces carbon dioxide which, in turn, mixes with gluten in flour to make the dough rise. Simply stated, without yeast your bread will be a flat, unleavened bread. Both active dry and fast-acting yeasts may be purchased either in envelopes (1 envelope equals approximately 2¼ tsp.) or in bulk. It is much cheaper to buy yeast in bulk in a jar or vacuum packed.

In recent yeast testing, the fast-acting yeast (sometimes called rapid or quick) consistently resulted in loaves that rose high than those made with the regular dry active yeast.

Yeast responds to ambient temperatures. It may be necessary to increase yeast in colder weather or to decrease it in very hot temperatures. Too much yeast may cause air pockets or air bubbles. Compressed (cake) yeast is not recommended for use in bread machines.

Liquids

Liquid ingredients should be warmed to lukewarm for the best performance. The liquid should be warm or comfortable to the inside of your wrist.— baby bottle temperature or about 110°.

Some ingredients which are used for liquid (fruits, cottage cheese) initially may be difficult to knead into the dough. It is helpful to take a rubber spatula and scrape down the sides of the pan and push the ingredients toward the kneading paddle. Once the paddle has picked up all ingredients, let it knead by itself for about 5 minutes and then check the dough consistency again for a smooth dough ball. If the process has taken quite a long time, you may wish to turn off the machine and start it again. This gives the dough with the correct consistency a longer kneading. Because the moisture must be pulled out of fruits (banana) or vegetables (potato or spinach) it may require a longer period of kneading before a judgment can be made as to whether to add more liquid. If lumps of the fruit, cheese or vegetable are still visible, chances are that you should let it knead longer before you add water. If you add water too early, you may end up with dough that is too moist. Should this happen, then you need to add flour, a tablespoon at a time, until a smooth ball of dough is obtained. Use very ripe bananas for the best moisture content.

Fats

In bread baking, fats provide flavor, make the bread moist and give it a soft crumb. Fats used interchangeably include margarine, butter, vegetable oil of any kind, shortening or lard. Some recipes specify olive oil as it imparts a distinctive taste; however, you may use any vegetable oil. Unlike conventional bread baking, butter or margarine need not be melted to be placed in the machine. Applesauce or apple and orange juice concentrates can be substituted tablespoon for tablespoon.

Sugar

A necessity in yeast bread baking, sugar feeds the yeast, enabling it to rise. In addition, it assists in the browning of the crust. Sugar substitutes for bread baking purposes include white or brown sugar, barley malt syrup, honey, molasses, maple syrup, and even jam, jellies or marmalades. Sugar substitutes used for diet purposes, such as NutraSweet, etc. should not be used since they break down during the heating process. Honey is also a natural preservative for your breads.

Salt

A growth-inhibitor of the yeast, salt provides a counterbalance for the sugar. It also brings out the flavor of the bread. If breads are not rising, the amount of salt may be cut.

Eggs

A nonessential ingredient, eggs are sometimes used in bread baking to add richness, color and flavor. Egg substitutes were used for testing with fractions of eggs. If you prefer not to use the fractions of egg or to round the fractions, you may adjust the consistency of the dough with milk or water or flour as needed. One yolk or white may easily be used for a half egg. One large egg equals approximately ¼ cup of liquid. Egg substitutes are based on this amount also. One half an egg equals approximately ⅛ cup or 2 tablespoons of liquid.

Flour

There are many different kinds of flours, grains or cereals which may be used for structure in your bread baking. As a general rule, white or bread flour should be at least 50 percent of the flour or grain used. A higher percentage will result in a low, heavy, dense bread. With the "rule" in mind, flours may be substituted cup for cup with other flours, grains or cereals. A detailed description of various grains and flours follows.

Prior to explaining the various flours and flour substitutes, some background information may be helpful. Any grain which has not yet had the hull, or outer lining, removed is called a groat. You will usually hear oats and buckwheat referred to in this way. Once the hulls are removed, the remaining kernel contains the bran, germ and endosperm. The bran and germ of any grain contain the majority of the nutrients. Up to 80 percent of the vitamins and minerals are lost by the grinding and refining of the grain into white flour (which consists of pure endosperm). A general rule is that the darker the flour (whether it is wheat, rye, rice, etc.), the more of the germ and bran are included and, hence, the more nutritional the bread. Any flour containing the germ and/or bran should be refrigerated for maximum freshness; at the very least, these flours should be stored in a dark, cool place.

While making yeast breads, you normally use a wheat flour base which, when kneaded, develops gluten. The gluten forms an elastic substance which traps the carbon dioxide released from the yeast. This is the key ingredient in the wheat which makes the dough rise. Other flours with less gluten must be mixed with wheat flour to a maximum ratio of 1 to 1. The higher the non- or low-gluten flour amount, the smaller and denser in texture your bread will be.

Wheat

The most common flour for bread baking is that obtained from wheat. One walk down the flour aisle of your local grocery store will tell you that there are several different kinds of wheat flours. Differences are due to where the wheat is grown (making it hard or soft), what section of the wheat kernel is used, or how the flour is milled and what treatments are provided after the milling.

All-Purpose Flour: A blend of hard and soft wheats that may be used for a variety of baking needs including breads and cakes. All-purpose loses many of its natural vitamins and nutrients during the milling process. Hence, it is usually "enriched" by replacing four of those nutrients: iron, thiamine, riboflavin and niacin. Bleached all-purpose flour is chemically whitened; unbleached flour is allowed to whiten naturally.

Bread Flour: The recommended flour for most of the recipes in this book. Bread flour is derived from hard wheat, meaning it is higher both in protein and gluten. You will find that bread flour will give you a finer grain bread. You may also hear this bread referred to as bromated, which is a dough conditioner used to enhance the gluten's development. If your grocery store does not carry bread flour, do not hesitate to ask the management to add it to their inventory. Bread flour is made by both Pillsbury and Gold Medal as well as many smaller mills, some of which sell via catalogs.

Whole Wheat Flour: Milled from the entire wheat kernel, it is light brown in color and contains all the natural nutrients. A healthy addition to bread, it is lower in gluten than the white flours and should not exceed 50 percent of the flour ingredients. You may also see this referred to as graham flour and sold in health food stores. Some mills label their graham flour differently than their whole wheat as the graham contains 100 percent of the kernel while the whole wheat may have had some minor cleaning and sifting. Every mill is different in its labeling, hence for our purposes, I call both whole wheat.

Gluten Flour/Gluten: The gluten protein is removed from wheat flour by rinsing off the starch. This is then dried and ground to be added to regular white flour. Pure gluten is slightly gray in color but does not affect the color of your bread. It may be purchased through a well- stocked health food store or by mail order. This is added in small amounts to your dry ingredients in low-gluten bread dough for a lighter texture.

Wheat Germ: One of the best parts of the wheat kernel, the germ is the embryo of the wheat berry. A wonderful source of protein, fat, vitamins and minerals, wheat germ can be added to all baked goods by placing 1 table-spoon in the bottom of your measuring cup prior to filling it with flour. It gives breads a slightly nutty flavor. Opened jars of wheat germ must be refrigerated.

Wheat Berry: Very high in protein and low in calories, this is the original form of the wheat grain before any grinding or milling. The berries must be soaked, preferably overnight, prior to use. They are the most common sprout-ed berry used for "sprout" bread. The berries may be bought in health food stores or ordered by mail. Store in a dry, cool place.

Cracked Wheat: Crushed, toasted wheat berries. Cracked wheat must be soaked a minimum of 1 hour prior to kneading. I always soak the cracked wheat right in the liquid called for in the recipe.

Wheat Bulghur: Parboiled, crushed and toasted wheat berries — some-times used interchangeably with cracked wheat, but does not need to be soaked.

Rolled Wheat Flakes: Similar to rolled oats, wheat flakes are available as a cereal at health food stores. They add a unique flavor and texture to bread.

Barley

Barley: Barley flour will only be found in health food stores. It has a very low gluten content and must be used in conjunction with a high gluten flour. Barley has a mild nutty flavor. Generally, barley flour is a low percentage of all flour used in bread recipes.

Barley Malt: A heavy syrup used in both bread baking and beer making, barley malt gives bread a rich, grainy flavor. Pure barley malt tastes similar to blackstrap molasses and the two may be used interchangeably. It is wonderful when used with seeds such as caraway, anise or fennel. The malt itself is made by soaking the whole barley grains, sprouting them, drying and grind-ing them. Available in a health food or beer-making store.

Corn

Cornmeal: Ground from corn kernels, cornmeal is found in any grocery store. Most commonly used is the yellow variety, but try also the white corn-meal which is milled from white corn. Corn is less nutritious by itself than many of its grain cousins.

Blue Corn: Used for both cornmeal and flour, blue corn is attributed to the Hopi Indians of the American Southwest. Blue cornmeal or flour may be used in place of any cornmeal. Blue corn is more nutritious than the yellow or white and has a subtle, sweet taste.

Oats

Rolled Oats: The grinding of oats leaves the bran and germ intact and, therefore, the nutrients. Fairly high in protein, oats are also high in vitamins B and E. Rolled oats are the most familiar form of oats to most of us. The grains are steamed, rolled into flakes and dried.

Oat Bran: Oat bran is nutritious and adds fiber to a diet. In baking of breads, oat bran will add a nice moisture to the texture.

Oat Flour: Milled or ground rolled oats. Try making your own in your food processor or blender: blend 1 cup at a time at high speed until a fine flour forms, about 1 minute. It is also available for purchase in health food stores or by mail order.

Rice

Rice Grains: Rice is no stranger to most of our dinner tables in the form of boiled grains. The most common grains found in grocery stores have had their hulls removed, hence most of their nutritional value.

Rice Flour: A low gluten flour, this must be used in conjunction with a white flour such as bread flour. You may find this in the Oriental section of your grocery store or in a health food store.

Rice Bran: This has recently been discovered to have the same qualities as oat bran in lowering blood cholesterol levels. As with all bran, it is the outer layer of the kernel and has high nutritional value.

Rice Syrup: A sweetener containing no fructose or sucrose. Syrup may be found in health food stores.

Rye

Rye Flour: Milled from the rye berry or the entire kernel, rye flour has a high nutrient content. The darker the color, the stronger the taste and the nutrient value. There is no gluten in rye flours; this must be used in combination with a white flour. The larger the percentage of rye, the smaller and denser the loaf will be.

Rye Meal: A coarser grind than flour of the rye kernel.

Rye Berry: The berry or kernel of rye, as wheat berries, may be sprouted and used in its entirety in bread for the highest nutritional content.

Soy

Soybeans: A very inexpensive source of high protein, soybeans are used in many different ways and foods.

Soy Flakes: Pressed soybeans which can be added to bread for crunchy, tasty bread.

Soy Flour: High in protein and low in calories, soy flour is often added to high protein, diet-type breads. It adds moisture and is a natural preservative. Soy flour is usually added in small amounts as the taste may be found to be somewhat overpowering.

Lesser Known Grains

Amaranth: Attributed to the Aztec Indians, amaranth is extremely high in protein, vitamins, minerals and calcium. You can find amaranth grain, cereals, etc., in your health food store and may find some in large grocery stores. The grains themselves may be cooked for a hot cereal, sprouted for salads or breads, toasted as nuts or even popped like popcorn. If you pop it, keep in mind that it may burn easily without a small amount of oil.

The history of amaranth is fascinating. When the Aztecs were conquered by the Spaniards, it was discovered that the Aztecs were mixing sacrificial blood with amaranth. In an attempt to end this practice, Cortez ordered all amaranth destroyed. It was during an archaeological expedition that some seeds were discovered and later replanted, giving us amaranth once again.

Buckwheat/Kasha: This grain has a very high protein count. It can be found in cereal form in many grocery and health food stores. Nutritionally, it is rich in vitamins B and E and has a high calcium content. Buckwheat flour is most commonly known for its use in pancakes.

Quinoa: Pronounced KEEN-wah, this is a fondly remembered grain from time I spent in Peru. Recently available in the United States, this grain is quickly catching on even though it is somewhat expensive. Extremely high in protein, (anywhere from 14 to 19 percent), quinoa is also an excellent source of calcium, and has a high lysine content, as well as vitamin C, thiamine, riboflavin and niacin. Quinoa grains may be cooked the same as rice. The flour is expensive but worth it in quinoa bread, which has a slightly nutty taste.

It also has an interesting history: Pizzaro attempted to destroy much of the crop in an effort to weaken the Incas during the conquest. As time passed, the Spaniards looked down upon quinoa as a grain for "heathens" and discounted the nutritional values. To this day, many upper-class Peruvians consider quinoa a grain suitable for the indigenous only!

Hints and Troubleshooting

If you have just received a bread machine and you are not sure how to use it, I strongly recommend reading two things:
1. The owner's manual which came with the machine.
2. The introductory chapters of this book.

Don't be afraid of the new machine. It really is as simple as 1-2-3-4-5:
1. Measure the ingredients and put them into the pan in the order specified (DAK and Welbilt read recipes from yeast up).

2. Choose the cycle and the setting.
3. Press the start button.
4. Check the dough after about 5 minutes of kneading to ensure that the dough has formed a round, smooth ball.
5. Remove the fully baked loaf of bread from the machine 2 to 4 hours later, depending on what machine you have.

Perhaps the single most important thing to check is the consistency of the dough after 5 to 10 minutes of kneading.

Many machines have a viewing window but if yours does not, don't be afraid to open it briefly during the kneading process. Open it long enough to check the consistency and then to make any adjustments necessary. Don't leave the lid open long and don't open it during the baking cycle.

There are variables which must be addressed whether bread is made by hand (the old-fashioned way) or by machine. The flour and other ingredients pick up the moisture from the air. The moisture content of the grain berries themselves may vary as will the absorbency of whole grain flour according to how it was milled. As a result, the dough may have too much liquid, which could result in an overflow or a sunken top.

When kneading dough by hand, you develop an ability to feel the right consistency. When kneading dough by machine, you can see the right consistency. If you have problems with consistency, allow the machine to knead the dough for approximately 5 minutes and then look at the dough. With few exceptions, it should form a nice, smooth ball. Sometimes the ball will be round and other times, it may take on more of a cylindrical shape which "tornadoes" up the side of the pan.

By watching the dough on a regular basis, you will soon develop a sense for what looks right. If you stick your finger in and touch it, it should feel moist but not really be sticky. Dough which is too dry will not mix properly or it may cause the machine to struggle (you'll hear it). It may be uneven (not smooth) or have two or more balls of dough. If this is the case, simply add whatever liquid you are using, one tablespoon at a time, until the required consistency is obtained. Conversely, dough which is too wet will not be able to form a ball, and flour should be added 1 tablespoon at a time until the required consistency is obtained.

If you hear the paddle rotating, but the ingredients on top of the dough are not moving —

Check to see that the paddle is inserted properly. Sometimes either the paddle was not placed on the kneading shaft correctly or it has slipped. The easiest way to check is to turn off the machine, reach in and feel whether the paddle is on correctly. It can usually just be pushed harder onto the shaft and the machine restarted without any difficulties (except for a messy hand!).

If the bread rises well but then collapses during baking —

It is either rising too fast in hot weather (cut yeast, sugar and/or increase salt or use a shorter cycle) or the size of the recipe is too large (use a smaller size recipe).

Too much moisture in the dough may cause a sunken top or a mushroom.

Cut back the amount of liquid by ¼ cup and add it slowly as the machine is kneading. Stop adding it when the dough forms a smooth round ball.

If the crust is too dark or brown —

Bake on "light" if your machine has crust control. If not, try removing the bread about 5 minutes prior to the end of the baking cycle. If your machine does not tell you how much time is left, try cutting the amount of sugar (which darkens the crust). If all of these methods fail, stop the machine at the end of the first kneading cycle and start the machine over again.

Brush butter or oil on the loaf while it is still hot to soften the crust. Milk will give a softer crust than water.

If the bread is not rising and/or is doughy (not baking properly) and heavy —

You should use the sweet or raisin cycle on your machine if available. Natural sugars found in fruits may actually inhibit the rising of bread and cause the bread to bake improperly. Cut down on fruits and other sugary substances. Too much butter or fat may cause a similar problem. While this may happen with any machine, it seems to happen more often with the glass-domed machines. If you have a glass-domed machine and have what I call "the doughy blues," you may also place a piece of aluminum foil on the glass dome (only) to maintain even heat. Do not block any air vents.

If the bread has large air bubbles —

Cut the amount of yeast used.

Some breads may be heavy and dense just because of the ingredients.

Nonwheat flours or meals such as rye, oat or corn do not contain as much gluten as wheat and will naturally be lower rising and denser than all wheat. In addition, ingredients such as wheat germ or bran actually break the gluten strands, causing breads to rise less. It may be helpful to add 1½ tsp. to 2 tbs. of vital (wheat) gluten to achieve a higher rise and/or a better texture when using large amounts of such grains. Other reasons for breads not rising include a large amount of salt which inhibits rising and/or not enough sugar or water.

Sometimes raisins or similar ingredients do not mix into the dough evenly.

Any dried fruit may be lightly floured to prevent pieces from sticking to each other. You may also add ingredients at the beginning of the second kneading cycle.

White Bread

This is a very rich bread — terrific for sandwiches. You'll find yourself going back for more and more. It is not, however, one of the more dietetic. Well worth the calories anyway! Use an egg white, egg yolk or 2 tbs. egg substitute for 1/2 egg.

	Small	**Medium**	**Large**
water	1/2 cup	3/4 cup	1 cup
margarine or butter	2 tbs.	2 1/2 tbs.	3 tbs.
egg	1/2	1	1
sugar	1 1/2 tbs.	2 tbs.	2 tbs.
salt	3/4 tsp.	1 tsp.	1 1/2 tsp.
bread flour	2 cups	3 cups	3 1/2 cups
dry milk powder	2 1/2 tbs.	1/4 cup	1/3 cup
yeast	1 tsp.	1 1/2 tsp.	2 tsp.

Sally Lunn

This very rich, European-tasting bread is loaded with butter and eggs and is not dietetic by any means! Make the 1 1/2 lb. size in glass-domed machines. Set the machine for a light crust. The eggs give it lots of terrific taste and color. Tradition says that a young Englishwoman, Sally Lunn, sold this bread on the streets of Bath. Most bread cookbooks contain a version of this, which attests to its wonderful flavor. This is one of those breads which will never last to see leftovers.

	Small	**Medium**	**Large**
milk	1/2 cup	2/3 cup	3/4 cup
margarine or butter	3 tbs.	4 tbs.	4 tbs.
eggs	1	2	2
salt	1 tsp.	1 1/2 tsp.	2 tsp.
sugar	2 1/2 tbs.	1/4 cup	1/3 cup
bread flour	2 cups	3 cups	3 1/2 cups
yeast	1 tsp.	1 1/2 tsp.	2 tsp.

Portuguese Sweet Bread

Sweet or Basic cycle

Maria and Manuel, from Portugal, are living here while Manuel completes his doctoral degree. She has experimented with recipes to closely resemble those of her country. This is one of my favorites.

	Small	Medium	Large
milk	½ cup	¾ cup	⅞ cup
eggs	1	1	2
margarine or butter	1 tbs.	1 ½ tbs.	2 tbs.
sugar	3 tbs.	¼ cup	⅓ cup
salt	½ tsp.	¾ tsp.	1 tsp.
bread flour	2 cups	2 ½ cups	3 cups
yeast	1 tsp.	1 ½ tsp.	2 tsp.

Portuguese White Bread

Basic cycle

A very light-colored, airy bread. Slightly difficult to cut while hot — but who can wait until it cools?

	Small	Medium	Large
water	¾ cup	1 cup	1 ¼ cups
margarine or butter	2 tbs.	3 tbs.	¼ cup
sugar	2 tsp.	1 tbs.	1 tbs.
salt	¾ tsp.	1 tsp.	1 ½ tsp.
bread flour	2 cups	3 cups	3 ½ cups
yeast	1 tsp.	1 ½ tsp.	2 tsp.

English Muffin Bread

Basic cycle

This is a really good, easy way to get that English muffin taste and texture. Great bread to set on the timer for a hot breakfast bread. In order to have the proper texture, there may be a sunken top to this bread.

	Small	Medium	Large
water	⅞ cup	1 ¼ cups	1 ½ cups
sugar	1 ½ tsp.	2 tsp.	1 tbs.
salt	¾ tsp.	1 tsp.	1 tsp.
baking soda	⅛ tsp.	¼ tsp.	½ tsp.
bread flour	2 cups	3 cups	3 ½ cups
dry milk powder	2 tbs.	3 tbs.	¼ cup
yeast	1 tsp.	1 ½ tsp.	2 tsp.

Peasant Bread

Basic cycle

This is a very moist, chewy bread with a light, crispy crust. Absolutely wonderful with butter or cheese. It is somewhat similar to English Muffin Bread but more moist. The dough will appear wet.

	Small	Medium	Large
water	7/8 cup	1 1/3 cups	1 1/2 cups
sugar	1 1/2 tsp.	2 tsp.	1 tbs.
salt	3/4 tsp.	1 tsp.	1 tsp.
bread flour	2 cups	3 cups	3 1/2 cups
yeast	1 1/2 tsp.	2 tsp.	2 1/2 tsp.

Sour Cream Bread

Basic cycle

Great sandwich bread with a nice texture and great taste. Warm the sour cream. Adjust the consistency with water as necessary and scrape the sides of the pan with a rubber spatula if you need to. As with any recipe with dairy products, do not use the timer.

	Small	Medium	Large
water	2 tbs.	2 1/2 tbs.	3 tbs.
sour cream	1 cup	1 1/3 cups	1 3/4 cups
salt	1/2 tsp.	3/4 tsp.	1 tsp.
baking soda	1/8 tsp.	1/4 tsp.	1/2 tsp.
sugar	1 tbs.	1 1/2 tbs.	2 tbs.
bread flour	2 1/2 cups	3 1/3 cups	4 cups
yeast	1 1/2 tsp.	2 tsp.	2 tsp.

Crusty Cuban Bread

French or Basic cycle

This ethnic bread is very similar to a French or Italian Bread. It tends to be low-rising due to the lack of oil and small amount of sugar. Keep an eye on the dough and add a tablespoon or two of water if the dough looks dry or if the machine sounds like it is struggling.

	Small	Medium	Large
water	3/4 cup	1 1/4 cups	1 1/2 cups
sugar	1 tsp.	1 1/2 tsp.	2 tsp.
salt	3/4 tsp.	1 tsp.	1 tsp.
bread flour	2 cups	3 cups	3 1/2 cups
yeast	1 1/2 tsp.	2 tsp.	2 1/2 tsp.

French Honey Bread
Basic cycle

This wonderful, slightly sweet French bread is lightly colored with a light, crispy crust. Expect a high-rising loaf.

	Small	Medium	Large
water	¾ cup	1⅛ cups	1¼ cups
honey	2 tsp.	1 tbs.	1½ tbs.
olive oil	2 tsp.	1 tbs.	1½ tbs.
salt	½ tsp.	¾ tsp.	1 tsp.
sugar	¾ tsp.	1 tsp.	1½ tsp.
bread flour	2 cups	3 cups	3½ cups
yeast	1½ tsp.	2 tsp.	2½ tsp.

Italian Bread
French or Basic cycle

The recipe for this light-colored bread has been revised to give the bread a better rise, but it has less ethnic flavor than the original one. Add a tablespoon or two of water if the dough appears dry, or if the machine sounds like it is struggling.

	Small	Medium	Large
water	⅞ cup	1¼ cups	1½ cups
sugar	1 tsp.	1½ tsp.	2 tsp.
salt	¼ tsp.	½ tsp.	¾ tsp.
bread flour	2 cups	3 cups	3½ cups
yeast	1½ tsp.	2 tsp.	2½ tsp.

Austrian Malt Bread
Basic cycle

A slight taste of malt gives this an exotic flavor. I found malted milk powder, made by Carnation, in the grocery store with other dry milk products.

	Small	Medium	Large
water	⅔ cup	1 cup	1¼ cups
margarine or butter	1½ tbs.	2 tbs.	2½ tbs.
sugar	1 tbs.	1½ tbs.	2 tbs.
salt	¾ tsp.	1 tsp.	1 tsp.
bread flour	2 cups	3 cups	3½ cups
malted milk powder	2 tbs.	3 tbs.	¼ cup
yeast	1½ tsp.	2 tsp.	2 tsp.

Buttermilk Bread

You get great taste and texture without fresh buttermilk.

	Small	Medium	Large
water	⅔ cup	1 cup	1¼ cups
margarine or butter	1 tbs.	2 tbs.	2 tbs.
sugar	1 tsp.	1½ tsp.	2 tsp.
salt	½ tsp.	¾ tsp.	1 tsp.
bread flour	2 cups	3 cups	3½ cups
buttermilk powder	3 tbs.	¼ cup	⅓ cup
yeast	1½ tsp.	2 tsp.	2½ tsp.

Cottage Cheese Bread

This rich, high-rising sandwich bread is a favorite of my husband. Warm the cottage cheese. Use an egg white or yolk or 2 tbs. egg substitute for ½ egg.

	Small	Medium	Large
water	3-4 tbs.	3-4 tbs.	¼-⅓ cup
cottage cheese	⅔ cup	¾ cup	1 cup
margarine or butter	1½ tbs.	1½ tbs.	2 tbs.
egg	½	1	1
sugar	2 tsp.	1 tbs.	1 tbs.
baking soda	⅛ tsp.	¼ tsp.	¼ tsp.
salt	¾ tsp.	1 tsp.	1 tsp.
bread flour	2 cups	2½ cups	3 cups
yeast	1½ tsp.	2 tsp.	2 tsp.

Cheddar Cheese Bread

This is a delicious bread. Use grated or shredded cheddar cheese and lightly pack it into the cup. The cheese may affect the consistency of the dough, so keep an eye on it and adjust the moisture if you need to.

	Small	Medium	Large
water or milk	⅔ cup	1 cup	1¼ cups
margarine or butter	1 tbs.	1 tbs.	1½ tbs.
cheddar cheese, grated or shredded	½ cup	⅔ cup	¾ cup
sugar	2 tsp.	1 tbs.	1½ tbs.
salt	½ tsp.	¾ tsp.	1 tsp.
bread flour	2 cups	3 cups	3½ cups
yeast	1 tsp.	1½ tsp.	2 tsp.

Ricotta Bread

Sweet or Basic cycle

This made a huge hit with friends and tasters who ranked it one of the best. It slices very well. Use an egg white, yolk or 2 tbs. egg substitute for ½ egg. Warm the cheese for a high rise, but puncture the dough on the second rise if it rises too high.

	Small	Medium	Large
milk	¼ cup	⅓ cup	½ cup
ricotta cheese	1 cup	1⅓ cups	1½ cups
margarine or butter	2 tbs.	2½ tbs.	3 tbs.
eggs	½	1	1
sugar	2½ tbs.	¼ cup	⅓ cup
salt	1 tsp.	1 tsp.	1½ tsp.
bread flour	2 cups	3 cups	3½ cups
yeast	1 tsp.	1½ tsp.	2 tsp.

Cream Cheese Bread

Basic cycle

This is more of a dessert bread or cake — delicious. Bring the cream cheese to room temperature for several hours or warm in the microwave. Scrape the sides of the pan if necessary and adjust the consistency with milk or water if you need to.

	Small	Medium	Large
milk	⅓ cup	⅓ cup	½ cup
cream cheese	4 oz.	6 oz.	8 oz.
margarine or butter	2 tbs.	2½ tbs.	3 tbs.
egg	½	1	1
sugar	2 tbs.	3 tbs.	3 tbs.
salt	¾ tsp.	1 tsp.	1½ tsp.
bread flour	2 cups	3 cups	3½ cups
yeast	1 tsp.	1½ tsp.	2 tsp.

About Whole Wheat, Grain and Cereal Breads

If you have difficulty with whole wheat or whole grain loaves, allow the machine to knead one time and then turn off the machine and start it again, producing a longer kneading time.

Whole Wheat 1
Whole Wheat, Sweet or Basic cycle

This is my favorite whole wheat. It's a high-rising bread that slices very well.

	Small	**Medium**	**Large**
water	½ cup	¾ cup	1 ¼ cups
margarine or butter	2 tbs.	3 tbs.	¼ cup
egg	1	1	1
sugar	1 ½ tbs.	2 tbs.	2 ½ tbs.
salt	¾ tsp.	1 tsp.	1 ½ tsp.
whole wheat flour	¾ cup	1 cup	1 ⅓ cups
bread flour	1 ½ cups	2 cups	2⅔ cups
yeast	1 tsp.	1 ½ tsp.	2 tsp.

Whole Wheat 11
Whole Wheat or Basic cycle

Here is a subtle, different whole wheat. The yogurt gives it a great flavor and dense texture. I have always enjoyed oats with whole wheat. Warm the yogurt and use the water to adjust the consistency.

	Small	**Medium**	**Large**
plain nonfat yogurt	1 cup	1 ¼ cups	1 ½ cups
water	¼ cup	⅓ cup	⅓ cup
margarine or butter	2 tbs.	2 ½ tbs.	3 tbs.
sugar	2 tbs.	2 ½ tbs.	3 tbs.
salt	1 tsp.	1 tsp.	1 ½ tsp.
oats	½ cup	⅔ cup	¾ cup
whole wheat flour	1 cup	1 ⅓ cups	1 ½ cups
bread flour	1 ½ cups	2 cups	2 ½ cups
yeast	1 ½ tsp.	2 tsp.	2 ½ tsp.

Whole Wheat III

This is a very good, low-fat bread.

	Small	Medium	Large
water	⅔ cup	1⅛ cups	1⅓ cups
margarine or butter	1 tbs.	1½ tbs.	2 tbs.
sugar	1 tbs.	1½ tbs.	2 tbs.
salt	½ tsp.	¾ tsp.	1 tsp.
whole wheat flour	1 cup	1½ cups	2 cups
bread flour	1 cup	1½ cups	2 cups
yeast	1 tsp.	1½ tsp.	2 tsp.

Sprout Bread

This is superb, and worth the trouble of sprouting the berries. The sprouts affect the amount of liquid required and it is likely that you will have to adjust the consistency with water or flour.

	Small	Medium	Large
water	⅔ cup	¾ cup	1 cup
margarine or butter	1½ tbs.	2 tbs.	2½ tbs.
sugar	2 tsp.	1 tbs.	1½ tbs.
salt	½ tsp.	¾ tsp.	1 tsp.
sprouted wheat berries	⅓ cup	½ cup	⅔ cup
bread flour	2 cups	2½ cups	3 cups
yeast	1 tsp.	1½ tsp.	2½ tsp.

Two to three days prior to making this bread, place ⅓ to ½ cup wheat berries in a sprouting jar (or any glass jar covered with cheesecloth tied down with a rubber band). Cover with water and allow to sit overnight (at least 12 hours). Drain and rinse again, right through the screen or cheesecloth, and set the jar mouth-side down at a 45-degree angle in a warm, dark place. Rinse sprouts twice a day. They are ready for use when you see small sprouts of about ⅛ to ¼ inch. (Wheat berry sprouts should be no longer than the berry itself.)

Nine-Grain Bread

Nine-grain cereal consists of cracked wheat, barley, corn, millet, oats, triti-cale, brown rice, soya and flax seed and is available for purchase either in bulk or packaged. It may be carried in a large grocery store or a natural food store. Seven-grain cereal can be used as a substitute. Some stores carry one and not the other. Another must-try.

	Small	Medium	Large
water	1 cup	1 1/3 cups	1 1/2 cups
margarine or butter	2 tbs.	2 1/2 tbs.	3 tbs.
brown sugar	1 1/2 tbs.	2 tbs.	2 1/2 tbs.
salt	1 tsp.	1 tsp.	1 tsp.
9-grain cereal	1 cup	1 1/3 cups	1 1/2 cups
bread flour	2 cups	2 2/3 cups	3 cups
yeast	1 tsp.	1 1/2 tsp.	2 tsp.

Cracked Wheat Bread

One of the best. This natural, great-tasting and high-rising bread has a bit of crunchiness. If in doubt about the size to make, make the smallest size.

	Small	Medium	Large
water	1 cup	1 1/4 cups	1 1/2 cups
cracked wheat	1/3 cup	1/2 cup	2/3 cup
vegetable oil	1 1/2 tbs.	2 tbs.	2 1/2 tbs.
honey	1 tbs.	1 tbs.	1 1/2 tbs.
salt	1/2 tsp.	1 tsp.	1 tsp.
whole wheat flour	3/4 cup	1 cup	1 1/3 cups
bread flour	1 cup	1 1/2 cups	2 cups
vital gluten, optional	1 tbs.	2 tbs.	2 tbs.
yeast	1 tsp.	1 1/2 tsp.	2 tsp.

Allow the cracked wheat to sit in the measured liquid for at least 1 hour. Add the water and cracked wheat with the liquid ingredients. Adjust the consistency with water or flour.

High Protein Diet (Cornell) Bread — *Whole Wheat or Basic cycle*

Much better than the commercial diet breads that use sawdust fiber as filler. This is a tasty, dense loaf. The recipe is based on a formula devised for superior nutrition in bread by Cornell University. Wheat germ, soy flour and dry milk powder are added to each cup of flour in the Cornell Formula; this recipe makes it easier.

	Small	**Medium**	**Large**
water	1 cup	1 1/4 cups	1 1/2 cups
vegetable oil	1 tbs.	1 1/2 tbs.	2 tbs.
honey	1 tbs.	1 1/2 tbs.	2 tbs.
salt	3/4 tsp.	1 tsp.	1 tsp.
wheat germ	2 tbs.	3 tbs.	1/4 cup
soy flour	1/4 cup	1/3 cup	1/2 cup
nonfat dry milk powder	1/4 cup	1/3 cup	1/2 cup
whole wheat flour	1 cup	1 1/3 cups	1 2/3 cups
bread flour	1 1/2 cups	1 2/3 cups	2 cups
vital gluten, optional	1 1/2 tsp.	2 tsp.	1 tbs.
yeast	1 1/2 tsp.	2 tsp.	2 1/2 tsp.

Bran 1 — *Whole Wheat or Basic cycle*

This wonderfully hearty bread is so healthy! Wheat bran is also known as millers' bran, and like oat bran, can be found in health food stores. Yes, the salt is the same amount for all sizes!

	Small	**Medium**	**Large**
water	1 cup	1 1/3 cups	1 1/2 cups
margarine or butter	2 tbs.	2 1/2 tbs.	3 tbs.
brown sugar	1 tbs.	1 1/2 tbs.	2 tbs.
salt	1 tsp.	1 tsp.	1 tsp.
wheat germ	1/4 cup	1/3 cup	1/2 cup
whole wheat flour	1/2 cup	2/3 cup	3/4 cup
oat or wheat bran	1 cup	1 1/3 cups	1 1/2 cups
bread flour	1 1/2 cups	2 cups	2 1/2 cups
vital gluten, optional	1 1/2 tsp.	2 tsp.	1 tbs.
yeast	1 1/2 tsp.	2 tsp.	2 1/2 tsp.

Bran II

Good tasting, good texture and good for you!

	Small	Medium	Large
water	1 cup	1⅓ cups	1½ cups
margarine or butter	1 tbs.	1½ tbs.	2 tbs.
sugar	1 tbs.	1½ tbs.	2 tbs.
salt	¾ tsp.	1 tsp.	1 tsp.
oat or wheat bran	¾ cup	1 cup	1¼ cups
bread flour	1¾ cups	2⅓ cups	2⅔ cups
vital gluten, optional	1½ tsp.	2 tsp.	1 tbs.
yeast	1½ tsp.	2 tsp.	2½ tsp.

Multi-Grain Bread

This hearty, somewhat dense, full-of-fiber bread is wonderful with a stew or homemade soup. You can substitute cracked wheat for bulgur. Scrape the sides of the pan with a rubber spatula if necessary.

	Small	Medium	Large
water	1⅛ cups	1⅓ cups	1½ cups
vegetable oil	1½ tbs.	2 tbs.	2½ tbs.
honey	2 tbs.	2½ tbs.	3 tbs.
salt	¾ tsp.	1 tsp.	1½ tsp.
bulgur wheat	¼ cup	⅓ cup	½ cup
wheat germ	2 tbs.	3 tbs.	¼ cup
wheat or oat bran	½ cup	⅔ cup	¾ cup
rye flour	½ cup	⅔ cup	¾ cup
oats	¼ cup	⅓ cup	½ cup
bread flour	1½ cups	2¼ cups	2½ cups
vital gluten	1½ tbs.	2 tbs.	2 tbs.
yeast	1½ tsp.	2 tsp.	2½ tsp.

Wheat Flake Bread

Whole Wheat or Basic cycle

Great bread — the wheat flakes, similar to oat flakes, give it a nice texture along with being nutritious. Expect a high-rising loaf.

	Small	**Medium**	**Large**
water	¾ cup	1⅛ cups	1⅓ cups
margarine or butter	1 tbs.	2 tbs.	2½ tbs.
brown sugar	2 tsp.	1 tbs.	1½ tbs.
salt	¼ tsp.	½ tsp.	¾ tsp.
rolled wheat flakes	⅓ cup	½ cup	⅔ cup
whole wheat flour	⅔ cup	1 cup	1⅓ cups
bread flour	1 cup	1½ cups	2 cups
vital gluten, optional	2 tsp.	1 tbs.	1 tbs.
yeast	1½ tsp.	2 tsp.	2½ tsp.

Wheat Germ Sesame Bread

Whole Wheat or Basic cycle

This high-rising bread is absolutely wonderful — light and airy. Use an egg yolk or white, or 2 tbs. egg substitute, for ½ egg. Keep an eye on the dough during the second rise and puncture it if necessary. If in doubt, make a smaller size. Substitute anise or fennel seeds for variety.

	Small	**Medium**	**Large**
water	⅔ cup	1 cup	1¼ cups
vegetable oil	2 tbs.	2½ tbs.	3 tbs.
honey	2 tbs.	2½ tbs.	3 tbs.
eggs	½	1	1
salt	½ tsp.	¾ tsp.	1 tsp.
wheat germ	2 tbs.	3 tbs.	¼ cup
sesame seeds	1 tbs.	1½ tbs.	2 tbs.
whole wheat flour	¾ cup	1 cup	1¼ cups
bread flour	1½ cups	2 cups	2½ cups
yeast	1 tsp.	1½ tsp.	2 tsp.

Whole Wheat Oatmeal Bread

Whole Wheat or Basic cycle

This great, wholesome bread slices well. It's one of my favorites.

	Small	Medium	Large
water	⅔ cup	1 cup	1⅓ cups
margarine or butter	2 tbs.	2 tbs.	3 tbs.
eggs	½	1	1
sugar	1½ tbs.	2 tbs.	3 tbs.
salt	½ tsp.	¾ tsp.	1 tsp.
oats	⅓ cup	½ cup	⅔ cup
wheat germ	3 tbs.	¼ cup	⅓ cup
whole wheat flour	½ cup	¾ cup	1 cup
bread flour	1½ cups	2 cups	3 cups
yeast	1½ tsp.	2 tsp.	2½ tsp.

Oatmeal Bread

Basic cycle

A terrific oatmeal loaf! Regular dry milk can be substituted for buttermilk powder.

	Small	Medium	Large
water	¾ cup	⅞ cup	1⅓ cups
margarine or butter	2 tbs.	2½ tbs.	3 tbs.
sugar	1½ tbs.	2 tbs.	3 tbs.
salt	½ tsp.	¾ tsp.	1 tsp.
buttermilk powder	3 tbs.	¼ cup	⅓ cup
oats	⅔ cup	1 cup	1⅓ cups
bread flour	1½ cups	2 cups	3 cups
yeast	1½ tsp.	2 tsp.	2½ tsp.

Variation: Cinnamon Oatmeal Bread

Add to the recipe:

	Small	Medium	Large
cinnamon	⅓ tsp.	½ tsp.	⅔ tsp.

Oat Wheat Bread

Whole Wheat or Basic cycle

Dip this bread in hot cheese (out of a microwave) for a great appetizer, similar to cheese fondue. Oat wheat flour is made by Gold Medal. If you can't find it, use equal parts of oat flour and whole wheat flour.

	Small	Medium	Large
water	⅞ cup	1 cup	1¼ cups
margarine or butter	1 tbs.	2 tbs.	2½ tbs.
sugar	1½ tbs.	2 tbs.	3 tbs.
salt	¾ tsp.	1 tsp.	1 tsp.
oat wheat flour	1 cup	1½ cups	2 cups
bread flour	1 cup	1½ cups	2 cups
yeast	1 tsp.	1½ tsp.	2 tsp.

Honey Nut Oatmeal Bread

Whole Wheat, Sweet or Basic cycle

While many grocery stores carry a honey nut oatmeal bread for sandwiches, this seems more of a dessert-type bread to me. Absolutely delicious and a must-try.

	Small	Medium	Large
water	⅔ cup	1 cup	1⅓ cups
vegetable or walnut oil	1 tbs.	2 tbs.	3 tbs.
honey	1 tbs.	2 tbs.	3 tbs.
salt	½ tsp.	1 tsp.	1 tsp.
oats	⅔ cup	1 cup	1⅓ cups
whole wheat flour	⅓ cup	½ cup	⅔ cup
bread flour	1 cup	1½ cups	2 cups
yeast	1 tsp.	1½ tsp.	2½ tsp.

At beep add: *(If National or Panasonic, add following first kneading)*

	Small	Medium	Large
chopped walnuts	⅓ cup	½ cup	⅔ cup

Almond Oatmeal Bread

Whole Wheat, Sweet or Basic cycle

This is a wonderful, tasty bread. The light almond taste combined with oats is a delightful combination. A must-try.

	Small	Medium	Large
milk	7/8 cup	1 1/8 cups	1 1/3 cups
margarine	2 tbs.	2 1/2 tbs.	3 tbs.
almond paste	1 1/2 tbs.	2 tbs.	2 1/2 tbs.
almond extract	1 1/2 tsp.	2 tsp.	1 tbs.
sugar	1 1/2 tsp.	2 tsp.	1 tbs.
salt	3/4 tsp.	1 tsp.	1 tsp.
oats	1 cup	1 1/3 cups	1 1/2 cups
bread flour	2 cups	2 2/3 cups	3 cups
yeast	1 1/2 tsp.	2 tsp.	2 1/2 tsp.

At beep add: (If National or Panasonic, add following first kneading)

	Small	Medium	Large
slivered almonds	1/4 cup	1/3 cup	1/2 cup

Almond Bread

Sweet or Basic cycle

Just a hint of almond flavor gives this bread a wonderful, sweet taste. Make this with or without the sliced almonds. The almond paste may affect the consistency. Watch the dough and add 1-2 tbs. milk if necessary. During the final rising, sprinkle top with slivered almonds for a decorative finish to the bread.

	Small	Medium	Large
milk	1/2 cup	7/8 cup	1 1/8 cups
margarine or butter	1 tbs.	1 1/2 tbs.	2 tbs.
almond paste	3 tbs.	1/4 cup	1/4 cup
salt	1/2 tsp.	1 tsp.	1 tsp.
bread flour	2 cups	3 cups	3 1/2 cups
yeast	1 1/2 tsp.	2 tsp.	2 1/2 tsp.
sliced almonds, optional	1/3 cup	1/2 cup	2/3 cup

Oat Bread

This is a terrific-tasting bread, and so good for you, too.

	Small	Medium	Large
water	1 cup	1 1/4 cups	1 1/3 cups
margarine or butter	1 tbs.	2 tbs.	2 1/2 tbs.
sugar	2 tbs.	3 tbs.	1/4 cup
salt	1/2 tsp.	3/4 tsp.	1 tsp.
oat bran	1/3 cup	1/2 cup	2/3 cup
oats	1/3 cup	1/2 cup	2/3 cup
bread flour	1 3/4 cups	2 1/2 cups	3 cups
vital gluten, optional	1 tbs.	1 1/2 tbs.	2 tbs.
yeast	1 1/2 tsp.	2 tsp.	2 1/2 tsp.

Oatmeal Sesame Bread

This delicious sweet bread is another good choice for breakfast.

	Small	Medium	Large
water	3/4 cup	1 cup	1 1/3 cups
margarine or butter	1 tbs.	1 1/2 tbs.	2 tbs.
brown sugar	1 tbs.	1 1/2 tbs.	2 tbs.
cinnamon, optional	1/2 tsp.	3/4 tsp.	1 tsp.
salt	1/2 tsp.	3/4 tsp.	1 tsp.
sesame seeds	3 tbs.	1/4 cup	1/3 cup
oats	1/3 cup	1/2 cup	2/3 cup
whole wheat flour	1/3 cup	1/2 cup	2/3 cup
bread flour	1 1/2 cups	2 cups	2 2/3 cups
yeast	1 tsp.	1 1/2 tsp.	2 1/2 tsp.

Grits Bread

The water is added while the machine is kneading to adjust the consistency. Leftover grits that have been refrigerated will be drier than freshly cooked.

	Small	Medium	Large
cooked grits	1 cup	1 ½ cups	1 ¾ cups
margarine	1 tbs.	1 ½ tbs.	2 tbs.
salt	¾ tsp.	1 tsp.	1 tsp.
sugar	2 tsp.	1 tbs.	1 tbs.
bread flour	2 cups	2 ¼ cups	2 ¾ cups
yeast	1 tsp.	1 ½ tsp.	2 tsp.
water	2-4 tbs.	⅓-½ cup	½-⅔ cup

Cream of Wheat Bread

You'll have people wondering what your secret ingredient is. This slices extremely well and makes excellent French toast. Some people use the flavored packets of Cream of Wheat for variety.

	Small	Medium	Large
milk	½ cup	1 cup	1 ¼ cups
margarine or butter	2 tbs.	¼ cup	5 tbs.
eggs	1	1	1
sugar	1 ½ tbs.	2 tbs.	2 ½ tbs.
salt	½ tsp.	¾ tsp.	1 tsp.
bread flour	1 ½ cups	2 cups	3 cups
Cream of Wheat, uncooked	⅔ cup	1 cup	1 ⅓ cups
vital gluten, optional	1 tbs.	1 tbs.	1 ½ tbs.
yeast	1 tsp.	1 ½ tsp.	2 tsp.

Shredded Wheat Bread

This is a very tasty, different bread. If you have another favorite cereal, try it in place of the shredded wheat. It's a great way to use up the end of the box! Grind the Shredded Wheat cereal in a food processor until finely crumbled. Or put it in a locking plastic storage bag and crush it with a rolling pin. Adjust the moisture if necessary.

	Small	Medium	Large
water	¾ cup	1 cup	1 ⅛ cups
vegetable oil	2 tbs.	3 tbs.	3 tbs.
honey	1 tbs.	1 ½ tbs.	2 tbs.
salt	½ tsp.	¾ tsp.	1 tsp.
Shredded Wheat cereal, finely crumbled	½ cup	⅔ cup	¾ cup
bread flour	2 ¼ cups	3 cups	3 ½ cups
dry milk powder	¼ cup	⅓ cup	⅓ cup
yeast	1 tsp.	1 ½ tsp.	2 tsp.

Grape Nuts Bread

It is not necessary to soak the Grape Nuts for this bread, but add them at the beep or appropriate time for your machine. The dough may be a little soft until the cereal is added. Any other of your favorite cereals can be substituted.

	Small	Medium	Large
water	1 cup	1 ⅓ cups	1 ½ cups
vegetable oil	2 tbs.	2 ½ tbs.	3 tbs.
sugar	1 tbs.	1 ¼ tbs.	1 ½ tbs.
salt	¾ tsp.	1 tsp.	1 tsp.
bread flour	2 cups	3 cups	3 ½ cups
yeast	1 ½ tsp.	2 tsp.	2 tsp.

At beep add: *(If National or Panasonic, add following first kneading)*

	Small	Medium	Large
Grape Nuts cereal	½ cup	⅔ cup	¾ cup

Kashi Bread

While usually found in the cereal section of a grocery store, kashi is actually a combination of the berries of seven grains. Several different cereals are sold by the same company — make sure you purchase the breakfast pilaf that requires cooking. Kashi may also be found in health food stores. Kashi requires approximately 30 minutes to cook in a water-to-grain ratio of 2:1. Adjust the dough with water if necessary.

	Small	Medium	Large
water	2/3 cup	3/4 cup	1 cup
margarine	1 tbs.	1 tbs.	1 1/2 tbs.
brown sugar	1 tbs.	1 1/2 tbs.	2 tbs.
salt	1/2 tsp.	3/4 tsp.	1 1/3 tsp.
cooked kashi	1/3 cup	1 1/2 cup	2/3 cup
whole wheat flour	1/3 cup	1/2 cup	2/3 cup
bread flour	1 3/4 cups	2 cups	2 2/3 cups
yeast	1 tsp.	1 1/2 tsp.	2 1/2 tsp.

New York Rye Bread

This is a low-rising, very dense, flavorful loaf just like you buy on the streets of New York. If you want a lighter, fluffier loaf, add the vital wheat gluten, which is available at health food stores. The caraway can be adjusted to taste.

	Small	Medium	Large
water	7/8 cup	1 1/8 cups	1 1/3 cups
vegetable oil	1 tsp.	1 1/3 tbs.	1 1/2 tbs.
honey	1 1/2 tbs.	2 tbs.	2 1/2 tbs.
salt	3/4 tsp.	1 tsp.	1 tsp.
caraway seeds	2 tsp.	1 tbs.	1 tbs.
rye flour	1 cup	1 1/3 cups	1 1/2 cups
bread flour	1 3/4 cups	2 1/4 cups	2 2/3 cups
vital gluten, optional	2 tsp.	1 tbs.	1 1/2 tbs.
dry milk powder	3 tbs.	1/4 cup	1/3 cup
yeast	1 1/2 tsp.	2 1/2 tsp.	1 tbs.

Swedish Rye Bread

Whole Wheat or Basic cycle

The taste is a cross between rye and whole wheat with a slight flavor of orange. Very good. Caraway and orange peel can be adjusted to taste.

	Small	Medium	Large
water	7/8 cup	1 cup	1 1/4 cups
honey	2 tbs.	3 tbs.	1/4 cup
margarine or butter	1 tbs.	1 1/2 tbs.	2 tbs.
salt	3/4 tsp.	1 tsp.	1 tsp.
caraway seeds	2 tsp.	1 tbs.	1 1/2 tbs.
grated orange peel	1/2 tsp.	3/4 tsp.	1 tsp.
rye flour	1 cup	1 1/3 cups	1 1/2 cups
bread flour	1 1/2 cups	2 cups	2 1/2 cups
yeast	1 1/2 tsp.	2 tsp.	2 1/2 tsp.

Norwegian Rye Bread

Whole Wheat, Sweet or Basic cycle

This is my favorite rye. There is a large amount of flour in this recipe. If the dough seems dry or the machine sounds like it is struggling, add 1-2 tbs. water.

	Small	Medium	Large
water	3/4 cup	1 cup	1 1/4 cups
molasses	1/3 cup	1/3 cup	1/2 cup
margarine or butter	2 tbs.	2 1/2 tbs.	3 tbs.
salt	1/4 tsp.	1/2 tsp.	3/4 tsp.
caraway seeds	2 tsp.	1 tbs.	1 1/2 tbs.
whole wheat flour	1/4 cup	1/3 cup	1/2 cup
rye flour	1 1/4 cups	1 2/3 cups	2 1/2 cups
bread flour	1 1/4 cups	1 2/3 cups	2 1/2 cups
yeast	1 1/2 tsp.	2 tsp.	2 1/2 tsp.

Light Pumpernickel

This is a wonderful, light pumpernickel; it makes great sandwiches.

	Small	Medium	Large
water	⅔ cup	1 cup	1⅓ cups
vegetable oil	1½ tbs.	2 tbs.	3 tbs.
molasses	1½ tbs.	2 tbs.	3 tbs.
sugar	2 tsp.	1 tbs.	1½ tbs.
salt	½ tsp.	¾ tsp.	1 tsp.
caraway seeds	1½ tsp.	2 tsp.	1 tbs.
unsweetened cocoa	1⅓ tbs.	2 tbs.	2½ tbs.
rye flour	1 cup	1½ cups	2 cups
bread flour	1 cup	1½ cups	2 cups
vital gluten, optional	2 tsp.	1 tbs.	1½ tbs.
yeast	1 tsp.	1½ tsp.	2½ tsp.

Dark Pumpernickel

This is a heavy, dense bread that is terrific with soup and or or salad.

	Small	Medium	Large
water	1 cup	1¼ cups	1½ cups
vegetable oil	2 tbs.	2½ tbs.	3 tbs.
molasses	3 tbs.	¼ cup	⅓ cup
unsweetened cocoa	1½ tbs.	2 tbs.	2½ tbs.
brown sugar	1 tbs.	1½ tbs.	2 tbs.
instant coffee granules	1 tsp.	1½ tsp.	2 tsp.
salt	¾ tsp.	1 tsp.	1½ tsp.
caraway seeds	2 tsp.	1 tbs.	1 tbs.
rye flour	¾ cup	1 cup	1¼ cups
whole wheat flour	¾ cup	1 cup	1¼ cups
bread flour	1½ cups	2 cups	2½ cups
yeast	1½ tsp.	2 tsp.	2½ tsp.

Russian Black Bread

Whole Wheat, Sweet or Basic cycle

Eat this wonderful hearty bread with soup and/ or salad or serve it as an appetizer with a crab dip! You can substitute dark molasses for barley malt syrup.

	Small	Medium	Large
water	1 cup	1⅓ cups	1⅓-1½ cups
vegetable oil	2 tbs.	3 tbs.	¼ cup
barley malt syrup	1 tbs.	1½ tbs.	2 tbs.
vinegar	1 tbs.	1½ tbs.	2 tbs.
sugar	¾ tsp.	1 tsp.	1½ tsp.
salt	¾ tsp.	1 tsp.	1 tsp.
unsweetened cocoa	1½ tbs.	2 tbs.	2½ tbs.
minced dried onion	½ tsp.	½ tsp.	¾ tsp.
instant coffee granules	¾ tsp.	1 tsp.	1 tsp.
caraway seed	2 tsp.	1 tbs.	1½ tbs.
fennel	½ tsp.	½ tsp.	¾ tsp.
bread flour	2 cups	2½ cups	3 cups
rye flour	1 cup	1¼ cups	1½ cups
yeast	1½ tsp.	2 tsp.	2½ tsp.

Cornmeal Bread

Whole Wheat or Basic cycle

Wonderful with a Southern or Mexican meal — if it makes it to the table. If you can find blue cornmeal in your health food store, try it. What a tasty, different treat! My bread testers thought at first that I was kidding but asked for more after trying it.

	Small	Medium	Large
water	¾ cup	1 cup	1⅓ cups
vegetable oil	1 tbs.	1½ tbs.	2 tbs.
eggs	1	1	1
sugar	1⅓ tbs.	2 tbs.	3 tbs.
salt	½ tsp.	1 tsp.	1 tsp.
yellow cornmeal	⅔ cup	1 cup	1⅓ cups
bread flour	1⅔ cups	2 cups	3 cups
yeast	1 tsp.	1½ tsp.	2½ tsp.

Honey Cornmeal Bread
Sweet or Basic cycle

This is a very tasty, slightly sweet cornmeal loaf. The dough may appear wet, but it should be high-rising and light in texture as a result.

	Small	Medium	Large
water	½ cup	¾ cup	1 cup
vegetable oil	1 tbs.	1½ tbs.	2 tbs.
honey	2 tbs.	3 tbs.	¼ cup
eggs	2	3	4
salt	½ tsp.	1 tsp.	1 tsp.
cornmeal	⅔ cup	1 cup	1⅓ cups
whole wheat flour	⅓ cup	½ cup	⅔ cup
bread flour	1 cup	1½ cups	2 cups
yeast	1 tsp.	1½ tsp.	2½ tsp.

Cornmeal Wheat Germ Bread
Whole Wheat, Sweet or Basic cycle

This cornmeal bread is very good, and great toasted. Expect a low-rising, dense loaf.

	Small	Medium	Large
water	¾ cup	1⅛ cups	1¼ cups
vegetable oil	1 tbs.	1½ tbs.	2 tbs.
honey	2 tbs.	2½ tbs.	3 tbs.
salt	½ tsp.	¾ tsp.	1 tsp.
cornmeal	½ cup	⅔ cup	¾ cup
wheat germ	¼ cup	⅓ cup	½ cup
bread flour	2¼ cups	3 cups	3½ cups
vital gluten, optional	1 tbs.	1½ tbs.	2 tbs.
yeast	1 tsp.	1½ tsp.	2 tsp.

Rice Bran Bread

This is absolutely delicious. The rice bran and flour give this a slightly sweet taste. It is said that rice bran has the same cholesterol-lowering qualities as oat bran. If you can't find rice bran in your grocery store, look for it in health food stores.

	Small	Medium	Large
water	¾ cup	1 cup	1⅓ cups
margarine or butter	1½ tbs.	2 tbs.	3 tbs.
sugar	2 tsp.	1 tbs.	1½ tbs.
salt	¾ tsp.	1 tsp.	1 tsp.
rice bran	⅓ cup	½ cup	⅔ cup
rice flour	⅓ cup	½ cup	⅔ cup
bread flour	1½ cups	2 cups	3 cups
vital gluten, optional	2 tsp.	1 tbs.	1 tbs.
yeast	1 tsp.	1½ tsp.	2 tsp.

Barley Bread

This is a delicious, light airy bread. Molasses can be used as a substitute for the barley malt syrup.

	Small	Medium	Large
water	¾ cup	1⅛ cups	1⅓ cups
margarine or butter	1 tbs.	2 tbs.	2½ tbs.
barley malt syrup	2 tbs.	3 tbs.	¼ cup
sugar	3 tbs.	⅓ cup	⅓ cup
salt	½ tsp.	1 tsp.	1 tsp.
cinnamon	¾ tsp.	1 tsp.	1½ tsp.
barley flour	⅓ cup	½ cup	⅔ cup
bread flour	2 cups	3 cups	3½ cups
yeast	1 tsp.	1½ tsp.	2½ tsp.

Buckwheat Bread

This is a strong-tasting bread, a must for buckwheat lovers.

	Small	**Medium**	**Large**
water	1 ⅛ cups	1 ¼ cups	1 ½ cups
vegetable oil	1 ½ tbs.	2 tbs.	3 tbs.
honey	1 tbs.	1 ½ tbs.	2 tbs.
salt	½ tsp.	1 tsp.	1 tsp.
buckwheat flour	½ cup	⅔ cup	¾ cup
whole wheat flour	1 cup	1 ⅓ cups	1 ½ cups
bread flour	1 ½ cups	2 cups	2 ½ cups
yeast	1 ½ tsp.	2 tsp.	2 tsp.

Buckwheat Cornmeal Bread

This wonderful mixture of buckwheat with cornmeal is one I think you'll like.

	Small	**Medium**	**Large**
water	½ cup	1 cup	1 cup
margarine or butter	2 tbs.	3 tbs.	3 tbs.
eggs	1	1	1
salt	½ tsp.	¾ tsp.	1 tsp.
brown sugar	1 tbs.	1 ½ tbs.	2 tbs.
buckwheat flour	3 tbs.	¼ cup	⅓ cup
cornmeal	⅓ cup	½ cup	⅔ cup
bread flour	1 ½ cups	2 ½ cups	3 cups
yeast	1 tsp.	1 ½ tsp.	2 ½ tsp.

Soy Flakes Bread

The soy flakes give this bread a unique texture and crunch. Kids love it. Soy flakes can be purchased at a health food store.

	Small	**Medium**	**Large**
water	⅔ cup	1 cup	1 ⅓ cups
vegetable oil	1 ½ tbs.	2 tbs.	3 tbs.
sugar	1 ½ tbs.	2 tbs.	3 tbs.
salt	½ tsp.	¾ tsp.	1 tsp.
soy flakes	⅓ cup	½ cup	⅔ cup
bread flour	1 ¾ cups	2 ½ cups	3 cups
yeast	1 tsp.	1 ½ tsp.	2 tsp.

Amaranth Bread

Basic cycle

Amaranth has a very unusual, distinct taste which is quite good and it is, of course, extremely nutritious. This is wonderful toasted.

	Small	Medium	Large
water	7/8 cup	1 cup	1 1/4 cups
margarine or butter	2 tbs.	3 tbs.	1/4 cup
sugar	2 tsp.	1 tbs.	1 1/2 tbs.
salt	1/2 tsp.	1 tsp.	1 tsp.
amaranth flour	1/3 cup	1/2 cup	2/3 cup
bread flour	2 cups	2 1/2 cups	3 1/2 cups
yeast	1 tsp.	1 1/2 tsp.	2 tsp.

Amaranth Cereal Bread

Sweet or Basic cycle

If you have never tried amaranth, this is a good bread for you. I use the amaranth cereal made by Health Valley which can be found in a health food store or in some grocery stores. Other amaranth cereals will work also. This is a must-try if you're looking for something a little different. Consistency may vary due to the brand of cereal used. Adjust with liquid if you need to.

	Small	Medium	Large
water	2/3-7/8 cup	1-1 1/4 cups	1 1/3-1 1/2 cups
vegetable oil	2 tbs.	3 tbs.	1/4 cup
sugar	1 tbs.	1 1/2 tbs.	2 tbs.
salt	1/2 tsp.	3/4 tsp.	1 tsp.
amaranth cereal	1/2 cup	3/4 cup	1 cup
bread flour	2 cups	2 1/2 cups	3 cups
yeast	1 tsp.	1 1/2 tsp.	2 tsp.

Amaranth Nut Bread

Sweet or Basic cycle

This wonderful nutty bread can be used for sandwiches, but it is more of a dessert bread. Use an egg white, yolk or 2 tbs. egg substitute for ½ egg.

	Small	**Medium**	**Large**
water	⅔ cup	1 cup	1¼ cups
vegetable oil	1 tbs.	2 tbs.	2½ tbs.
honey	2 tbs.	3 tbs.	¼ cup
egg	½	1	1
vanilla extract	½ tsp.	1 tsp.	1 tsp.
salt	½ tsp.	1 tsp.	1½ tsp.
dry milk powder	2 tbs.	3 tbs.	¼ cup
amaranth flour	⅓ cup	½ cup	⅔ cup
bread flour	1¾ cups	2½ cups	3⅓ cups
yeast	1 tsp.	1½ tsp.	2 tsp.

At beep add: *(If National or Panasonic, add following first kneading)*

chopped walnuts	⅓ cup	½ cup	⅔ cup

Three Seed Bread

Whole Wheat or Basic cycle

This bread has a wonderful taste and texture. Feel free to experiment with different seeds. Try combinations of anise, fennel, caraway or any other seeds which you may have on hand!

	Small	**Medium**	**Large**
water	1 cup	1½ cups	1¾ cups
vegetable oil	1½ tbs.	2 tbs.	3 tbs.
honey	1½ tsp.	2 tsp.	1 tbs.
salt	½ tsp.	¾ tsp.	1 tsp.
sunflower seeds	3 tbs.	¼ cup	⅓ cup
sesame seeds	1½ tbs.	2 tbs.	3 tbs.
poppy seeds	1 tbs.	1½ tbs.	2 tbs.
whole wheat flour	1 cup	1⅓ cups	1½ cups
bread flour	2 cups	2¾ cups	3 cups
dry milk powder	3 tbs.	¼ cup	¼ cup
yeast	1 tsp.	2 tsp.	2½ tsp.

Ancient Grain Bread

Whole Wheat or Basic cycle

This bread is a variation of Three Seed Bread. It has great texture with the wonderful tastes of quinoa, amaranth, sesame seeds and poppy seeds. The quinoa and amaranth make this an extremely nutritious, healthy bread. In place of the seeds in Three Seed Bread, substitute:

	Small	Medium	Large
quinoa grains	1 1/3 tbs.	2 tbs.	2 2/3 tbs.
amaranth grains	1 1/3 tbs.	2 tbs.	2 2/3 tbs.
sesame seeds	2 tsp.	1 tbs.	1 1/3 tbs.
poppy seeds	1 1/4 tsp.	2 tsp.	2 1/2 tsp.

Quinoa Bread

Basic cycle

The quinoa gives this bread a nutty flavor. It's a good source of protein and calcium — worth trying. Ancient Harvest packages quinoa flour and it should be available through a good health food store.

	Small	Medium	Large
water	3/4 cup	1 1/8 cups	1 1/4 cups
margarine or butter	2 tbs.	1/4 cup	1/4 cup
sugar	1 1/2 tsp.	2 tsp.	1 tbs.
salt	1/2 tsp.	1 tsp.	1 1/2 tsp.
quinoa flour	1/3 cup	1/2 cup	3/4 cup
bread flour	2 cups	2 1/2 cups	3 cups
yeast	1 tsp.	1 1/2 tsp.	2 tsp.

About Sourdough Breads

As the early day pioneers traveled west across the United States, they carried a mixture of flour and milk or water, which was used to leaven bread. As the mixture or starter aged, it became more sour and, hence, so did the bread.

A true sourdough starter is nothing more than the flour and milk or water which sits at room temperature for several days and catches live yeast bacteria from the air. Most starter recipes today include yeast as an original ingredient as it is much easier and less time-consuming. In addition, many sourdough bread recipes also indicate usage of yeast itself, as it does provide a higher-rising, lighter loaf.

A sourdough starter should be kept in a glass or plastic bowl that has a tight-fitting lid. I recommend a bowl instead of a jar as you can feed your starter right in the bowl easily.

Sourdough Starter

To make your starter, mix together:

2 cups lukewarm milk
2 cups bread flour
2½ tsp. (1 package) yeast.

I mix the starter with an electric, hand-held mixer on the lowest setting. Cover your starter and place in a warm, draft-free location for 4 to 7 days, gently stirring it once a day. You may notice that the mixture bubbles and in some cases it may even overflow your bowl. This is an indication that you have a healthy fermenting process going on. A sour-smelling liquid may form on top of the starter which should simply be stirred back in.

If your starter ever changes colors, to purple, for example, discard and start another one.

After allowing your starter to sit for 4 to 7 days, it is ready to be used. Take out whatever portion your recipe calls for and put it into the machine as you would any liquid ingredient. After removing a portion from the starter, the starter must be fed. Simply add equal portions of milk or water and flour as was used. For example, if you used 1 cup of starter, replace it with 1 cup of water and 1 cup of bread flour.

Some hints on feeding your starter: Always use the same kind of flour. If you used bread flour in your original starter, use bread flour to feed it. Also, alternate between milk and water for each feeding. Since your original liquid ingredient was milk, the first liquid feeding should be with water. If you forget which you used last, that's okay, but try to alternate at least every other time. After feeding your starter, let it sit at room temperature for approximately 1 day and then refrigerate.

Many cookbooks suggest stirring the starter once a day even when being refrigerated; I find that it is not necessary. You must, however, use a portion of the starter at least once a week. If you choose not to bake sourdough breads that often, then remove a cup of your starter and feed it as though you used some during the week. If this is not done, your starter will turn rancid and have to be replaced. Should you be away on vacation or otherwise unable to tend to the starter, freeze it. Upon your return, thaw it in the refrigerator and then remove a portion and feed it as soon as you are able.

You may be thinking that this sounds too complicated, but it really is not, nor is the starter overly fragile. A friend of mine had the same starter for 14 years!

My first few loaves of sourdough were not very sour and I feared it was my starter. After allowing the starter to mellow a little by sitting in the refrigerator and using only once a week, it and the breads became more sour.

Another hint is to put the ingredients on the timer cycle for early morning baking. The milk put in the night before adds a little more sour taste. If the bread is getting too sour for you, feed with water more often than milk.

Always check the consistency of the dough. The starter itself may vary from one day to the next and it is not uncommon to have to adjust the dough with water or flour.

If you use your starter frequently and/or it is very active and strong, it may be necessary to decrease the amount of yeast given in the recipe. This will require experimentation. It may even be possible to omit the yeast altogether if the bread is rising sufficiently with just the sourdough starter.

Many of the recipes in this chapter were adapted from ethnic recipes which called for a high amount of salt. If you feel the bread is too salty, you can safely cut the amount of salt to approximately 1 tsp. for a large size recipe.

Sourdough Bread

This compares favorably to the famous San Francisco sourdoughs. Adjust the consistency with the milk while the dough is kneading.

	Small	Medium	Large
starter	¾ cup	1 cup	1⅓ cups
margarine or butter	1 tbs.	2 tbs.	2 tbs.
sugar	1½ tbs.	2 tbs.	2½ tbs.
salt	1 tsp.	1½ tsp.	1½ tsp.
bread flour	2 cups	3 cups	3½ cups
yeast	1 tsp.	1½ tsp.	2 tsp.
milk	3 tbs.-⅓ cup	¼-⅔ cup	¼-¾ cup

Sourdough Wheat Bread

This is a delicious sourdough with the benefits of whole wheat flour. Adjust the consistency with the milk while the dough is kneading.

	Small	Medium	Large
starter	⅞ cup	1 cup	1½ cups
margarine or butter	1 tbs.	2 tbs.	2½ tbs.
sugar	1½ tbs.	2 tbs.	2½ tbs.
salt	1 tsp.	1½ tsp.	1½ tsp.
whole wheat flour	¾ cup	1 cup	1½ cups
bread flour	1½ cups	2 cups	2½ cups
yeast	1 tsp.	2 tsp.	2 tsp.
milk	3 tbs.-⅓ cup	½-⅔ cup	¼-¾ cup

Sourdough French Bread

This is absolutely delicious — great for sandwiches. Adjust the consistency with the water while the dough is kneading.

	Small	Medium	Large
starter	⅔ cup	1 cup	1⅓ cups
sugar	1 tsp.	1½ tsp.	2 tsp.
salt	½ tsp.	¾ tsp.	1 tsp.
bread flour	2 cups	3 cups	4 cups
yeast	1 tsp.	1½ tsp.	2 tsp.
water	¼-⅓ cup	½-⅔ cup	⅔-¾ cup

Sourdough Pizza Crust

Dough cycle

This is an interesting change-of-pace in pizza making.

	Small	Medium	Large
starter	½ cup	¾ cup	1 cup
olive oil	1 ½ tbs.	2 ¼ tbs.	3 tbs.
salt	½ tsp.	¾ tsp.	1 tsp.
all-purpose flour	2 cups	3 cups	4 cups
yeast	1 tsp.	1 ½ tsp.	2 tsp.
water	as needed	as needed	as needed

Roll dough into a rectangle or circle, depending on the pan to be used. Place dough on pan and turn excess under, forming a raised edge. Brush very lightly with olive oil. Cover and let rise about 30 minutes. Top with pizza sauce and desired toppings. Place in a preheated 500° oven and bake until crust is brown and cheese is melted, about 5 to 10 minutes.

Sourdough Cornmeal Bread

Basic cycle

This one is a unique, delicious bread. Adjust the consistency with the milk while the dough is kneading.

	Small	Medium	Large
starter	⅔ cup	1 cup	1 ⅓ cups
margarine or butter	1 tbs.	1 ½ tbs.	2 tbs.
sugar	1 tbs.	1 ½ tbs.	2 tbs.
salt	½ tsp.	¾ tsp.	1 tsp.
cornmeal	⅔ cup	1 cup	1 ⅓ cups
bread flour	1 ½ cups	2 ½ cups	2 ⅔ cups
yeast	1 tsp.	1 ½ tsp.	2 ½ tsp.
milk	2-4 tbs.	¼-⅓ cup	⅓-½ cup

Sourdough Oatmeal

This is a very moist sourdough bread. Adjust the consistency with the milk while the dough is kneading.

	Small	Medium	Large
starter	¾ cup	1 cup	1¼ cups
margarine or butter	1 tbs.	1½ tbs.	2 tbs.
sugar	1 tbs.	1½ tbs.	2 tbs.
salt	¾ tsp.	1 tsp.	1 tsp.
oats	¾ cup	1 cup	1¼ cups
bread flour	2¼ cups	3 cups	3½ cups
yeast	1½ tsp.	2 tsp.	2 tsp.
milk	⅓-½ cup	½-⅔ cup	⅔-¾ cup

Sourdough Rye Bread

This slightly sour loaf of rye is very light. It is somewhat different than many of the other sourdoughs as it has its own starter, which is used in its entirety in the recipe. Molasses can be substituted for the barley malt syrup.

	Small	Medium	Large
rye starter*			
warm milk (115°)	½ cup	¾ cup	1 cup
rye flour	½ cup	¾ cup	1 cup
yeast	1 tsp.	1 tsp.	1½ tsp.

To prepare starter: Sprinkle yeast over warm milk and stir until dissolved; stir in rye flour. Cover and let stand at room temperature for 3 days, stirring once a day. Use the entire starter in the bread recipe.

	Small	Medium	Large
rye starter	*	*	*
water	⅓ cup	½ cup	⅔ cup
egg	½	1	1
vegetable oil	1 tbs.	1½ tbs.	2 tbs.
barley malt syrup	1 tbs.	1½ tbs.	2 tbs.
salt	1 tsp.	1½ tsp.	2 tsp.
caraway seeds	2 tsp.	1 tbs.	1⅓ tbs.
bread flour	1¾ cups	2½ cups	3 cups
rye flour	½ cup	¾ cup	1 cup
yeast	1 tsp.	1½ tsp.	2½ tsp.

About Fruit and Vegetable Breads

Fruits and vegetables often vary in their liquid content. Check the dough after 5 to 10 minutes of kneading and add water or flour if necessary.

Apple Butter Bread
Sweet or Basic cycle

Bake the apple butter right into the bread. Try substituting any favorite jam or jelly for the apple butter. This is a high-rising bread. If in doubt, make a smaller size.

	Small	Medium	Large
water	¾ cup	1 cup	1⅓ cups
vegetable oil	1½ tbs.	2 tbs.	3 tbs.
apple butter	⅓ cup	½ cup	⅔ cup
sugar	2 tsp.	1 tbs.	1½ tbs.
salt	¾ tsp.	1 tsp.	1 tsp.
whole wheat flour	⅔ cup	1 cup	1⅓ cups
bread flour	1½ cups	2 cups	2¾ cups
yeast	1 tsp.	1½ tsp.	2 tsp.

Apple Chunk Bread
Sweet or Basic cycle

You'll think you're eating an apple pie. This is an absolute must-try. The apples add moisture to the dough. Add the apples at the beginning of the second kneading cycle. If your machine has only one main kneading cycle, add apples at the beginning. Add 1-2 tbs. flour to adjust consistency if necessary. This dessert bread should be served warm (it probably won't last long enough to get cold anyway).

	Small	Medium	Large
milk	⅔ cup	1 cup	1¼ cups
vegetable oil	2 tbs.	3 tbs.	3 tbs.
sugar	1½ tbs.	2 tbs.	2½ tbs.
cinnamon	½ tsp.	½ tsp.	1 tsp.
salt	1 tsp.	1½ tsp.	1½ tsp.
bread flour	2 cups	3 cups	3½ cups
yeast	1 tsp.	1½ tsp.	2 tsp.
medium apple, peeled and diced	½	1½	1½

Applesauce Bread

Sweet or Basic cycle

This bread made a huge hit at a neighborhood potluck — especially the children kept going back for more. Very moist.

	Small	Medium	Large
applesauce	1 cup	1 1/4 cups	1 3/4 cups
margarine or butter	2 tbs.	2 tbs.	3 tbs.
sugar	1 tbs.	1 1/2 tbs.	2 tbs.
salt	1 tsp.	1 tsp.	1 1/2 tsp.
cinnamon, optional	1 tsp.	1 tsp.	1 1/2 tsp.
whole wheat flour	3/4 cup	1 cup	1 1/4 cups
bread flour	1 1/2 cups	2 cups	2 1/2 cups
yeast	1 1/2 tsp.	2 tsp.	2 1/2 tsp.

Banana Oatmeal Bread

Sweet or Basic cycle

This low-rising bread has a slight taste of banana with the texture of oatmeal. The flavor of the banana seems to be stronger when the bread is toasted. Use fully ripe bananas and adjust the dough consistency with the extra water if you need to.

	Small	Medium	Large
water	1/3-1/2 cup	1/2-2/3 cup	1/2-3/4 cup
mashed banana	3/4 cup	1 cup	1 1/4 cups
vegetable oil	2 tbs.	2 1/2 tbs.	3 tbs.
sugar	1 tbs.	1 1/2 tbs.	2 tbs.
salt	1 tsp.	1 tsp.	1 1/2 tsp.
oats	1 cup	1 1/3 cups	1 3/4 cups
bread flour	2 cups	2 2/3 cups	3 cups
yeast	1 1/2 tsp.	2 tsp.	2 1/2 tsp.

Blueberry Bread

Sweet or Basic cycle

Delicious — try blue cornmeal, although yellow will do nicely too. If using frozen blueberries, they must be well thawed and tightly packed into your measuring cup. Adjust the consistency with the water as the dough is kneading. This low-rising, dense bread is full of flavor.

	Small	**Medium**	**Large**
cottage cheese	½ cup	⅔ cup	¾ cup
margarine or butter	1 ½ tbs.	2 tbs.	2 tbs.
blueberries	¾ cup	1 cup	1 ¼ cups
sugar	2 tbs.	2 ½ tbs.	3 tbs.
salt	1 tsp.	1 ½ tsp.	1 ½ tsp.
blue cornmeal	1 cup	1 ⅓ cups	1 ½ cups
bread flour	2 cups	2 ⅔ cups	3 cups
yeast	1 ½ tsp.	2 tsp.	2 ½ tsp.
water	2-4 tbs.	3 tbs.-⅓ cup	¼-½ cup

Carrot Bread

Sweet or Basic cycle

This delicious, healthy bread is a good way to get your beta carotene!

	Small	**Medium**	**Large**
water	¾ cup	⅞ cup	1 ¼ cups
vegetable oil	1 tbs.	1 ½ tbs.	2 tbs.
grated carrot	½ cup	⅔ cup	¾ cup
brown sugar	1 ½ tbs.	2 tbs.	2 ½ tbs.
salt	1 tsp.	1 tsp.	1 ½ tsp.
oats	1 cup	1 ⅓ cups	1 ½ cups
whole wheat flour	½ cup	⅔ cup	¾ cup
bread flour	1 ½ cups	2 cups	2 ½ cups
dry milk powder	3 tbs.	¼ cup	⅓ cup
yeast	1 tsp.	1 ½ tsp.	2 tsp.

Coconut Pineapple Bread

Wonderful. A must for Sunday brunch or dessert, and it's really fun for a Hawaiian Luau dinner. Adjust the consistency of the dough with the water as the dough is kneading.

	Small	Medium	Large
cream cheese	4 oz.	6 oz.	8 oz.
can (8 oz.) crushed pineapple, drained	½ can	1 can	1 can
pineapple extract	1 tsp.	1½ tsp.	2 tsp.
vegetable oil	2 tbs.	3 tbs.	3 tbs.
sugar	2 tbs.	3 tbs.	3 tbs.
salt	¾ tsp.	1 tsp.	1 tsp.
grated coconut	3 tbs.	¼ cup	⅓ cup
bread flour	2 cups	3 cups	3½ cups
yeast	1 tsp.	1½ tsp.	2 tsp.
water	1-3 tbs.	2-4 tbs.	¼-⅓ cup

Lemon Bread

This lightly colored bread has a subtle, pleasing flavor. The lemon peel can be adjusted to taste.

	Small	Medium	Large
water	⅔ cup	1 cup	1¼ cups
margarine or butter	1 tbs.	2 tbs.	2 tbs.
grated lemon peel	¾ tsp.	1 tsp.	1½ tsp.
sugar	½ tsp.	¾ tsp.	1 tsp.
salt	¼ tsp.	½ tsp.	¾ tsp.
bread flour	2 cups	3 cups	3½ cups
dry milk powder	2 tbs.	¼ cup	⅓ cup
yeast	1 tsp.	1½ tsp.	2 tsp.

Onion Bread

Even if you typically do not like onions, you'll like this bread. It is a great accompaniment to barbecue dinners — especially chicken or burgers. Onions vary in moisture content, so you may have to adjust the consistency.

	Small	Medium	Large
water	½ cup	¾ cup	1 cup
margarine or butter	1 tbs.	1½ tbs.	2 tbs.
grated fresh onion	⅓ cup	½ cup	⅔ cup
sugar	2 tsp.	1 tbs.	1½ tbs.
salt	¾ tsp.	1 tsp.	1½ tsp.
whole wheat flour	⅓ cup	½ cup	⅔ cup
bread flour	1¾ cups	2½ cups	3⅓ cups
yeast	1 tsp.	1½ tsp.	2½ tsp.

Orange Banana Bread

This unique breakfast bread is just as good toasted as fresh out of the oven. Use very ripe bananas and adjust the consistency with additional orange juice if necessary.

	Small	Medium	Large
orange juice	½ cup	¾ cup	⅞ cup
margarine or butter	½ tbs.	1 tbs.	1 tbs.
mashed banana	⅓ cup	½ cup	⅔ cup
sugar	2 tsp.	1 tbs.	1½ tbs.
grated orange peel	½ tsp.	¾ tsp.	1 tsp.
salt	½ tsp.	¾ tsp.	1 tsp.
bread flour	2 cups	3 cups	3½ cups
yeast	1½ tsp.	2 tsp.	2 tsp.

Orange Cinnamon Bread

Sweet or Basic cycle

This makes delicious breakfast bread. Set it on the timer cycle and wake up to it hot from the oven, or have it toasted the next day, if it lasts that long. Both the cinnamon and the orange peel can be adjusted to taste.

	Small	Medium	Large
orange juice	¾ cup	1⅛ cups	1⅓ cups
margarine or butter	1 tbs.	2 tbs.	2 tbs.
cinnamon	1 tsp.	2 tsp.	1 tbs.
grated orange peel	¾ tsp.	1 tsp.	1 tsp.
salt	½ tsp.	¾ tsp.	1 tsp.
sugar	1 tsp.	2 tsp.	1 tbs.
bread flour	2 cups	3 cups	3½ cups
yeast	1½ tsp.	2 tsp.	2½ tsp.

Peanut Butter and Jelly Bread

Sweet, Raisin or Basic cycle

Kids love this bread! Watch this dough carefully and add water or scrape the sides of the pan if necessary. Jam seems to have too high a sugar content, so make sure to use a jelly. This is a high-rising loaf. If in doubt about the size, use the next smaller recipe. People with glass-domed machines should make the medium size for best results.

	Small	Medium	Large
water	⅔ cup	1 cup	1⅓ cups
vegetable oil	1 tbs.	1½ tbs.	2 tbs.
peanut butter	⅓ cup	½ cup	⅔ cup
jelly	⅓ cup	½ cup	⅔ cup
sugar	2 tsp.	1 tbs.	1⅓ tbs.
salt	⅔ tsp.	1 tsp.	1 tsp.
whole wheat flour	⅔ cup	1 cup	1⅓ cups
bread flour	1⅓ cups	2 cups	2⅔ cups
yeast	1 tsp.	1½ tsp.	2½ tsp.

Poppy Seed Bread

Sweet or Basic cycle

Expect a high-rising loaf when you make this very light, airy bread. Eat it alone or try it topped with hot ham and cheese.

	Small	Medium	Large
water	⅔ cup	1 cup	1¼ cups
vegetable oil	1 tbs.	1½ tbs.	2 tbs.
vanilla extract	½ tsp.	1 tsp.	1 tsp.
butter flavoring	½ tsp.	1 tsp.	1 tsp.
almond extract	½ tsp.	1 tsp.	1 tsp.
salt	¾ tsp.	1 tsp.	1 tsp.
sugar	2 tbs.	3 tbs.	¼ cup
poppy seeds	1½ tbs.	2 tbs.	3 tbs.
bread flour	2 cups	3 cups	3½ cups
yeast	1 tsp.	1½ tsp.	2 tsp.

Potato Bread

Basic cycle

This potato bread is really good alone or as sandwich bread. The potatoes give it just a little extra flavor. This is high-rising. If in doubt about the size, use a smaller size. This bread slices very well. Use an egg yolk, white or 2 tbs. egg substitute for the ½ egg.

	Small	Medium	Large
potato water	½ cup	⅔ cup	¾ cup
margarine or butter	2 tbs.	2½ tbs.	3 tbs.
egg	½	½	1
mashed potatoes	⅓ cup	⅓ cup	½ cup
sugar	1½ tbs.	2 tbs.	2 tbs.
salt	¾ tsp.	1 tsp.	1 tsp.
bread flour	2 cups	2½ cups	3 cups
yeast	1 tsp.	1½ tsp.	2 tsp.

Boil 1-2 peeled potatoes. Save water to use in bread. Mash potatoes, without milk or butter, and let cool to lukewarm or room temperature.

Pumpkin or Winter Squash Bread

Sweet or Basic cycle

Spicy squash bread uses those leftover squashes. Here is a great way to hide vegetables from finicky eaters. Canned pumpkin can be used if desired. Watch the consistency.

	Small	Medium	Large
water	½ cup	¾ cup	1 cup
winter squash, cooked and mashed (acorn, butternut, pumpkin, etc.)	⅓ cup	⅔ cup	¾ cup
vegetable oil	1½ tbs.	2 tbs.	3 tbs.
honey	1½ tbs.	2 tbs.	3 tbs.
salt	1 tsp.	1½ tsp.	2 tsp.
cinnamon	¾ tsp.	1 tsp.	1⅓ tsp.
allspice	¼ tsp.	½ tsp.	¾ tsp.
nutmeg	⅛ tsp.	¼ tsp.	½ tsp.
ground cloves	⅛ tsp.	¼ tsp.	½ tsp.
whole wheat flour	⅓ cup	½ cup	⅔ cup
bread flour	1⅔ cups	2½ cups	3⅓ cups
yeast	1 tsp.	1½ tsp.	2½ tsp.

Pistachio Raisin Bread

Sweet or Basic cycle

You won't believe how good this one is!

	Small	Medium	Large
water	⅔ cup	1 cup	1⅓ cups
vegetable oil	1 tbs.	1½ tbs.	2 tbs.
honey	1 tbs.	1½ tbs.	2 tbs.
salt	½ tsp.	1 tsp.	1 tsp.
whole wheat flour	½ cup	¾ cup	1 cup
bread flour	1½ cups	2¼ cups	3 cups
yeast	1 tsp.	1½ tsp.	2 tsp.

At beep add: *(If National or Panasonic, add following first kneading)*

	Small	Medium	Large
raisins	2 tbs.	3 tbs.	¼ cup
pistachio nuts	2 tbs.	3 tbs.	¼ cup

Raisin Bread

A friend of mine tasted this bread and went out the next day to buy an automatic bread machine. Need I say more?

	Small	Medium	Large
water	¾ cup	1⅛ cups	1¼ cups
margarine or butter	1½ tbs.	2 tbs.	2 tbs.
sugar	1½ tbs.	2 tbs.	2½ tbs.
salt	¾ tsp.	1 tsp.	1 tsp.
bread flour	2 cups	3 cups	3½ cups
yeast	1 tsp.	1½ tsp.	2 tsp.

At beep add: *(If National or Panasonic, add following first kneading)*

	Small	Medium	Large
raisins	½ cup	¾ cup	1 cup

Raisin Bread Variations

All ingredients are put in the machine when it beeps (or during the rest period after the first kneading in National or Panasonic machines).

Cinnamon Raisin Bread	Small	Medium	Large
raisins	½ cup	¾ cup	1 cup
cinnamon	2 tsp.	1 tbs.	1 tbs.
Apricot Bread			
dried apricots, chopped	½ cup	¾ cup	1 cup
Mixed Dried Fruit Bread			
mixed dried fruit, chopped	½ cup	¾ cup	1 cup
Orange Raisin Bread			
raisins	½ cup	¾ cup	1 cup
grated orange peel	⅓ tsp.	½ tsp.	1 tsp.

Irish Soda Bread

While at first you may wonder about the caraway seed or raisin combination, once you've tried it, you'll be hooked. This is a must-try.

	Small	Medium	Large
buttermilk	¾ cup	1⅛ cups	1⅓ cups
margarine or butter	1½ tbs.	2 tbs.	3 tbs.
sugar	1½ tbs.	2 tbs.	2½ tbs.
salt	¾ tsp.	1 tsp.	1 tsp.
baking soda	¼ tsp.	½ tsp.	½ tsp.
caraway seeds	1½ tsp.	2 tsp.	1 tbs.
bread flour	2 cups	3 cups	3½ cups
yeast	1½ tsp.	2 tsp.	2½ tsp.

At beep add: *(If National or Panasonic, add following first kneading)*

	Small	Medium	Large
raisins	¼ cup	⅓ cup	½ cup

Sunflower Bread

The sunflower seeds make an interesting change from a raisin bread and provide terrific flavor. Try substituting pumpkin seeds for another interesting, tasty variation.

	Small	Medium	Large
water	⅔ cup	1 cup	1⅓ cups
vegetable oil	1 tbs.	1½ tbs.	2 tbs.
honey	1½ tbs.	2 tbs.	2½ tbs.
salt	½ tsp.	¾ tsp.	1 tsp.
oats	⅓ cup	½ cup	⅔ cup
whole wheat flour	⅓ cup	½ cup	⅔ cup
bread flour	1½ cups	2 cups	2⅔ cups
yeast	1 tsp.	1½ tsp.	2 tsp.

At beep add: *(If National or Panasonic, add following first kneading)*

	Small	Medium	Large
sunflower seeds	⅓ cup	½ cup	⅔ cup
raisins	¼ cup	¼ cup	⅓ cup

Stollen

If this bread does not bake properly in your machine, next time reduce the amount of fruits.

	Small	**Medium**	**Large**
milk	½-⅔ cup	⅔-¾ cup	⅞-1 cup
margarine or butter	2 tbs.	3 tbs.	¼ cup
egg	1	1	1
almond extract	¼ tsp.	¼ tsp.	½ tsp.
rum extract	¼ tsp.	¼ tsp.	½ tsp.
sugar	2 tbs.	3 tbs.	¼ cup
salt	¾ tsp.	1 tsp.	1 tsp.
mace	⅛ tsp.	⅛ tsp.	¼ tsp.
cardamom	dash	dash	⅛ tsp.
grated lemon peel	1½ tsp.	2 tsp.	1 tbs.
grated orange peel	1½ tsp.	2 tsp.	1 tbs.
bread flour	2 cups	3 cups	3½ cups
yeast	1 tsp.	1½ tsp.	2 tsp.

At beep add: *(If National or Panasonic, add following first kneading)*

slivered almonds	¼ cup	⅓ cup	½ cup
mixed dried fruit, chopped	¼ cup	⅓ cup	½ cup

Panettone

Candied fruit is traditionally used in Panettone recipes, but some machines have difficulty baking the high sugar content. Try dried mixed fruits instead. People with glass-domed machines should make the medium size.

	Small	**Medium**	**Large**
water	½ cup	⅔ cup	¾ cup
margarine or butter	3 tbs.	¼ cup	5 tbs.
eggs	1	1½	1½
sugar	3 tbs.	¼ cup	⅓ cup
salt	½ tsp.	¾ tsp.	1 tsp.
grated lemon peel	1 tsp.	1½ tsp.	1½ tsp.
bread flour	2 cups	3 cups	3½ cups
yeast	1 tsp.	1½ tsp.	2 tsp.

At beep add: *(If National or Panasonic, add following first kneading)*

mixed dried fruits, chopped	2 tbs.	3 tbs.	¼ cup
chopped nuts	2 tbs.	3 tbs.	¼ cup

Salsa Cornmeal Bread

Basic cycle

This wonderful cornmeal bread has just a hint of hot and spicy salsa. Serve this low-rising bread with any Mexican meal. Adjust the consistency of the dough if necessary.

	Small	Medium	Large
milk	⅔ cup	⅞ cup	1 cup
salsa	2 tbs.	3 tbs.	¼ cup
margarine or butter	1½ tbs.	2 tbs.	2½ tbs.
egg	1	1	1
sugar	2 tsp.	1 tbs.	1½ tbs.
salt	¾ tsp.	1 tsp.	1½ tsp.
yellow cornmeal	⅔ cup	1 cup	1⅓ cups
bread flour	2 cups	2½ cups	3 cups
yeast	1 tsp.	1½ tsp.	2 tsp.

Strawberry Banana Bread

Sweet or Basic cycle

This wonderful, light loaf has just the right hint of both strawberries and banana. Use ripe bananas and adjust the consistency with additional milk or flour if necessary.

	Small	Medium	Large
milk	¼ cup	⅓ cup	½ cup
mashed strawberries	¼ cup	⅓ cup	½ cup
mashed bananas	¼ cup	⅓ cup	½ cup
margarine	1 tbs.	1½ tbs.	2 tbs.
sugar	1 tsp.	1½ tsp.	2 tsp.
salt	½ tsp.	¾ tsp.	1 tsp.
bread flour	2 cups	2½ cups	3½ cups
yeast	1 tsp.	1½ tsp.	2½ tsp.

Sweet Potato Bread

Sweet or Basic cycle

Just a hint of sweet potatoes makes this a perfect accompaniment to a turkey dinner and is great later for the leftover sandwiches. Cinnamon or nutmeg can be adjusted to taste if desired. Be sure to save the water used to cook the sweet potatoes for the first ingredient.

	Small	Medium	Large
sweet potato water	½ cup	¾ cup	⅞ cup
mashed sweet potatoes	⅓ cup	½ cup	⅔ cup
margarine or butter	2 tbs.	3 tbs.	3 tbs.
brown sugar	2 tbs.	3 tbs.	¼ cup
salt	¾ tsp.	1 tsp.	1½ tsp.
cinnamon or nutmeg	½ tsp.	¾ tsp.	1 tsp.
bread flour	2 cups	3 cups	3½ cups
yeast	1 tsp.	1½ tsp.	2 tsp.

Zucchini Wheat Bread

Sweet or Basic cycle

Zucchini lovers will be especially happy with this bread. Toasting brings out a stronger flavor. Watch the consistency and adjust with water or flour as needed.

	Small	Medium	Large
shredded zucchini	½ cup	¾ cup	1 cup
water	½ cup	¾ cup	1 cup
vegetable oil	2 tbs.	3 tbs.	¼ cup
honey	2 tbs.	3 tbs.	¼ cup
salt	½ tsp.	¾ tsp.	1 tsp.
grated orange peel	¾ tsp.	1 tsp.	1½ tsp.
wheat germ	3 tbs.	¼ cup	⅓ cup
whole wheat flour	1 cup	1½ cups	2 cups
bread flour	1 cup	1½ cups	2 cups
yeast	1 tsp.	1½ tsp.	2 tsp.

Oregano Bread

This is an absolute must with spaghetti or lasagna — an often-requested bread. Once you have this you'll never go back to plain old garlic bread! Several bread testers have placed orders for this when entertaining with Italian meals.

	Small	Medium	Large
water	¾ cup	1 ⅛ cups	1 ½ cups
olive oil	2 tbs.	¼ cup	⅓ cup
Parmesan cheese, grated	3 tbs.	¼ cup	⅓ cup
sugar, optional	1 tsp.	1 ½ tsp.	2 tsp.
salt	½ tsp.	¾ tsp.	1 tsp.
oregano, dried	2 tsp.	1 tbs.	1 ½ tbs.
bread flour	2 cups	3 cups	3 ½ cups
dry milk powder	3 tbs.	¼ cup	⅓ cup
yeast	1 ½ tsp.	2 tsp.	2 ½ tsp.

Herb Bread

Basic cycle

This spicy bread perks up a meal, and is especially good with chicken or fish.

	Small	Medium	Large
water	⅔ cup	1 ⅛ cups	1 ¼ cups
egg	1	1	1
margarine or butter	1 tbs.	2 tbs.	2 ½ tbs.
salt	¼ tsp.	½ tsp.	1 tsp.
sugar	1 tbs.	1 ½ tbs.	2 tbs.
oregano, dried	¼ tsp.	½ tsp.	1 tsp.
thyme, dried	¼ tsp.	½ tsp.	1 tsp.
black pepper	¼ tsp.	½ tsp.	1 tsp.
parsley, dried	¼ tsp.	½ tsp.	1 tsp.
celery seed	dash	⅛ tsp.	¼ tsp.
sage	dash	⅛ tsp.	¼ tsp.
wheat germ	3 tbs.	¼ cup	⅓ cup
oats	3 tbs.	¼ cup	⅓ cup
bread flour	2 cups	3 cups	3 ½ cups
yeast	1 ½ tsp.	2 cups	2 ½ tsp.

Parsley Herb Bread

Basic cycle

This is another good bread to serve with chicken. Not as spicy as the preceding Herb Bread, it nevertheless adds a nice flavor to the meal.

	Small	Medium	Large
water	¾ cup	1 cup	1¼ cups
olive oil	1 tbs.	1½ tbs.	2 tbs.
sugar	1 tsp.	1½ tsp.	2 tsp.
salt	½ tsp.	1 tsp.	1 tsp.
parsley, dried	1½ tsp.	2 tsp.	1 tbs.
chives	¼ tsp.	½ tsp.	1 tsp.
tarragon	¼ tsp.	½ tsp.	1 tsp.
bread flour	2 cups	3 cups	3½ cups
yeast	1 tsp.	1½ tsp.	2 tsp.

Dill Bread

Basic cycle

The dill flavor makes an outstanding bread, especially good with with either pasta or fish. It's one of our favorites, and another often-requested bread. The amount of cottage cheese is the same for all sizes; the eggs provide additional moisture. This loaf is high-rising.

	Small	Medium	Large
cottage cheese	1 cup	1 cup	1 cup
eggs	1	2	3
sugar	1½ tbs.	2 tbs.	3 tbs.
dill weed, dried	2 tsp.	1 tbs.	1½ tbs.
salt	½ tsp.	½ tsp.	1 tsp.
baking soda	¼ tsp.	¼ tsp.	½ tsp.
bread flour	2 cups	2½ cups	3 cups
yeast	1 tsp.	1½ tsp.	2 tsp.

Garlic Parmesan Bread

If you're a garlic bread lover, this is for you. Feel free to increase or decrease the amount of garlic powder to suit your taste. Very aromatic and great, of course, with Italian meals. Make sure the garlic powder is fresh (it gets bitter if it sits on your shelf too long), and use freshly grated Parmesan.

	Small	Medium	Large
water	⅔ cup	1 cup	1⅛ cups
margarine or butter	2 tbs.	2½ tbs.	3 tbs.
honey	2 tsp.	1 tbs.	1½ tbs.
Parmesan cheese, grated	½ cup	⅔ cup	¾ cup
salt	½ tsp.	¾ tsp.	1 tsp.
garlic powder	1 tsp.	1½ tsp.	2 tsp.
bread flour	2 cups	3 cups	3½ cups
yeast	1 tsp.	1½ tsp.	2 tsp.

Anadama Bread

Here is a very different tasting bread — the molasses gives it just the right oomph. Legend has it that a fisherman, tired of his wife's cooking, devised this recipe. As he sat down to eat, he mumbled "Anna, damn her," and from then on this was Anadama bread.

	Small	Medium	Large
water	⅞ cup	1 cup	1⅛ cups
molasses	2 tbs.	¼ cup	⅓ cup
margarine or butter	1 tbs.	1 tbs.	1½ tbs.
salt	½ tsp.	¾ tsp.	1 tsp.
yellow cornmeal	3 tbs.	¼ cup	⅓ cup
bread flour	2 cups	3 cups	3½ cups
yeast	1½ tsp.	2 tsp.	2½ tsp.

Christmas Anise Bread

Sweet or Basic cycle

The flavor of anise adds nice flavor to this bread but is not overwhelming. If you want a stronger-tasting bread, you can safely double the amount of anise and other spices.

	Small	**Medium**	**Large**
milk	⅔ cup	1 cup	1¼ cups
margarine or butter	2 tbs.	2½ tbs.	3 tbs.
sugar	1 tbs.	1½ tbs.	2 tbs.
salt	½ tsp.	¾ tsp.	1 tsp.
anise seeds	1 tsp.	1½ tsp.	2 tsp.
mace	dash	⅛ tsp.	¼ tsp.
nutmeg	dash	⅛ tsp.	¼ tsp.
grated lemon peel	½ tsp.	¾ tsp.	1 tsp.
grated orange peel	½ tsp.	¾ tsp.	1 tsp.
bread flour	2 cups	3 cups	3½ cups
yeast	1½ tsp.	2 tsp.	2½ tsp.

Christmas Bread

Sweet or Basic cycle

This is a delicious hearty bread for Christmas or any morning. Also wonderful with soup or stew.

	Small	**Medium**	**Large**
water	½ cup	¾ cup	1 cup
molasses	2½ tbs.	¼ cup	⅓ cup
honey	1½ tbs.	2 tbs.	3 tbs.
margarine or butter	1 tbs.	1½ tbs.	2 tbs.
salt	¾ tsp.	1 tsp.	1½ tsp.
oats	¼ cup	⅓ cup	½ cup
bread flour	2 cups	3 cups	3½ cups
yeast	1 tsp.	1½ tsp.	2 tsp.

Coffee Spice Bread

Basic cycle

This is similar in taste to a brown bread and a great way to use up that leftover coffee — regular or decaf.

	Small	Medium	Large
brewed coffee	½ cup	¾ cup	1 cup
vegetable oil	2 tbs.	2½ tbs.	3 tbs.
egg	1	1	1
sugar	2 tbs.	3 tbs.	¼ cup
salt	¾ tsp.	1 tsp.	1 tsp.
cinnamon	¾ tsp.	1 tsp.	1 tsp.
ground cloves	⅛ tsp.	¼ tsp.	½ tsp.
allspice	⅛ tsp.	¼ tsp.	½ tsp.
bread flour	2 cups	3 cups	3½ cups
yeast	1 tsp.	1½ tsp.	2 tsp.

About the Dough Cycle

The dough cycle kneads the dough and lets it rise one time. Upon completion of the cycle, the dough is removed from the machine, shaped by hand, allowed to rise again and then baked in a conventional oven. If you have a DAK, Citizen or Welbilt 100, remove the dough after allowing the dough to rise for about 1 hour and before the second kneading. All machines are capable of kneading up to 4 cups of flour, even a 1-pound machine. Please do not try to bake these recipes in your machine.

Brioche

Dough cycle

These make marvelous coffee rolls — very rich texture. It's worth using butter instead of margarine. Be sure to make plenty, as people will go back for seconds and even thirds! This dough will be somewhat moist, which results in a light end product. Add only enough flour to prevent sticking, either while the machine is kneading or after the dough has been removed. Makes 12.

1 cup milk	1 tsp. salt
1/4 cup butter	3-3 1/2 cups bread flour
2 eggs	1 1/2 tsp. yeast
3 tbs. sugar	

Remove dough from machine. Form dough into 12 large balls and 12 small balls. Place large balls of dough into muffin cups; press down in the center of each one to form an indentation into which you place a small ball of dough. Cover and let rise for about 40 minutes. Brush tops with a mixture of 1 beaten egg and 1 tbs. sugar. Bake in a preheated 375° oven for 15 to 20 minutes, until golden brown.

Croissants

The making of croissants is time-consuming; however, most of the time involved is actually in the rising and the chilling of the dough. Should you decide to make them in the minimum amount of time allowed, you will need approximately 5½ hours. If you desire hot croissants in the morning, you must start the process about 3 hours before refrigerating the dough overnight; and then you need approximately 1 hour in the morning. Makes 16.

1⅛ cups milk	1 tsp. salt
1 tbs. vegetable oil	2½ -3 cups all-purpose flour
2 tsp. sugar	1½ tsp. yeast

Have ready but do not put in the machine:
1 cup butter, cold

Allow dough to sit in the machine past the stop time with the lid down, so that the total first-rising time should be at least 2 to 2½ hours. Cover dough right in the pan, and put it in the refrigerator for a minimum of 20 minutes.

Using a lightly floured plastic cutting board, a baking pan or other portable surface, roll dough out into a rectangular shape.

While dough rests just a few seconds, knead butter while holding it under cold running water. You should be able to make it into a ball easily. Spread butter over rectangle of dough, using a flat utensil such as a pastry knife or spatula. Leave about ¼ to ½ inch unbuttered around the edges.

Fold dough into thirds, much as you would fold an 8½ x 11 piece of paper to fit into a business envelope. Roll dough into another rectangle, fold it into thirds and repeat again so that dough has been rolled and folded a total of 3 times. Cover dough loosely with plastic wrap and refrigerate for a minimum of 1½ hours, or overnight if you want croissants in the morning.

Repeat the procedure for rolling dough into a rectangle and folding 3 more times. You may need to sprinkle flour on dough and/or rolling pin for ease of rolling. Roll dough into another rectangle and cut into squares (about 4-5 inches, depending on the size of croissant you want). Cut each square in half, forming a triangle. Roll each triangle into a crescent shape and place on a well greased baking sheet.

Chill for 20 to 60 minutes. Bake in a preheated 400° oven for 10 minutes, drop the temperature to 350° and bake for another 10 to 15 minutes until done.

Variation: Almond Croissants

Mix 3 tbs. amond paste with cold butter. Brush the top of ready-to-be-baked croissants with beaten egg white and sprinkle with slivered almonds.

Almond Butter Crescents

About half of my testers said these were just as good as the croissants. They are extremely simple to make, too. Makes 8.

½ cup milk
¼ cup butter
1½ tsp. almond extract
2 eggs

⅓ cup sugar
½ tsp. salt
3-3¼ cups all-purpose flour
1½ tsp. yeast

Filling
2 tbs. butter, melted
1 tsp. almond extract

Glaze
1 egg beaten with 1 tbs. water

On a lightly floured surface, roll dough into a large circle. Brush mixture of melted butter and almond extract over dough. Cut circle into 8 pieces, as you would a pie. Roll each piece from wide end to tip of triangle so that it forms a crescent. Brush each roll with glaze. Place on a cornmeal-covered baking sheet, cover and let rise for about 1 hour. Bake in a preheated 350° oven for 15 to 20 minutes, or until golden.

Variation: Almond Nut Crescents

Sprinkle about ¼ cup chopped almonds on top of melted butter-almond extract mixture before you cut circle of dough.

Sweet Rolls

These are wonderful topped with jam. A special treat. Makes 12.

¾ cup milk
¼ cup margarine or butter
1 egg
¼ cup sugar

1 tsp. salt
3 cups all-purpose flour
2 tsp. yeast

After completion of dough cycle, shape dough into 12 balls and place in muffin cups. Cover and let rise for 45 to 60 minutes. Bake in a preheated 350° oven for 15 to 20 minutes or until done.

Croissant Loaf

This loaf has flaky layers similar to croissants. Delicious.

½ cup water
2 tbs. margarine or butter
1 tsp. vanilla extract
2 eggs
¼ cup sugar

¾ tsp. salt
3 cups all-purpose flour
2 tsp. yeast
3 tbs. butter or margarine to spread
    over dough

Roll dough into a ½-inch thick rectangle. Cut ½ of the butter or margarine into small pieces and place in the middle third of dough. Fold one third over onto top of butter. Place remaining butter, cut into small pieces, on top of folded-over third and fold remaining third over butter. All butter is now encased in dough.

Roll dough into another rectangle and fold into thirds, as you would a business letter. Wrap dough loosely in waxed paper and refrigerate for approximately 20 minutes.

Roll dough into a rectangle and fold into thirds 3 more times. Chill dough in the refrigerator if it seems sticky and difficult to work with.

Lightly knead dough, shaping into a ball. Place dough in a greased loaf pan (or 2). Cover and let rise for 50 to 60 minutes or until doubled in bulk. Bake in a preheated 350° oven for 30 to 35 minutes or until golden brown.

Parker House Dinner Rolls

Now synonymous with American dinner rolls, these were originated by The Parker House in Boston. Makes 12.

1 cup milk
2 tbs. margarine or butter
1 egg
1 tbs. sugar

½ tsp. salt
2½-3 cups all-purpose flour
2 tsp. yeast
3-4 tbs. butter, melted, for brushing

Glaze
1 egg, beaten

After completion of dough cycle, knead dough by hand for approximately 5 minutes. Roll out and cut with a biscuit cutter (or cup). Brush with melted butter. Fold circles in half and place in buttered muffin cups. Cover and let rise for 35 to 45 minutes. Brush tops with glaze and bake in a preheated 350° oven for 20 to 25 minutes.

Cinnamon Rolls

Dough cycle

These rolls are very good and not overly sweet. About ⅔ of the testers liked them as is; the others wanted them sweeter. If you want a sweeter bun, make a glaze out of milk and confectioners' sugar to spread over the tops while still warm. Baking these rolls in muffin cups makes them rise beautifully and look uniform. Makes 12.

1 cup milk
2 tbs. butter
1 egg
2 tbs. sugar
½ tsp. salt
3-3½ cups all-purpose flour
1½ tsp. yeast

Filling
 Mix together:
¼ cup sugar
1½ tbs. cinnamon
½ cup raisins, optional
2 tbs. melted butter for brushing

Remove dough from machine. Roll dough into a rectangle, brush with melted butter and spread cinnamon mixture over butter. Roll dough as a jellyroll and cut into slices of about 1½ inches wide. Place each slice in a muffin cup, cover and let rise for 35 to 40 minutes. Brush tops lightly with melted butter if desired. Bake in a preheated 400° oven for 20 to 25 minutes.

Hamburger or Hot Dog Rolls

Dough cycle

These are the best. Make plenty and freeze the extras for the next time, if you have any left, that is! Wonderful as is, but good with variations as well. Makes 12.

1 cup water
2 tbs. margarine or butter
2 tbs. sugar
2 tsp. salt

3-3¼ cups bread flour
3 tbs. dry milk powder
2 tsp. yeast

Remove dough from machine. Punch it down and let it rest for 20 minutes. Form into 12 balls, make bun shapes and flatten. Cover and let rise for 1 hour. Bake in a preheated 375° oven for 15 to 20 minutes or until golden.

Variations

Add 1½ tbs. of one of the following to the dough: sesame seeds, poppy seeds, chives or minced onion. You can also brush the tops of the buns with a beaten egg and sprinkle on sesame seeds immediately prior to baking.

Lithuanian Coffee Bread

Dough cycle

Tom and Rasa, friends of Lithuanian descent, said this tasted just like the coffee breads their mothers used to make.

½ cup milk
¼ cup margarine or butter
2 eggs
1 tsp. vanilla extract
½ tsp. salt

½ cup sugar
1 tsp. grated lemon peel
3-3¼ cups bread flour
1½ tsp. yeast

Filling
¼ cup sugar
¼ cup chopped walnuts
½ cup raisins

Glaze
1 egg, beaten

After completion of dough cycle, divide and roll dough into 3 rectangles. Spread ⅓ of mixed filling ingredients onto middle of each rectangle and fold dough over filling to encase it. Braid rectangles together and place in a lightly greased loaf pan. Let rise for about 30 minutes. Brush with beaten egg. Bake in a preheated 350° oven for 30 to 35 minutes until brown.

Crusty Pizza Dough

Dough cycle

If you once make pizza dough in your bread machine, you will probably never buy commercial pizza again! One of our favorites includes leftover turkey and frozen mixed vegetables as toppings. Truly a great way to use leftovers! The small size will make one 14-inch pizza; medium will make one 14-16-inch pizza; depending on thickness of crust, large will make two 14-inch pizzas.

	Small	Medium	Large
water	⅔ cup	1 cup	1⅓ cups
olive oil	1 tbs.	1½ tbs.	2 tbs.
salt	½ tsp.	½ tsp.	¾ tsp.
all-purpose flour	1 cup	1½ cups	2 cups
whole wheat flour	1 cup	1½ cups	2 cups
yeast	1 tsp.	1½ tsp.	2 tsp.

Roll dough into rectangle or circle, depending on the pan to be used. Place on pan and turn excess under, forming a crust on the side. Brush very lightly with olive oil. (For a thicker, chewy crust, cover and let rise for about 30 minutes.) Top with pizza sauce, cheese and other desired toppings. Bake in a preheated 500° oven for 5 to 10 minutes, or until crust is brown and cheese is melted.

Challah

Challah is a very light and wonderful-tasting bread. The dough is some-what moist, and you should add only enough flour to prevent sticking, either while the machine is kneading or after the dough has been removed.

2/3 cup water
2 eggs
2 tbs. vegetable oil
2 tbs. sugar
1 tsp. salt

3-3 1/4 cups bread flour
1 1/2 tsp. yeast

Glaze
1 egg, beaten
poppy seeds, optional

Remove dough from machine and divide into 3 pieces; roll each piece into a rope about 14 inches long and braid on a greased baking sheet. Cover and let rise for about 45 minutes. Brush top with egg glaze and sprinkle with poppy seeds, if you wish. Bake in a preheated 350° oven for 45 minutes.

Hot Cross Buns

You needn't wait for Easter to come around to enjoy these — with or without the frosting cross. Absolutely delicious. Makes 12.

3/4 cup milk
2 eggs
3 tbs. margarine or butter
1/4 cup sugar
1/2 tsp. salt

1 tsp. cinnamon
3-3 1/4 cups all-purpose flour
1 1/2 tsp. yeast
       Add at end of kneading:
3/4 cup raisins

About 5 minutes prior to the end of machine kneading, add raisins, or knead them in by hand at the completion of the cycle. After a short kneading, let dough rest for about 10 minutes. Cut dough into 12 pieces, shape each into a ball and place in a greased baking dish. Cover and let rise about 35 minutes or until doubled in bulk. Brush with a mixture of egg yolk and 2 tsp. water. Bake in a preheated 350° oven for 20 to 25 minutes. If desired, after buns are completely cool, drizzle with frosting in the shape of a cross.

Frosting
1 cup confectioners' sugar
1/2 tsp. vanilla extract
1 tbs. milk

Mix ingredients together.

Sandwich Rolls

These are wonderful hot out of the oven whether you make sandwiches with them or not. Makes 10-12.

1¼ cups water
2 tbs. vegetable oil
2 tsp. sugar
1 tsp. salt

3-3¼ cups bread flour
⅓ cup dry milk powder or buttermilk
  powder
1½ tsp. yeast

Remove dough from machine. Form into 10 or 12 balls, shape into rolls and let rise for 40 to 50 minutes on a lightly greased baking sheet. Bake in a preheated 375° oven for 20 minutes or until golden.

Whole Wheat Sandwich Rolls

Wonderfully tasty as well as nutritious. To vary this recipe, use one of the flavored olive oils, such as garlic, or use walnut oil. Makes 12.

1⅛ cups water
2 tbs. vegetable oil
1 tbs. honey
1½ tsp. salt
1 cup whole wheat flour

2 tbs. wheat or oat bran
¼ cup wheat germ
2 cups bread flour
1½ tsp. yeast

Remove dough from machine. Form into 12 balls, make into desired shape of rolls and let rise for 50 to 60 minutes on a lightly greased baking sheet. Bake in a preheated 375° oven for 20 minutes or until done.

Pita Bread

This is a definite must-try, and well worth the few minutes involved to make. The pitas are easy to have done in time for lunch sandwiches. Makes 10.

1⅓ cups water
3 tbs. olive oil
1½ tbs. sugar
1 tsp. salt

2 cups bread flour
1½ cups whole wheat flour
2 tsp. yeast

Upon completion of the dough cycle, divide dough into 10 pieces and roll into balls. Flatten each ball into a disk, rolling each one into a circle of about 6 inches. Place on a baking sheet, let rise for about 20 minutes and bake in a preheated 500° oven for 8 to 10 minutes.

Cheese Pizza Dough

Dough cycle

The cheese gives this pizza crust an interesting taste and texture.

	Small	Medium	Large
water	2/3 cup	1 cup	1 1/3 cups
olive oil	2 tsp.	1 tbs.	1 1/3 tbs.
shredded mozzarella cheese	1/3 cup	1/2 cup	2/3 cup
salt	1/2 tsp.	1/2 tsp.	3/4 tsp.
all-purpose flour	1 cup	1 1/2 cups	2 cups
whole wheat flour	1 cup	1 1/2 cups	2 cups
yeast	1 tsp.	1 1/2 tsp.	2 1/2 tsp.

Roll dough into a rectangle or circle, depending on the pan to be used. Place on pan and turn excess under, forming a crust on the edges. Brush very lightly with olive oil. (For a thicker, chewy crust, cover and let rise about 30 minutes.) Top with pizza sauce, cheese and other desired toppings. Bake in a preheated 500° oven for 5 to 10 minutes, or until crust is brown and cheese is melted.

Breadsticks

Dough cycle

Far better than the ones you buy in the store. Bake enough to keep on hand. Each of the different toppings changes the flavor of the sticks — try them all.

1 1/3 cups water
1 tbs. margarine or butter
1 1/2 tbs. sugar

1 1/2 tsp. salt
4 cups bread flour
2 tsp. yeast

Glaze
1 egg white mixed with 1 tbs. water

Cut dough into small egg-sized pieces and roll them into ropes. Cover and let rise 20 minutes. Brush each one with glaze. Sprinkle with salt or seeds. Bake in a preheated 400° oven for 15 minutes or until golden brown. The shorter the baking time, the softer they are; the longer the baking time, the crunchier.

Suggested Toppings

Coarse salt, sesame seeds, poppy seeds, anise seeds, dried onion bits

Bagels

I was ready to give up on a bagel recipe until my frustration finally led me to a local bagel bakery where they shared some hints with me. Here is the successful result. Makes 12.

1 cup water	1 cup whole wheat flour
1½ tbs. honey	2 cups bread flour
1 tsp. salt	1½ tsp. yeast

Let the machine knead the dough once, and then let dough rise for 20 minutes only in machine. Even if your cycle runs longer, simply remove dough after 20 minutes and turn off the machine. Divide dough into 12 pieces. Roll each piece into a rope and form a circle, pressing ends together. You may find it necessary to wet one end slightly to help seal ends together.

Place bagels on a well-greased baking sheet, cover and let rise for only 15 to 20 minutes. Meanwhile, bring about 2 inches of water to a slight boil in a nonaluminum pan (I use a cast iron frying pan). Carefully lower 3 or 4 bagels at a time into water, cooking for about 30 seconds on each side. Remove bagels, drain on a towel and sprinkle with topping, if desired. Return to greased baking sheet and bake in a preheated 550° oven for 8 minutes.

Suggested Toppings

Sesame seeds, poppy seeds, anise seeds, dried onion bits

Pretzels

I bet you can't eat just one! Makes 15 to 24, depending on size.

1⅓ cups water	2½ tsp. yeast
2 tbs. margarine or butter	For boiling:
1½ tbs. sugar	4 cups water
¾ tsp. salt	1½ tbs. baking soda
4 cups all-purpose flour	

Cut dough into short strips, roll into ropes and shape into pretzels. Cover and let rise on a greased baking sheet for about 45 minutes.

In a cast iron or other nonaluminum pan, bring water and baking soda almost to a boil. Gently lower (by hand or slotted spoon) pretzels into water for about 1 minute, turning once. Do not let water come to a full boil. Remove pretzels and return to greased baking sheet. Sprinkle with coarse salt or kosher salt. Bake in a preheated 475° oven for about 12 minutes.

The
Bread
Machine
Cookbook II

White Bread

This is a basic, no-frills white bread. It's low in fat, sugar and sodium and it's really good!

	1 lb.	1½ lb.	1¾-2 lb.
milk or water	⅔ cup	1 cup	1¼ cups
vegetable oil	1½ tbs.	2 tbs.	3 tbs.
honey	1½ tbs.	2 tbs.	3 tbs.
salt	½ tsp.	¾ tsp.	1 tsp.
bread flour	2 cups	3 cups	3½ cups
yeast	1 tsp.	1½ tsp.	2 tsp.

Rice Bread

This delicious twist on white bread makes good sandwiches. The moisture of the rice affects the moisture of the dough. Check the dough 5 to 10 minutes into the first kneading period and add water or flour if necessary. Any type of rice can be used.

	1 lb.	1½ lb.	1¾-2 lb.
cooked rice	⅔ cup	1 cup	1¼ cups
water	⅔ cup	1 cup	1¼ cups
margarine or butter	1 tbs.	1½ tbs.	2 tbs.
sugar	1 tsp.	1½ tsp.	2 tsp.
salt	¼ tsp.	½ tsp.	¾ tsp.
bread flour	2 cups	3 cups	3½ cups
yeast	1 tsp.	1½ tsp.	2 tsp.

Cola Bread

This is a very easy, unique bread that picks up the flavor of whatever cola you use. "Flatten" the cola by warming it in the microwave to remove some of the bubbles. If the dough looks dry while kneading, add more cola — different brands of cola react differently. Substitute any flavor soda, diet or regular, if desired.

	1 lb.	1½ lb.	1¾-2 lb.
cola	¾ cup	1⅛ cups	1⅓ cups
margarine or butter	1½ tbs.	2 tbs.	2 tbs.
bread flour	2 cups	3 cups	3½ cups
yeast	1 tsp.	1½ tsp.	2 tsp.

Semolina Bread

Although semolina is usually thought of as a pasta flour in this country, it also makes delicious bread. You'll find the color slightly yellow and the taste nutty. It's a super sandwich bread.

	1 lb.	1½ lb.	1¾-2 lb.
water	1 cup	1⅓ cups	1⅔ cups
olive oil	1 tbs.	1½ tbs.	2 tbs.
sugar	1 tsp.	2 tsp.	1 tbs.
salt	¾ tsp.	1 tsp.	1 tsp.
semolina flour	¾ cup	1 cup	1½ cups
bread flour	2¼ cups	3 cups	3½ cups
yeast	1½ tsp.	2 tsp.	2½ tsp.

Cheese Bread

Here's a rich, absolutely wonderful cheese bread. Use Gruyère, Swiss or sharp cheddar cheese.

	1 lb.	1½ lb.	1¾-2 lb.
water	¼ cup	⅓ cup	½ cup
margarine or butter	6 tbs.	½ cup	½ cup
eggs	3	4	4
sugar	½ tsp.	¾ tsp.	1 tsp.
salt	½ tsp.	¾ tsp.	1 tsp.
bread flour	2 cups	3 cups	3½ cups
yeast	1 tsp.	1½ tsp.	2 tsp.
*grated cheese	¾ cup	1 cup	1 cup

*Add ingredients after dough has formed a smooth ball, about 5 minutes into the first kneading period.

Cheddar Cheese and Bacon Bread
Raisin, Sweet or Basic cycle

Make sure you make the largest loaf your machine allows — it will go fast!
Fresh bacon is preferable to bacon bits. If you use bacon bits, be sure to use
those made from real bacon.

	1 lb.	1½ lb.	1¾-2 lb.
milk	⅔ cup	1 cup	1¼ cups
margarine or butter	1 tbs.	1½ tbs.	2 tbs.
sugar	2 tsp.	1 tbs.	1½ tbs.
salt	½ tsp.	¾ tsp.	1 tsp.
bread flour	2 cups	3 cups	3½ cups
yeast	1 tsp.	1½ tsp.	2 tsp.
*grated cheddar cheese	½ cup	⅔ cup	¾ cup
*cooked, crumbled bacon	½ cup	⅔ cup	¾ cup

*Add ingredients as soon as dough has formed a ball. Allow to knead for
3 to 4 minutes. Adjust liquid or flour content if necessary.

Cheese Herb Bread
Sweet or Basic cycle

*This is wonderful with a fish or chicken dinner or for a picnic lunch. Use
freshly grated Parmesan cheese. For a variation, use grated cheddar cheese or
a combination of cheddar and Swiss. The herbs can be adjusted to taste.*

	1 lb.	1½ lb.	1¾-2 lb.
water	⅔ cup	1 cup	1⅓ cups
margarine or butter	1 tbs.	1½ tbs.	2 tbs.
sugar	1½ tsp.	1 tbs.	1 tbs.
salt	½ tsp.	¾ tsp.	1 tsp.
basil, dried	¼ tsp.	½ tsp.	½ tsp.
parsley, dried	½ tsp.	1 tsp.	1 tsp.
whole wheat flour	½ cup	¾ cup	1 cup
bread flour	1½ cups	2¼ cups	3 cups
yeast	1 tsp.	1½ tsp.	2 tsp.
*grated Swiss cheese	⅓ cup	½ cup	⅔ cup
*grated Parmesan cheese	2 tbs.	3 tbs.	¼ cup

*Add ingredients after dough has formed a smooth ball, about 5
minutes into the first kneading period. Adjust liquid or flour content if
necessary.

Jalapeño Cheese Bread

Sweet or Basic cycle

This bread's a must for jalapeño lovers. Serve it with a Mexican-type meal for instant success. The jalapeños can be adjusted to taste. Check the consistency of the dough during kneading and adjust with flour or water if necessary.

	1 lb.	1½ lb.	1¾-2 lb.
milk	⅔ cup	1 cup	1¼ cups
margarine or butter	1½ tbs.	2 tbs.	2 tbs.
chopped jalapeños	1	1½	2
sugar	2 tsp.	1 tbs.	1½ tbs.
salt	½ tsp.	¾ tsp.	1 tsp.
bread flour	2 cups	3 cups	3½ cups
yeast	1 tsp.	1½ tsp.	2 tsp.
*grated pepper Jack cheese	½ cup	⅔ cup	¾ cup

*Add ingredients after dough has formed a smooth ball, about 5 minutes into the first kneading period.

Wine and Cheese Bread

Sweet or Basic cycle

This loaf is terrific as an appetizer with cheese. I much prefer white wine, although red wine can be used. Use a good-quality, sharp cheddar cheese.

	1 lb.	1½ lb.	1¾-2 lb.
water	⅓ cup	½ cup	⅔ cup
wine	⅓ cup	½ cup	½ cup
margarine or butter	1 tbs.	2 tbs.	3 tbs.
sugar	1 tbs.	1½ tbs.	2 tbs.
salt	¾ tsp.	1 tsp.	1 tsp.
bread flour	2 cups	3 cups	3½ cups
yeast	1½ tsp.	2 tsp.	2½ tsp.
*grated cheddar cheese	⅔ cup	¾ cup	1 cup

*Add ingredients after dough has formed a smooth ball, about 5 minutes into the first kneading period.

Quick Sourdough

Here's a way to enjoy a sourdough-flavored bread without having a full starter on hand. Check the dough's consistency as it is kneading and adjust if necessary.

	1 lb.	1½ lb.	1¾-2 lb.
water	⅔ cup	1 cup	1¼ cups
bread flour	⅔ cup	1 cup	1½ cups
sugar	¼ tsp.	½ tsp.	1 tsp.
yeast	1½ tsp.	1½ tsp.	1½ tsp.

Stir ingredients together in the order given to make a starter. Cover with plastic and let sit in a warm location for 6 to 8 hours, or overnight. Place in the bread machine pan, add the following and proceed.

milk	3 tbs.	¼ cup	⅓ cup
vinegar	¾ tsp.	1 tsp.	1 tsp.
vegetable oil	2 tsp.	1 tbs.	1½ tbs.
sugar	1½ tsp.	2 tsp.	1 tbs.
salt	½ tsp.	½ tsp.	1 tsp.
bread flour	2 cups	3 cups	3½ cups
yeast	1½ tsp.	1½ tsp.	2 tsp.

100% Whole Wheat Bread
Whole Wheat, Sweet or Basic cycle

A pure whole wheat bread will not rise as much as one that uses a combination of white and whole wheat flour. This is a delicious, wheaty bread.

	1 lb.	1½ lb.	1¾-2 lb.
water	1⅛ cups	1½ cups	1¾ cups
vegetable oil	1 tbs.	1½ tbs.	2 tbs.
honey	3 tbs.	¼ cup	⅓ cup
salt	½ tsp.	½ tsp.	1 tsp.
whole wheat flour	3 cups	4 cups	5 cups
vital gluten, optional	1 tbs.	1½ tbs.	2 tbs.
yeast	2 tsp.	2½ tsp.	1 tbs.

Classic Whole Wheat Bread
Whole Wheat or Basic cycle

This makes a really good, basic whole wheat loaf.

	1 lb.	1½ lb.	1¾-2 lb.
water	1 cup	1½ cups	1¾ cups
margarine or butter	1½ tbs.	2 tbs.	3 tbs.
brown sugar, packed	1½ tbs.	2 tbs.	3 tbs.
salt	½ tsp.	¾ tsp.	1 tsp.
whole wheat flour	1½ cups	2 cups	2½ cups
bread flour	1½ cups	2 cups	2½ cups
yeast	1½ tsp.	2 tsp.	2½ tsp.

Whole Wheat with Bran
Whole Wheat or Basic cycle

This whole wheat bread is great for sandwiches. Choose either wheat or oat bran.

	1 lb.	1½ lb.	1¾-2 lb.
water	1⅛ cups	1⅓ cups	1⅔ cups
vegetable oil	2 tbs.	3 tbs.	¼ cup
honey	2 tbs.	3 tbs.	¼ cup
salt	¾ tsp.	1 tsp.	1 tsp.
wheat or oat bran	¼ cup	⅓ cup	½ cup
whole wheat flour	1 cup	1½ cups	2 cups
bread flour	1½ cups	2 cups	2½ cups
yeast	1½ tsp.	2 tsp.	2½ tsp.

Rye Beer Bread

This subtly flavored loaf has a great texture. It slices well for sandwiches. Open the beer and let it sit for 15 to 20 minutes to "flatten" it. Or, heat it in the microwave for 1 to 2 minutes and cool to lukewarm before adding other ingredients. This is a low-rising, dense loaf of bread.

	1 lb.	1 1/2 lb.	1 3/4-2 lb.
beer	1 1/4 cups	1 2/3 cups	1 7/8 cups
vegetable oil	2 tbs.	3 tbs.	1/4 cup
sugar	1 tsp.	1 1/2 tsp.	2 tsp.
salt	1/2 tsp.	1/2 tsp.	1 tsp.
rye flour	1 1/2 cups	2 cups	2 1/2 cups
bread flour	2 cups	2 1/2 cups	3 cups
yeast	2 tsp.	2 1/2 tsp.	2 1/2 tsp.

Note: For a regular beer bread, you can substitute bread flour for rye flour. Do not, however, use more than 2 to 3 cups of bread flour in your machine.

Multi-Grain Bread

This is a moist, dense, low-rising loaf. It is low in fat and has lots of nutrients.

	1 lb.	1 1/2 lb.	1 3/4-2 lb.
water	1 cup	1 1/3 cups	1 2/3 cups
vegetable oil	1 tbs.	1 1/2 tbs.	2 tbs.
honey	1 tbs.	1 1/2 tbs.	2 tbs.
salt	1/4 tsp.	1/2 tsp.	3/4 tsp.
wheat germ	2 tbs.	3 tbs.	1/4 cup
wheat or oat bran	2 tbs.	3 tbs.	1/4 cup
whole wheat flour	1/4 cup	1/3 cup	1/2 cup
wheat flakes	1/4 cup	1/3 cup	1/2 cup
oat flour	1/4 cup	1/3 cup	1/2 cup
oats	1/4 cup	1/3 cup	1/2 cup
bread flour	2 cups	2 1/2 cups	3 cups
yeast	1 1/2 tsp.	2 tsp.	2 1/2 tsp.

Maple Wheat Bread

Sweet, Whole Wheat or Basic cycle

Here's a tasty, sweet bread — the flavor of maple syrup is delicious. For variety, substitute oat flakes for wheat flakes and oat flour for whole wheat flour. It's easy to measure syrup when you spray a measuring spoon or cup with nonstick cooking spray first.

	1 lb.	1 ½ lb.	1 ¾-2 lb.
water	¾ cup	1 cup	1 ¼ cups
margarine or butter	1 tbs.	1 ½ tbs.	2 tbs.
maple syrup	3 tbs.	¼ cup	⅓ cup
salt	½ tsp.	¾ tsp.	1 tsp.
wheat flakes	½ cup	¾ cup	1 cup
whole wheat flour	½ cup	¾ cup	1 cup
bread flour	2 cups	2 ½ cups	3 cups
dry milk powder	1 tbs.	1 ½ tbs.	2 tbs.
yeast	1 ½ tsp.	2 tsp.	2 ½ tsp.

Honey Bread

Whole Wheat, Sweet or Basic cycle

This bread is great whether eaten alone or used to make sandwiches.

	1 lb.	1 ½ lb.	1 ¾-2 lb.
water	1 cup	1 ¼ cups	1 ½ cups
vegetable oil	1 tbs.	1 ½ tbs.	2 tbs.
honey	3 tbs.	¼ cup	⅓ cup
salt	¾ tsp.	1 tsp.	1 tsp.
oats	¾ cup	1 cup	1 ½ cups
bread flour	2 cups	3 cups	3 ½ cups
yeast	1 ½ tsp.	2 tsp.	2 ½ tsp.

Whole Wheat Cinnamon Raisin Nut Bread

This bread is particularly good toasted for breakfast and for sandwiches.

	1 lb.	1 ½ lb.	1 ¾-2 lb.
water	1 cup	1 ¼ cups	1 ½ cups
margarine or butter	1 tbs.	1 ½ tbs.	2 tbs.
brown sugar, packed	1 tbs.	1 ½ tbs.	2 tbs.
salt	¼ tsp.	½ tsp.	½ tsp.
cinnamon	½ tsp.	¾ tsp.	1 tsp.
wheat or oat bran	¼ cup	⅓ cup	½ cup
wheat or oat flakes	½ cup	¾ cup	1 cup
whole wheat flour	½ cup	¾ cup	1 cup
bread flour	1 ½ cups	2 cups	3 cups
yeast	1 ½ tsp.	2 tsp.	2 ½ tsp.
*raisins	⅓ cup	½ cup	⅔ cup
*chopped walnuts or pecans	⅓ cup	½ cup	⅔ cup

*Add ingredients at the beginning of the second kneading period.

Granola Bread

Use your favorite granola cereal for a wonderful change of pace.

	1 lb.	1 ½ lb.	1 ¾-2 lb.
water	⅞ cup	1 ⅛ cups	1 ⅓ cups
vegetable oil	1 ½ tbs.	2 tbs.	3 tbs.
honey	1 ½ tbs.	2 tbs.	3 tbs.
salt	½ tsp.	½ tsp.	¾ tsp.
grated orange peel	½ tsp.	¾ tsp.	1 tsp.
granola cereal	1 cup	1 ½ cups	2 cups
bread flour	2 cups	3 cups	3 ½ cups
yeast	1 tsp.	1 ½ tsp.	2 tsp.
*raisins, optional	¼ cup	⅓ cup	½ cup
*sunflower kernels, optional	¼ cup	⅓ cup	½ cup

*Add ingredients at the beginning of the second kneading period.

Cracked Wheat Oat Bread
Whole Wheat, Sweet or Basic cycle

This wonderful variation on cracked wheat has a nice, nutty taste and texture. Wheat flakes can be substituted for cracked wheat for a delicious variation. Check the dough after 5 minutes of kneading and adjust the liquid or flour if necessary.

	1 lb.	1½ lb.	1¾-2 lb.
water	1 cup	1⅓ cups	1½ cups
cracked wheat	½ cup	¾ cup	1 cup
vegetable oil	1½ tbs.	2 tbs.	3 tbs.
honey	1 tbs.	1½ tbs.	2 tbs.
salt	¼ tsp.	½ tsp.	½ tsp.
oats	½ cup	¾ cup	1 cup
bread flour	2 cups	2½ cups	3 cups
yeast	1 tsp.	1½ tsp.	2 tsp.

Note: The cracked wheat must sit in the liquids for at least 1 hour. I usually make this bread on the timer cycle on all machines except DAK or Welbilt, which have holes in the bottom of the pan. In these machines, soak the cracked wheat in the water prior to placing the mixture in the machine.

Cracked Wheat Almond Bread
Whole Wheat, Raisin, Sweet or Basic cycle

This is soon to be one of your favorites, as it is at my house. Wheat flakes can be substituted for the cracked wheat for a delicious variation.

	1 lb.	1½ lb.	1¾-2 lb.
water	1 cup	1⅓ cups	1½ cups
cracked wheat	½ cup	¾ cup	1 cup
margarine or butter	2 tbs.	3 tbs.	¼ cup
brown sugar, packed	1 tbs.	1½ tbs.	2 tbs.
salt	½ tsp.	¾ tsp.	1 tsp.
whole wheat flour	½ cup	¾ cup	1 cup
bread flour	2 cups	2½ cups	3 cups
dry milk powder	2 tbs.	3 tbs.	¼ cup
yeast	1½ tsp.	2 tsp.	2½ tsp.
*chopped almonds	½ cup	¾ cup	1 cup

Note: See Cracked Wheat Oat Bread for instructions on soaking cracked wheat.

*Add ingredients at the beginning of the second kneading period

Honey Wheat Berry Bread

Whole Wheat, Raisin, Sweet or Basic cycle

This is an absolutely wonderful bread! The honey-soaked wheat berries are a terrific addition to this nutritious loaf.

	1 lb.	1½ lb.	1¾-2 lb.
water	⅔ cup	1 cup	1¼ cups
vegetable oil	1½ tbs.	2 tbs.	2 tbs.
honey	2 tbs.	3 tbs.	¼ cup
salt	½ tsp.	¾ tsp.	1 tsp.
wheat germ	1½ tbs.	2 tbs.	2½ tbs.
soaked wheat berries*	*	*	*
whole wheat flour	½ cup	¾ cup	1 cup
bread flour	1½ cups	2½ cups	3 cups
dry milk powder	2 tbs.	3 tbs.	¼ cup
yeast	1 tsp.	1½ tsp.	2 tsp.

*Soaked Wheat Berries

	1 lb.	1½ lb.	1¾-2 lb.
wheat berries	⅓ cup	½ cup	⅔ cup
water	1 cup	1½ cups	2 cups
honey	1½ tbs.	2 tbs.	3 tbs.

Combine ingredients in a saucepan and bring to a boil. Reduce heat to medium low and simmer for about 1 hour, stirring occasionally, adding water if necessary. Remove from heat, cover and let stand for 6 to 12 hours. Drain any standing water before adding wheat berries to the dough.

Walnut Rye

Whole Wheat, Raisin, Sweet or Basic cycle

You will love this absolutely superb combination of rye flour and walnuts.

	1 lb.	1½ lb.	1¾-2 lb.
water	1⅛ cups	1⅓ cups	1¾ cups
walnut oil	2 tbs.	3 tbs.	¼ cup
sugar	¾ tsp.	1 tsp.	1½ tsp.
salt	¾ tsp.	1 tsp.	1 tsp.
whole wheat flour	½ cup	¾ cup	1 cup
rye flour	½ cup	¾ cup	1 cup
bread flour	2 cups	3 cups	3½ cups
yeast	1½ tsp.	2 tsp.	2½ tsp.
*chopped walnuts	½ cup	¾ cup	1 cup

*Add ingredients at the beginning of the second kneading period.

Raisin Pumpernickel

Whole Wheat, Raisin, Sweet or Basic cycle

Raisins are a delicious addition to this pumpernickel. It's great spread with cream cheese. This is a very moist, low-rising bread.

	1 lb.	1 1/2 lb.	1 3/4-2 lb.
water	1 1/8 cups	1 1/2 cups	1 3/4 cups
vegetable oil	1 1/2 tbs.	2 tbs.	3 tbs.
molasses	1 1/2 tbs.	2 tbs.	3 tbs.
salt	1/2 tsp.	3/4 tsp.	1 tsp.
cocoa powder	1 1/2 tbs.	2 tbs.	3 tbs.
instant coffee granules	1 tsp.	1 1/2 tsp.	2 tsp.
caraway seeds	1 tbs.	1 1/2 tbs.	2 tbs.
cornmeal	1/3 cup	1/2 cup	2/3 cup
rye flour	1 1/4 cups	1 1/2 cups	2 cups
bread flour	1 1/2 cups	2 cups	3 cups
yeast	1 1/2 tsp.	2 tsp.	2 1/2 tsp.
*raisins	1/2 cup	2/3 cup	3/4 cup

*Add ingredients at the beginning of the second kneading period.

Whole Wheat Raisin Oatmeal Bread

Whole Wheat, Raisin, Sweet or Basic cycle

A combination of whole wheat, oatmeal and raisins makes a great loaf of bread.

	1 lb.	1 1/2 lb.	1 3/4-2 lb.
water	1 cup	1 1/3 cups	1 2/3 cups
vegetable oil	1 1/2 tbs.	2 tbs.	3 tbs.
honey	1 1/2 tbs.	2 tbs.	3 tbs.
salt	1/2 tsp.	3/4 tsp.	1 tsp.
oats	3/4 cup	1 cup	1 1/4 cups
whole wheat flour	3/4 cup	1 cup	1 1/4 cups
bread flour	1 1/2 cups	2 cups	2 1/2 cups
yeast	1 1/2 tsp.	2 tsp.	2 1/2 tsp.
*raisins	1/2 cup	2/3 cup	3/4 cup
*chopped nuts, optional	1/2 cup	2/3 cup	3/4 cup

*Add ingredients at the beginning of the second kneading period.

Rye Cornmeal Bread

Whole Wheat, Sweet or Basic cycle

Rye flour and cornmeal make a delicious combination in this low-rising bread.

	1 lb.	1 ½ lb.	1 ¾-2 lb.
water	1 ⅛ cups	1 ½ cups	1 ¾ cups
vegetable oil	1 ½ tbs.	2 tbs.	3 tbs.
molasses	2 ½ tbs.	3 tbs.	¼ cup
salt	½ tsp.	¾ tsp.	1 tsp.
rye flour	¾ cup	1 cup	1 ¼ cups
cornmeal	¾ cup	1 cup	1 ¼ cups
bread flour	2 cups	2 ½ cups	3 cups
yeast	1 ½ tsp.	2 tsp.	2 ½ tsp.

Raisin Rye

Whole Wheat, Raisin, Sweet or Basic cycle

This low-rising bread is particularly good with cream cheese.

	1 lb.	1 ½ lb.	1 ¾-2 lb.
water	1 cup	1 ⅓ cups	1 ⅔ cups
vegetable oil	1 ½ tbs.	2 tbs.	3 tbs.
molasses	2 tbs.	2 ½ tbs.	3 tbs.
salt	½ tsp.	¾ tsp.	1 tsp.
cocoa powder	1 ½ tbs.	2 tbs.	2 ½ tbs.
caraway seeds, optional	1 tbs.	1 ½ tbs.	2 tbs.
rye flour	1 cup	1 ½ cups	2 cups
bread flour	2 cups	3 cups	3 ½ cups
yeast	1 ½ tsp.	2 tsp.	2 ½ tsp.
*raisins	½ cup	⅔ cup	¾ cup

*Add ingredients at the beginning of the second kneading period.

88   Bread Machine II ~ Whole Grain Breads

Four Seed Bread

The seeds add lots of flavor to this loaf.

	1 lb.	1½ lb.	1¾-2 lb.
water	1 cup	1⅓ cups	1⅔ cups
vegetable oil	2 tbs.	2½ tbs.	3 tbs.
honey	2 tbs.	2½ tbs.	3 tbs.
salt	½ tsp.	¾ tsp.	1 tsp.
fennel seeds	1 tsp.	1½ tsp.	2 tsp.
caraway seeds	1 tsp.	1½ tsp.	2 tsp.
anise seeds	1 tsp.	1½ tsp.	2 tsp.
celery seeds	1 tsp.	1½ tsp.	2 tsp.
whole wheat flour	1½ cups	2 cups	2½ cups
bread flour	1½ cups	2 cups	2½ cups
yeast	1½ tsp.	2 tsp.	2½ tsp.

Kasha Bread

This hearty, flavorful bread is made from roasted buckwheat groats, also known as kasha. Put the raisins in at the beginning so that they will be crushed.

	1 lb.	1½ lb.	1¾-2 lb.
water	1 cup	1⅓ cups	1¾ cups
vegetable oil	1½ tbs.	2 tbs.	3 tbs.
raisins	¼ cup	⅓ cup	½ cup
salt	¾ tsp.	1 tsp.	1 tsp.
buckwheat groats	¼ cup	⅓ cup	½ cup
whole wheat flour	¾ cup	1 cup	1½ cups
bread flour	1½ cups	2½ cups	3 cups
yeast	1½ tsp.	2 tsp.	2 tsp.

Quick Sour Rye

This recipe makes a delicious, dense loaf. Adjust the water in the second stage as necessary.

	1 lb.	**1 1/2 lb.**	**1 3/4-2 lb.**
water	3/4 cup	1 1/8 cups	1 1/2 cups
rye flour	1 cup	1 1/2 cups	2 cups
yeast	1 tsp.	1 1/2 tsp.	2 tsp.

Stir ingredients together in the order given to make a starter. Cover with plastic and let sit in a warm location for 6 to 8 hours, or overnight. Place in the machine, add the following and proceed.

water	1/4 cup	1/3 cup	1/2 cup
vegetable oil	1 tbs.	1 1/2 tbs.	2 tbs.
honey	1 tbs.	1 1/2 tbs.	2 tbs.
salt	1/4 tsp.	1/2 tsp.	1/2 tsp.
caraway seeds	2 tsp.	1 tbs.	1 tbs.
bread flour	2 cups	3 cups	3 1/2 cups
yeast	1 tsp.	1 1/2 tsp.	2 tsp.

Berry Bread

Raisin, Sweet, Whole Wheat or Basic cycle

For this recipe, you can use any type of berry puree or berry syrup — choose your favorite. Whirl fresh or frozen unsweetened whole berries with a blender or food processor to make puree. Set crust color to light.

	1 lb.	1 ½ lb.	1 ¾-2 lb.
raspberry or strawberry puree	1 cup	1 ⅓ cups	1 ½ cups
vegetable oil	1 ½ tbs.	2 tbs.	3 tbs.
raspberry or strawberry syrup	1 ½ tbs.	2 tbs.	3 tbs.
salt	½ tsp.	¾ tsp.	1 tsp.
whole wheat flour	1 ½ cups	2 cups	2 ½ cups
bread flour	1 ½ cups	2 cups	2 ½ cups
yeast	1 ½ tsp.	2 tsp.	2 ½ tsp.
*chopped walnuts or pecans, optional	⅓ cup	½ cup	⅔ cup

*Add ingredients at the beginning of the second kneading period.

Banana, Coconut and Macadamia Bread

Raisin, Whole Wheat, Sweet or Basic cycle

This bread is a favorite. Use fully or overly ripe bananas. Adjust the consistency of the dough while it's kneading if necessary. Vanilla extract can be substituted for the coconut extract and almonds for the macadamia nuts. Set crust color to light.

	1 lb.	1 ½ lb.	1 ¾-2 lb.
mashed bananas	1 cup	1 ⅓ cups	1 ½ cups
vegetable oil	1 ½ tbs.	2 tbs.	3 tbs.
honey	1 ½ tbs.	2 tbs.	3 tbs.
coconut extract	1 ½ tsp.	2 tsp.	1 tbs.
salt	¾ tsp.	1 tsp.	1 tsp.
grated lemon peel	¾ tsp.	1 tsp.	1 tsp.
flaked coconut	¾ cup	1 cup	1 ¼ cups
whole wheat flour	1 cup	1 ½ cups	2 cups
bread flour	1 ½ cups	2 ½ cups	3 cups
yeast	1 ½ tsp.	2 tsp.	2 ½ tsp.
*chopped macadamia nuts	½ cup	⅔ cup	¾ cup

*Add ingredients at the beginning of the second kneading period.

Peach Bread

Raisin, Whole Wheat, Sweet or Basic cycle

Here's a great way to use fresh peaches, although canned peaches work nicely, too. Puree peeled fresh or rinsed canned peaches with a food processor or blender. Set crust color to light.

	1 lb.	1½ lb.	1¾-2 lb.
peach puree	¾ cup	1¼ cups	1½ cups
vegetable oil	1 tbs.	1½ tbs.	2 tbs.
eggs	1	1	2
honey	1 tbs.	1½ tbs.	2 tbs.
salt	½ tsp.	½ tsp.	¾ tsp.
cinnamon	⅛ tsp.	¼ tsp.	½ tsp.
whole wheat flour	1 cup	1½ cups	2 cups
bread flour	1 cup	1½ cups	2 cups
yeast	1 tsp.	1½ tsp.	2 tsp.
*chopped dried peaches	⅓ cup	½ cup	⅔ cup

*Add ingredients at the beginning of the second kneading period.

Hawaiian Macadamia Nut Bread

Raisin, Sweet or Basic cycle

This superb bread will receive rave reviews. The macadamia nuts give it a wonderful flavor. If desired, you can substitute Mauna Lài or a similar juice for the water, and sliced almonds for the macadamia nuts. This is a high-rising loaf. Set crust color to light.

	1 lb.	1½ lb.	1¾-2 lb.
water	⅔ cup	⅞ cup	1⅛ cups
margarine or butter	1½ tbs.	2 tbs.	3 tbs.
eggs	1	2	2
sugar	3 tbs.	¼ cup	⅓ cup
salt	¾ tsp.	1 tsp.	1 tsp.
bread flour	2 cups	3 cups	3½ cups
yeast	1 tsp.	1½ tsp.	2 tsp.
*chopped macadamia nuts	¾ cup	1 cup	1 cup

*Add ingredients at the beginning of the second kneading period.

Date Nut Bread

Raisin, Whole Wheat, Sweet or Basic cycle

This dark-colored, flavorful loaf will have you going back for more. You'll love this even if you think you don't like dates! Set crust color to light.

	1 lb.	1½ lb.	1¾-2 lb.
water	1⅛ cups	1½ cups	1⅔ cups
vegetable oil	2 tbs.	2½ tbs.	3 tbs.
molasses	1 tbs.	1½ tbs.	2 tbs.
salt	¾ tsp.	1 tsp.	1 tsp.
cocoa powder	2 tbs.	2½ tbs.	3 tbs.
whole wheat flour	1½ cups	2 cups	2½ cups
bread flour	1½ cups	2 cups	2½ cups
yeast	1½ tsp.	2 tsp.	2½ tsp.
*chopped dates	¼ cup	⅓ cup	½ cup
*chopped walnuts	¼ cup	⅓ cup	½ cup

*Add ingredients at the beginning of the second kneading period.

Orange Bread

Sweet or Basic cycle

For this delicious breakfast bread, make sure the Mandarin orange segments are tightly packed into the measuring cup. Orange juice concentrate is found in the freezer case of the grocery store. Thaw it before using. Watch the dough while it's kneading and add flour or water if necessary. Set crust color to light.

	1 lb.	1½ lb.	1¾-2 lb.
Mandarin orange segments	1 cup	1⅓ cups	1½ cups
margarine or butter	1½ tbs.	2 tbs.	2 tbs.
orange juice concentrate	1½ tbs.	2 tbs.	2 tbs.
sugar	3 tbs.	¼ cup	¼ cup
salt	¾ tsp.	1 tsp.	1 tsp.
bread flour	2 cups	3 cups	3½ cups
yeast	1½ tsp.	2 tsp.	2 tsp.

Raisin Nut Cocoa Bread
Raisin, Whole Wheat, Sweet or Basic cycle

A must for chocolate lovers, this is a wonderful change-of-pace raisin bread. Set crust color to light.

	1 lb.	1 ½ lb.	1¾-2 lb.
milk	1 cup	1 ⅓ cups	1 ½ cups
margarine or butter	1 ½ tbs.	2 tbs.	3 tbs.
brown sugar, packed	3 tbs.	¼ cup	⅓ cup
salt	½ tsp.	¾ tsp.	1 tsp.
cocoa powder	1 ½ tbs.	2 tbs.	3 tbs.
oats	¾ cup	1 cup	1 ¼ cups
whole wheat flour	¾ cup	1 cup	1 ¼ cups
bread flour	1 ½ cups	2 cups	2 ½ cups
yeast	1 ½ tsp.	2 tsp.	2 ½ tsp.
*raisins	½ cup	⅔ cup	¾ cup
*chopped walnuts	½ cup	⅔ cup	¾ cup

*Add ingredients at the beginning of the second kneading period.

Walnut Raisin Bread
Raisin, Whole Wheat, Sweet or Basic cycle

Try this toasted for breakfast and you'll be hooked. Any vegetable oil can be used in place of the walnut oil. Set crust color to light.

	1 lb.	1 ½ lb.	1¾-2 lb.
milk	1 cup	1 ⅓ cups	1 ½ cups
walnut oil	1 ½ tbs.	2 tbs.	3 tbs.
honey	1 ½ tbs.	2 tbs.	3 tbs.
salt	¾ tsp.	1 tsp.	1 tsp.
whole wheat flour	1 ½ cups	2 cups	2 ½ cups
bread flour	1 ½ cups	2 cups	2 ½ cups
yeast	1 ½ tsp.	2 tsp.	2 ½ tsp.
*raisins	½ cup	⅔ cup	¾ cup
*chopped walnuts	½ cup	⅔ cup	¾ cup

*Add ingredients at the beginning of the second kneading period.

Vegetable Bread

Raisin, Sweet, Whole Wheat or Basic cycle

What a great way to hide vegetables from finicky eaters! Set crust color to light.

	1 lb.	1 1/2 lb.	1 3/4-2 lb.
water	1 cup	1 1/3 cups	1 1/2 cups
grated carrots	1/3 cup	1/2 cup	2/3 cup
margarine or butter	1 1/2 tbs.	2 tbs.	3 tbs.
sugar	3/4 tsp.	1 tsp.	1 1/2 tsp.
salt	1/2 tsp.	3/4 tsp.	1 tsp.
celery seeds	1 1/2 tsp.	2 tsp.	1 tbs.
whole wheat flour	1 1/2 cups	2 cups	2 1/2 cups
bread flour	1 1/2 cups	2 cups	2 1/2 cups
yeast	1 1/2 tsp.	2 tsp.	2 tsp.
*chopped sun-dried tomatoes, optional	1/4 cup	1/3 cup	1/2 cup
*diced bell pepper, optional	1/4 cup	1/3 cup	1/2 cup

*Add ingredients at the beginning of the second kneading period.

Corny Bread

Sweet or Basic cycle

This is based on my father's recipe, which he devised using corn that was freshly scraped off the cob. It's a delicious twist on cornbread. Adjust the dough consistency during kneading if necessary.

	1 lb.	1 1/2 lb.	1 3/4-2 lb.
creamed corn	1 cup	1 1/2 cups	1 3/4 cups
vegetable oil	1 1/2 tbs.	2 tbs.	3 tbs.
vanilla extract	3/4 tsp.	1 tsp.	1 tsp.
brown sugar, packed	1 1/2 tbs.	2 tbs.	3 tbs.
salt	1/2 tsp.	3/4 tsp.	1 tsp.
nutmeg	1/2 tsp.	3/4 tsp.	1 tsp.
cornmeal	3/4 cup	1 cup	1 1/4 cups
bread flour	2 cups	3 cups	3 1/2 cups
yeast	1 1/2 tsp.	2 tsp.	2 1/2 tsp.

Note: For fresh creamed corn, fill the measuring cup with cooked, freshly scraped corn kernels. Add milk up to the correct measurement.

Potato Bread

Some people swear there is no better bread than potato bread. For another tasty variety, Cheese Potato Bread, add grated cheddar cheese. Potato water is the water in which you cooked the potatoes. If you don't have any, use regular tap water.

	1 lb.	1½ lb.	1¾-2 lb.
mashed potatoes	¾ cup	1 cup	1¼ cups
potato water	¾ cup	1 cup	1¼ cups
vegetable oil	2 tbs.	2½ tbs.	3 tbs.
sugar	1 tbs.	1½ tbs.	2 tbs.
salt	¾ tsp.	1 tsp.	1 tsp.
whole wheat flour	1½ cups	2 cups	2½ cups
bread flour	1½ cups	2 cups	2½ cups
yeast	1 tsp.	1½ tsp.	2 tsp.
*grated cheddar cheese, optional	⅓ cup	½ cup	⅔ cup

*Add ingredients after dough has formed a smooth ball, about 5 minutes into the first kneading period.

Spicy Bell Pepper Bread

You'll find red pepper flakes (called crushed red pepper) and white pepper on the spice shelf at the grocery store.

	1 lb.	1½ lb.	1¾-2 lb.
water	1 cup	1⅓ cups	1½ cups
olive oil	1½ tbs.	2 tbs.	3 tbs.
sugar	¾ tsp.	1 tsp.	1 tsp.
salt	¾ tsp.	1 tsp.	1 tsp.
red pepper flakes	¾ tsp.	1 tsp.	1 tsp.
ground white pepper	½ tsp.	½ tsp.	¾ tsp.
whole wheat flour	1½ cups	2 cups	2½ cups
bread flour	1½ cups	2 cups	2½ cups
yeast	1½ tsp.	2 tsp.	2 tsp.
*diced bell peppers	¾ cup	1 cup	1¼ cups

*Add ingredients at the beginning of the second kneading period. Adjust dough consistency if necessary.

Lentil Bread

Whole Wheat, Sweet or Basic cycle

Here's a great, tasty way to increase the protein in your bread. It's especially good for vegetarians. Instead of lentils, try using beans from a 9- or 13-bean soup combination package. Or, use your favorite variety of beans, such as kidney, black or navy. Cook lentils or beans according to package directions. Cool them to room temperature and pack them tightly into the measuring cup. Canned beans should be rinsed with cold water and drained well before using.

	1 lb.	1 ½ lb.	1 ¾-2 lb.
water	1 cup	1 ⅓ cups	1 ½ cups
cooked lentils	¾ cup	1 cup	1 ¼ cups
olive oil	1 ½ tbs.	2 tbs.	3 tbs.
honey	1 ½ tbs.	2 tbs.	3 tbs.
salt	¾ tsp.	1 tsp.	1 tsp.
whole wheat flour	1 ½ cups	2 cups	2 ½ cups
bread flour	1 ½ cups	2 cups	2 ½ cups
yeast	1 ½ tsp.	2 tsp.	2 ½ tsp.

Orange Oatmeal Bread

Sweet or Basic cycle

This delicious, nutritious bread is great for breakfast or any other time of the day. If you use fresh orange peel (zest), strip it directly into the bread machine pan.

	1 lb.	1 ½ lb.	1 ¾-2 lb.
orange juice	¾ cup	1 ⅛ cups	1 ⅓ cups
vegetable oil	1 ½ tbs.	2 tbs.	3 tbs.
honey	1 ½ tbs.	2 tbs.	3 tbs.
salt	¾ tsp.	1 tsp.	1 tsp.
grated orange peel	¾ tsp.	1 tsp.	1 ½ tsp.
oats	½ cup	⅔ cup	¾ cup
bread flour	2 cups	3 cups	3 ½ cups
yeast	1 ½ tsp.	2 tsp.	2 ½ tsp.

Whole Grain Orange Bread

This is a dense, hearty bread. It's wonderful served with a tossed green salad made with Mandarin oranges, red onions and walnuts. If you use fresh orange peel (zest), strip it directly into the bread machine pan.

	1 lb.	1 1/2 lb.	1 3/4-2 lb.
orange juice	1 cup	1 1/3 cups	1 1/2 cups
vegetable oil	2 tbs.	3 tbs.	1/4 cup
honey	2 tbs.	3 tbs.	1/4 cup
salt	1/2 tsp.	3/4 tsp.	1 tsp.
grated orange peel	1 1/2 tsp.	2 tsp.	1 tbs.
oats	1/3 cup	1/2 cup	2/3 cup
whole wheat flour	1/3 cup	1/2 cup	2/3 cup
rye flour	1/3 cup	1/2 cup	2/3 cup
bread flour	2 cups	3 cups	3 1/2 cups
yeast	2 tsp.	2 1/2 tsp.	2 1/2 tsp.

Apricot Almond Bread

This outstanding combination of flavors is a must for apricot lovers.

	1 lb.	1 1/2 lb.	1 3/4-2 lb.
water	1 cup	1 1/3 cups	1 1/2 cups
vegetable oil	2 tbs.	3 tbs.	1/4 cup
egg	1	1	1
honey	2 tbs.	3 tbs.	1/4 cup
salt	1/2 tsp.	3/4 tsp.	1 tsp.
grated lemon peel	1/2 tsp.	3/4 tsp.	1 tsp.
oats	2/3 cup	3/4 cup	1 cup
whole wheat flour	2/3 cup	3/4 cup	1 cup
bread flour	2 cups	3 cups	3 1/2 cups
yeast	1 1/2 tsp.	2 tsp.	2 1/2 tsp.
*chopped dried apricots	1/3 cup	1/2 cup	2/3 cup
*raisins	1/3 cup	1/2 cup	2/3 cup
*chopped almonds	3 tbs.	1/4 cup	1/3 cup

*Add ingredients at the beginning of the second kneading period.

Apple Oatmeal Bread

Raisin, Whole Wheat, Sweet or Basic cycle

This bread is so good it could be eaten for dessert. Try it toasted for breakfast for a great early morning treat.

	1 lb.	1½ lb.	1¾-2 lb.
applesauce	1 cup	1⅓ cups	1½ cups
vegetable oil	1½ tbs.	2 tbs.	3 tbs.
honey	1½ tbs.	2 tbs.	3 tbs.
salt	½ tsp.	¾ tsp.	1 tsp.
cinnamon	½ tsp.	¾ tsp.	1 tsp.
oats	1 cup	1½ cups	2 cups
bread flour	2 cups	3 cups	3½ cups
yeast	1½ tsp.	2 tsp.	2½ tsp.
*chopped dried apples	⅓ cup	½ cup	⅔ cup

*Add ingredients at the beginning of the second kneading period.

Apple Oatmeal Raisin Bread

Raisin, Sweet, Whole Wheat or Basic cycle

This is a wonderful breakfast bread. It's also good for sandwiches.

	1 lb.	1½ lb.	1¾-2 lb.
apple juice	1⅛ cups	1⅓ cups	1½ cups
margarine or butter	1½ tbs.	2 tbs.	3 tbs.
brown sugar, packed	1½ tbs.	2 tbs.	3 tbs.
salt	¾ tsp.	1 tsp.	1 tsp.
cinnamon	½ tsp.	1 tsp.	1½ tsp.
oat bran	3 tbs.	¼ cup	⅓ cup
oats	¾ cup	1 cup	1½ cups
bread flour	2 cups	3 cups	3½ cups
yeast	1½ tsp.	2 tsp.	2½ tsp.
*raisins	½ cup	⅔ cup	¾ cup
*chopped apples	½ cup	⅔ cup	¾ cup
*chopped nuts, optional	⅓ cup	½ cup	⅔ cup

*Add ingredients at the beginning of the second kneading period.

Apple Carrot Bread

Raisin, Sweet, Whole Wheat or Basic cycle

Here is a great way to sneak those carrots in for finicky eaters. Delicious!

	1 lb.	1 1/2 lb.	1 3/4-2 lb.
apple juice	7/8 cup	1 1/8 cups	1 1/3 cups
grated carrots	1/3 cup	1/2 cup	2/3 cup
vegetable oil	1 1/2 tbs.	2 tbs.	3 tbs.
honey	1 1/2 tbs.	2 tbs.	3 tbs.
salt	1/2 tsp.	3/4 tsp.	1 tsp.
whole wheat flour	1 1/2 cups	2 cups	2 1/2 cups
bread flour	1 1/2 cups	2 cups	2 1/2 cups
yeast	1 1/2 tsp.	2 tsp.	2 1/2 tsp.
*chopped dried apples	1/4 cup	1/3 cup	1/2 cup
*raisins, optional	1/4 cup	1/3 cup	1/2 cup
*chopped nuts, optional	1/4 cup	1/3 cup	1/2 cup

*Add ingredients at the beginning of the second kneading period.

Carrot, Cherry and Coconut Bread

Raisin, Sweet, Whole Wheat or Basic cycle

Serve this for dessert, or toasted for breakfast. Regular milk can be substituted for the coconut milk if desired.

	1 lb.	1 1/2 lb.	1 3/4-2 lb.
unsweetened coconut milk	2/3 cup	1 cup	1 1/4 cups
grated carrots	1/3 cup	1/2 cup	2/3 cup
maraschino cherries	12	16	20
vegetable oil	2 1/2 tbs.	1/4 cup	1/4 cup
sugar	1 1/2 tbs.	2 tbs.	2 1/2 tbs.
salt	3/4 tsp.	1 tsp.	1 tsp.
flaked coconut	3 tbs.	1/4 cup	1/3 cup
cinnamon	1/2 tsp.	1/2 tsp.	3/4 cup
bread flour	2 cups	3 cups	3 1/2 cups
yeast	1 1/2 tsp.	2 tsp.	2 1/2 tsp.
*chopped walnuts	1/3 cup	1/2 cup	2/3 cup

*Add ingredients at the beginning of the second kneading period.

Carrot Pineapple Bread
Raisin, Sweet, Whole Wheat or Basic cycle

I use well-drained canned pineapple for this interesting, delicious bread.

	1 lb.	1½ lb.	1¾-2 lb.
water	⅓ cup	½ cup	⅔ cup
drained crushed pineapple	¾ cup	1 cup	1¼ cups
grated carrots	½ cup	⅔ cup	¾ cup
margarine or butter	1½ tbs.	2 tbs.	3 tbs.
vanilla extract	¾ tsp.	1 tsp.	1 tsp.
brown sugar, packed	1½ tbs.	2 tbs.	2½ tbs.
salt	½ tsp.	¾ tsp.	1 tsp.
oats	¾ cup	1 cup	1¼ cups
whole wheat flour	¾ cup	1 cup	1¼ cups
bread flour	1½ cups	2 cups	2½ cups
yeast	1½ tsp.	2 tsp.	2½ tsp.
*chopped nuts	⅓ cup	½ cup	⅔ cup
*raisins	⅓ cup	½ cup	⅔ cup

*Add ingredients at the beginning of the second kneading period.

Peanut Butter Banana Bread
Sweet, Whole Wheat or Basic cycle

This delightful bread slices well and is great for sandwiches. Try it toasted with banana slices on top for a wonderful early-morning treat. Use fully ripe bananas, which add both flavor and moisture to the bread. Check the consistency of the dough after 5 minutes of kneading and add water if necessary.

	1 lb.	1½ lb.	1¾-2 lb.
mashed bananas	1⅛ cups	1½ cups	1¾ cups
peanut butter	⅓ cup	½ cup	⅔ cup
eggs	1	1	2
sugar	1½ tbs.	2 tbs.	3 tbs.
salt	¾ tsp.	1 tsp.	1 tsp.
whole wheat flour	1½ cups	2 cups	2½ cups
bread flour	1½ cups	2 cups	2½ cups
yeast	1½ tsp.	2 tsp.	2½ tsp.

Peanut Butter Chocolate Chip Bread

Use a favorite candy bar flavor combination to make a really different dessert bread. Set crust color to light.

	1 lb.	1 1/2 lb.	1 3/4-2 lb.
milk	1 1/8 cups	1 1/2 cups	1 3/4 cups
peanut butter	1/2 cup	2/3 cup	3/4 cup
honey	1 1/2 tbs.	2 tbs.	3 tbs.
salt	1/2 tsp.	3/4 tsp.	1 tsp.
whole wheat flour	1 1/2 cups	2 cups	2 1/2 cups
bread flour	1 1/2 cups	2 cups	2 1/2 cups
yeast	1 tsp.	1 1/2 tsp.	2 tsp.
*chocolate chips	1/2 cup	2/3 cup	3/4 cup

*Add ingredients at the beginning of the second kneading period.

Sunflower Bread

This tasty, nutty bread is great for sandwiches or toast.

	1 lb.	1 1/2 lb.	1 3/4-2 lb.
water	1 cup	1 1/3 cups	1 1/2 cups
vegetable oil	2 1/2 tbs.	3 tbs.	1/4 cup
honey	2 1/2 tbs.	3 tbs.	1/4 cup
salt	3/4 tsp.	1 tsp.	1 tsp.
whole wheat flour	1 1/2 cups	2 cups	2 1/2 cups
bread flour	1 1/2 cups	2 cups	2 1/2 cups
yeast	1 1/2 tsp.	2 tsp.	2 1/2 tsp.
*sunflower kernels	1/3 cup	1/2 cup	2/3 cup

*Add ingredients at the beginning of the second kneading period.

Walnut Bread

This hearty loaf of bread is superb served with cheese and red wine. Walnut oil can be found in a well-stocked grocery store. Any vegetable oil can be substituted. Adjust the rosemary to taste if desired.

	1 lb.	1 1/2 lb.	1 3/4-2 lb.
water or beer	1 cup	1 1/3 cups	1 1/2 cups
walnut oil	1 1/2 tbs.	2 tbs.	3 tbs.
finely chopped onion	1/3 cup	1/2 cup	1/2 cup
sugar	1 tbs.	1 1/2 tbs.	2 tbs.
salt	3/4 tsp.	1 tsp.	1 tsp.
dried rosemary	1/4 tsp.	1/2 tsp.	3/4 tsp.
whole wheat flour	3/4 cup	1 cup	1 1/4 cups
rye flour	3/4 cup	1 cup	1 1/4 cups
bread flour	1 1/2 cups	2 cups	2 1/2 cups
yeast	1 1/2 tsp.	2 tsp.	2 1/2 tsp.
*chopped walnuts	1/3 cup	1/2 cup	2/3 cup

*Add ingredients at the beginning of the second kneading period.

Scallion Bread

This is a great accompaniment to a barbecue meal or picnic lunch. Check the consistency of the dough after 5 minutes of kneading and add flour if necessary.

	1 lb.	1 1/2 lb.	1 3/4-2 lb.
water	3/4 cup	1 cup	1 1/4 cups
margarine or butter	1 tbs.	1 1/2 tbs.	2 tbs.
chopped scallions	2/3 cup	3/4 cup	1 cup
eggs	1	2	2
sugar	1 tsp.	1 1/2 tsp.	2 tsp.
salt	3/4 tsp.	1 tsp.	1 tsp.
garlic powder	1/2 tsp.	1/2 tsp.	3/4 tsp.
black pepper	1/2 tsp.	1/2 tsp.	3/4 tsp.
whole wheat flour	1 cup	1 1/2 cups	2 cups
bread flour	1 3/4 cups	2 cups	2 1/2 cups
yeast	1 1/2 tsp.	2 tsp.	2 tsp.

Walnut Onion Mushroom Bread

Raisin, Sweet, Whole Wheat or Basic cycle

For a full meal, serve this loaf with some hot soup and a salad.

	1 lb.	1½ lb.	1¾-2 lb.
water	¾ cup	1 cup	1⅓ cups
walnut oil	1 tbs.	1½ tbs.	2 tbs.
chopped onion	3 tbs.	¼ cup	⅓ cup
sautéed sliced mushrooms	⅓ cup	½ cup	⅔ cup
honey	1 tbs.	1½ tbs.	2 tbs.
salt	¾ tsp.	1 tsp.	1 tsp.
whole wheat flour	¾ cup	1 cup	1¼ cups
bread flour	2 cups	3 cups	3½ cups
yeast	1½ tsp.	2 tsp.	2½ tsp.
*chopped walnuts	3 tbs.	¼ cup	⅓ cup

Note: Sauté mushrooms in 1 to 2 tsp. walnut oil until liquid is gone. If walnut oil is unavailable, any vegetable oil can be substituted.

*Add ingredients at the beginning of the second kneading period.

Onion Rye

Whole Wheat, Sweet or Basic cycle

This variation on onion bread is terrific — you'll make it more than once. Check the consistency of the dough during kneading and adjust with water or flour if necessary. This low-rising loaf is packed with flavor.

	1 lb.	1½ lb.	1¾-2 lb.
water	¾ cup	1 cup	1¼ cups
vegetable oil	1 tbs.	1½ tbs.	2 tbs.
chopped onion	½ cup	⅔ cup	¾ cup
honey	1 tbs.	1½ tbs.	2 tbs.
salt	¾ tsp.	1 tsp.	1 tsp.
rye flour	1 cup	1½ cups	2 cups
bread flour	2 cups	2½ cups	3 cups
yeast	1½ tsp.	2 tsp.	2½ tsp.

Onion Poppy Seed Bread

Whole Wheat, Sweet or Basic cycle

Even someone who does not like onions will like this bread. The poppy seed and onion combination is a true winner. Adjust the consistency of the dough while it's kneading if necessary.

	1 lb.	1 ½ lb.	1 ¾-2 lb.
water	¾ cup	1 cup	1 ¼ cups
margarine or butter	1 ½ tbs.	2 tbs.	2 tbs.
chopped onion	½ cup	⅔ cup	¾ cup
sugar	1 ½ tsp.	2 tsp.	1 tbs.
salt	¾ tsp.	1 tsp.	1 tsp.
poppy seeds	1 ½ tbs.	2 tbs.	3 tbs.
whole wheat flour	1 ½ cups	2 cups	2 ½ cups
bread flour	1 ½ cups	2 cups	2 ½ cups
yeast	1 tsp.	1 ½ tsp.	2 tsp.

Black Pepper Bread

Sweet or Basic cycle

This loaf is a great accompaniment to a grilled steak dinner or sandwiches. Warm the cottage cheese as you would milk. Ricotta cheese can be substituted for the cottage cheese if desired. Add milk, 1 tbs. at a time, only if necessary, after 10 full minutes of kneading. If you desire a spicier bread, double the amount of pepper used.

	1 lb.	1½ lb.	1¾-2 lb.
cottage cheese	1 cup	1½ cups	1¾ cups
margarine or butter	2 tbs.	3 tbs.	¼ cup
egg	1	1	1
sugar	1 tbs.	1½ tbs.	2 tbs.
salt	¾ tsp.	1 tsp.	1 tsp.
coarsely ground black pepper	¾ tsp.	1 tsp.	1½ tsp.
dried chives	1 tsp.	1½ tsp.	2 tsp.
bread flour	2 cups	3 cups	3½ cups
yeast	1 tsp.	1½ tsp.	2 tsp.
milk, optional	2 tbs.	¼ cup	¼ cup

Honey Curry Bread

Whole Wheat, Sweet or Basic cycle

This bread is great with chicken at dinner or on a picnic.

	1 lb.	1½ lb.	1¾-2 lb.
water	1⅛ cups	1½ cups	1⅔ cups
vegetable oil	1 tbs.	1½ tbs.	2 tbs.
honey	1½ tbs.	2 tbs.	2½ tbs.
salt	¾ tsp.	1 tsp.	1 tsp.
curry powder	1½ tsp.	2 tsp.	1 tbs.
whole wheat flour	1½ cups	2 cups	2½ cups
bread flour	1½ cups	2 cups	2½ cups
yeast	1½ tsp.	2 tsp.	2½ tsp.

Oatmeal Ginger Bread

Sweet, Whole Wheat or Basic cycle

This tasty, low-rising loaf is great with chicken salad for brunch. Spray the measuring cup with nonstick cooking spray before measuring the molasses.

	1 lb.	1 1/2 lb.	1 3/4-2 lb.
water	7/8 cup	1 1/8 cups	1 1/2 cups
vegetable oil	1 1/2 tbs.	2 tbs.	3 tbs.
molasses	3 tbs.	1/4 cup	1/3 cup
salt	3/4 tsp.	1 tsp.	1 tsp.
ground ginger	3/4 tsp.	1 tsp.	1 1/2 tsp.
oats	1 cup	1 1/2 cups	2 cups
bread flour	2 cups	3 cups	3 1/2 cups
yeast	1 1/2 tsp.	2 tsp.	2 1/2 tsp.

Saffron Bread

Raisin, Sweet, Whole Wheat or Basic cycle

Saffron is one of the world's most expensive spices, but only a little bit is needed to produce this wonderful, tasty bread. It's equally delicious without the raisins. The nutmeg can be adjusted to taste.

	1 lb.	1 1/2 lb.	1 3/4-2 lb.
milk	1/2 cup	7/8 cup	1 1/8 cups
margarine or butter	2 tbs.	3 tbs.	1/4 cup
egg	1	1	1
sugar	2 1/2 tbs.	3 tbs.	1/4 cup
salt	1/2 tsp.	3/4 tsp.	1 tsp.
nutmeg	1/2 tsp.	1/2 tsp.	3/4 tsp.
powdered saffron	1/16 tsp.	1/8 tsp.	1/4 tsp.
bread flour	2 cups	3 cups	3 1/2 cups
yeast	1 1/2 tsp.	2 tsp.	2 1/2 tsp.
*dried currants or raisins	1/3 cup	1/2 cup	2/3 cup

*Add ingredients at the beginning of the second kneading period.

Basil Parmesan Bread

Raisin, Sweet, Whole Wheat or Basic cycle

This bread is out of this world! It's a must with an Italian meal. While pre-grated Parmesan cheese can be used in this recipe, freshly grated Parmesan cheese is much better. If using fresh basil, triple the amount called for.

	1 lb.	1½ lb.	1¾-2 lb.
water	1⅛ cups	1½ cups	1¾ cups
olive oil	1½ tbs.	2 tbs.	3 tbs.
sugar	1 tbs.	1½ tbs.	2 tbs.
salt	½ tsp.	¾ tsp.	1 tsp.
basil, dried	1 tbs.	1½ tbs.	2 tbs.
whole wheat flour	1½ cups	2 cups	2½ cups
bread flour	2 cups	2½ cups	3 cups
yeast	1½ tsp.	2 tsp.	2½ tsp.
*grated Parmesan cheese	⅓ cup	½ cup	⅔ cup

*Add ingredients after dough has formed a smooth ball, about 5 minutes into the first kneading period.

Pizza Bread

Raisin, Sweet, Whole Wheat or Basic cycle

This makes a great snack bread. Add 1 or 2 of the optional ingredients at the beep.

	1 lb.	1½ lb.	1¾-2 lb.
pizza sauce	1⅛ cups	1½ cups	1¾ cups
olive oil	2½ tbs.	3 tbs.	3 tbs.
salt	½ tsp.	¾ tsp.	1 tsp.
dried oregano	¾ tsp.	1 tsp.	1 tsp.
whole wheat flour	1½ cups	2 cups	2½ cups
bread flour	1½ cups	2 cups	2½ cups
yeast	1½ tsp.	2 tsp.	2½ tsp.
*grated mozzarella cheese, optional	½ cup	⅔ cup	¾ cup
*diced pepperoni, optional	½ cup	⅔ cup	¾ cup
*chopped mushrooms, optional	½ cup	⅔ cup	¾ cup
*chopped sun-dried tomatoes, optional	3 tbs.	¼ cup	⅓ cup

*Add ingredients at the beginning of the second kneading period.

Pepperoni Bread

Raisin, Sweet, Whole Wheat or Basic cycle

Serve this as a snack with some beer or on a picnic. It's a must-try.

	1 lb.	1½ lb.	1¾-2 lb.
water	1 cup	1⅓ cups	1½ cups
olive oil	1½ tbs.	2 tbs.	3 tbs.
sugar	¾ tsp.	1 tsp.	1½ tsp.
salt	½ tsp.	¾ tsp.	1 tsp.
dried oregano	1 tsp.	1½ tsp.	2 tsp.
garlic powder	½ tsp.	¾ tsp.	1 tsp.
basil, dried	½ tsp.	¾ tsp.	1 tsp.
whole wheat flour	1 cup	1½ cups	2 cups
bread flour	2 cups	2½ cups	3 cups
yeast	1½ tsp.	2 tsp.	2½ tsp.
*diced pepperoni	¾ cup	1 cup	1½ cups

*Add ingredients at the beginning of the second kneading period.

Variation: Pepperoni Jalapeño Bread

Add the following to Pepperoni Bread as soon as the dough forms a ball. If desired, adjust the jalapeños to taste.

	1 lb.	1½ lb.	1¾-2 lb.
grated pepper Jack cheese	½ cup	⅔ cup	¾ cup
diced jalapeños	1	1½	2

Minted Herb Bread

French, Sweet or Basic cycle

This is an absolutely superb bread. Don't forget to triple amount of herbs if you use fresh ones. Use freshly grated Parmesan cheese.

	1 lb.	1½ lb.	1¾-2 lb.
water	⅔ cup	1 cup	1¼ cups
olive oil	2 tbs.	3 tbs.	¼ cup
sugar	1 tsp.	1½ tsp.	2 tsp.
salt	¾ tsp.	1 tsp.	1 tsp.
basil, dried	1½ tsp.	2 tsp.	1 tbs.
parsley, dried	1½ tsp.	2 tsp.	1 tbs.
dried mint	1½ tsp.	2 tsp.	1 tbs.
bread flour	2 cups	3 cups	3½ cups
yeast	1½ tsp.	2 tsp.	2½ tsp.
*grated Parmesan cheese	3 tbs.	¼ cup	⅓ cup

*Add ingredients after dough has formed a smooth ball, about 5 minutes into the first kneading period.

Easter Bread

Raisin, Sweet, Whole Wheat or Basic cycle

Thanks to Marcia Germaine for sharing her grandmother's recipe. Some of the anise seeds will be incorporated into the bread, while the rest will remain whole to lend a crunchy texture.

	1 lb.	1½ lb.	1¾-2 lb.
milk	¼ cup	⅓ cup	½ cup
water	⅓ cup	⅓ cup	½ cup
eggs	1	2	2
margarine or butter	¼ cup	6 tbs.	½ cup
sugar	¼ cup	⅓ cup	⅓ cup
salt	½ tsp.	¾ tsp.	1 tsp.
anise seeds	½ tsp.	¾ tsp.	1 tsp.
bread flour	2 cups	3 cups	3½ cups
yeast	1 tsp.	1½ tsp.	2 tsp.
*anise seeds	½ tsp.	¾ tsp.	1 tsp.

*Add ingredients at the beginning of the second kneading period.

Greek Kouloura Bread

Sweet or Basic cycle

Traditionally, this loaf is twisted and has a topping of sesame seeds. It's a great breakfast or brunch bread. If desired, open the machine briefly during the second rising period and sprinkle sesame seeds on the top of the dough. Be careful not to spill any into the machine itself.

	1 lb.	1½ lb.	1¾-2 lb.
milk	⅔ cup	1 cup	1⅛ cups
vegetable oil	1 tbs.	1 tbs.	1½ tbs.
egg	1	1	1
sugar	1 tbs.	1½ tbs.	2 tbs.
salt	½ tsp.	¾ tsp.	1 tsp.
bread flour	2¼ cups	3 cups	3½ cups
yeast	1½ tsp.	2 tsp.	2½ tsp.

St. Basil's Bread

Sweet or Basic cycle

This classic Greek bread is traditionally served with a coin hidden inside, which is rumored to bestow luck upon the finder. Instead, add a single raisin or nut at the beep. St. Basil's Bread is a delicious, sweet bread that disappears quickly.

	1 lb.	1½ lb.	1¾-2 lb.
milk	½ cup	¾ cup	⅞ cup
margarine or butter	2 tbs.	3 tbs.	¼ cup
eggs	1	2	2
sugar	¼ cup	⅓ cup	½ cup
salt	½ tsp.	¾ tsp.	1 tsp.
grated lemon peel	½ tsp.	¾ tsp.	1 tsp.
cinnamon	⅛ tsp.	¼ tsp.	½ tsp.
nutmeg	¼ tsp.	½ tsp.	¾ tsp.
ground cloves	1/16 tsp.	⅛ tsp.	⅛ tsp.
bread flour	2 cups	3 cups	3½ cups
yeast	1½ tsp.	2 tsp.	2½ tsp.

Greek Sunday Bread

Sweet or Basic cycle

Here's another wonderful Greek bread! If desired, open the machine during the second rising period and place sesame seeds on top of the dough.

	1 lb.	1½ lb.	1¾-2 lb.
milk	½ cup	1 cup	1¼ cups
margarine or butter	2 tbs.	3 tbs.	¼ cup
egg	1	1	1
sugar	1½ tbs.	2 tbs.	3 tbs.
salt	½ tsp.	¾ tsp.	1 tsp.
cinnamon	⅛ tsp.	⅛ tsp.	¼ tsp.
anise seeds	⅛ tsp.	⅛ tsp.	¼ tsp.
grated orange peel	⅛ tsp.	⅛ tsp.	¼ tsp.
ground allspice	1/16 tsp.	1/16 tsp.	⅛ tsp.
bread flour	2 cups	3 cups	3½ cups
yeast	1 tsp.	1½ tsp.	2 tsp.

Greek Easter Bread (Lambropsomo)

Sweet or Basic cycle

This wonderful, sweet bread is good any time of the year. The spices can be adjusted to taste.

	1 lb.	1 ½ lb.	1¾-2 lb.
milk	½ cup	⅞ cup	1 ⅛ cups
margarine or butter	2 tbs.	3 tbs.	¼ cup
egg	1	1	1
sugar	¼ cup	⅓ cup	⅓ cup
salt	¾ tsp.	1 tsp.	1 tsp.
grated lemon peel	⅛ tsp.	⅛ tsp.	¼ tsp.
cinnamon	¼ tsp.	¼ tsp.	½ tsp.
ground allspice	⅛ tsp.	⅛ tsp.	¼ tsp.
bread flour	2 cups	3 cups	3½ cups
yeast	1 ½ tsp.	1 ½ tsp.	2 tsp.

Portuguese Easter Bread

Sweet or Basic cycle

My daughter, Rachel, refused to let me give any of this bread away to tasters — she loves it for sandwiches! The dough should be slightly wet.

	1 lb.	1 ½ lb.	1¾-2 lb.
milk	⅔ cup	⅞ cup	1 cup
margarine or butter	1 ½ tbs.	2 tbs.	3 tbs.
eggs	1	2	2
sugar	⅓ cup	½ cup	½ cup
salt	¾ tsp.	1 tsp.	1 tsp.
bread flour	2 cups	3 cups	3½ cups
yeast	1 ½ tsp.	2 tsp.	2½ tsp.

Portuguese Cornbread (Broa)

Whole Wheat, Sweet or Basic cycle

This Portuguese cornmeal bread is outstanding. White cornmeal makes this a very distinctive, delicious loaf. Most recipes for broa stipulate using white cornmeal. Yellow or blue cornmeal can be used as a variation.

	1 lb.	1 1/2 lb.	1 3/4-2 lb.
water	1 cup	1 1/3 cups	1 2/3 cups
olive oil	2 tbs.	3 tbs.	1/4 cup
sugar	1 tsp.	1 1/2 tsp.	2 tsp.
salt	3/4 tsp.	1 tsp.	1 tsp.
white cornmeal	1 cup	1 1/3 cups	1 1/2 cups
bread flour	2 cups	2 2/3 cups	3 1/2 cups
yeast	1 1/2 tsp.	2 tsp.	2 1/2 tsp.

French Pear Bread

Sweeet or Basic cycle

It is well worth the time involved to make the pear puree for this bread. Fresh pears should be poached in water until soft; canned pears should be rinsed. Puree pears with a blender or food processor. The pepper can be omitted for a different taste, and dried pears can be added for another variation.

	1 lb.	1 1/2 lb.	1 3/4-2 lb.
pear puree	3/4 cup	1 cup	1 1/4 cups
vegetable oil	1 1/2 tbs.	2 tbs.	2 1/2 tbs.
eggs	1	2	2
honey	1 1/2 tbs.	2 tbs.	2 1/2 tbs.
salt	1/2 tsp.	3/4 tsp.	1 tsp.
coarsely ground black pepper	1/8 tsp.	1/4 tsp.	1/4 tsp.
bread flour	2 cups	3 cups	3 1/2 cups
yeast	1 1/2 tsp.	2 tsp.	2 1/2 tsp.
*chopped dried pears, optional	1/3 cup	1/2 cup	2/3 cup

* Add ingredients at the beginning of the second kneading period.

German Easter Bread

Raisin, Sweet, Whole Wheat or Basic cycle

This bread is traditionally formed into a braided circle and served with dyed Easter eggs placed in the center. Here is a wonderful lazy way to make it.

	1 lb.	1½ lb.	1¾-2 lb.
milk	½ cup	⅔ cup	⅞ cup
margarine or butter	3 tbs.	¼ cup	5 tbs.
eggs	1	2	2
almond extract	¾ tsp.	1 tsp.	1 tsp.
sugar	3 tbs.	¼ cup	⅓ cup
salt	½ tsp.	¾ tsp.	1 tsp.
grated lemon peel	½ tsp.	¾ tsp.	1 tsp.
anise seeds	½ tsp.	¾ tsp.	1 tsp.
bread flour	2 cups	3 cups	3½ cups
yeast	1½ tsp.	2 tsp.	2½ tsp.
*golden raisins	⅓ cup	½ cup	⅔ cup
*sliced almonds	3 tbs.	¼ cup	⅓ cup

*Add ingredients at the beginning of the second kneading period.

Italian Easter Bread

Raisin, Sweet or Basic cycle

This rich, cheesy bread is not as sweet as many of the other Easter breads.

	1 lb.	1½ lb.	1¾-2 lb.
milk	½ cup	¾ cup	1 cup
olive oil	2½ tbs.	3 tbs.	¼ cup
margarine or butter	3 tbs.	¼ cup	5 tbs.
eggs	1	2	2
sugar	¾ tsp.	1 tsp.	1½ tsp.
salt	½ tsp.	¾ tsp.	1 tsp.
freshly ground black pepper	⅛ tsp.	¼ tsp.	½ tsp.
bread flour	2 cups	3 cups	3½ cups
yeast	1½ tsp.	2 tsp.	2½ tsp.
*grated Parmesan cheese	¾ cup	1 cup	1¼ cups

*Add ingredients after dough has formed a smooth ball, about 5 minutes into the first kneading period.

Italian Spring Bread

Anise imparts an exotic flavor to this bread.

	1 lb.	**1½ lb.**	**1¾-2 lb.**
water	⅔ cup	1 cup	1¼ cups
vegetable oil	1½ tbs.	2 tbs.	3 tbs.
honey	1½ tsp.	2 tsp.	1 tbs.
salt	½ tsp.	¾ tsp.	1 tsp.
anise seeds	3 tbs.	¼ cup	⅓ cup
bread flour	2 cups	3 cups	3½ cups
yeast	1 tsp.	1½ tsp.	2 tsp.
*golden raisins	½ cup	⅔ cup	¾ cup

*Add ingredients at the beginning of the second kneading period.

English Good Friday Bread

Most people equate caraway seeds with rye — that is, until they try this bread!

	1 lb.	**1½ lb.**	**1¾-2 lb.**
water	¾ cup	1 cup	1¼ cups
margarine or butter	3 tbs.	¼ cup	5 tbs.
sugar	1 tbs.	1½ tbs.	2 tbs.
salt	¾ tsp.	1 tsp.	1 tsp.
caraway seeds	1 tsp.	1½ tsp.	2 tsp.
bread flour	2 cups	3 cups	3½ cups
yeast	1½ tsp.	2 tsp.	2½ tsp.

English New Year's Rum Bread

Sweet or Basic cycle

This traditional bread is served with a hidden coin to bestow luck upon the finder. If you wish, you can use a single raisin or nut.

	1 lb.	1 ½ lb.	1¾-2 lb.
water	⅔ cup	1 cup	1⅛ cups
light rum	1 tbs.	1½ tbs.	2 tbs.
margarine or butter	2 tbs.	3 tbs.	¼ cup
sugar	3 tbs.	¼ cup	⅓ cup
salt	¾ tsp.	1 tsp.	1 tsp.
bread flour	2 cups	3 cups	3½ cups
yeast	1 tsp.	1½ tsp.	2 tsp.

Welsh Yeast Cake (Bara Brith)

Raisin, Sweet or Basic cycle

This is a rich cake-like bread. It's a real treat.

	1 lb.	1 ½ lb.	1¾-2 lb.
milk	½ cup	¾ cup	1 cup
margarine or butter	¼ cup	6 tbs.	½ cup
egg	1	1	1
molasses	1½ tsp.	2 tsp.	1 tbs.
sugar	2 tbs.	3 tbs.	¼ cup
salt	½ tsp.	¾ tsp.	1 tsp.
caraway seeds	½ tsp.	¾ tsp.	1 tsp.
bread flour	2 cups	3 cups	3½ cups
yeast	1½ tsp.	2 tsp.	2½ tsp.
*raisins	¼ cup	⅓ cup	½ cup
*chopped nuts	¼ cup	⅓ cup	½ cup

*Add ingredients at the beginning of the second kneading period.

Swedish Christmas Bread (Julbrod)

Raisin, Sweet, Whole Wheat or Basic cycle

The cardamom in this recipe imparts a distinctive, delicious taste.

	1 lb.	1 1/2 lb.	1 3/4-2 lb.
milk	2/3 cup	7/8 cup	1 1/8 cups
margarine or butter	2 tbs.	3 tbs.	1/4 cup
egg	1	1	1
sugar	2 tbs.	3 tbs.	1/4 cup
salt	3/4 tsp.	1 tsp.	1 tsp.
ground cardamom	1/2 tsp.	3/4 tsp.	1 tsp.
bread flour	2 cups	3 cups	3 1/2 cups
yeast	1 1/2 tsp.	2 tsp.	2 1/2 tsp.
*raisins	1/3 cup	1/2 cup	2/3 cup
*chopped citron	1/3 cup	1/2 cup	2/3 cup
*sliced almonds	1 tbs.	1 1/2 tbs.	2 tbs.

*Add ingredients at the beginning of the second kneading period.

Swedish Chocolate Bread

Raisin, Sweet, Whole Wheat or Basic cycle

Traditionally, this bread is made as a chocolate-filled coffee bread. Here is a variation devised for ease in bread machines. Use hazelnuts or walnuts.

	1 lb.	1 1/2 lb.	1 3/4-2 lb.
milk	1/2 cup	7/8 cup	1 1/8 cups
margarine or butter	2 tbs.	3 tbs.	1/4 cup
egg	1	1	1
sugar	1/4 cup	1/3 cup	1/3 cup
salt	1/2 tsp.	3/4 tsp.	1 tsp.
cocoa powder	1 tbs.	1 1/2 tbs.	2 tbs.
cinnamon	1/4 tsp.	1/2 tsp.	3/4 tsp.
bread flour	2 cups	3 cups	3 1/2 cups
yeast	1 tsp.	1 1/2 tsp.	2 tsp.
*chopped nuts	1/4 cup	1/3 cup	1/2 cup

*Add ingredients at the beginning of the second kneading period.

Scandinavian Rye

This bread is similar to a Swedish limpa. The fennel gives it a wonderful, uplifting flavor.

	1 lb.	1½ lb.	1¾-2 lb.
water	1 cup	1⅓ cups	1⅔ cups
vegetable oil	2½ tbs.	3 tbs.	¼ cup
molasses	2½ tbs.	3 tbs.	¼ cup
salt	¾ tsp.	1 tsp.	1 tsp.
baking soda	⅛ tsp.	¼ tsp.	¼ tsp.
fennel seeds	1 tsp.	1½ tsp.	2 tsp.
caraway seeds	1 tsp.	1½ tsp.	2 tsp.
grated orange peel	1 tsp.	1½ tsp.	2 tsp.
rye flour	1 cup	1½ cups	2 cups
bread flour	2 cups	3 cups	3½ cups
yeast	1½ tsp.	2 tsp.	2½ tsp.

Finnish Easter Bread

Rye flour makes this a unique Easter bread.

	1 lb.	1½ lb.	1¾-2 lb.
milk	⅔ cup	⅞ cup	1⅛ cups
margarine or butter	3 tbs.	¼ cup	5 tbs.
eggs	1	2	2
sugar	3 tbs.	¼ cup	⅓ cup
salt	½ tsp.	¾ tsp.	1 tsp.
ground cardamom	¾ tsp.	1 tsp.	1 tsp.
grated lemon peel	¾ tsp.	1 tsp.	1 tsp.
grated orange peel	¾ tsp.	1 tsp.	1 tsp.
rye flour	¾ cup	1 cup	1¼ cups
bread flour	2 cups	3 cups	3½ cups
yeast	1½ tsp.	2 tsp.	2½ tsp.
*golden raisins	⅓ cup	½ cup	⅔ cup
*chopped almonds	⅓ cup	½ cup	⅔ cup

*Add ingredients at the beginning of the second kneading period.

Finnish Pulla

Raisin, Sweet or Basic cycle

Cardamom is common in Scandinavian breads and lends a sweet flavor.

	1 lb.	1½ lb.	1¾-2 lb.
milk	½ cup	¾ cup	⅞ cup
margarine or butter	¼ cup	6 tbs.	7 tbs.
egg	1	1	1
sugar	¼ cup	⅓ cup	⅓ cup
salt	¾ tsp.	1 tsp.	1 tsp.
ground cardamom	¾ tsp.	1 tsp.	1 tsp.
bread flour	2 cups	3 cups	3½ cups
yeast	1½ tsp.	2 tsp.	2½ tsp.
*raisins	½ cup	⅔ cup	¾ cup

*Add ingredients at the beginning of the second kneading period.

Moroccan Bread

Whole Wheat, Sweet or Basic cycle

*This bread is traditionally made as a large, round and puffy loaf. Try it —
you'll like it! If the dough does not knead easily, scrape the sides of the pan
with a rubber spatula to help push the dough toward the kneading paddle.
After the machine has kneaded the dough once, stop the machine and start
the entire process over from the beginning.*

	1 lb.	1½ lb.	1¾-2 lb.
water	1 cup	1⅓ cups	1¾ cups
olive oil	2 tbs.	3 tbs.	¼ cup
sugar	1 tsp.	1½ tsp.	2 tsp.
salt	¾ tsp.	1 tsp.	1 tsp.
anise seeds	2 tsp.	1 tbs.	1½ tbs.
sesame seeds	½ tsp.	¾ tsp.	1 tsp.
whole wheat flour	½ cup	⅔ cup	¾ cup
rye flour	½ cup	⅔ cup	¾ cup
semolina flour	½ cup	⅔ cup	¾ cup
bread flour	1½ cups	2 cups	2½ cups
yeast	1 tsp.	1½ tsp.	2 tsp.

Moroccan Anise Bread

Sweet or Basic cycle

This is an outstanding change-of-pace bread. The anise gives it nice flavor.

	1 lb.	1½ lb.	1¾-2 lb.
water	¾ cup	1⅛ cups	1¼ cups
margarine or butter	3 tbs.	¼ cup	5 tbs.
sugar	3 tbs.	¼ cup	⅓ cup
salt	½ tsp.	¾ tsp.	1 tsp.
anise seeds	1 tsp.	1½ tsp.	2 tsp.
bread flour	2 cups	3 cups	3½ cups
yeast	1½ tsp.	2 tsp.	2½ tsp.

Ethiopian Honey Bread

Sweet or Basic cycle

This is an adaptation of one of our family's favorite breads from pre-machine days. You, too, will soon love this.

	1 lb.	1½ lb.	1¾-2 lb.
water	⅝ cup	¾ cup	1 cup
vegetable oil	2 tbs.	3 tbs.	¼ cup
honey	3 tbs.	¼ cup	⅓ cup
salt	½ tsp.	½ tsp.	¾ tsp.
ground coriander	1 tsp.	1½ tsp.	2 tsp.
cinnamon	½ tsp.	¾ tsp.	1 tsp.
ground cloves	⅛ tsp.	¼ tsp.	½ tsp.
bread flour	2¼ cups	3 cups	3½ cups
dry milk powder	3 tbs.	¼ cup	⅓ cup
yeast	1½ tsp.	2 tsp.	2½ tsp.

Mexican Sweet Bread

Sweet or Basic cycle

This wonderful bread is often used for sandwiches in this household of kids.

	1 lb.	1½ lb.	1¾-2 lb.
milk	⅔ cup	1 cup	1¼ cups
margarine or butter	3 tbs.	¼ cup	¼ cup
egg	1	1	1
sugar	3 tbs.	¼ cup	⅓ cup
salt	¾ tsp.	1 tsp.	1 tsp.
bread flour	2 cups	3 cups	3½ cups
yeast	1 tsp.	1½ tsp.	1½ tsp.

West Indies Banana Bread

Raisin, Sweet or Basic cycle

This is an adaptation of a delicious quick bread from the West Indies. Vanilla extract can be substituted for coconut extract. Use fully or overly ripe bananas. Check the consistency of the dough while it's kneading and add water if necessary.

	1 lb.	1 ½ lb.	1 ¾-2 lb.
mashed bananas	¾ cup	1 ⅛ cups	1 ⅓ cups
margarine or butter	¼ cup	6 tbs.	7 tbs.
egg	1	1	1
coconut extract	¾ tsp.	1 tsp.	1 tsp.
sugar	2 tbs.	2 ½ tbs.	3 tbs.
salt	½ tsp.	¾ tsp.	1 tsp.
cinnamon	½ tsp.	¾ tsp.	1 tsp.
nutmeg	⅛ tsp.	¼ tsp.	½ tsp.
flaked coconut	1 ½ tbs.	2 tbs.	3 tbs.
bread flour	2 cups	3 cups	3 ½ cups
yeast	1 ½ tsp.	2 tsp.	2 ½ tsp.
*raisins	¼ cup	½ cup	⅔ cup

*Add ingredients at the beginning of the second kneading period.

Mexican King's Bread

Sweet or Basic cycle

Rum adds a subtle yet distinctive taste. This delicious bread is traditionally served on the twelfth day of Christmas to mark the arrival of the three kings in Bethlehem. A small porcelain doll is hidden inside and whoever receives the doll must give a party during the holiday season.

	1 lb.	1 ½ lb.	1 ¾-2 lb.
milk	⅔ cup	⅔ cup	1 cup
light rum	2 tsp.	1 tbs.	1 ½ tbs.
margarine or butter	2 ½ tbs.	¼ cup	5 tbs.
eggs	1	2	2
sugar	2 ½ tbs.	¼ cup	⅓ cup
salt	¾ tsp.	1 tsp.	1 tsp.
grated orange peel	¾ tsp.	1 tsp.	1 ½ tsp.
bread flour	2 cups	3 cups	3 ½ cups
yeast	1 ½ tsp.	2 tsp.	2 ½ tsp.

Mexican Christmas Bread

Raisin, Sweet or Basic cycle

The candied cherries give this bread wonderful color and flavor.

	1 lb.	1 1/2 lb.	1 3/4-2 lb.
milk	5/8 cup	7/8 cup	1 cup
margarine or butter	1 tbs.	1 1/2 tbs.	2 tbs.
egg	1	1	1
sugar	1 1/2 tbs.	2 tbs.	3 tbs.
salt	1/2 tsp.	3/4 tsp.	1 tsp.
grated orange peel	1/4 tsp.	1/2 tsp.	3/4 tsp.
bread flour	2 cups	3 cups	3 1/2 cups
yeast	1 tsp.	1 1/2 tsp.	2 tsp.
*chopped candied cherries	1/3 cup	1/2 cup	2/3 cup
*chopped walnuts	2 tbs.	3 tbs.	1/4 cup

*Add ingredients at the beginning of the second kneading period.

Brazilian Easter Bread

Raisin, Sweet or Basic cycle

Brazil nuts give this bread a wonderful, distinctive flavor.

	1 lb.	1 1/2 lb.	1 3/4-2 lb.
milk	1/2 cup	1 cup	1 1/8 cups
margarine or butter	3 tbs.	1/4 cup	5 tbs.
egg	1	1	1
sugar	2 1/2 tbs.	3 tbs.	1/4 cup
salt	1/2 tsp.	3/4 tsp.	1 tsp.
cinnamon	1/2 tsp.	3/4 tsp.	1 tsp.
nutmeg	1/8 tsp.	1/4 tsp.	1/2 tsp. (scant)
ground allspice	1/8 tsp.	1/4 tsp.	1/2 tsp. (scant)
bread flour	2 cups	3 cups	3 1/2 cups
yeast	1 1/2 tsp.	2 tsp.	2 tsp.
*golden raisins	3 tbs.	1/4 cup	1/3 cup
*chopped dried apricots	3 tbs.	1/4 cup	1/3 cup
*chopped Brazil nuts	3 tbs.	1/4 cup	1/3 cup

*Add ingredients at the beginning of the second kneading period.

Bread of the Dead (Pan de Muertos)
Sweet or Basic cycle

This is the bread carried to and eaten at the graves of relatives on All Souls Day. Traditionally, it is round and decorated with bones made from the dough. This is almost like eating a cake instead of bread — not one of your more dietetic loaves!

	1 lb.	1 1/2 lb.	1 3/4-2 lb.
water	1/3 cup	1/2 cup	1/2 cup
margarine or butter	2 tbs.	3 tbs.	1/4 cup
eggs	2	3	4
sugar	1/4 cup	1/4 cup	1/3 cup
salt	3/4 tsp.	1 tsp.	1 tsp.
grated orange peel	1/2 tsp.	3/4 tsp.	1 tsp.
anise seeds	1/8 tsp.	1/4 tsp.	1/2 tsp.
bread flour	2 1/4 cups	3 cups	3 1/2 cups
yeast	1 tsp.	1 tsp.	1 1/2 tsp.

Russian Easter Bread (Kulich)
Raisin, Sweet or Basic cycle

Soak the raisins in the sherry or amaretto for at least 15 minutes. Drain before adding to the dough. Use one or all of the remaining additions.

	1 lb.	1 1/2 lb.	1 3/4-2 lb.
milk	2/3 cup	7/8 cup	1 cup
margarine or butter	1 tbs.	1 1/2 tbs.	2 tbs.
eggs	1	1	2
salt	1/2 tsp.	3/4 tsp.	1 tsp.
sugar	1/4 cup	1/3 cup	1/2 cup
grated lemon peel (zest)	3/4 tsp.	1 tsp.	1 1/2 tsp.
bread flour	2 cups	3 cups	3 1/2 cups
yeast	1 tsp.	1 1/2 tsp.	2 tsp.
*sherry or amaretto	1 tbs.	1 1/2 tbs.	2 tbs.
*golden or dark raisins	2 tbs.	3 tbs.	1/4 cup
*chopped candied cherries	2 tbs.	3 tbs.	1/4 cup
*chopped candied pineapple	2 tbs.	3 tbs.	1/4 cup
*chopped almonds	2 tbs.	3 tbs.	1/4 cup

*Add ingredients at the beginning of the second kneading period.

Russian Krendl

Traditionally, this is a filled, coffeecake-type bread. Here's a shortcut.

	1 lb.	1½ lb.	1¾-2 lb.
milk	¼ cup	⅓ cup	½ cup
margarine or butter	1½ tbs.	2 tbs.	2 tbs.
sautéed diced apples	1 cup	1½ cups	1½ cups
egg	1	1	1
vanilla extract	¾ tsp.	1 tsp.	1½ tsp.
sugar	1½ tbs.	2 tbs.	2½ tbs.
salt	¾ tsp.	1 tsp.	1 tsp.
bread flour	2 cups	3 cups	3½ cups
yeast	1 tsp.	1½ tsp.	2 tsp.
*chopped prunes, optional	2 tbs.	3 tbs.	¼ cup
*chopped dried apricots, optional	2 tbs.	3 tbs.	¼ cup

Note: Sauté apples in 1 to 2 tbs. each butter (or margarine) and sugar until just soft. Drain excess liquid; cool to room temperature prior to adding to machine.

*Add ingredients at the beginning of the second kneading period.

Ukrainian Black Bread

This is a very moist bread. The consistency reminds me of an English muffin or peasant bread. If the machine has difficulty kneading this dough, stop it after the first kneading period and start it over from the beginning.

	1 lb.	1½ lb.	1¾-2 lb.
strong brewed coffee	1 cup	1⅓ cups	1⅔ cups
vegetable oil	1 tbs.	1½ tbs.	2 tbs.
molasses	1 tbs.	1½ tbs.	2 tbs.
salt	½ tsp.	¾ tsp.	1 tsp.
rye flour	1 cup	1½ cups	2 cups
bread flour	2 cups	3 cups	3½ cups
vital gluten, optional	1½ tsp.	2 tsp.	1 tbs.
yeast	2 tsp.	2½ tsp.	1 tbs.

Viennese Easter Bread

Raisin, Sweet or Basic cycle

Here is a delectable bread with a light and airy form. If citron is unavailable, double the amount of golden raisins.

	1 lb.	1½ lb.	1¾-2 lb.
milk	⅔ cup	¾ cup	1 cup
rum	1 tbs.	1½ tbs.	2 tbs.
margarine or butter	3 tbs.	3 tbs.	¼ cup
eggs	1	2	2
sugar	3 tbs.	¼ cup	¼ cup
salt	½ tsp.	¾ tsp.	1 tsp.
bread flour	2¼ cups	3 cups	3½ cups
yeast	1 tsp.	1½ tsp.	2 tsp.
*golden raisins	1½ tbs.	2 tbs.	3 tbs.
*chopped citron	1½ tbs.	2 tbs.	3 tbs.
*slivered almonds	1½ tbs.	2 tbs.	3 tbs.

*Add ingredients at the beginning of the second kneading period.

Vienna Bread

French or Basic cycle

You'll really enjoy this flavorful bread. The dough makes superb dinner rolls, too.

	1 lb.	1½ lb.	1¾-2 lb.
water	⅞ cup	1¼ cups	1½ cups
vegetable oil	2 tsp.	1 tbs.	1½ tbs.
sugar	1 tsp.	1½ tsp.	2 tsp.
salt	½ tsp.	¾ tsp.	1 tsp.
bread flour	2 cups	3 cups	3½ cups
dry milk powder	2 tbs.	3 tbs.	¼ cup
yeast	1½ tsp.	2 tsp.	2½ tsp.

Coffee Breads: General Instructions

All breads in this chapter are made on the dough cycle, removed and shaped according to one of the following directions.

Jelly Roll - Remove the dough from the machine and roll into a rectangle about ⅛-inch thick. Spread filling evenly on top. Roll in a jelly roll-fashion starting at the wide end. Pinch the seam closed. Place roll on a greased baking sheet, cover and let rise for about 30 to 45 minutes (unless otherwise specified). Bake according to recipe.

Monkey Bread - Remove the dough from the machine and separate into as many 1- to 1½-inch balls as possible. Roll the balls in the melted butter and the topping ingredients. Place the balls in a loaf pan, tube pan or holiday-shaped pan (such as a heart-shaped pan for Valentine's Day), cover and let rise for about 1 hour. Bake in a preheated 350° oven for 30 to 40 minutes or until golden brown.

Wreath - Remove the dough from the machine. If there is a filling, follow directions for shaping a jelly roll. If there is no filling, shape the dough into a rope-shaped roll. Form the filled or unfilled roll into a circle, pinching the seam closed. With scissors, cut roll into ⅔- to 1-inch pieces. Place pieces cut-side up on a greased baking sheet, cover and let rise for about 45 minutes. Bake in a preheated 350° oven for 30 to 40 minutes or until golden brown (unless otherwise specified).

Amaretto Bread

This is superb for a buffet — it's both attractive and delicious. It's great during the Christmas holidays or any other time of year. Follow the directions for monkey bread or wreath. The Small recipe makes 1 large bread; the Medium recipe makes 2 small breads; the Large recipe makes 2 large breads.

Dough	Small	Medium	Large
water	½ cup	½ cup	1 cup
amaretto	¼ cup	⅓ cup	½ cup
margarine or butter	1 tbs.	1½ tbs.	2 tbs.
eggs	1	2	2
almond extract	½ tsp.	¾ tsp.	1 tsp.
sugar	1 tbs.	1½ tbs.	2 tbs.
salt	½ tsp.	½ tsp.	¾ tsp.
bread flour	2 cups	3 cups	4 cups
yeast	1 tsp.	1½ tsp.	2½ tsp.
Topping			
melted butter	¼ cup	6 tbs.	½ cup
chopped almonds	½ cup	⅔ cup	1 cup

Poppy Seed Monkey Bread

This makes an attractive addition to any picnic or buffet. Follow the directions for monkey bread or wreath. Or, make Parmesan Monkey Bread: substitute grated Parmesan cheese for poppy seeds, and cut the sugar in half.

Dough	Small	Medium	Large
milk or water	½ cup	⅔ cup	1 cup
margarine or butter	1 tbs.	1½ tbs.	2 tbs.
eggs	1	2	2
almond or vanilla extract	1 tsp.	1½ tsp.	2 tsp.
sugar	2 tbs.	3 tbs.	¼ cup
salt	½ tsp.	½ tsp.	¾ tsp.
bread flour	2 cups	3 cups	4 cups
yeast	1 tsp.	1½ tsp.	2 tsp.
Topping			
melted butter	¼ cup	6 tbs.	½ cup
poppy seeds	¼ cup	⅓ cup	½ cup

Pumpkin Cheese Nut Roll

Dough cycle

This fabulous coffee bread is festive for fall. People will ask you for the recipe, I am sure. Use either canned pumpkin or cooked, pureed fresh pumpkin. Adjust the consistency of the dough during kneading if required. The Small recipe makes 1 large roll; the Medium recipe makes 2 small rolls; the Large recipe makes 2 Large rolls.

Dough	Small	Medium	Large
water	¼ cup	⅓ cup	½ cup
pumpkin	⅔ cup	1 cup	1⅓ cups
vegetable oil	1 tbs.	1½ tbs.	2 tbs.
honey	2 tbs.	3 tbs.	¼ cup
salt	½ tsp.	¾ tsp.	1 tsp.
cinnamon	½ tsp.	¾ tsp.	1 tsp.
ground allspice	¼ tsp.	½ tsp.	½ tsp.
nutmeg	¼ tsp.	½ tsp.	½ tsp.
ground cloves	⅛ tsp.	⅛ tsp.	¼ tsp.
bread flour	2 cups	3 cups	4 cups
yeast	1 tsp.	1½ tsp.	2 tsp.

Filling			
softened cream cheese	4 oz.	6 oz.	8 oz.
vanilla extract	¼ tsp.	½ tsp.	½ tsp.
confectioners' sugar	½ cup	¾ cup	1 cup
chopped walnuts or pecans	½ cup	¾ cup	1 cup

Mix ingredients together. Follow directions for jelly roll or wreath, page 126. Bake in a preheated 350° oven for 35 to 40 minutes or until golden brown.

Polish Walnut and Poppy Seed Buns

Dough cycle

These buns are well worth the time it takes to prepare the filling. Better make lots — you'll need them!

Dough	Small (9)	Medium (14)	Large (18)
milk	¼ cup	½ cup	¾ cup
margarine or butter	1 tbs.	2 tbs.	3 tbs.
egg	1	1	1
sugar	1 tbs.	1 ½ tbs.	2 tbs.
salt	½ tsp.	¾ tsp.	1 tsp.
bread flour	1 ½ cups	2 ¼ cups	3 cups
yeast	1 tsp.	1 ½ tsp.	2 tsp.
Filling			
milk	2 tbs.	¼ cup	6 tbs.
honey	1 tbs.	1 ½ tbs.	2 tbs.
sugar	1 ½ tsp.	1 tbs.	1 ½ tbs.
bread flour	1 ½ tsp.	1 tbs.	1 ½ tbs.
poppy seeds	1 ½ tbs.	2 tbs.	3 tbs.
chopped walnuts	⅔ cup	1 cup	1 ⅓ cups

In a saucepan, bring all filling ingredients to a boil over medium heat; set aside to cool. Follow shaping directions for jelly roll, page 126. Cut into the appropriate number of slices. Place each slice in a well-greased muffin cup, cover and let rise for about 30 minutes. Bake in a preheated 375° oven for 20 to 25 minutes.

Bread Cookies

Dough cycle

I make these all the time with my kids — they're so easy in the machine — and they don't have a lot of sugar! These cookies are great for snacks or parties.

	Small	Medium	Large
milk or water	⅔ cup	1 cup	1 ⅓ cups
margarine or butter	1 tbs.	1 ½ tbs.	2 tbs.
sugar	2 tbs.	2 ½ tbs.	3 tbs.
salt	½ tsp.	½ tsp.	¾ tsp.
bread flour	2 cups	3 cups	4 cups
yeast	1 tsp.	1 ½ tsp.	2 tsp.

Remove dough from machine and roll to a thickness of ¼ inch. Cut shapes with cookie cutters and place shapes on a greased baking sheet. Let rise for 10 to 15 minutes. Bake in a preheated 375° oven for 10 to 15 minutes. If desired, turn cookies over once during baking to achieve a golden brown appearance on both sides. Cookies will puff during baking.

French Chocolate Buns

These buns are a chocolate-lover's dream come true.

Dough	Small (8)	Medium (12)	Large (16)
milk	½ cup	⅞ cup	1 cup
margarine or butter	2 tbs.	3 tbs.	¼ cup
eggs	1	1	2
vanilla extract	¾ tsp.	1 tsp.	1½ tsp.
sugar	1 tbs.	1½ tbs.	2 tbs.
salt	¼ tsp.	⅓ tsp.	½ tsp.
bread flour	2 cups	3 cups	4 cups
yeast	1 tsp.	1½ tsp.	2 tsp.

Filling			
semisweet chocolate chips	½ cup	¾ cup	1 cup

Roll dough into a large rectangle, about ¼-inch thick. With a pastry wheel or knife, cut into squares. Place about 1 tbs. of the chocolate chips in the center of each square and fold dough to encase chocolate. Place buns on a greased baking sheet and bake in a preheated 350° oven for 20 to 25 minutes.

Cinnamon Swirl Bread

This was a childhood favorite of my brother-in-law, Larry.

Dough	Small (1)	Medium (1)	Large (2)
water	⅝ cup	¾ cup	1⅛ cups
margarine or butter	1 tbs.	1½ tbs.	2 tbs.
raisins	⅓ cup	½ cup	⅔ cup
sugar	1 tbs.	1½ tbs.	2 tbs.
salt	½ tsp.	¾ tsp.	1 tsp.
bread flour	1½ cups	2 cups	3 cups
yeast	1 tsp.	1½ tsp.	2 tsp.
Filling			
melted margarine	3 tbs.	¼ cup	6 tbs.
cinnamon	2 tsp.	1 tbs.	1⅓ tbs.
brown sugar, packed	2½ tbs.	3 tbs.	5 tbs.
chopped walnuts	1½ tbs.	2 tbs.	3 tbs.

Mix filling ingredients together. Follow directions for jelly roll, page 126. Bake in a preheated 350° oven for 18 to 25 minutes or until golden brown. Bread should make a hollow sound when tapped.

Glaze			
confectioners' sugar	about ½ cup	about ¾ cup	about 1 cup
milk	1½ tsp.	2 tsp.	3 tsp.
vanilla extract	⅛ tsp.	⅛ tsp.	¼ tsp.

Mix glaze ingredients until smooth and fairly thick. Add more confectioners' sugar if necessary. Pour over baked bread while still hot.

Pizza, Meat Pies and Handpies: General Instructions

The recipes in this chapter could be served as entrées for lunch, brunch or dinner, accompanied by a tossed salad or a bowl of soup. If you have a Panasonic SDBT6P or a National SDBT6N you can make some of these on the Variety Bread Cycle. This cycle enables you to remove the dough, place fillings into it and return it to the machine for baking. Follow the directions in your owner's manual. Owners of all other machines should make these recipes on the dough cycle, remove, fill according to the following directions and bake in a conventional oven. A small amount of flour can be used when rolling the dough to prevent it from sticking.

Calzones - Remove the dough from the machine and divide it into equal portions according to the recipe. Roll portions into circles about 8 inches in diameter. Spread filling on ½ of each circle leaving a border around the edge for sealing. Seal the calzone by folding the unfilled side over the filled side and crimping the edge closed with your fingers or a fork. Place calzones on a lightly greased baking or pizza pan. Let rise for about 30 minutes. Bake according to recipe.

For appetizers, roll the dough to a thickness of ⅛ inch and cut into circles with a glass or biscuit cutter (about 3 inches). Fill and seal them as you would the large calzones, but bake in a preheated 450° oven for 25 to 30 minutes.

Jelly Roll - Remove the dough from the machine and roll into a rectangle about ⅛-inch thick. Spread or layer filling on top. Starting from the wide end, roll the dough jelly roll-fashion to encase filling and pinch seam closed. Place on a nonstick baking pan, cover and let rise for about 30 minutes. Bake according to recipe.

Stromboli - Remove the dough from the machine and roll into a rectangle about ¼-inch thick. Spread filling ingredients over the middle ⅓ of the rectangle so it runs the length of the wide end. Fold ⅓ of the dough over the filling; then, fold the remaining ⅓ over the top. Pinch seam closed. Place stromboli seam-side down on a lightly greased baking sheet, cover and let rise for about 30 minutes. Lightly brush top with olive oil and bake in a preheated 350° oven for 20 to 30 minutes, or until done (unless otherwise specified).

Pizza - Remove the dough from the machine and roll into 1 or 2 pizza pan-sized circles. Place on a lightly greased pizza pan and turn any excess dough under itself to form a high crust. Cover and let rise for about 30 minutes. Spread desired sauce and toppings on top. Place pan in a cold oven, turn oven to 500° and bake for about 20 to 30 minutes, or until crust is golden brown and cheese, if using, is melted. If using Three Cheese Filling, bake in a preheated 400° oven for 25 to 30 minutes.

Italian Turnovers (Calzones)

Dough cycle

Large calzones make a wonderful meal, or make smaller versions for appetizers. Stromboli fillings, can also be used.

Dough	Small (4)	Medium (6)	Large (8)
water	2/3 cup	1 cup	1 1/3 cups
olive oil	1 tbs.	1 1/2 tbs.	2 tbs.
salt	1/4 tsp.	1/2 tsp.	3/4 tsp.
dried oregano	1/4 tsp.	1/2 tsp.	1/2 tsp.
bread flour	2 cups	3 cups	4 cups
yeast	1 tsp.	1 1/2 tsp.	2 tsp.
Filling			
ricotta cheese	6 tbs.-1/2 cup	9 tbs.-3/4 cup	12 tbs.-1 cup
grated mozzarella cheese	6 tbs.-1/2 cup	9 tbs.-3/4 cup	12 tbs.-1 cup

Follow directions for calzone, page 132. Brush tops lightly with olive oil and bake in a preheated 500° oven for about 15 to 20 minutes or until puffed and golden.

Sausage Bread

Dough cycle

This bread is terrific hot or cold. Serve it sliced at a picnic or tailgate party with red wine.

Dough	Medium	Large
water	2/3 cup	1 cup
margarine or butter	1 tbs.	1 1/2 tbs.
sugar	3/4 tsp.	1 tsp.
salt	3/4 tsp.	1 tsp.
bread flour	2 cups	3 cups
yeast	1 1/2 tsp.	2 1/2 tsp.
Filling		
cooked, chopped sausage	2/3 lb.	1 lb.
grated provolone cheese	2 oz.	3 oz.
grated mozzarella cheese	2 oz.	3 oz.
garlic powder	1/8 tsp.	1/4 tsp.
salt and pepper	to taste	to taste

Drain sausage well. Mix filling ingredients together. Follow directions for jelly roll, page 132. Bake for 30 to 35 minutes in a preheated 350° oven.

Meat Roll

My children went wild over this recipe and now want it every night for supper.

Dough	Medium	Large
water	⅔ cup	1 cup
vegetable oil	2 tsp.	1 tbs.
sugar	¾ tsp.	1 tsp.
salt	¼ tsp.	½ tsp.
whole wheat flour	⅔ cup	1 cup
bread flour	1⅓ cups	2 cups
dry milk powder	2 tbs.	3 tbs.
yeast	1 tsp.	1½ tsp.

Filling		
cooked, chopped sausage	⅓ lb.	½ lb.
cooked, crumbled ground beef or turkey	⅓ lb.	½ lb.
processed American cheese, such as Velveeta	⅓ lb.	½ lb.
salt and pepper	to taste	to taste

Drain sausage and ground beef well. Keep warm. Cut cheese into 1-inch cubes and mix with meats. If cheese is not melting, warm filling in a microwave for 1 to 2 minutes. Cheese should be warm enough to serve as the glue for the filling. Follow directions for jelly roll or stromboli, page 132. Bake in a preheated 350° oven for 20 to 25 minutes.

 *Bread Quiche*

A bread crust, instead of a pastry crust, cuts the richness of this dish a bit, and is a nice change of pace. The Medium recipe makes one 8- to 9-inch quiche. The Large recipe makes two 8- to 9-inch quiches.

Dough	Medium	Large
water	½ cup	⅔ cup
vegetable oil	¾ tsp.	1 tsp.
sugar	¼ tsp.	½ tsp.
salt	⅛ tsp.	⅛ tsp.
parsley, dried, optional	¼ tsp.	½ tsp.
bread flour	1 ½ cups	2 cups
dry milk powder	2 tsp.	1 tbs.
yeast	1 tsp.	1 tsp.

Filling		
chopped scallions, optional	¼ cup	½ cup
margarine or butter, optional	1 tsp.	2 tsp.
eggs, beaten	3	6
cream or milk	½ cup	1 cup
nutmeg	to taste	to taste
salt and pepper	to taste	to taste
cooked, crumbled bacon, optional	¼ cup	½ cup
grated Swiss or Gruyère cheese	1 cup	2 cups

Remove dough from machine and roll into an 8- or 9-inch circle. Place dough into a greased 8- or 9-inch pie pan.

Lightly sauté scallions in margarine or butter. In a large bowl, mix together eggs, cream or milk, nutmeg, salt and pepper. Add scallions, bacon, if using, and grated cheese. Pour filling into dough and bake in a preheated 375° oven for 35 to 40 minutes or until filling is set in the middle.

Mexican Turnovers (Empanadas)

While empanadas are usually made from pastry dough, you'll love this yeasted version. These can be eaten hot or cold.

Dough	Medium (6)	Large (12)
water	½ cup	1 cup
margarine or butter	1 tbs.	2 tbs.
sugar	½ tsp.	1 tsp.
salt	½ tsp.	1 tsp.
whole wheat flour	¾ cup	1½ cups
bread flour	¾ cup	1½ cups
yeast	1 tsp.	1½ tsp.

Filling		
ground beef or turkey	½ lb.	1 lb.
chopped onion	½	1
vegetable oil	as needed	as needed
paprika	1 tsp.	2 tsp.
ground cumin	½ tsp.	1 tsp.
salt	¼ tsp.	½ tsp.

Sauté meat and onions in oil until meat is no longer pink and onion is soft. Stir in seasonings. Follow directions for calzone, page 132. Bake in a preheated 350° oven for 20 to 25 minutes.

Pizza Dough

Pizza will quickly become an often-served meal in your home with this delicious, easy recipe. If you prefer, you can replace the whole wheat flour with bread flour. The Small recipe makes 1 small pizza crust; the Medium recipe makes 1 large crust; and the Large recipe makes 2 small crusts.

	Small	Medium	Large
water	⅔ cup	1 cup	1⅓ cups
olive oil	2 tsp.	1 tbs.	1½ tbs.
salt	¼ tsp.	½ tsp.	¾ tsp.
dried oregano, optional	1 tsp.	1½ tsp.	2 tsp.
whole wheat flour	1 cup	1½ cups	2 cups
bread flour	1 cup	1½ cups	2 cups
yeast	1 tsp.	1½ tsp.	2 tsp.

Follow directions for pizza, page 132.

Note: This can also be made in jelly roll-style, using any pizza topping. Brush roll lightly with olive oil and bake in a preheated 400° oven for about 30 minutes.

Italian Handpies (Stromboli)

Thanks to Lt. Morro, USN, for sharing a family recipe on which this is based. It's soon to become one of your family favorites too!

Dough	Medium (1)	Large (2)
water	¾ cup	1⅛ cups
margarine or butter	1 tbs.	2 tbs.
sugar	¾ tsp.	1½ tsp.
salt	½ tsp.	1 tsp.
coarsely ground black pepper	1 tsp.	2 tsp.
bread flour	2 cups	3 cups
yeast	1½ tsp.	2 tsp.

Choose Spinach or Broccoli Filling, Meat Filling, or Three Cheese Filling. Follow instructions for stromboli, page 132.

Variation 1: Spinach or Broccoli Filling

	Medium (1)	Large (2)
frozen chopped spinach or broccoli, thawed	1 pkg. (10 oz.)	2 pkg. 10 oz. each)
olive oil	1 tbs.	2 tbs.
minced garlic	1 tsp.	2 tsp.
grated provolone cheese	about ½ cup	about 1 cup
grated mozzarella cheese	about ½ cup	about 1 cup

Sauté spinach or broccoli with olive oil and garlic until moisture has evaporated. Mix in cheese.

Variation 2: Meat Filling

	Medium (1)	Large (2)
grated provolone cheese	¼-⅓ cup	½-⅔ cup
grated mozzarella cheese	¼-⅓ cup	½-⅔ cup
diced hard Italian salami	¼-⅓ cup	½-⅔ cup
diced Italian ham	¼-⅓ cup	½-⅔ cup

Mix ingredients together.

Variation 3: Three Cheese Filling or Sauce

This is an excellent topping for pizza or a filling for calzones or stromboli. Don't forget, freshly grated Parmesan is always better than pre-grated Parmesan.

	Small	Medium	Large
ricotta cheese	1 cup	1 ½ cups	2 cups
grated Parmesan cheese	½ cup	¾ cup	1 cup
grated mozzarella cheese	½ cup	¾ cup	1 cup
eggs	1	1	2
parsley, dried	¾ tsp.	1 tsp.	1 ½ tsp.
basil, dried	¾ tsp.	1 tsp.	1 ½ tsp.
coarsely ground black pepper	¼ tsp.	½ tsp.	¾ tsp.

Mix cheeses and eggs together until well blended. Add remaining ingredients and stir until just mixed.

Focaccia

Dough cycle

(Say foh-CAH-chee-ah.) This cousin to pizza, cut into small wedges or squares, is the perfect accompaniment to soups or salads. Or, serve it as an appetizer or on a buffet. It's delicious served hot or cold, as a snack or with a meal. The Small, Medium and Large recipes make 1 large sheet, 2 small sheets and 2 large sheets of focaccia respectively.

Dough	Small	Medium	Large
water	½ cup	¾ cup	1 cup
vegetable oil	¼ cup	⅓ cup	½ cup
sugar	1 ½ tsp.	2 tsp.	1 tbs.
salt	¼ tsp.	½ tsp.	½ tsp.
chopped fresh basil or rosemary	2 tsp.	1 tbs.	1 ½ tbs.
bread flour	2 cups	3 cups	4 cups
yeast	1 tsp.	1 ½ tsp.	2 tsp.

Remove dough from machine and press on a lightly greased pizza pan or baking sheet. Cover and let rise for about 30 minutes.

Topping	Small	Medium	Large
minced garlic	½ tsp.	¾ tsp.	1 tsp.
olive oil	2 tbs.	3 tbs.	¼ cup
chopped fresh basil or rosemary	2 tbs.	3 tbs.	¼ cup
sea salt or coarse salt	1 tsp.	1 ½ tsp.	2 tsp.

Mix ingredients together. Spread topping over dough and bake in a pre-heated 375° oven for about 30 minutes.

Reuben Roll

This is a quick and easy way to make several Reubens. They're great for picnics or tailgating parties. Substitute mustard for Thousand Island dressing if preferred.

Dough	Small	Medium	Large
water	⅔ cup	1 cup	1⅓ cups
vegetable oil	2 tsp.	1 tbs.	1½ tbs.
sugar	¼ tsp.	½ tsp.	½ tsp.
salt	¼ tsp.	½ tsp.	½ tsp.
cocoa powder	1 tbs.	1½ tbs.	2 tbs.
caraway seeds	1 tsp.	1½ tsp.	2 tsp.
rye flour	⅔ cup	1 cup	1⅓ cups
bread flour	1⅓ cups	2 cups	2⅔ cups
yeast	1 tsp.	1½ tsp.	2 tsp.

Filling	Small	Medium	Large
Thousand Island dressing	2 tbs.	3 tbs.	¼ cup
drained sauerkraut	⅓ cup	½ cup	⅔ cup
grated Swiss cheese	⅓ cup	½ cup	⅔ cup
cooked, cubed corned beef	½ cup	¾ cup	1 cup

Layer filling ingredients on dough, following directions for jelly roll or stromboli, page 132. Bake in a preheated 350° oven for 25 to 30 minutes.

Mini Cheese Breads

This recipe is based on a recipe for a Turkish cheese bread. These are great as an appetizer, lunch or light dinner with a salad. I even pack these for school or work lunches for a nice change of pace. Serve them either hot or cold. Calzone dough, page 133, will work also.

Dough	Small (5)	Medium (8)	Large (10)
Pizza Dough, page 136	Small	Medium	Large

Filling			
cream cheese	4 oz.	6 oz.	8 oz.
ricotta cheese	¾ cup	1⅛ cups	1½ cups
grated Parmesan cheese	½ cup	⅔ cup	1 cup
chopped parsley	1 tbs.	1½ tbs.	2 tbs.
dried chives	2 tsp.	1 tbs.	1½ tbs.

Divide dough into balls and roll into disks or small rectangles of desired thickness. Fold edge(s) up to form a small crust. Mix filling ingredients and spread evenly on dough. Place on a greased baking sheet, let rise for 20 minutes and bake in a preheated 375° oven for 25 minutes or until golden brown.

The
Bread
Machine
Cookbook III

White Potato Bread

Basic cycle

Here is a different and incredibly easy way to enjoy potato bread. The loaf is low-rising, easy to cut and great for sandwiches or with a spicy stew. The potato should be uncooked, peeled and diced or grated.

	Small	Medium	Large
milk	⅔ cup	⅞ cup	1 cup
potato	¼ cup	¼+ cup	⅓ cup
vegetable oil	1 tsp.	1¼ tsp.	1½ tsp.
sugar	1 tbs.	1½ tbs.	2 tbs.
salt	⅓ tsp.	⅔ tsp.	1 tsp.
bread flour	2 cups	2½ cups	3 cups
yeast	1 tsp.	1½ tsp.	2 tsp.

No Fat White Bread

Basic cycle

This is a light sandwich bread with a nice fluffy texture and a pleasant flavor.

	Small	Medium	Large
water	⅔ cup	¾ cup	1 cup
egg	1	1	1½
sugar	1 tsp.	1¼ tsp.	1½ tsp.
salt	⅛ tsp.	⅛+ tsp.	¼ tsp.
bread flour	2 cups	2½ cups	3 cups
yeast	1 tsp.	1½ tsp.	2 tsp.

No Sugar Sweet Bread

Sweet or Basic cycle

For those who cannot or prefer not to eat refined sugar, this delicious recipe uses natural fructose, found in grocery stores or health food stores. One tester experimented with her recipe by substituting Sugar Twin for the fructose. She recommends using 1 tbs., 1½ tbs. or 2 tbs. for a regular loaf and doubling that amount for a sweeter loaf.

	Small	Medium	Large
milk	⅔ cup	¾ cup	1 cup
eggs	1	1½	2
margarine or butter	1 tbs.	1½ tbs.	2 tbs.
fructose	2 tsp.	1⅛ tbs.	1½ tbs.
salt	⅛ tsp.	⅛+ tsp.	¼ tsp.
bread flour	2 cups	2½ cups	3 cups
yeast	1 tsp.	1½ tsp.	2 tsp.

Fruit-Flavored Basic White Bread
Basic cycle

A delicious white bread, this uses no refined sugar or fat. Select your favorite fruit juice concentrate to lightly flavor the bread. I use frozen juice concentrate (orange or apple), thawed.

	Small	Medium	Large
milk or water	¾ cup	1 cup	1⅛ cups
fruit juice concentrate	2 tbs.	2½ tbs.	3 tbs.
salt	¼ tsp.	⅓ tsp.	½ tsp.
bread flour	2 cups	2½ cups	3 cups
yeast	1 tsp.	1½ tsp.	2 tsp.

Coffee Can Bread
Sweet or Basic cycle

Karen Adler has made this bread for at least 20 years. She has adapted the recipe to her bread machine and no longer needs the coffee cans! She says it reminds her of challah, a Jewish egg bread. It is not one of the most dietetic. Karen has a DAK machine and makes the large loaf without suffering from the "doughy blues." If your machine is prone to doughiness, I recommend cutting the oil in half and replacing it with milk.

	Small	Medium	Large
milk	¼ cup	5 tbs.	⅜ cup
vegetable oil	¼ cup	5 tbs.	⅜ cup
eggs	1½	1½	2
sugar	2 tbs.	2½ tbs.	3 tbs.
salt	½ tsp.	⅔ tsp.	¾ tsp.
bread flour	2 cups	2½ cups	3 cups
yeast	1 tsp.	1½ tsp.	2 tsp.

Cheese and Poppy Seed Bread

This is worth the extra calories as a special treat. Suggested cheeses are Swiss or cheddar. This dough will be stickier and more moist than normal. It is a very high-rising loaf. The cheese should be lightly packed in the measuring cup.

	Small	Medium	Large
milk	½ cup	⅝ cup	⅔ cup
eggs	2½	3	4
margarine or butter	5 tbs.	6½ tbs.	8 tbs.
lemon extract	⅔ tsp.	¾ tsp.	1 tsp.
grated cheese	⅔ cup	¾ cup	1 cup
sugar	1 tsp.	1½ tsp.	2 tsp.
salt	½ tsp.	⅔ tsp.	1 tsp.
lemon peel	⅔ tsp.	¾ tsp.	1 tsp.
poppy seeds	1⅓ tbs.	1½ tbs.	2 tbs.
bread flour	2 cups	2½ cups	3 cups
yeast	1 tsp.	1½ tsp.	2 tsp.

Buttermilk Cheese Bread

Buttermilk helps to produce an absolutely delicious, light and airy bread. I made the medium-sized recipe using a 2-cup machine and it hit the lid of the machine and mushroomed. It was still completely edible and delicious but the lid required cleaning! Cheddar is my favorite cheese to use in this.

	Small	Medium	Large
buttermilk	⅔ cup	¾ cup	1 cup
margarine or butter	1 tbs.	1½ tbs.	2 tbs.
egg(s)	1	1½	2
grated cheese	½ cup	¾ cup	1 cup
sugar	1 tsp.	1½ tsp.	2 tsp.
salt	⅛-¼ tsp.	¼-½ tsp.	½-¾ tsp.
baking soda	¼ tsp.	⅓ tsp.	½ tsp.
bread flour	2 cups	2½ cups	3 cups
yeast	1 tsp.	1½ tsp.	2 tsp.

Cheddar Raisin Bread

The testers give this one four stars! It has a light texture with a pretty color and wonderful flavor. If the dough appears crumbly, add a tablespoon or so of milk, but don't add too much.

	Small	Medium	Large
milk	⅔ cup	¾ cup	1 cup
margarine or butter	1⅓ tbs.	1½ tbs.	2 tbs.
grated cheddar cheese	⅔ cup	¾ cup	1 cup
sugar	2 tsp.	1 tbs.	1⅓ tbs.
salt	¼ tsp.	⅓ tsp.	½ tsp.
paprika	⅔ tsp.	¾ tsp.	1 tsp.
bread flour	2 cups	2½ cups	3 cups
yeast	1 tsp.	1½ tsp.	2 tsp.
*raisins (dark)	⅓ cup	½ cup	⅔ cup

*Add ingredients at the beginning of the second kneading period.

Dated Peasant Bread

The bread has just a hint of different flavor and has no fat or refined sugar. Due to the high liquid content, the texture is open and coarse. If desired, chopped dates can be added on the raisin or mix cycle, at the beeps (or when appropriate for your machine). Also, brown or granulated maple sugar could be used in place of the date sugar.

	Small	Medium	Large
water	1 cup	1¼ cups	1½ cups
date sugar	1 tsp.	1¼ tsp.	1½ tsp.
salt	⅛ tsp.	⅛+ tsp.	¼ tsp.
bread flour	2 cups	2½ cups	3 cups
yeast	1 tsp.	1½ tsp.	2 tsp.
*chopped dates, optional	2-3 tbs.	3 tbs.	3-4 tbs.

*Add ingredients at the beginning of the second kneading period.

Easy Cake Bread

Rebecca O'Dea had her bread machine for only 10 days when she experimented with this recipe. She says it reminds her of the Hawaiian bread from a local deli. The bread rises quite a bit during the baking program, and is very light and fluffy with a crisp crust. The variations to this are endless — try using different cake mixes such as devil's food, white or vanilla, etc. Orange or lemon peel (1/4-1 tsp.) could be added, or even an extract (1/4-1/2 tsp.) for added flavor. This is an easy bread to make as all the sugar and salt are in the cake mix.

	Small	Medium	Large
water or milk	7/8 cup	1 cup	1 1/4 cups
butter or margarine	1 tbs.	1 1/2 tbs.	2 tbs.
yellow cake mix	2/3 cup	3/4 cup	1 cup
bread flour	1 1/4 cups	1 3/4 cups	2 1/2 cups
yeast	1 tsp.	1 1/2 tsp.	2 tsp.

Haitian Bread

This is a beautiful, high-rising, fluffy loaf which is sweet but not overly so. Nutmeg can be adjusted to taste, if desired. If you have never tried freshly grated nutmeg, I urge you to do so (even though my motto is, "make it simple and easy." Whole nutmegs are available in the spice section of a well-stocked grocery. Simply grate it on a basic kitchen food grater. Try serving with ham and pineapple for a real treat! If desired, cinnamon can be substituted for the nutmeg.

	Small	Medium	Large
water	2/3 cup	3/4 cup	1 cup
vegetable oil	1 tbs.	1 1/3 tbs.	1 1/2 tbs.
honey	2 tbs.	2 1/2 tbs.	3 tbs.
salt	1/4 tsp.	1/4+ tsp.	1/3 tsp.
nutmeg	1/3 tsp.	1/3+ tsp.	1/2 tsp.
bread flour	2 cups	2 1/2 cups	3 cups
yeast	1 tsp.	1 1/2 tsp.	2 tsp.

Blue Cheese Bread

Basic cycle

This tangy bread is a wonderful accompaniment to soup and salad. Should you have leftovers, try making croutons. It's a high-rising, light loaf.

	Small	Medium	Large
water	2/3 cup	7/8 cup	1 cup
butter or margarine	1 tbs.	1 1/4 tbs.	1 1/2 tbs.
blue cheese	1/3 cup	scant 1/2 cup	1/2 cup heaped
sugar	1 tbs.	1 1/4 tbs.	1 1/2 tbs.
celery seeds	1/4 tsp.	1/3 tsp.	scant 1/2 tsp.
salt	1/4-1/2 tsp.	1/3-2/3 tsp.	1/2-1 tsp.
bread flour	2 cups	2 1/2 cups	3 cups
yeast	1 tsp.	1 1/2 tsp.	2 tsp.

Broccoli and Cheese Bread

Raisin or Basic cycle

Here's a bread with good flavor and a wonderful aroma. Serve with pork chops or soup and salad. The broccoli should be cooked and chopped; the amount can be adjusted to taste if desired. Suggested cheeses are Swiss or cheddar; pack cheese lightly in the cup.

	Small	Medium	Large
milk	3/4 cup	1 1/8 cups	1 1/2 cups
margarine	1 tbs.	1 1/2 tbs.	2 tbs.
sugar	1 tsp.	1 1/2 tsp.	2 tsp.
salt	1/4 tsp.	1/3 tsp.	1/2 tsp.
whole wheat flour	1 cup	1 1/2 cups	2 cups
bread flour	1 cup	1 1/2 cups	2 cups
yeast	1 tsp.	1 1/2 tsp.	2 tsp.
broccoli	1/2 cup	3/4 cup	1 cup
*cheese, grated	1/3 cup	1/2 cup	2/3 cup

*Add ingredients at the beginning of the second kneading period.

Buttermilk Honey Wheat Bread

Peg Timney of southern California shares her favorite recipe.

	Small	Medium	Large
buttermilk	1 cup	1 1/4 cups	1 1/2 cups
butter or margarine	1 tbs.	1 1/3 tbs.	1 1/2 tbs.
honey	2 tbs.	2 1/2 tbs.	3 tbs.
salt	3/4 tsp.	1 tsp.	1 1/2 tsp.
baking soda	1/4 tsp.	1/3 tsp.	1/2 tsp.
whole wheat flour	2/3 cup	3/4 cup	1 cup
bread flour	1 1/3 cups	1 3/4 cups	2 cups
yeast	1 tsp.	1 1/2 tsp.	2 tsp.

Honey Whole Wheat No Fat

This is in response to many requests for nonfat or very low-fat breads. The honey is a natural preservative as well as a sweetener. Great toasted.

	Small	Medium	Large
water	3/4 cup	1 1/8 cups	1 1/2 cups
honey	2 tbs.	3 tbs.	1/4 cup
salt	1/4 tsp.	1/3 tsp.	1/2 tsp.
whole wheat flour	1 cup	1 1/2 cups	2 cups
bread flour	1 cup	1 1/2 cups	2 cups
yeast	1 tsp.	1 1/2 tsp.	2 tsp.

Carris' Wheat Bread

Carris House Jr. has been baking bread for many years. He recommends using a blend of 50% Pillsbury bread flour and 50% Gold Medal bread flour. He also recommends using stone ground wheat flour, if you can find it!

	Small	Medium	Large
milk	1/4 cup	3/8 cup	1/2 cup
water	1/2 cup	3/4 cup	1 cup
margarine or butter	1 tbs.	1 1/2 tbs.	2 tbs.
molasses	2 tsp.	1 tbs.	1 1/3 tbs.
sugar	1 1/3 tbs.	2 tbs.	2 2/3 tbs.
salt	2/3 tsp.	1 tsp.	1 1/3 tsp.
whole wheat flour	2/3 cup	1 cup	1 1/3 cups
bread flour	1 1/3 cups	2 cups	2 2/3 cups
yeast	1 tsp.	1 1/2 tsp.	2 tsp.

Creamy Buttermilk Wheat Bread

Sweet or Basic cycle

Buttermilk again makes an outstanding bread. For variations, add 1, 1 1/2 or 2 tablespoons of dried dill, chives, mint, basil or oregano (triple this amount for fresh).

	Small	Medium	Large
buttermilk	1/2 cup	3/4 cup	1 cup
heavy cream	2 1/2 tbs.	1/4 cup	1/3 cup
butter	1 tbs.	1 1/2 tbs.	2 tbs.
egg	1	1 1/2	2
sugar	1 tbs.	1 1/2 tbs.	2 tbs.
salt	1/8-1/4 tsp.	1/4-1/3 tsp.	1/3-1/2 tsp.
baking soda	1/4 tsp.	1/3 tsp.	1/2 tsp.
whole wheat flour	1 cup	1 1/2 cups	2 cups
bread flour	1 cup	1 1/2 cups	2 cups
yeast	1 tsp.	1 1/2 tsp.	2 tsp.

Porcupine Bread

Basic cycle

Don Downer adapted this recipe to his bread machine and receives rave reviews. Near the end of the second rising, Don lifts the lid and brushes the top of the loaf with an egg wash and sprinkles on additional sunflower and sesame seeds.

	Small	Medium	Large
buttermilk	3/4 cups	1 1/8 cups	1 1/2 cups
butter or margarine	1 tbs.	1 1/2 tbs.	2 tbs.
sugar	1 tbs.	1 1/2 tbs.	2 tbs.
salt	1/2 tsp.	3/4 tsp.	1 tsp.
baking soda	1/4 tsp.	1/3 tsp.	1/2 tsp.
cinnamon	1 tsp.	1 1/2 tsp.	2 tsp.
sesame seeds	1 tbs.	1 1/2 tbs.	2 tbs.
sunflower seeds	2 tbs.	3 tbs.	4 tbs.
raisins	1/4 cup	1/3 cup	1/2 cup
oats	1/4 cup	1/3 cup	1/2 cup
bread flour	1 3/4 cups	2 2/3 cups	3 1/2 cups
yeast	1 tsp.	1 1/2 tsp.	2 tsp.

Irish Brown Bread

Whole Wheat or Basic cycle

This bread has a crisp crust with a firm yet airy inside. Rises nicely.

	Small	Medium	Large
water	¾ cup	1⅛ cups	1½ cups
brown sugar	2 tbs.	3 tbs.	¼ cup
salt	⅓ tsp.	½ tsp.	⅔ tsp.
buttermilk powder	2 tbs.	3 tbs.	¼ cup
vital gluten, optional	2 tbs.	3 tbs.	¼ cup
oats	⅓ cup	½ cup	⅔ cup
whole wheat flour	¾ cup	1 cup	1½ cups
bread flour	1 cup	1½ cups	2 cups
yeast	1½ tsp.	2 tsp.	2½ tsp.

Oatmeal Honey Raisin Bread

Raisin or Basic cycle

Patricia Harper of Louisiana dreamed this one up. She actually uses more raisins, but I cut them back as some machines have more difficulty cooking properly with too many raisins or similar ingredients. If desired, use fresh buttermilk in place of the water, omit the powder and add ⅛ to ¼ tsp. baking soda. This bread is also delicious without the raisins! Use quick-cooking or regular oats.

	Small	Medium	Large
water	⅞ cup	1¼ cups	1¾ cups
vegetable oil	1 tbs.	1½ tbs.	2 tbs.
honey	1⅓ tbs.	2 tbs.	2½ tbs.
salt	½ tsp.	¾ tsp.	1 tsp.
buttermilk powder	1⅓ tbs.	2 tbs.	2½ tbs.
oats	⅔ cup	1 cup	1⅓ cups
bread flour	1⅓ cups	2 cups	2⅔ cups
yeast	1 tsp.	1½ tsp.	2 tsp.
*raisins	½ cup	¾ cup	1 cup

*Add ingredients at the beginning of the second kneading period.

Healthy Whole Wheat Bread

Sweet or Basic cycle

This is an especially healthy, sweet whole wheat bread from Conrad Feierabend.

	Small	Medium	Large
water	⅝ cup	1 cup	1¼ cups
vegetable oil	1⅓ tbs.	2 tbs.	2½ tbs.
molasses	1½ tbs.	2⅓ tbs.	3 tbs.
salt	½ tsp.	¾ tsp.	1 tsp.
fructose	2 tsp.	1 tbs.	1½ tbs.
sesame seeds	½ tsp.	¾ tsp.	1 tsp.
oat groats, cracked	1½ tsp.	2 tsp.	1 tbs.
wheat germ	2 tsp.	1 tbs.	1⅓ tbs.
oat bran	2 tsp.	1 tbs.	1⅓ tbs.
wheat flakes	2 tsp.	1 tbs.	1⅓ tbs.
oats	1 tbs.	1½ tbs.	2 tbs.
whole wheat flour	½ cup	¾ cup	1 cup
bread flour	1 cup	1½ cups	2 cups
yeast	1½ tsp.	2 tsp.	2½ tsp.

Coconut Cornbread

Raisin, Sweet or Basic cycle

This recipe is based on a recipe from the Dominican Republic. Soak the raisins in the rum for at least 30 minutes before putting them into the machine at the normal time.

	Small	Medium	Large
milk or water	¾ cup	1⅛ cups	1½ cups
butter or margarine	1 tbs.	1½ tbs.	2 tbs.
sugar	2 tbs.	3 tbs.	¼ cup
salt	½ tsp.	¾ tsp.	1 tsp.
cinnamon	½ tsp.	¾ tsp.	1 tsp.
ground cloves	¼ tsp.	⅓ tsp.	½ tsp.
shredded coconut	½ cup	¾ cup	1 cup
cornmeal	½ cup	¾ cup	1 cup
bread flour	1½ cups	2¼ cups	3 cups
yeast	1 tsp.	1½ tsp.	2 tsp.
*rum	1 tbs.	1½ tbs.	2 tbs.
*raisins	¼ cup	⅓ cup	½ cup

*Add ingredients at the beginning of the second kneading period.

Bimini Bread

Gerry Milot had this bread at the Bimini Boat Yard restaurant in Ft. Lauderdale. He soaks oats, molasses and butter in hot water for 2 minutes and then adds them to the bread machine. I put everything in all at once, unsoaked.

	Small	Medium	Large
water	¾ cup	1 ⅛ cups	1 ½ cups
vegetable oil	1 tbs.	1 ½ tbs.	2 tbs.
molasses	1 ½ tbs.	1 ⅓ tbs.	3 tbs.
salt	⅓ tsp.	½ tsp.	⅔ tsp.
oats	½ cup	¾ cup	1 cup
bread flour	1 ½ cups	2 ¼ cups	3 cups
yeast	1 tsp.	1 ½ tsp.	2 tsp.

Anadama Bread

Anadama is one of those breads which have many variations. Each recipe uses molasses and cornmeal. Katherine Kuckens adapted her mother's recipe for use in her bread machine. A hearty bread to serve with soup and salad!

	Small	Medium	Large
water	1 cup	1 ¼ cups	1 ½ cups
oil or butter	1 ½ tsp.	2 tsp.	2 ¼ tsp.
molasses	¼ cup	5 tbs.	6 tbs.
salt	½ tsp.	⅔ tsp.	¾ tsp.
cornmeal	¼ cup	⅓ cup	⅜ cup
bread flour	2 cups	2 ½ cups	3 cups
yeast	1 ½ tsp.	2 tsp.	2 ½ tsp.

Cornmeal English Muffin Bread

Dee Iuliano of New Mexico makes this cornbread. It's similar to the English muffin bread; hence, the name. For variety, try using blue cornmeal.

	Small	Medium	Large
water	¾ cup	1 ⅛ cups	1 ½ cups
egg	½	1 small	1 large
sugar	2 tsp.	1 tbs.	1 ⅓ tbs.
salt	½ tsp.	¾ tsp.	1 tsp.
cornmeal	½ cup	¾ cup	1 cup
bread flour	1 ½ cups	2 ¼ cups	3 cups
yeast	1 ½ tsp.	2 tsp.	2 ½ tsp.

Jalapeño Cornbread

Here's an outstanding bread for jalapeño lovers. Use either cheddar or Monterey Jack cheese. The jalapeños can be adjusted to taste; the amount of buttermilk may require some adjusting to compensate for more or less liquid from the peppers. Green chiles can be substituted if desired. I use either drained corn or frozen kernels which have been thawed. If fresh corn is available, that would be even better.

	Small	Medium	Large
buttermilk	¾ cup	1⅛ cups	1½ cups
corn kernels	⅓ cup	½ cup	⅔ cup
grated cheese	¼ cup	⅓ cup	½ cup
diced jalapeños	1	1½	2
honey	½ tsp.	¾ tsp.	1 tsp.
salt	¼ tsp.	⅓ tsp.	½ tsp.
baking soda	¼ tsp.	⅓ tsp.	½ tsp.
cornmeal	½ cup	¾ cup	1 cup
bread flour	1½ cups	2¼ cups	3 cups
yeast	1½ tsp.	2 tsp.	2½ tsp.

Three Seed Barley Rye

This rye has a distinctive taste, due to the seed and barley combination, that is great with cream cheese. Sprinkle some seeds on top of cheese for added flavor if desired. Since the high percentage of rye flour causes this to be a low-rising loaf, adding the vital gluten will help. Molasses or honey can be substituted for the barley malt.

	Small	Medium	Large
water	⅔ cup	1 cup	1⅓ cups
vegetable oil	1½ tbs.	2¼ tbs.	3 tbs.
barley malt syrup	1½ tbs.	2¼ tbs.	3 tbs.
salt	⅛-¼ tsp.	¼-⅓ tsp.	⅓-½ tsp.
anise seeds	½ tsp.	¾ tsp.	1 tsp.
fennel seeds	½ tsp.	¾ tsp.	1 tsp.
caraway seeds	½ tsp.	¾ tsp.	1 tsp.
vital gluten, optional	1-2 tbs.	1½-3 tbs.	2-4 tbs.
rye flour	1 cup	1½ cups	2 cups
bread flour	1 cup	1½ cups	2 cups
yeast	1½ tsp.	2 tsp.	2½ tsp.

Orange Potato Rye

What a combination — a potato bread with rye for a superb treat! Try substituting other seeds, such as anise or fennel, for a flavorful change of pace. Instead of mashing a potato, use a 4, 6 or 8 oz. cooked potato and let the machine mash it for you.

	Small	Medium	Large
mashed potato	½ cup	¾ cup	1 cup
potato water	⅓ cup	½ cup	⅔ cup
vegetable oil	1 tbs.	1½ tbs.	2 tbs.
honey or molasses	1 tbs.	1½ tbs.	2 tbs.
orange peel	¼ tsp.	⅓ tsp.	½ tsp.
salt	⅓ tsp.	½ tsp.	⅔ tsp.
caraway seeds, optional	1 tsp.	1½ tsp.	2 tsp.
rye flour	½ cup	¾ cup	1 cup
whole wheat flour	½ cup	¾ cup	1 cup
bread flour	1 cup	1½ cups	2 cups
yeast	1 tsp.	1½ tsp.	2 tsp.

Rye and Cracked Wheat Bread

This is a low dense loaf without the gluten. If desired, add anise, fennel or caraway seeds for extra flavor (½ to 2 tsp. depending on taste). The cracked wheat must sit in the water for at least 1 hour. With the exception of the DAK, Welbilt and National/Panasonic machines, the cracked wheat can be soaked right in the pan if using the timer.

	Small	Medium	Large
water	¾ cup	1⅛ cups	1½ cups
cracked wheat	½ cup	¾ cup	1 cup
vegetable oil	1 tbs.	1½ tbs.	2 tbs.
honey	2 tsp.	1 tbs.	1⅓ tbs.
salt	⅛ tsp.	⅛+ tsp.	¼ tsp.
bread flour	1 cup	1½ cups	2 cups
rye flour	½ cup	¾ cup	1 cup
vital gluten, optional	1-2 tbs.	1½-3 tbs.	2-4 tbs.
yeast	1½ tsp.	2 tsp.	2½ tsp.

Rye Berry Bread

This densely textured bread makes great sandwiches or toast. Watch the dough and add a tablespoon or two more of milk if needed to form a well rounded ball.

	Small	Medium	Large
water	1 cup	1 ½ cups	2 cups
rye berries	⅓ cup	½ cup	⅔ cups

Bring berries and water to a boil for approximately 5 minutes. Cover, remove from heat and allow to stand for about 6 to 8 hours or overnight. Drain berries prior to using.

milk	½ cup	¾ cup	1 cup
vegetable oil	1 tbs.	1 ½ tbs.	2 tbs.
honey	1 tbs.	1 ½ tbs.	2 tbs.
salt	1/16 tsp.	⅛ tsp.	⅛+ tsp.
caraway	1 tsp.	1 ½ tsp.	2 tsp.
vital gluten, optional	1 tbs.	1 ½ tbs.	2 tbs.
whole wheat flour	⅓ cup	½ cup	⅔ cup
rye flour	⅓ cup	½ cup	⅔ cup
bread flour	1 cup	1 ½ cups	2 cups
yeast	1 ½ tsp.	2 tsp.	2 ½ tsp.

Rye Herb Bread

This is a really flavorful bread. The pepper, rosemary and parsley amounts can be adjusted to taste if desired. If using fresh herbs, triple the amount given. I use coarsely ground black pepper. Vital gluten makes it a light, high-rising rye.

	Small	Medium	Large
water	¾ cup	1 ⅛ cups	1 ½ cups
butter or margarine	2 tbs.	3 tbs.	4 tbs.
brown sugar	1 tbs.	1 ½ tbs.	2 tbs.
salt	¼ tsp.	⅓ tsp.	½ tsp.
black pepper	½ tsp.	¾ tsp.	1 tsp.
rosemary	½ tsp.	¾ tsp.	1 tsp.
parsley, dried	1 tsp.	1 ½ tsp.	2 tsp.
vital gluten, optional	1-2 tbs.	1 ½-3 tbs.	2-4 tbs.
whole wheat flour	⅔ cup	1 cup	1 ⅓ cups
rye flour	⅔ cup	1 cup	1 ⅓ cups
bread flour	⅔ cup	1 cup	1 ⅓ cups
yeast	1 ½ tsp.	2 tsp.	2 ½ tsp.

Bean Flake Rye Bread

Whole Wheat, Sweet or Basic cycle

This is a really superb loaf of bread, moist and tasty. Black bean flakes can be found in health food and some grocery stores. I use just the flakes but have seen black bean flake soup/dip mixes available. If using a mix, check the amount of salt and reduce or even delete the salt from this recipe, if necessary.

	Small	Medium	Large
water or milk	¾ cup	1 ⅛ cups	1 ½ cups
vegetable oil	1 tbs.	1 ½ tbs.	2 tbs.
molasses	2 tbs.	3 tbs.	¼ cup
salt	¼ tsp.	⅓ tsp.	½ tsp.
black bean flakes	¼ cup	⅓ cup	½ cup
caraway seeds	1 tsp.	1 ½ tsp.	2 tsp.
orange peel, optional	¼ tsp.	⅓ tsp.	½ tsp.
vital gluten, optional	1-2 tbs.	1 ½-3 tbs.	2-4 tbs.
rye flour	¾ cup	1 cup	1 ½ cups
bread flour	1 ¼ cups	2 cups	2 ½ cups
yeast	1 tsp.	1 ½ tsp.	2 tsp.

Bean Flake Pumpernickel

Whole Wheat, Sweet or Basic cycle

Black bean flakes provide this bread with some of its coloring as well as a distinctive taste and, of course, lots of added nutrients. Barley malt can be substituted for the molasses if desired. This is one of my favorites.

	Small	Medium	Large
water or milk	¾ cup	1 ⅛ cups	1 ½ cups
vegetable oil	1 tbs.	1 ½ tbs.	2 tbs.
molasses	2 tbs.	3 tbs.	¼ cup
salt	¼ tsp.	⅓ tsp.	½ tsp.
black bean flakes	¼ cup	⅓ cup	½ cup
instant coffee granules	1 tbs.	1 ½ tbs.	2 tbs.
unsweetened cocoa	1 tbs.	1 ½ tbs.	2 tbs.
caraway seeds	1 tsp.	1 ½ tsp.	2 tsp.
rye flour	½ cup	¾ cup	1 cup
whole wheat flour	½ cup	¾ cup	1 cup
bread flour	1 cup	1 ½ cups	2 cups
yeast	1 tsp.	1 ½ tsp.	2 tsp.

Mustard Rye

Whole Wheat, Sweet or Basic cycle

Kit Bie says to make sure to use a Dijon with the coarsely ground mustard seeds as it gives the bread a nicer texture. Mustard seeds can be added if desired. It's a very moist bread which rises nicely and has a great taste as well as aroma! A must-try.

	Small	Medium	Large
water	2/3 cup	1 cup	1 1/3 cups
vegetable oil	2 tsp.	1 tbs.	1 1/3 tbs.
honey	1 tbs.	1 1/2 tbs.	2 tbs.
Dijon mustard	2 tbs.	3 tbs.	1/4 cup
salt	1/3 tsp.	1/2 tsp.	2/3 tsp.
mustard seeds, optional	1/2 tsp.	3/4 tsp.	1 tsp.
caraway or fennel, optional	1 tsp.	1 1/2 tsp.	2 tsp.
vital gluten, optional	1-2 tbs.	1 1/2-3 tbs.	2-4 tbs.
rye flour	2/3 cup	1 cup	1 1/3 cups
whole wheat flour	1/3 cup	1/2 cup	2/3 cup
bread flour	1 cup	1 1/2 cups	2 cups
yeast	1 1/2 tsp.	2 tsp.	2 1/2 tsp.

Jewish Rye Cornmeal Bread

Whole Wheat, Sweet or Basic cycle

A very small amount of gluten in both the rye and cornmeal results in a low-rising loaf of bread. I recommend using the vital gluten in this recipe. The combination of rye and cornmeal along with the wheat flour makes a very nutritious loaf of bread.

	Small	Medium	Large
water	3/4 cup	1 1/8 cups	1 1/2 cups
vegetable oil	1 tbs.	1 1/2 tbs.	2 tbs.
honey	2 tbs.	2 1/3 tbs.	3 tbs.
salt	1/4 tsp.	1/3 tsp.	1/2 tsp.
caraway, optional	1 tsp.	1 1/2 tsp.	2 tsp.
vital gluten, optional	1-2 tbs.	1 1/2-3 tbs.	2-4 tbs.
cornmeal	1/4 cup	1/3 cup	1/2 cup
rye flour	1/2 cup	2/3 cup	1 cup
bread flour	1 1/4 cups	2 cups	2 1/2 cups
yeast	1 1/2 tsp.	2 tsp.	2 1/2 tsp.

Slightly Rye Bread

Whole Wheat, Sweet or Basic cycle

If using the caraway, it can be adjusted to your taste. Other seeds such as anise, fennel or sesame can be substituted. This is a low-rising, densely textured loaf with the distinct flavor of the seed and a slight rye taste. Wheat flakes are rolled, just like the oats, and can be found in health food stores.

	Small	Medium	Large
milk or water	¾ cup	1⅛ cups	1½ cups
vegetable oil	1½ tbs.	2¼ tbs.	3 tbs.
honey or molasses	2 tbs.	3 tbs.	¼ cup
salt	⅓ tsp.	½ tsp.	⅔ tsp.
caraway, optional	1½ tsp.	2 tsp.	1 tbs.
orange peel	¼ tsp.	⅓ tsp.	½ tsp.
vital gluten, optional	1-2 tbs.	1½-3 tbs.	2-4 tbs.
oat or wheat flakes	¾ cup	1⅛ cups	1½ cups
rye flour	¼ cup	⅓ cup	½ cup
bread flour	1 cup	1½ cups	2 cups
yeast	1 tsp.	1½ tsp.	2 tsp.

Dated Rye

Whole Wheat or Basic cycle

Date sugar (available in health food stores) replaces refined sugar in this great sandwich bread.

	Small	Medium	Large
water	¾ cup	1⅛ cups	1½ cups
egg	1	1½	2
vegetable oil	1 tbs.	1½ tbs.	2 tbs.
date sugar	1 tsp.	1½ tsp.	2 tsp.
salt	⅛-¼ tsp.	¼-⅓ tsp.	⅓-½ tsp.
caraway seed	1½ tsp.	2¼ tsp.	3 tsp.
vital gluten	1-2 tbs.	1½-3 tbs.	2-4 tbs.
rye flour	1 cup	1½ cups	2 cups
bread flour	1 cup	1½ cups	2 cups
yeast	1½ tsp.	2 tsp.	2½ tsp.

Stout Bread

This recipe was developed by Paul Dudley of Pillsford, NY. He uses chocolate malted barley which he purchases from a beer making supply company. Or use barley malt syrup, available from any health food store. Paul says that this bread is a wonderful accompaniment to any sandwich. The bread rises nicely.

	Small	Medium	Large
water	¾ cup	1 cup	1½ cups
vegetable oil	2 tsp.	1 tbs.	1½ tbs.
barley malt syrup	2 tsp.	1 tbs.	1½ tbs.
sugar (white or brown)	2 tsp.	1 tbs.	1½ tbs.
salt	⅓ tsp.	½ tsp.	¾ tsp.
Roman meal	1½ tbs.	2⅓ tbs.	3 tbs.
whole wheat flour	1½ tbs.	2⅓ tbs.	3 tbs.
rye flour	1½ tbs.	2⅓ tbs.	3 tbs.
oats	1½ tbs.	2⅓ tbs.	3 tbs.
bread flour	1⅓ cups	1¾ cups	2⅔ cups
yeast	1½ tsp.	2 tsp.	2½ tsp.

Rye Flake Bread

Janice Buttress adapted her mother's recipe to her bread machine. She suggests using the variations as well. This is a very high rising, chewy bread. Rye flakes are similar to oat flakes (such as Quaker Oats) and can be found in health food stores.

	Small	Medium	Large
water	¾ cup	1⅛ cups	1½ cups
vegetable oil	1 tsp.	1½ tsp.	2 tsp.
honey	1 tsp.	1½ tsp.	2 tsp.
salt	⅓ tsp.	½ tsp.	⅔ tsp.
bread flour	1¾ cups	2⅔ cup	3½ cups
rye flakes	¼ cup	⅓ cup	½ cup
yeast	1 tsp.	1½ tsp.	2 tsp.

Variations: Add 1 of the following, or 2 if you cut the amounts in half:

	Small	Medium	Large
cracked wheat	2 tbs.	3 tbs.	¼ cup
9-grain cereal	2 tbs.	3 tbs.	¼ cup
wheat germ	1¼ tbs.	2 tbs.	2½ tbs.

Wheat Soy Sesame Bread
Whole Wheat, Sweet or Basic cycle

Janice Quinn made this bread before she discovered the wonders of bread machines. It's a low-rising loaf with lots of taste and an easy-to-cut texture.

	Small	Medium	Large
water	2/3 cup	1 cup	1 1/3 cups
vegetable oil	1 1/3 tbs.	2 tbs.	2 2/3 tbs.
honey	1 1/3 tbs.	2 tbs.	2 2/3 tbs.
sesame seeds	1/4 cup	1/3 cup	1/2 cup
soy powder or flour	2 2/3 tbs.	1/4 cup	5 1/3 tbs.
grits	2 tsp.	1 tbs.	1 1/3 tbs.
whole wheat flour	2/3 cup	1 cup	1 1/3 cups
bread flour	7/8 cup	1 1/4 cups	1 3/4 cups
yeast	1 tsp.	1 1/2 tsp.	2 tsp.

Whole Wheat Peasant Bread
Basic cycle

This is a basic nonfat, no-refined-sugar bread, with a nice flavor. Either brown or maple sugar can be substituted for the date sugar.

	Small	Medium	Large
water	1 cup	1 1/2 cups	2 cups
date sugar	1 tsp.	1 1/2 tsp.	2 tsp.
salt	1/4 tsp.	1/3 tsp.	1/2 tsp.
whole wheat flour	1 cup	1 1/2 cups	2 cups
bread flour	1 cup	1 1/2 cups	2 cups
yeast	1 tsp.	1 1/2 tsp.	2 tsp.

Maple Bran Bread
Raisin, Sweet or Basic cycle

The maple syrup imparts a delicate, sweet taste to this great loaf of bread.

	Small	Medium	Large
milk	3/4 cup	1 1/8 cups	1 1/2 cups
vegetable oil	1 tbs.	1 1/2 tbs.	2 tbs.
maple syrup	2 tbs.	3 tbs.	1/4 cup
salt	1/4 tsp.	1/3 tsp.	1/2 tsp.
oat or wheat bran	1/4 cup	1/3 cup	1/2 cup
whole wheat flour	1/2 cup	3/4 cup	1 cup
bread flour	1 1/2 cups	2 1/4 cups	3 cups
yeast	1 1/2 tsp.	2 tsp.	2 1/2 tsp.
*raisins, optional	1/4 cup	1/3 cup	1/2 cup

*Add ingredients at the beginning of the second kneading period.

About Sourdough

Sourdough recipes have been among the most requested. One thing that I keep hearing, however, is that people want it to be easy — making and caring for the starter initially seems intimidating. The solution is very simple as starters can be purchased easily. For testing purposes, I used two different starters. Baker's Catalog from King Arthur Flour sells a starter that is in a liquid form. It is a compilation of several different starters, including one each from San Francisco, Alaska and the New England area. Ordered through their mail order catalog, they cannot ship during the hot summer months. The other starter I used is more readily available in grocery and gourmet stores as well as by mail order. Called Goldrush Sourdough Starter, this is a dried starter that is purchased in small packets. The contents of both starters are mixed with just flour and water (fed) and are ready for use within a day or so; follow the directions with your purchased starter. I was very pleased with both. Each starter had a different thickness which may be adjusted by simply adding more or less liquid during feedings. Over most of the testing period the starters were used individually but towards the end they were combined for a new taste.

To make your own starter, mix together in a glass or plastic bowl:
2 cups lukewarm (110°-115°) water or milk
2 cups bread or unbleached all-purpose flour
2 1/2 tsp. (1 pkg.) yeast

Cover the bowl and allow to sit in a warm, draft-free location for 4 to 7 days, gently stirring once a day. You may notice that the mixture bubbles and may even overflow the bowl; this is an indication of the fermentation going on. It is also common for the starter to bubble up and then collapse if moved or jarred somehow. A sour smelling liquid may form on top of the starter which may simply be stirred back into the starter prior to use. It is generally recommended that you stir your starter with a wooden or plastic spoon.

To use your starter, simply remove the amount called for in the recipe and add to the other ingredients. Replace the amount removed with equal amounts of water or milk and bread or unbleached all-purpose flour. I always use bread flour. For example, if one cup of starter is used in your recipe, stir one cup of water and one cup of flour back into the mixture; this is called "feeding" your starter. Allow the starter to sit in a warm, draft-free location for approximately 24 hours after which time it can be used again or refrigerated.

A starter must be used at least once a week; or remove a portion (usually 1 cup) and throw that away. Feed as usual. If this is not done, your starter will become rancid as it requires fresh flour to feed on. Should you be away from your starter, freeze it and then thaw it in the refrigerator upon your return. As soon as it is thawed, it can be fed as above.

The longer the starter is used, the stronger it becomes in flavor. For many people developing and using their own starter is part of the fun and excitement; for other people, it seems easier and more fun to purchase one which already has lots of flavor and strength and has a story behind it.

IMPORTANT! Sourdough starters develop their own personalities and flavors; some may be thicker than others depending on variables such as the type of flour and liquid used. For this reason it is imperative to watch the dough as it kneads. I recommend that you allow the machine to knead the dough for approximately 3-5 minutes and then check it to see if it has formed a nice round dough ball. If not, add a tablespoon of water or flour at a time until it does so.

You may even want to keep notes if necessary. Once you have a good "feel" for the need to add more water or flour than the recipes call for, you could begin to use the timer cycle with your changes already made.

Sourdough Onion Rye
Whole Wheat, Sweet or Basic cycle

This is truly delicious. Use anise instead of caraway for a wonderful twist on an old favorite. As with any rye bread, this tends to be a low-rising loaf.

	Small	Medium	Large
starter	½ cup	¾ cup	1 cup
water or milk	⅓ cup	½ cup	⅔ cup
diced onion	¼ cup	⅓ cup	½ cup
vegetable oil	1 tbs.	1½ tbs.	2 tbs.
molasses	2 tbs.	3 tbs.	¼ cup
salt	½ tsp.	¾ tsp.	1 tsp.
caraway seeds, optional	2 tsp.	1 tbs.	1⅓ tbs.
vital gluten	1-2 tbs.	1½-3 tbs.	2-4 tbs.
rye flour	½ cup	¾ cup	1 cup
bread flour	1½ cups	2¼ cups	3 cups
yeast	1 tsp.	1½ tsp.	2 tsp.

Sourdough Pumpernickel

Whole Wheat, Sweet or Basic cycle

Outstanding! The cocoa and instant coffee granules provide color for this bread; black bean flour could be substituted for the cocoa if available. (I grind my own in an electric flour mill). Caraway can be adjusted to taste.

	Small	Medium	Large
starter	½ cup	¾ cup	1 cup
water	½ cup	¾ cup	1 cup
vegetable oil	1 tbs.	1½ tbs.	2 tbs.
molasses	2 tbs.	3 tbs.	¼ cup
unsweetened cocoa	1 tbs.	1½ tbs.	2 tbs.
instant coffee granules	1 tsp.	1½ tsp.	2 tsp.
salt	½ tsp.	¾ tsp.	1 tsp.
caraway seeds, optional	2 tsp.	1 tbs.	1⅓ tbs.
rye flour	½ cup	¾ cup	1 cup
whole wheat flour	½ cup	¾ cup	1 cup
bread flour	1 cup	1½ cups	2 cups
yeast	1½ tsp.	2 tsp.	2½ tsp.

Sourdough French Bread

Dough cycle

This delicious, pungent sour French bread goes nicely with cheese and wine.

	Small	Medium	Large
starter	½ cup	¾ cup	1 cup
water	½ cup	¾ cup	1 cup
salt	½ tsp.	¾ tsp.	1 tsp.
sugar	⅓ tsp.	½ tsp.	⅔ tsp.
whole wheat flour	1 cup	1½ cups	2 cups
all-purpose flour	1 cup	1½ cups	2 cups
yeast	1 tsp.	1½ tsp.	2 tsp.
cornmeal for shaping			

Allow the dough to rise in the machine for at least 1½ hours, even if the machine has stopped. Punch down the dough while it is still in the pan in the machine and allow it to rise in the turned off but still warm machine or other warm, draft-free location for 30 to 40 minutes. See page 200 for shaping and baking guidelines.

Sourdough Peasant Bread

Whole Wheat, Sweet or Basic cycle

Art Cazares took two of his favorite breads and combined them to come up with this one. Art uses much more water than I have listed. Increase the water if necessary to make the dough the right consistency.

	Small	Medium	Large
starter	¾ cup	1⅛ cups	1½ cups
water	⅓ cup	½ cup	⅔ cup
sugar	1 tsp.	1¼ tsp.	1½ tsp.
salt	½ tsp.	¾ tsp.	1 tsp.
bread flour	1½ cups	2¼ cups	3 cups
yeast	1 tsp.	1½ tsp.	2 tsp.

Sourdough French Bread

Dough cycle

This delicious, pungent sour French bread goes nicely with cheese and wine.

	Small	Medium	Large
starter	½ cup	¾ cup	1 cup
water	½ cup	¾ cup	1 cup
salt	½ tsp.	¾ tsp.	1 tsp.
sugar	⅓ tsp.	½ tsp.	⅔ tsp.
whole wheat flour	1 cup	1½ cups	2 cups
all-purpose flour	1 cup	1½ cups	2 cups
yeast	1 tsp.	1½ tsp.	2 tsp.
cornmeal for shaping			

Allow the dough to rise in the machine for at least 1½ hours, even if the machine has stopped. Punch down the dough while it is still in the pan in the machine and allow it to rise in the turned off but still warm machine or other warm, draft-free location for 30 to 40 minutes. See page 200 for shaping and baking guidelines.

Maple Walnut Sourdough
Raisin, Whole Wheat, Sweet or Basic cycle

A twist on a basic sourdough, this is good even without the nuts!

	Small	Medium	Large
starter	½ cup	¾ cup	1 cup
milk or water	½ cup	¾ cup	1 cup
walnut oil	1 tbs.	1 ½ tbs.	2 tbs.
maple syrup	2 tbs.	3 tbs.	¼ cup
cinnamon, optional	¼ tsp.	⅓ tsp.	½ tsp.
salt	⅓ tsp.	½ tsp.	⅔ tsp.
whole wheat flour	1 cup	1 ½ cups	2 cups
bread flour	1 cup	1 ½ cups	2 cups
yeast	1 tsp.	1 ½ tsp.	2 tsp.
*chopped walnuts	¼ cup	⅓ cup	½ cup
*raisins, optional	¼ cup	⅓ cup	½ cup

*Add ingredients at the beginning of the second kneading period.

Quick Sour Pumpernickel
Whole Wheat, Sweet or Basic cycle

You'll enjoy this easy sourdough.

	Small	Medium	Large
starter			
milk	¾ cup	1 ⅛ cups	1 ½ cups
rye flour	1 cup	1 ½ cups	2 cups
vital gluten	1 tbs.	1 ½ tbs.	2 tbs.
yeast	1 tsp.	1 ½ tsp.	2 tsp.

Let starter ingredients knead for about 10 minutes and then sit in the pan in the machine overnight or for 6 to 8 hours. Add remaining ingredients and start machine as usual.

	Small	Medium	Large
coffee	¼ cup	⅓ cup	½ cup
vegetable oil	1 tbs.	1 ½ tbs.	2 tbs.
molasses	2 tbs.	3 tbs.	¼ cup
unsweetened cocoa	1 tbs.	1 ½ tbs.	2 tbs.
salt	¼ tsp.	⅓ tsp.	½ tsp.
caraway or fennel seeds	1 tsp.	1 ½ tsp.	2 tsp.
vital gluten, optional	1 tbs.	1 ½ tbs.	2 tbs.
whole wheat flour	½ cup	¾ cup	1 cup
bread flour	⅔ cup	1 cup	1 ⅓ cups

Quick Sour French

This is light and crisp outside with a light fluffy inside. Wonderful! If desired, this can also be made on the dough cycle. See shaping and baking guidelines, page 200.

	Small	**Medium**	**Large**
sour cream	½ cup	⅝ cup	¾ cup
milk	½ cup	⅝ cup	¾ cup
vinegar	1 tbs.	1 ½ tbs.	2 tbs.
sugar	1 tsp.	1 ½ tsp.	2 tsp.
salt	⅔ tsp.	1 tsp.	1 ⅓ tsp.
baking soda	⅛ tsp.	⅛+ tsp.	¼ tsp.
bread flour	2 cups	2½ cups	3 cups
yeast	1 ½ tsp.	2 tsp.	2½ tsp.

Refrigerated Sourdough

Wow! This rises and cuts nicely. The starter is moist and sticky when removing it from the pan to refrigerate. The bread has a light, fluffy texture and taste. Good for sandwiches, toast or anything; a versatile bread.

starter	**Small**	**Medium**	**Large**
water (110°-115°)	½ cup	¾ cup	1 cup
bread flour	1 cup	1 ½ cups	2 cups
vital gluten, optional	1 tsp.	1 ½ tsp.	2 tsp.
yeast	1 tsp.	1 ½ tsp.	2 tsp.

Place in machine (any cycle) as usual and allow to knead for 5 to 10 minutes. (Stop machine at that time by using your stop or reset button or by unplugging.) Dough will be very soft and gooey. Remove from pan and place in a glass bowl, cover with plastic and refrigerate overnight (up to a day and a half is okay). Bring to room temperature prior to starting machine. The dough needs to be watched and more water added if necessary. Start with the amount given and add more, 1 tablespoon at a time, until a soft, round ball is formed.

dough			
starter (see above)			
water	⅓ cup	½ cup	⅔ cup
vegetable oil	1 tbs.	1 ½ tbs.	2 tbs.
sugar	½ tsp.	¾ tsp.	1 tsp.
salt	⅛-⅓ tsp.	¼-½ tsp.	⅓-¾ tsp.
oats	⅓ cup	½ cup	⅔ cups
bread flour	⅔ cup	1 cup	1 ⅓ cups
yeast	½ tsp.	1 tsp.	1 ½ tsp.

Apple Cinnamon Bread

Whole Wheat, Sweet or Basic cycle

This is a delicious breakfast bread. The cinnamon can be increased or decreased to your taste. The applesauce replaces butter or margarine in this recipe. I use frozen apple juice concentrate which has been thawed. The bread has a moist texture with light flavor and a crisp crust. Kids love it. Try adding chopped apple (fresh or dried) and nuts.

	Small	Medium	Large
water	½ cup	¾ cup	1 cup
apple juice concentrate	2½ tbs.	3¾ tbs.	5 tbs.
applesauce	¼ cup	⅓ cup	½ cup
cinnamon	½ tsp.	¾ tsp.	1 tsp.
brown sugar	2 tsp.	1 tbs.	1⅓ tbs.
salt	¼ tsp.	⅓ tsp.	½ tsp.
whole wheat flour	1 cup	1½ cups	2 cups
vital gluten, optional	1-2 tbs.	1½-3 tbs.	2-4 tbs.
bread flour	1 cup	1½ cups	2 cups
yeast	1 tsp.	1½ tsp.	2 tsp.

Cranberry Orange Bread

Raisin, Sweet or Basic cycle

What a festive bread for fall! Use the dried cranberries to enjoy during the rest of the year. Testing was done in the off season using dried cranberries. If using fresh cranberries, they should be finely chopped.

	Small	Medium	Large
orange juice concentrate	⅓ cup	½ cup	⅔ cup
water	½ cup	¾ cup	1 cup
honey	1 tbs.	1½ tbs.	2 tbs.
salt	¼ tsp.	⅓ tsp.	½ tsp.
whole wheat flour	1 cup	1½ cups	2 cups
bread flour	1 cup	1½ cups	2 cups
yeast	1 tsp.	1½ tsp.	2 tsp.
*cranberries	¼ cup	⅓ cup	½ cup

*Add ingredients at the beginning of the second kneading period.

Pineapple Cranberry Bread

Sweet or Basic cycle

This is a full-bodied bread with lots of flavor. If desired, add chopped nuts and/or dried cranberries on the raisin or mix cycle. One tester recommended adding coconut flakes in addition to the oats and flour (¼, ⅓ or ½ cup).

	Small	Medium	Large
cranberry juice	½ cup	¾ cup	1 cup
crushed pineapple	⅓ cup	½ cup	⅔ cup
butter or margarine	1 tbs.	1½ tbs.	2 tbs.
salt	¼ tsp.	⅓ tsp.	½ tsp.
oats	½ cup	¾ cups	1 cup
bread flour	1½ cups	2¼ cups	3 cups
yeast	1 tsp.	1½ tsp.	2 tsp.

Buttermilk Berry Bread

Sweet or Basic cycle

The buttermilk produces a light airy bread, and the berries add just a hint of berry flavor. Use your favorite berries, pureed with a blender or food processer. As with any fruit bread, much of the liquid is derived from the fruit itself, so watch the dough and add more buttermilk or flour if necessary. Serve toasted with cream cheese and berries. If desired, use regular milk cup for cup for the buttermilk and omit the baking soda.

	Small	Medium	Large
buttermilk	⅓ cup	⅓+ cup	½ cup
berry puree	⅓ cup	⅓+ cup	½ cup
egg	1	1½	2
butter	1 tbs.	1½ tbs.	2 tbs.
sugar	1 tbs.	1½ tbs.	2 tbs.
baking soda	¼ tsp.	⅓ tsp.	½ tsp.
salt	¼ tsp.	⅓ tsp.	½ tsp.
bread flour	2 cups	2½ cups	3 cups
yeast	1 tsp.	1½ tsp.	2 tsp.

Creamed Chocolate Coconut Bread

Raisin, Sweet or Basic cycle

This recipe is a twist on an old favorite. The coconut and oats give the bread a moist, chewy texture. This bread would be a wonderful holiday gift. Four stars!

	Small	Medium	Large
heavy cream	⅔ cup	1 cup	1⅓ cups
egg	1	1½	2
butter or margarine	2 tbs.	3 tbs.	4 tbs.
sugar	2 tbs.	3 tbs.	¼ cup
unsweetened cocoa	1 tbs.	1½ tbs.	2 tbs.
salt	¼ tsp.	⅓ tsp.	½ tsp.
coconut flakes	¼ cup	⅓ cup	½ cup
oats	1 cup	1½ cups	2 cups
bread flour	1 cup	1½ cups	2 cups
yeast	1 tsp.	1½ tsp.	2 tsp.
chocolate chips	⅓ cup	½ cup	⅔ cup
chopped nuts	¼ cup	⅓ cup	½ cup

Blueberry Bread

Sweet or Basic cycle

This is wonderful, with nice blueberry flavor and a dense texture. It's perfect for breakfast or a late morning coffee. Blueberries are pureed by processing with a blender or food processor.

	Small	Medium	Large
blueberry puree	⅔ cup	¾ cup	1 cup
egg	1	1½	2
margarine or butter	2 tbs.	3 tbs.	4 tbs.
sugar	2 tbs.	3 tbs.	¼ cup
salt	¼ tsp.	⅓ tsp.	½ tsp.
bread flour	2 cups	2½ cups	3 cups
yeast	1 tsp.	1½ tsp.	2 tsp.

Sour Cream Lemon Bread

Sweet or Basic cycle

This bread is rich, with a hint of lemon. Try serving it toasted, topped with lemon curd, for a delectable treat.

	Small	Medium	Large
sour cream	3 tbs.	¼ cup	⅓ cup
milk	⅓ cup	½ cup	⅔ cup
butter or margarine	1 ½ tbs.	2 tbs.	3 tbs.
eggs	1 small	1	1 ½
baking soda	⅛+ tsp.	¼ tsp.	⅓ tsp.
grated lemon peel	¼ tsp.	⅓ tsp.	½ tsp.
sugar	1 ½ tbs.	2 tbs.	3 tbs.
salt	½ tsp.	¾ tsp.	1 tsp.
bread flour	1 ½ cups	2 cups	3 cups
yeast	1 tsp.	1 ½ tsp.	2 tsp.

Lemon Ginger Bread

Sweet or Basic cycle

This is a light, airy loaf with a delicate taste. The ginger can be increased to taste if desired. A must for lemon lovers!

	Small	Medium	Large
water	½ cup	⅔ cup	¾ cup
lemon juice	2 tbs.	2 ½ tbs.	3 tbs.
butter or margarine	2 tbs.	2 ½ tbs.	3 tbs.
maple syrup	1 tbs.	1 ¼ tbs.	1 ½ tbs.
ground ginger	¼ tsp.	⅓ tsp.	½ tsp.
brown sugar	2 tbs.	2 ½ tbs.	3 tbs.
salt	¼ tsp.	⅓ tsp.	½ tsp.
bread flour	2 cups	2 ½ cups	3 cups
yeast	1 tsp.	1 ½ tsp.	2 tsp.

Chocolate Banana Bread

Raisin, Sweet or Basic cycle

As with any bread that derives liquid from the fruit, watch the dough and add milk or water, if necessary, one tablespoon at a time, until a nice round ball of dough is formed. The chocolate-banana combo is outstanding. Nuts are optional.

	Small	Medium	Large
mashed banana	2/3 cup	3/4 cup	1 cup
egg	1	1	1 1/2
butter or margarine	2 tbs.	2 1/2 tbs.	3 tbs.
vanilla extract	1 tsp.	1 1/4 tsp.	1 1/2 tsp.
salt	1/8 tsp.	1/8 tsp.	1/4 tsp.
cinnamon	1/3 tsp.	1/3 tsp.	1/2 tsp.
unsweetened cocoa	1 tbs.	1 1/4 tbs.	1 1/2 tbs.
sugar	2 tbs.	2 1/2 tbs.	3 tbs.
bread flour	2 cups	2 1/2 cups	3 cups
yeast	1 tsp.	1 1/2 tsp.	2 tsp.
*chopped walnuts	2 tbs.	2 1/2 tbs.	3 tbs.

*Add ingredients at the beginning of the second kneading period.

Orange Ginger Bread

Sweet or Basic cycle

This is wonderful! The aroma alone is worth it, and the flavor is light and gingery but not too sweet.

	Small	Medium	Large
orange juice	2/3 cup	1 cup	1 1/3 cups
butter or margarine	2 tbs.	3 tbs.	4 tbs.
brown sugar	2 tbs.	3 tbs.	1/4 cup
cinnamon	2/3 tsp.	1 tsp.	1 1/3 tsp.
ground ginger	1 tsp.	1 1/2 tsp.	2 tsp.
ground cloves	1/3 tsp.	1/2 tsp.	2/3 tsp.
salt	1/8 tsp.	1/8+ tsp.	1/4 tsp.
bread flour	1 cup	1 1/2 cup	2 cups
whole wheat flour	1 cup	1 1/2 cups	2 cups
yeast	1 tsp.	1 1/2 tsp.	2 tsp.

Ginger Cream Bread

Sweet or Basic cycle

This recipe makes a rich bread with a good creamy flavor. The crystallized ginger should be finely chopped; I use a food processor or blender.

	Small	Medium	Large
cream	⅔ cup	¾ cup	1 cup
butter	2 tbs.	2½ tbs.	3 tbs.
egg	1	1½	2
vanilla extract	1 tsp.	1¼ tsp.	1½ tsp.
crystallized ginger	1 tbs.	1¼ tbs.	1½ tbs.
brown sugar	1 tbs.	1¼ tbs.	1½ tbs.
salt	¼ tsp.	¼+ tsp.	⅓ tsp.
bread flour	2 cups	2½ cups	3 cups
yeast	1 tsp.	1½ tsp.	2 tsp.

Amaretto Raisin Bread

Raisin, Sweet or Basic cycle

This wonderful, light fluffy bread has a crisp crust and a hint of amaretto. Soak raisins in amaretto for approximately 1 hour and add to your dough at the proper time for your machine.

	Small	Medium	Large
water	⅔ cup	¾ cup	1 cup
almond extract	⅔ tsp.	¾ tsp.	1 tsp.
vegetable oil	2 tsp.	2½ tsp.	1 tbs.
honey	1 tsp.	1¼ tsp.	1½ tsp.
salt	¼ tsp.	⅓ tsp.	½ tsp.
bread flour	2 cups	2½ cups	3 cups
yeast	1 tsp.	1¼ tsp.	1½ tsp.
*amaretto	1 tbs.	1½ tbs.	2 tbs.
*raisins	¼ cup	⅓ cup	½ cup
*chopped almonds, optional	2 tbs.	2½ tbs.	3 tbs.

*Add ingredients at the beginning of the second kneading period.

Chocolate Strawberry Bread

Raisin, Sweet or Basic cycle

Serve this decadent bread with ice cream, fresh strawberries and melted chocolate drizzled on top. Or make French toast and serve with a strawberry syrup and fresh strawberries. Strawberries can be pureed by processing them in a food processor (steel blade) or blender for a minute or two. As with any bread using a fruit as part of the liquid, watch the dough and add water if necessary.

	Small	**Medium**	**Large**
strawberry puree	⅔ cup	⅞ cup	1 cup
butter	2 tbs.	2½ tbs.	3 tbs.
sugar	2 tbs.	2½ tbs.	3 tbs.
unsweetened cocoa	1 tbs.	1¼ tbs.	1½ tbs.
salt	¼ tsp.	⅓ tsp.	½ tsp.
bread flour	2 cups	2½ cups	3 cups
yeast	1 tsp.	1½ tsp.	2 tsp.
*chocolate chips	⅓ cup	½ cup	⅔ cup

*Add ingredients at the beginning of the second kneading period.

Bimini Coconut Bread

Sweet or Basic cycle

This is based on a recipe given to me by my father-in-law, a (rare) native Floridian. This is an outstanding bread, great with coffee or alone as a snack. Mary Vollendorf adds more coconut flakes, white chocolate chips and chopped nuts to this (a few tablespoons of each). This works great in some machines, but not those which are prone to "doughy blues."

	Small	**Medium**	**Large**
milk	⅔ cup	¾ cup	1 cup
coconut extract	2 tsp.	2½ tsp.	1 tbs.
butter or margarine	1 tbs.	1¼ tbs.	1½ tbs.
egg	1	1	1½
sugar	2 tbs.	2½ tbs.	3 tbs.
salt	¼-½ tsp.	⅓-⅔ tsp.	½-1 tsp.
coconut flakes	¼ cup	¼+ cup	⅓ cup
bread flour	2 cups	2½ cups	3 cups
yeast	1 tsp.	1½ tsp.	2 tsp.

Lemon Saffron Bread

Saffron produces a distinctive-tasting bread with a wonderful yellow color. Serve with lemon curd or any of the wonderful lemon toppings.

	Small	Medium	Large
water or milk	¾ cup	1 ⅛ cups	1 ½ cups
lemon juice concentrate	1 tbs.	1 ⅓ tbs.	1 ½ tbs.
sugar	2 tbs.	2 ½ tbs.	3 tbs.
salt	¼ tsp.	⅓ tsp.	½ tsp.
lemon peel	¼ tsp.	⅓ tsp.	⅓+ tsp.
ground saffron	⅛ tsp.	⅛+ tsp.	¼ tsp.
bread flour	2 cups	2 ½ cups	3 cups
yeast	1 tsp.	1 ½ tsp.	2 tsp.

Pumpkin Apple Bread

Who could ask for a better bread to enjoy on a nice fall day? The pumpkin pie spice can be adjusted to taste. For a delectable treat, try this as a sandwich bread with cream cheese and apple or pumpkin butter. Dried apple and nuts are optional.

	Small	Medium	Large
apple juice	¼ cup	⅓ cup	½ cup
pumpkin	⅔ cup	1 cup	1 ⅓ cups
apple juice concentrate	1 tbs.	1 ½ tbs.	2 tbs.
brown or maple sugar	2 tbs.	3 tbs.	¼ cup
pumpkin pie spice	1 tsp.	1 ½ tsp.	2 tsp.
salt	⅓ tsp.	¼ tsp.	⅔ tsp.
oats	½ cup	¾ cup	1 cup
bread flour	1 ½ cups	2 ¼ cups	3 cups
yeast	1 tsp.	1 ½ tsp.	2 tsp.
*dried apple, diced	¼ cup	⅓ cup	½ cup
*ground nuts	2 tbs.	3 tbs.	¼ cup

*Add ingredients at the beginning of the second kneading period.

Irish Soda Bread

Bettie Cooper has adapted this recipe to her bread machine and says it is a favorite with all of her friends. It is required that she take it to any get-togethers.

	Small	Medium	Large
vinegar	1 tbs.	1 1/4 tbs.	1 1/2 tbs.
skim milk*	1 cup	1 1/4 cups	1 1/2 cups
canola oil	1 tbs.	1 1/4 tbs.	1 1/2 tbs.
raisins	1/4 cup	5 tbs.	1/3 cup
sugar	2 tbs.	2 1/2 tbs.	3 tbs.
salt	2/3 tsp.	3/4 tsp.	1 tsp.
caraway seeds	2 tbs.	2 1/2 tbs.	3 tbs.
whole wheat flour	1 cup	1 1/4 cups	1 1/2 cups
bread flour	1 1/4 cups	1 2/3 cups	1 7/8 cups
yeast	1 1/2 tsp.	2 tsp.	2 1/2 tsp.
**raisins	1/3 cup	1/2 cup	2/3 cups

*Measure the vinegar into your liquid measuring cup. Add skim milk. Or substitute fresh buttermilk for vinegar and skim milk.

**Add ingredients at the beginning of the second kneading period.

Sweet Raisin Bread

Golden raisins tend to be sweeter than the darker ones. You can use whichever ones you prefer. This dough is very wet, which results in an extremely light, high-rising loaf. The raisins can be increased if your machine has no problems cooking fruited loaves completely.

	Small	Medium	Large
milk or water	2/3 cup	1 cup	1 1/3 cup
butter or margarine	1 tbs.	1 1/2 tbs.	2 tbs.
sugar	1 1/2 tbs.	2 1/3 tbs.	3 tbs.
salt	1/2 tsp.	2/3 tsp.	1 tsp.
grated lemon peel	1/2 tsp.	3/4 tsp.	1 tsp.
bread flour	1 1/2 cups	2 1/4 cups	3 cups
yeast	1 tsp.	1 1/2 tsp.	2 tsp.
*golden raisins	1/3 cup	1/2 cup	2/3 cup
*chopped nuts, optional	1/4 cup	1/3 cup	1/2 cup

*Add ingredients at the beginning of the second kneading period.

Poppy Seed Bread

Sweet or Basic cycle

Poppy seeds are a favorite in everything from cakes to bread. Unlimited versions abound; here's another one to enjoy. Poppy seeds can be purchased in bulk (much more economical) from mail order catalogs or gourmet shops.

	Small	Medium	Large
milk	⅔ cup	¾ cup	1 cup
butter or margarine	2 tbs.	2½ tbs.	3 tbs.
salt	⅔ tsp.	¾ tsp.	1 tsp.
lemon peel, optional	1 tsp.	1¼ tsp.	1½ tsp.
sugar	2 tbs.	2½ tbs.	3 tbs.
poppy seeds	2 tbs.	2½ tbs.	3 tbs.
bread flour	2 cups	2½ cups	3 cups
yeast	1 tsp.	1½ tsp.	2 tsp.

Prune Bread

Raisin, Sweet or Basic cycle

Priscilla Ward of Delaware shares her favorite bread, which she developed using her bread machine. She says that she snips each prune into 8 pieces; I let the machine mash them for me. I also cut back on the amount of juice she uses.

	Small	Medium	Large
cran-raspberry juice	¾ cup	1 cup	1½ cups
margarine or butter	1¼ tbs.	1⅔ tbs.	2½ tbs.
sugar	1½ tbs.	2¼ tbs.	3 tbs.
salt	½ tsp.	¾ tsp.	1 tsp.
whole wheat flour	½ cup	¾ cup	1 cup
bread flour	1½ cups	2¼ cups	3 cups
yeast	1 tsp.	1½ tsp.	2 tsp.
*snipped pitted prunes	⅓-½ cup	½-⅔ cup	⅔-¾ cup

*Add ingredients at the beginning of the second kneading period.

Squaw Bread

Karen Pennington adapted this version of an often-requested bread for the bread machines. It's a nice, sweet bread. Karen mixes the first five ingredients together in a blender until liquified; I simply put them in all at once and let the machine mash the raisins. A few tablespoons of sunflower seeds can be added for variation.

	Small	Medium	Large
water	2/3 cup	1 1/8 cups	1 1/3 cups
vegetable oil	1 1/3 tbs.	2 tbs.	2 2/3 tbs.
honey	1 tbs.	1 1/2 tbs.	2 tbs.
brown or maple sugar	1 tbs.	1 1/2 tbs.	2 tbs.
raisins	1 tbs.	1 1/2 tbs.	2 tbs.
salt	1/2-2/3 tsp.	2/3-1 tsp.	1-1 1/2 tsp.
rye flour	1/2 cup	3/4 cup	1 cup
whole wheat flour	1/2 cup	3/4 cup	1 cup
bread flour	1 cup	1 1/2 cups	2 cups
yeast	1 1/2 tsp.	2 tsp.	2 1/2 tsp.

Orange Sherry Raisin Bread

The raisins are plumped in sherry for a tasty treat and are still fat and juicy after baking! The orange peel really gives this zing! Great with cream cheese. Soak the raisins in the sherry overnight or for at least 6 to 8 hours. When starting the dough, drain the sherry into the pan with the other liquid ingredients.

	Small	Medium	Large
orange juice	2/3 cup	1 cup	1 1/3 cups
vegetable oil	2 tbs.	3 tbs.	1/4 cup
honey	2 tbs.	3 tbs.	1/4 cup
orange peel	1/3 tsp.	1/2 tsp.	2/3 tsp.
whole wheat flour	1 cup	1 1/2 cups	2 cups
bread flour	1 cup	1 1/2 cups	2 cups
yeast	1 tsp.	1 1/2 tsp.	2 tsp.
*dry sherry	2 tbs.	3 tbs.	1/4 cup
*raisins	1/3 cup	1/2 cup	2/3 cup

*Add ingredients at the beginning of the second kneading period.

Apricot Cornmeal Bread

Raisin, Sweet or Basic cycle

This winning combination will please the apricot lover in your family.

	Small	Medium	Large
milk or water	⅔ cup	1 cup	1⅓ cups
apricot nectar	1 tbs.	1½ tbs.	2 tbs.
honey	1 tbs.	1½ tbs.	2 tbs.
salt	⅔ tsp.	1 tsp.	1⅓ tsp.
cornmeal	½ cup	¾ cup	1 cup
bread flour	1½ cups	2¼ cups	3 cups
yeast	1 tsp.	1½ tsp.	2 tsp.
*diced dried apricots	¼ cup	⅓ cup	½ cup

*Add ingredients at the beginning of the second kneading period.

Banana Amaranth Bread

Raisin, Sweet or Basic cycle

Amaranth is a great source of protein and combines nicely with banana in this loaf. If necessary, add water to mashed banana to equal amount in recipe. Watch the kneading of the dough and add water, 1 tbs. at a time until ball is formed.

	Small	Medium	Large
milk	⅔ cup	1 cup	1⅓ cups
mashed banana	¼ cup	⅓ cup	½ cup
walnut oil	2 tsp.	1 tbs.	1⅓ tbs.
honey	2 tbs.	3 tbs.	¼ cup
salt	¼ tsp.	⅓ tsp.	½ tsp.
cinnamon	⅛ tsp.	⅛+ tsp.	¼ tsp.
amaranth flour	¼ cup	⅓ cup	½ cup
whole wheat flour	½ cup	¾ cup	1 cup
bread flour	1¼ cups	1⅔ cups	2½ cups
vital gluten, optional	1 tbs.	1½ tbs.	2 tbs.
yeast	1½ tsp.	2 tsp.	2½ tsp.
*chopped nuts, optional	¼ cup	⅓ cup	½ cup

*Add ingredients at the beginning of the second kneading period.

Fruit Cocktail Bread

Sweet or Basic cycle

The coconut flakes really add that special touch to this bread. Serve this toasted with ice cream and coconut flakes for a different dessert treat. Do not drain the fruit cocktail.

	Small	Medium	Large
fruit cocktail	¾ cup	1⅛ cups	1½ cups
vegetable oil	1 tbs.	1½ tbs.	2 tbs.
fruit juice concentrate	2 tbs.	3 tbs.	¼ cup
salt	¼ tsp.	⅓ tsp.	½ tsp.
coconut flakes	¼ cup	⅓ cup	½ cup
whole wheat flour	1 cup	1½ cups	2 cups
bread flour	1 cup	1½ cups	2 cups
yeast	1 tsp.	1½ tsp.	2 tsp.

Orange Rye Cornmeal Bread

Whole Wheat, Sweet or Basic cycle

This is a tasty but very low-rising loaf of bread. The combination is unbeatable! Tip: 1⅞ cups equals 2 cups less 2 tbs.

	Small	Medium	Large
orange juice	¾ cup	1⅛ cups	1½ cups
orange juice concentrate	2 tbs.	3 tbs.	¼ cup
honey	1 tbs.	1½ tbs.	2 tbs.
salt	⅓ tsp.	½ tsp.	⅔ tsp.
cornmeal	½ cup	¾ cup	1 cup
rye flour	¼ cup	⅓ cup	½ cup
bread flour	1¼ cups	1⅞ cups	2½ cups
vital gluten	1-2 tbs.	1½-3 tbs.	2-4 tbs.
yeast	1 tsp.	1½ tsp.	2 tsp.

Chocolate Chocolate Chip Bread

Raisin, Sweet or Basic cycle

For all the chocoholics of the world! This has a good chocolate flavor without being too sweet. One tester replaced the sugar with date sugar and highly recommends it.

	Small	Medium	Large
milk	½ cup	¾ cup	1 cup
margarine or butter	1 tbs.	1½ tbs.	2 tbs.
eggs	1	1½	2
vanilla extract	1 tsp.	1½ tsp.	2 tsp.
sugar	2 tbs.	3 tbs.	4 tbs.
unsweetened cocoa	1 tbs.	1½ tbs.	2 tbs.
salt	¼ tsp.	⅓ tsp.	½ tsp.
bread flour	1½ cups	2¼ cups	3 cups
yeast	1 tsp.	1½ tsp.	2 tsp.
*chocolate chips	¼-⅓ cup	⅓-½ cup	½-⅔ cup

*Add ingredients at the beginning of the second kneading period.

Chocolate Chip Banana Coconut Bread

Raisin, Sweet or Basic cycle

This flavorful sweet bread could be served for brunch, or for dessert with ice cream. The chips may become mashed in the bread which gives it a chocolate appearance instead of the visible chips. Either way, it is just as good.

	Small	Medium	Large
milk	½ cup	¾ cup	1 cup
mashed banana	¼ cup	⅓ cup	½ cup
butter or margarine	1 tbs.	1½ tbs.	2 tbs.
sugar	1 tbs.	1½ tbs.	2 tbs.
salt	¼ tsp.	⅓ tsp.	½ tsp.
coconut flakes	¼ cup	⅓ cup	½ cup
oats	½ cup	¾ cup	1 cup
bread flour	1½ cups	2¼ cups	3 cups
yeast	1 tsp.	1½ tsp.	2 tsp.
*chocolate chips	¼ cup	⅓ cup	½ cup

*Add ingredients at the beginning of the second kneading period.

Orange Bourbon Bread

Here is a great holiday and gift bread. Soak raisins in bourbon for 30 minutes or longer prior to starting the machine. Pour off any excess liquid and add to other liquid ingredients; add raisins at the normal time. Try freshly grated nutmeg — it's much better!

	Small	Medium	Large
bourbon	2 tbs.	3 tbs.	1/4 cup
orange juice	1/2 cup	3/4 cup	1 cup
eggs	1	1 1/2	2
butter or margarine	2 tbs.	3 tbs.	4 tbs.
sugar	2 tbs.	3 tbs.	4 tbs.
salt	1/4 tsp.	1/3 tsp.	1/2 tsp.
nutmeg	1/8 tsp.	1/8+ tsp.	1/4 tsp.
whole wheat flour	1 cup	1 1/2 cups	2 cups
bread flour	1 cup	1 1/2 cups	2 cups
yeast	1 tsp.	1 1/2 tsp.	2 tsp.
*raisins	1/3 cup	1/2 cup	2/3 cup
*bourbon	2 tbs.	3 tbs.	1/4 cup

*Add ingredients at the beginning of the second kneading period.

Orange Cottage Cheese Bread

This low-rising bread has great taste and texture. Allow the dough to knead for at least 5 minutes before looking to see if added liquids (orange segments) are required. I use canned Mandarin orange segments that have been drained. Try this toasted with orange marmalade!

	Small	Medium	Large
orange segments	1/2 cup	3/4 cup	1 cup
cottage cheese	1/4 cup	1/3 cup	1/2 cup
vegetable oil	1 tbs.	1 1/2 tbs.	2 tbs.
honey	1 tbs.	1 1/2 tbs.	2 tbs.
salt	1/4 tsp.	1/3 tsp.	1/2 tsp.
baking soda	1/4 tsp.	1/3 tsp.	1/2 tsp.
oats	1/2 cup	3/4 cup	1 cup
bread flour	1 1/2 cups	2 1/4 cups	3 cups
yeast	1 tsp.	1 1/2 tsp.	2 tsp.

Oregano Bread — No Cheese

Basic cycle

Due to so many requests for reduced fat, I have revised one of our all-time favorites. Fructose can be used in place of the sugar if the amount is cut to: 1, 1¼ or 2 tsp. Basil or another favorite herb can be substituted for the oregano. This flavorful bread is terrific with lasagna or a similar meal.

	Small	**Medium**	**Large**
water	⅔ cup	¾ cup	1 cup
olive oil	1 tbs.	1½ tbs.	2 tbs.
egg	1	1	1½
sugar	1 tbs.	1⅓ tbs.	1½ tbs.
salt	¼-⅓ tsp.	⅓-½ tsp.	½-⅔ tsp.
oregano, dried	1 tbs.	1½ tbs.	2 tbs.
bread flour	2 cups	2½ cups	3 cups
yeast	1 tsp.	1½ tsp.	2 tsp.

Ginger Bread

Sweet or Basic cycle

A wonderful aroma fills the house while this bakes and the taste is just as good!

	Small	**Medium**	**Large**
buttermilk	¾ cup	1⅛ cups	1½ cups
vegetable oil	1 tbs.	1½ tbs.	2 tbs.
molasses	1 tbs.	1½ tbs.	2 tbs.
egg	1	1½	2
salt	⅓ tsp.	½ tsp.	⅔ tsp.
baking soda	¼ tsp.	⅓ tsp.	½ tsp.
ground ginger	1 tsp.	1½ tsp.	2 tsp.
cinnamon	1 tsp.	1½ tsp.	2 tsp.
ground cloves	⅓ tsp.	½ tsp.	⅔ tsp.
nutmeg	⅓ tsp.	½ tsp.	⅔ tsp.
orange peel	¼ tsp.	⅓ tsp.	½ tsp.
whole wheat flour	1 cup	1½ cups	2 cups
bread flour	1 cup	1½ cups	2 cups
yeast	1 tsp.	1½ tsp.	2 tsp.

Cayenne Cornbread

Sweet or Basic cycle

Here's a hot, spicy cornbread with a consistency similar to corn muffins.

	Small	**Medium**	**Large**
milk or water	¾ cup	1⅛ cups	1½ cups
margarine or butter	1 tbs.	1½ tbs.	2 tbs.
brown sugar	1 tbs.	1½ tbs.	2 tbs.
salt	⅛ tsp.	⅛+ tsp.	¼ tsp.
cayenne pepper	½ tsp.	¾ tsp.	1 tsp.
cornmeal	½ cup	¾ cup	1 cup
bread flour	1½ cups	2¼ cups	3 cups
yeast	1 tsp.	1½ tsp.	2 tsp.

Mexican Cornbread

Sweet or Basic cycle

Wow! This will soon become a favorite in your house too. I ran out of creamed corn during my testing once so I filled my measuring cup with thawed frozen corn and then poured in milk to top it off; worked great. Both the corn and the salsa can throw off the liquid/flour ratio, so check the dough about 3 to 5 minutes into the kneading and add more water or flour as necessary.

	Small	**Medium**	**Large**
creamed corn	⅔ cup	1 cup	1⅓ cups
vegetable oil	1 tbs.	1½ tbs.	2 tbs.
honey	2 tsp.	1 tbs.	1⅓ tbs.
grated cheddar cheese	¼ cup	⅓ cup	½ cup
salsa	¼ cup	⅓ cup	½ cup
salt	⅓ tsp.	½ tsp.	⅔ tsp.
cornmeal	½ cup	¾ cup	1 cup
bread flour	1½ cups	2¼ cups	3 cups
yeast	1 tsp.	1½ tsp.	2 tsp.

Herb Cornbread

This is a delightful, flavorful bread to serve with chicken and a green salad or a Mexican-style dinner. It is also good toasted with honey. For variety, try omitting the three herbs and using paprika (1 tsp., 1 1/2 tsp., 2 tsp.).

	Small	**Medium**	**Large**
milk or water	¾ cup	1 ⅛ cups	1 ½ cups
vegetable oil	1 tbs.	1 ½ tbs.	2 tbs.
honey or maple syrup	1 tbs.	1 ½ tbs.	2 tbs.
salt	¼ tsp.	⅓ tsp.	½ tsp.
thyme	¼ tsp.	⅓ tsp.	½ tsp.
oregano	¼ tsp.	⅓ tsp.	½ tsp.
celery seeds	⅛ tsp.	⅛+ tsp.	¼ tsp.
cornmeal	½ cup	¾ cup	1 cup
bread flour	1 ½ cups	2 ¼ cups	3 cups
yeast	1 tsp.	1 ½ tsp.	2 tsp.

Cornmeal Cheese Bread

This hearty loaf is great with a Mexican dish. The cheese adds wonderful flavor to cornmeal. Try serving this toasted, topped with melted cheese and salsa.

	Small	**Medium**	**Large**
buttermilk	¾ cup	1 ⅛ cups	1 ½ cups
grated cheese	⅓ cup	½ cup	⅔ cup
butter or margarine	1 tbs.	1 ½ tbs.	2 tbs.
baking soda	¼ tsp.	⅓ tsp.	½ tsp.
sugar	1 tbs.	1 ½ tbs.	2 tbs.
salt	¼ tsp.	⅓ tsp.	½ tsp.
caraway seeds	1 tsp.	1 ½ tsp.	2 tsp.
cornmeal	½ cup	¾ cup	1 cup
bread flour	1 ½ cups	2 ¼ cups	3 cups
yeast	1 tsp.	1 ½ tsp.	2 tsp.

Hungarian Onion Bread

Basic cycle

Paprika adds both flavor and color to this wonderful, aromatic onion bread. Serve with cream cheese as an appetizer or toast slices of this bread on the grill and serve with hamburgers for a delightful change from buns. Liquid is provided by the diced onion; watch the dough and add more water if necessary to form a well-rounded ball of dough.

	Small	Medium	Large
water	½ cup	⅔ cup	¾ cup
butter or margarine	1 tbs.	1¼ tbs.	1½ tbs.
finely diced onion	¼ cup	¼+ cup	⅓ cup
sugar	½ tsp.	⅔ tsp.	¾ tsp.
salt	⅛ tsp.	⅛+ tsp.	¼ tsp.
paprika	⅔ tsp.	¾ tsp.	1 tsp.
bread flour	2 cups	2½ cups	3 cups
yeast	1 tsp.	1½ tsp.	2 tsp.

Herb Sally Lunn

Sweet or Basic cycle

This is a nice variation on a plain Sally Lunn. Oregano or rosemary can be used as well, if desired. Evaporated skim milk can be substituted for the cream if you're counting calories.

	Small	Medium	Large
heavy cream	½ cup	⅝ cup	¾ cup
milk	¼ cup	⅜ cup	⅓ cup
eggs	1	1½	2
butter or margarine	2 tbs.	2½ tbs.	3 tbs.
sugar	2 tbs.	2½ tbs.	3 tbs.
salt	½ tsp.	¾ tsp.	1 tsp.
basil, dried	1 tsp.	1¼ tsp.	1½ tsp.
bread flour	2 cups	2½ cups	3 cups
yeast	1 tsp.	1½ tsp.	2 tsp.

Dill Parsley Bread

Basic cycle

Heather Smith adapted this favorite recipe for her bread machine. Wonderful served with turkey or chicken.

	Small	Medium	Large
water	⅔ cup	¾ cup	1 cup
olive oil	¼ cup	¼+ cup	⅓ cup
sugar	½ tsp.	⅔ tsp.	¾ tsp.
salt	¼ tsp.	⅓ tsp.	½ tsp.
parsley, dried	1 tbs.	1⅓ tbs.	1½ tbs.
dill weed, dried	1 tbs.	1⅓ tbs.	1½ tbs.
dry milk powder	3 tbs.	¼ cup	5 tbs.
bread flour	2 cups	2½ cups	3 cups
yeast	1½ tsp.	2 tsp.	2½ tsp.

Scallion Sesame Bread

Basic cycle

Serve this interesting, Oriental-flavored bread with a curry chicken or similar meal. For a real twist, try adding raisins (¼, ⅓ or ½ cup). The loaf is low-rising with a heavy texture that cuts nicely.

	Small	Medium	Large
milk	¾ cup	1⅛ cups	1½ cups
sesame oil	½ tsp.	¾ tsp.	1 tsp.
scallions, chopped	¼ cup	⅓ cup	½ cup
brown sugar	¼ tsp.	⅓ tsp.	½ tsp.
sesame seeds	2 tsp.	1 tbs.	1⅓ tbs.
salt	⅛ tsp.	⅛+ tsp.	¼ tsp.
garlic powder	⅛ tsp.	⅛+ tsp.	¼ tsp.
whole wheat flour	1 cup	1½ cups	2 cups
bread flour	1 cup	1½ cups	2 cups
yeast	1 tsp.	1½ tsp.	2 tsp.

Sesame Onion Cheese Bread

Sweet or Basic cycle

This beautiful loaf has a nice hearty sesame flavor. I like using a sharp cheddar in this recipe.

	Small	Medium	Large
milk	2/3 cup	1 cup	1 1/3 cups
diced onion	1/4 cup	1/3 cup	1/2 cup
grated cheese	1/3 cup	1/2 cup	2/3 cup
butter or margarine	1 tbs.	1 1/2 tbs.	2 tbs.
sugar	1 tbs.	1 1/2 tbs.	2 tbs.
salt	1/3 tsp.	1/2 tsp.	2/3 tsp.
sesame seeds	2 tsp.	1 tbs.	1 1/3 tbs.
whole wheat flour	1 cup	1 1/2 cups	2 cups
bread flour	1 cup	1 1/2 cups	2 cups
yeast	1 tsp.	1 1/2 tsp.	2 tsp.

Turkey Stuffing Bread

Sweet or Basic cycle

Joan Garneau makes this bread just to stuff turkey with, or to serve as a dressing on the side with a turkey breast. The bread is a treat as is, too!

	Small	Medium	Large
water	2/3 cup	1 cup	1 1/3 cups
egg	1 small	1 large	2 small
butter or margarine	2 tbs.	3 tbs.	4 tbs.
diced onion	1/4 cup	1/3 cup	1/2 cup
brown or white sugar	1 1/2 tsp.	2 1/4 tsp.	1 tbs.
salt	1/3 tsp.	1/2 tsp.	2/3 tsp.
black pepper (coarse)	1/4 tsp.	1/3 tsp.	1/2 tsp.
sage, dried	2/3 tsp.	1 tsp.	1 1/3 tsp.
celery seeds	2/3 tsp.	1 tsp.	1 1/3 tsp.
poultry seasoning	1/2 tsp.	3/4 tsp.	1 tsp.
cornmeal	1/2 cup	2/3 cup	1 cup
bread flour	1 2/3 cups	2 1/2 cups	3 1/3 cups
yeast	1 tsp.	1 1/2 tsp.	2 tsp.

Favorite Fennel Bread

Sweet or Basic cycle

This light fluffy bread has a great flavor of fennel; adjust amounts to taste.

	Small	Medium	Large
milk or water	¾ cup	1 cup	1⅛ cups
butter or margarine	1 tbs.	1⅓ tbs.	1½ tbs.
sugar	1 tbs.	1⅓ tbs.	1½ tbs.
baking soda	¼ tsp.	⅓ tsp.	½ tsp.
salt	¼ tsp.	⅓ tsp.	½ tsp.
fennel seeds	1 tsp.	1½ tsp.	2 tsp.
bread flour	2 cups	2½ cups	3 cups
yeast	1 tsp.	1½ tsp.	2 tsp.

Italian Herb Bread

Sweet or Basic cycle

This light loaf is out of this world. For variation, substitute rosemary for basil.

	Small	Medium	Large
water	⅔ cup	1 cup	1⅓ cups
olive oil	1 tbs.	1½ tbs.	2 tbs.
sugar	2 tsp.	1 tbs.	1⅓ tbs.
salt	⅓ tsp.	½ tsp.	⅔ tsp.
basil, dried	½ tsp.	¾ tsp.	1 tsp.
golden or dark raisins	1-2 tbs.	1½-3 tbs.	2-4 tbs.
bread flour	1½ cups	2¼ cups	3 cups
yeast	1 tsp.	1½ tsp.	2 tsp.

Tomato Herb Bread

Sweet or Basic cycle

Carol Ashman of California developed this recipe. For those of us who don't have fresh herbs, substitute dried herbs (⅓ the amount listed). The tomato juice is the juice and seeds taken from fresh tomatoes; water can be added if necessary. If using canned tomato juice, delete salt from the recipe.

	Small	Medium	Large
tomato juice	¾ cup	1 cup	1⅛ cups
vegetable oil	1 tbs.	2⅔ tbs.	3 tbs.
sugar	1 tbs.	1⅓ tbs.	1½ tbs.
tarragon or basil, dried	1½ tbs.	2 tbs.	2⅓ tbs.
salt	½ tsp.	⅔ tsp.	¾ tsp.
bread flour	2 cups	2⅔ cups	3 cups
yeast	1 tsp.	1½ tsp.	2 tsp.

Pepperoni Bread

Ann Goss makes this bread for a friend who loves pizza. Good alone, or layer a slice of mozzarella cheese, pizza sauce and any other desired ingredients on top of a slice of this bread. Pop it under the broiler just to melt the cheese and heat. The pepperoni should have the skin removed and be ground or diced in a food processor and added at the beginning so that it is evenly distributed. Premixed Italian spices or oregano or basil can be added to taste if desired (½ to 2 tsp.)

	Small	Medium	Large
water or milk	¾ cup	1 ⅛ cups	1 ½ cups
olive oil or butter	1 tbs.	1 ½ tbs.	2 tbs.
pepperoni	3 oz.	4 ½ oz.	6 oz.
sugar	2 tbs.	3 tbs.	¼ cup
Italian spices, optional	to taste	to taste	to taste
salt	½ tsp.	¾ tsp.	1 tsp.
whole wheat flour	1 cup	1 ½ cups	2 cups
bread flour	1 cup	1 ½ cups	2 cups
yeast	1 ½ tsp.	2 tsp.	2 ½ tsp.

Golden Cheese Bread

This is out of this world, an absolute must-try. The combination of cheeses and spices is unbeatable. Four stars!

	Small	Medium	Large
buttermilk	⅔ cup	1 cup	1 ⅓ cups
butter or margarine	1 tbs.	1 ½ tbs.	2 tbs.
egg	1	1 ½	2
grated cheddar cheese	¼ cup	⅓ cup	½ cup
crumbled blue cheese	2 tbs.	3 tbs.	¼ cup
salt	¼ tsp.	⅓ tsp.	½ tsp.
coarse black pepper	⅛ tsp.	⅛+ tsp.	¼ tsp.
caraway seeds	1 tsp.	1 ½ tsp.	2 tsp.
wheat or oat flakes	½ cup	¾ cup	1 cup
bread flour	1 ½ cups	2 ¼ cups	3 cups
yeast	1 tsp.	1 ½ tsp.	2 tsp.

Maple Walnut Bread

Raisin, Sweet or Basic cycle

It is worth buying walnut oil to enjoy in this nutty tasting bread. Of course, any vegetable oil can be substituted, but will not have quite the flavor.

	Small	Medium	Large
water	¾ cup	1 ⅛ cups	1 ½ cups
walnut oil	1 tbs.	1 ½ tbs.	2 tbs.
maple syrup	2 tbs.	3 tbs.	¼ cup
cinnamon	⅛ tsp.	⅛+ tsp.	¼ tsp.
salt	¼ tsp.	⅓ tsp.	½ tsp.
whole wheat	1 cup	1 ½ cups	2 cups
bread flour	1 cup	1 ½ cups	2 cups
yeast	1 tsp.	1 ½ tsp.	2 tsp.
*chopped walnuts	⅓ cup	½ cup	⅔ cup

*Add ingredients at the beginning of the second kneading period.

Wheat Rye Nut Bread

Raisin, Sweet or Whole Wheat cycle

Use hazelnuts or Brazil nuts to give this a distinctive flavor. If using walnuts, try using walnut oil; otherwise, your normal vegetable oil will do.

	Small	Medium	Large
milk or water	¾ cup	1 ⅛ cups	1 ½ cups
vegetable oil	1 tbs.	1 ½ tbs.	2 tbs.
honey	1 tbs.	1 ½ tbs.	2 tbs.
salt	⅓ tsp.	½ tsp.	⅔ tsp.
whole wheat flour	¾ cup	1 ⅛ cups	1 ½ cups
rye flour	½ cup	¾ cup	1 cup
vital gluten, optional	1 ½ tbs.	2 ⅓ tbs.	3 tbs.
bread flour	¾ cup	1 ⅛ cups	1 ½ cups
yeast	1 ½ tsp.	2 tsp.	2 ½ tsp.
*chopped nuts	¼ cup	⅓ cup	½ cup

*Add ingredients at the beginning of the second kneading period.

Wheat Nut Raisin Bread

Raisin, Sweet or Basic cycle

This nutty wheat bread is great toasted for breakfast or a snack, with butter and jam or cream cheese and fruit.

	Small	Medium	Large
water	¾ cup	1 ⅛ cups	1 ½ cups
walnut oil	2 tbs.	3 tbs.	¼ cup
molasses	2 tbs.	3 tbs.	¼ cup
brown sugar	1 tbs.	1 ⅓ tbs.	2 tbs.
salt	¼ tsp.	⅓ tsp.	½ tsp.
whole wheat flour	2 cups	3 cups	4 cups
vital gluten, optional	1-2 tbs.	1 ½-3 tbs.	2-4 tbs.
yeast	1 ½ tsp.	2 tsp.	2 ½ tsp.
*raisins	¼ cup	⅓ cup	½ cup
*chopped walnuts	¼ cup	⅓ cup	½ cup

*Add ingredients at the beginning of the second kneading period.

Almond Poppy Seed Bread

Raisin, Sweet or Basic cycle

A must-try! Four stars! This one is worth making for the aroma alone. It's an outstanding bread for dessert or brunch.

	Small	Medium	Large
buttermilk	¾ cup	⅞ cup	1 ⅛ cups
butter or margarine	3 tbs.	3 ½ tbs.	4 tbs.
almond extract	1 tbs.	1 ⅓ tbs.	1 ½ tbs.
brown sugar	1 ⅓ tbs.	1 ½ tbs.	2 tbs.
salt	¼ tsp.	⅓ tsp.	½ tsp.
poppy seeds	1 tbs.	1 ⅓ tbs.	1 ½ tbs.
baking soda	¼ tsp.	⅓ tsp.	½ tsp.
bread flour	2 cups	2 ½ cups	3 cups
yeast	1 tsp.	1 ½ tsp.	2 tsp.
*chopped almonds	⅓ cup	½ cup	⅔ cup

*Add ingredients at the beginning of the second kneading period.

Orange Pistachio Bread

Raisin, Sweet or Basic cycle

Here is a wonderful combination of flavors. Serve toasted with pistachio ice cream. It's a medium-rising loaf of bread.

	Small	Medium	Large
orange juice concentrate	2 tbs.	3 tbs.	1/4 cup
orange segments	2/3 cup	1 cup	1 1/3 cups
butter or margarine	2 tbs.	3 tbs.	4 tbs.
grated orange peel	1/4 tsp.	1/3 tsp.	1/2 tsp.
salt	1/8 tsp.	1/8+ tsp.	1/4 tsp.
whole wheat flour	1 cup	1 1/2 cups	2 cups
bread flour	1 cup	1 1/2 cups	2 cups
yeast	1 tsp.	1 1/2 tsp.	2 tsp.
*chopped pistachios	1/3 cup	1/2 cup	2/3 cup

*Add ingredients at the beginning of the second kneading period.

Apple Date Nut Bread

Raisin, Sweet or Basic cycle

Not only a very aromatic bread, this also has lots of rich flavor. If fresh apples are unavailable, dried apples can be substituted; adjust milk or water if necessary. A great breakfast bread.

	Small	Medium	Large
milk or water	2/3 cup	1 cup	1 1/3 cups
apple juice concentrate	2 tbs.	3 tbs.	1/4 cup
applesauce	1 tbs.	1 1/2 tbs.	2 tbs.
salt	1/4 tsp.	1/3 tsp.	1/2 tsp.
cinnamon	1/4 tsp.	1/3 tsp.	1/2 tsp.
whole wheat flour	1 cup	1 1/2 cups	2 cups
bread flour	1 cup	1 1/2 cups	2 cups
yeast	1 tsp.	1 1/2 tsp.	2 tsp.
*diced, peeled apple	1/4 cup	1/3 cup	1/2 cup
*chopped dates	2-3 tbs.	1/4 cup	1/3 cup
*chopped nuts	1/4 cup	1/3 cup	1/2 cup

*Add ingredients at the beginning of the second kneading period.

White Chocolate Bread

This is a wonderful dessert bread. The chips and or or nuts may be adjusted to taste. Coconut or vanilla extract can be substituted for the almond extract if desired.

	Small	Medium	Large
milk	½ cup	⅝ cup	¾ cup
egg	1	1	1½
butter or margarine	2 tbs.	2½ tbs.	3 tbs.
almond extract	1 tsp.	1¼ tsp.	1½ tsp.
salt	¼ tsp.	⅓ tsp.	½ tsp.
sugar	2 tbs.	2½ tbs.	3 tbs.
bread flour	2 cups	2½ cups	3 cups
yeast	1 tsp.	1½ tsp.	2 tsp.
*white chocolate chips	¼ cup	⅓ cup	½ cup
*chopped nuts	¼ cup	⅓ cup	½ cup

*Add ingredients at the beginning of the second kneading period.

Poulsbo Bread

Gaye Levy shares this recipe for Poulsbo bread. This bread, originally developed based on Biblical references to bread, has put Poulsbo, Washington on the map. This is a must-try — one of the best!

	Small	Medium	Large
water	¾ cup	1⅛ cups	1½ cups
margarine or oil	1 tbs.	1½ tbs.	2 tbs.
molasses	1⅓ tbs.	2 tbs.	2⅔ tbs.
sugar	1⅓ tbs.	2 tbs.	2⅔ tbs.
salt	½ tsp.	¾ tsp.	1 tsp.
powdered buttermilk	1 tbs.	1½ tbs.	2 tbs.
7-grain cereal	½ cup	¾ cup	1 cup
whole wheat flour	¼ cup	⅓ cup	½ cup
bread flour	1½ cups	2¼ cups	3 cups
yeast	1 tsp.	1½ tsp.	2 tsp.
*sunflower seeds	⅓ cup	½ cup	⅔ cup

*Add ingredients at the beginning of the second kneading period.

Pecan Gouda Bread

Raisin, Sweet or Basic cycle

A devoted fan of bread machines, Wendy Ceracche has been cooking up a storm with her Panasonic for many years now. I know you'll enjoy this. Walnuts can be substituted for the pecans.

	Small	Medium	Large
water or milk	½ cup	¾ cup	1 cup
margarine or butter	1½ tsp.	2¼ tsp.	1 tbs.
grated Gouda cheese	⅓ cup	½ cup	⅔ cup
sugar	1½ tsp.	2¼ tsp.	1 tbs.
salt	¼ tsp.	⅓ tsp.	½ tsp.
bread flour	1½ cups	2¼ cups	3 cups
yeast	1 tsp.	1½ tsp.	2 tsp.
*chopped pecans	¼ cup	⅓ cup	½ cup

*Add ingredients at the beginning of the second kneading period.

Mexican Date Pecan Bread

Raisin, Sweet or Basic cycle

This is a scrumptious sweet bread. Serve with amaretto coffee and whipped cream for a special treat. It also makes great toast or French toast.

	Small	Medium	Large
milk	⅔ cup	¾ cup	1 cup
butter or margarine	1 tbs.	1½ tbs.	2 tbs.
salt	¼ tsp.	⅓ tsp.	½ tsp.
sugar (white)	2 tbs.	2½ tbs.	3 tbs.
cinnamon	½ tsp.	⅔ tsp.	¾ tsp.
nutmeg	⅛ tsp.	⅛+ tsp.	¼ tsp.
bread flour	2 cups	2½ cups	3 cups
yeast	1 tsp.	1½ tsp.	2 tsp.
*chopped dates	⅓ cup	⅓+ cup	½ cup
*chopped pecans	¼ cup	⅓ cup	⅓+ cup

*Add ingredients at the beginning of the second kneading period.

Black Walnut Bread

Raisin, Sweet or Basic cycle

Black walnuts are richer and more flavorful than the English walnuts. This bread takes full advantage of the distinctive black walnut taste.

	Small	Medium	Large
buttermilk	¾ cup	scant 1 cup	1⅛ cups
walnut oil	1 tbs.	1⅓ tbs.	1½ tbs.
honey	2 tbs.	2½ tbs.	3 tbs.
salt	¼ tsp.	⅓ tsp.	½ tsp.
baking soda	¼ tsp.	¼+ tsp.	⅓ tsp.
coconut flakes	¼ cup	¼+ cup	⅓ cup
oats	½ cup	⅝ cup	¾ cup
bread flour	1½ cups	1⅞ cups	2¼ cups
yeast	1 tsp.	1½ tsp.	2 tsp.
*chopped black walnuts	⅓ cup	½ cup	⅔ cup

*Add ingredients at the beginning of the second kneading period.

Macadamia Nut Bread

Raisin, Sweet or Basic cycle

This is a must-try — a delicious sweet bread which is great toasted for breakfast or brunch, or served with dessert.

	Small	Medium	Large
buttermilk	¾ cup	1⅛ cups	1½ cups
butter or margarine	1 tbs.	1½ tbs.	2 tbs.
maple or brown sugar	2 tbs.	3 tbs.	¼ cup
salt	⅓ tsp.	½ tsp.	⅔ tsp.
baking soda	¼ tsp.	⅓ tsp.	½ tsp.
ground ginger	¼ tsp.	⅓ tsp.	½ tsp.
oats	½ cup	¾ cup	1 cup
coconut flakes	¼ cup	⅓ cup	½ cup
bread flour	1½ cups	2¼ cups	3 cups
yeast	1 tsp.	1½ tsp.	2 tsp.
*chopped macadamias	⅓ cup	½ cup	⅔ cup

*Add ingredients at the beginning of the second kneading period.

Sunflower Honey Bread

Sweet or Basic cycle

Heather Smith of Southern California adapted this recipe and receives rave reviews. The sunflower seeds, in this case, replace some of the flour. If you have sunflower oil, use it as the vegetable oil for extra flavoring. The salt can be halved if desired.

	Small	**Medium**	**Large**
milk or water	⅔ cup	1 cups	1⅓ cups
vegetable oil	1⅓ tbs.	2 tbs.	2⅔ tbs.
honey	1⅓ tbs.	2 tbs.	2⅔ tbs.
salt	⅔ tsp.	1 tsp.	1⅓ tsp.
whole wheat flour	½ cup	¾ cup	1 cup
sunflower seeds	¼ cup	⅓ cup	½ cup
bread flour	1 cup	1½ cups	2 cups
yeast	1 tsp.	1½ tsp.	2 tsp.

Cherry Nut Bread

Raisin, Sweet or Basic cycle

This colorful loaf really picks up the flavor of the cherries. Dried cherries are available in large groceries, through gourmet shops and mail order catalogs

	Small	**Medium**	**Large**
milk	¾ cup	1⅛ cups	1½ cups
vegetable oil	1 tbs.	1½ tbs.	2 tbs.
honey	2 tbs.	3 tbs.	¼ cup
salt	⅓ tsp.	½ tsp.	⅔ tsp.
oats	½ cup	¾ cup	1 cup
bread flour	1½ cups	2¼ cups	3 cups
yeast	1 tsp.	1½ tsp.	2 tsp.
*dried cherries	⅓ cup	½ cup	⅔ cup
*chopped nuts	¼ cup	⅓ cup	½ cup

*Add ingredients at the beginning of the second kneading period.

Orange Nut Bread

Raisin or Sweet cycle

This is one of our favorite combinations. Use your favorite nuts — I like Brazil nuts with this bread. Of course, the bread is also delicious without the nuts. For variation, substitute raisins or dried cranberries for the nuts.

	Small	**Medium**	**Large**
buttermilk	¾ cup	1⅛ cups	1½ cups
orange juice concentrate	2 tbs.	3 tbs.	4 tbs.
honey	2 tbs.	3 tbs.	4 tbs.
salt	⅓ tsp.	½ tsp.	⅔ tsp.
baking soda	¼-½ tsp.	⅓-¾ tsp.	½-1 tsp.
oats	½ cup	¾ cup	1 cup
bread flour	1½ cups	2¼ cups	3 cups
yeast	1 tsp.	1½ tsp.	2 tsp.
*chopped nuts	⅓ cup	½ cup	⅔ cup

*Add ingredients at the beginning of the second kneading period.

White Chocolate Macadamia Bread

Raisin, Sweet or Basic cycle

The result of many requests, this has become a favorite in our house. If macadamia nuts are unavailable or too expensive, almonds can also be used.

	Small	**Medium**	**Large**
milk	½ cup	⅔ cup	¾ cup
white chocolate chips	¼ cup	⅓ cup	½ cup
egg	1	1½	1½
butter or margarine	2 tbs.	2½ tbs.	3 tbs.
almond extract	1 tsp.	1¼ tsp.	1½ tsp.
sugar	2 tbs.	2½ tbs.	3 tbs.
salt	¼ tsp.	⅓ tsp.	½ tsp.
bread flour	2 cups	2½ cups	3 cups
yeast	1 tsp.	1½ tsp.	2 tsp.
*chopped macadamias	⅓ cup	½ cup	⅔ cup

*Add ingredients at the beginning of the second kneading period.

Creamed Cinnamon Raisin Nut Bread

Raisin, Sweet or Basic cycle

This is a wonderful raisin nut bread. Top with confectioners' sugar for a major hit in your house. If watching calories, evaporated skim milk can be substituted for the whipping cream.

	Small	Medium	Large
whipping cream	¾ cup	1⅛ cups	1½ cups
butter or margarine	2 tbs.	3 tbs.	4 tbs.
egg	1	1½	2
sugar	2 tsp.	1 tbs.	1⅓ tbs.
cinnamon	½ tsp.	¾ tsp.	1 tsp.
salt	¼ tsp.	⅓ tsp.	½ tsp.
whole wheat flour	1 cup	1½ cups	2 cups
bread flour	1 cup	1½ cups	2 cups
yeast	1 tsp.	1½ tsp.	2 tsp.
*raisins	¼ cup	⅓ cup	½ cup
*nuts, chopped	3 tbs.	4½ tbs.	6 tbs.

*Add ingredients at the beginning of the second kneading period.

Coconut Chocolate Bread

Raisin, Sweet or Basic cycle

This is so yummy! Chips may become ground up depending on which machine you have, but either way it is equally delicious. Eat it as a dessert, snack or for breakfast or brunch. You can substitute walnuts or pecans for macadamias.

	Small	Medium	Large
water	⅔ cup	⅞ cup	1 cup
vegetable oil	2 tsp.	1 tbs.	1⅓ tbs.
coconut extract	2 tsp.	1 tbs.	1⅓ tbs.
salt	⅛-¼ tsp.	⅛+⅓ tsp.	¼-½ tsp.
coconut flakes	⅓ cup	½ cup	⅔ cup
bread flour	2 cups	2½ cups	3 cups
yeast	1 tsp.	1½ tsp.	2 tsp.
*chocolate chips	⅓ cup	½ cup	⅔ cup
*chopped macadamias	¼ cup	⅓ cup	½ cup

*Add ingredients at the beginning of the second kneading period.

About Rolls and Coffeecakes

One of the joys of owning a bread machine is the ability to make delicious yeasted coffeecakes or rolls with relatively little effort. The machine does the initial kneading (the hardest part) and allows the dough to rise for the first time. Once the dough is removed from the machine, it can be filled and shaped and allowed to rise a second time prior to baking in a conventional oven.

This chapter has several sweet and non-sweet dough recipes which can be used with fillings found on pages 216–218. You can pick and choose both the dough and the filling you want and follow any of the suggested shaping and baking guidelines to achieve your desired coffeecake or rolls. All dough recipes are made using the basic dough cycle. Various washes, which are brushed on the loaves or rolls just prior to baking, are also provided as suggestions. If you have DAK or Welbilt ABM 100, turn the machine off after approximately 1 hour and remove the dough.

If the dough is too sticky to roll, simply add flour a little at a time until it can be handled. Don't overflour. Remember that ovens vary and that cooking times may also vary. As with any baking, keep an eye on the oven to avoid burning.

Shaping and Baking Guidelines

Crescents: Remove dough from machine and roll into 1 or 2 circles. Brush with melted butter or a very thin filling and cut circles into 8 pieces. Roll each piece, starting from thick end, into the center, forming a crescent shape. Brush top with any remaining butter. Place on a greased baking sheet, cover and let rise for approximately 30 minutes. Bake in a preheated 325° oven for about 20 minutes or until golden brown.

Coffeecake Rolls: Punch down dough and divide in half if making the medium or large recipe. On a lightly floured surface, roll the dough into a rectangle and spread with filling ingredients. Jelly-roll starting at the wide end, pinch the ends and cut into rolls. Place in 1 or 2 greased 9-inch round or square cake pans. An alternative is to place each roll in a greased muffin tin. Cover and let rise in a warm, draft-free location approximately 1 hour. Brush with wash if desired and bake in a preheated 350° oven for 20 to 25 minutes.

Monkey Bread (Pull-Apart): Remove dough from machine and separate into as many 1- to 1½-inch balls as you can. Roll the balls in melted butter and then a coating such as finely chopped nuts, grated Parmesan cheese or even herbs. Place the balls in a greased loaf pan, tube pan or holiday-shaped pan (such as a Christmas tree), cover and let rise for approximately 1 hour. Brush with wash if desired, and bake in a preheated 350° oven for 30 to 40 minutes or until golden brown.

Wreath: Remove the dough from the machine. Roll the dough into 1 or 2 rectangles and spread filling (if applicable) on top. Roll in a jelly-roll fashion starting at the wide end. Form this into 1 or 2 circles, pinching the seam closed. With scissors, cut at ⅔- to 1-inch intervals and turn cut sections up. Place on a greased baking sheet, cover and let rise for approximately 45 minutes. Brush with wash if desired and bake in a preheated 350° oven for 30 to 40 minutes or until golden brown.

Jelly Roll: Remove dough from machine and roll into 1 or 2 rectangles. Spread filling evenly on top. Roll in a jelly-roll fashion starting at the wide end. Pinch seams closed. Place seam side down on a greased baking sheet or in a greased bread pan (or 2), cover and let rise about 30 to 45 minutes. Brush with wash if desired and bake in a preheated 350° oven for approximately 30 to 40 minutes or until golden and it sounds hollow when tapped.

Stromboli Roll: Remove dough from machine and roll into 1 or 2 rectangles. Spread filling mixture on top of middle third of rectangle and fold each side over top of filling so that it is encased. Pinch ends closed and place fold side down on a well greased baking sheet. Brush top with wash if desired. Bake in a preheated 350° for 20 to 30 minutes or until golden brown.

Pizza: One trick to a thin, crispy pizza crust is rolling the dough as thin as you can. Trim it to fit your pan. Using a pizza stone or a pizza pan with holes in the bottom will result in a crispier crust. If desired, the leftover dough may be used to make bread sticks.

Remove the dough from the machine and roll into a circle or rectangle depending on what pan you are using. Place on your greased or cornmeal covered pan and top as desired. Do not let rise a second time. There are two thoughts on baking pizza. The first is to put it into a cold oven and turn the oven on to 500°; bake until golden brown and cheese is melted. The second is to bake on a pizza stone or the bottom (not the rack) of a preheated 500° oven until the pizza is golden brown and cheese is melted. This could range from 10 to 30 minutes depending on which method you use.

A tip: I keep pizza dough in a plastic bag in the refrigerator and use as needed. It makes for a quick throw-together meal with spaghetti sauce or pizza sauce and grated cheese. The dough lasts for several days this way. I just remove it and roll it out while it is still cold.

English Muffins: Remove dough from machine upon its completion. Roll or press the dough so that it is approximately ⅓- to ½-inch thick on a greased and cornmeal- covered baking sheet. Cut into circles of approximately 3 inches in diameter, using a biscuit or cookie cutter, removing excess dough. (A tuna fish-size can would be perfect as well!) Leave the dough as is, cover and place in a warm, draft-free location for approximately 1 to 2 hours. Sprinkle with more cornmeal if desired and then cook the muffins in a lightly greased frying pan or griddle for 5 to 7 minutes on each side until both sides are golden brown. Be sure not to burn. Allow to cool on a wire rack.

French Bread: Remove dough from machine and roll on a cornmeal-covered surface into one or two rectangles. Jelly-roll the rectangles, starting at a wide end; pinch ends closed. Place the loaves on a greased baking sheet which has been sprinkled with cornmeal to prevent sticking. (I use a pizza pan with holes in the bottom which makes the crust crustier.) Cover and let rise in a warm location for 40 to 50 minutes.

Slash the dough 5 or 6 times with a sharp knife or razor blade and brush with cold water. Bake in a preheated 400° oven for 15 minutes, lower temperature to 350° and bake for 5 to 10 minutes or until golden brown and bread sounds hollow when tapped.

Coconut Sweet Dough

Dough Cycle

Try this with the following fillings: Orange Coconut, page 217, and Orange, page 216.

	Small	Medium	Large
buttermilk	⅔ cup	1 cup	1 ⅓ cups
butter or margarine	1 tbs.	1 ½ tbs.	2 tbs.
egg	1	1 ½	2
sugar	2 tbs.	3 tbs.	¼ cup
baking soda	¼ tsp.	⅓ tsp.	½ tsp.
salt	⅓ tsp.	½ tsp.	⅔ tsp.
coconut flakes	½ cup	¾ cup	1 cup
bread flour	2 cups	3 cups	4 cups
yeast	1 tsp.	1 ½ tsp.	2 tsp.
wash with:			
melted butter	1 tbs.	1 ½ tbs.	2 tbs.
coconut extract	¼ tsp.	⅓ tsp.	½ tsp.

Orange Sweet Dough

Dough Cycle

Try this dough with Orange Coconut filling, page 217, Praline Rolling Filling, page 217 or Orange Filling, page 216.

	Small	Medium	Large
milk	½ cup	¾ cup	1 cup
butter or margarine	2 tbs.	3 tbs.	4 tbs.
orange extract	½ tsp.	¾ tsp.	1 tsp.
egg	1	1 ½	2
orange peel	⅛ tsp.	⅛+ tsp.	¼ tsp.
sugar	2 tbs.	3 tbs.	4 tbs.
salt	¼ tsp.	⅓ tsp.	½ tsp.
bread flour	2 cups	3 cups	4 cups
yeast	1 tsp.	1 ½ tsp.	2 tsp.

Sourdough Dough

Dough Cycle

Say this ten times really fast! This basic dough goes well with anything and everything.

	Small	Medium	Large
starter	½ cup	¾ cup	1 cup
milk or water	½ cup	¾ cup	1 cup
olive oil	2 tsp.	1 tbs.	1 ⅓ tbs.
sugar	⅔ tsp.	1 tsp.	1 ⅓ tsp.
salt	¼ tsp.	⅓ tsp.	½ tsp.
bread flour	2 cups	3 cups	4 cups
yeast	1 tsp.	1 ½ tsp.	2 tsp.

Buttermilk Dough

This dough goes nicely with everything from pizza to sweets.

	Small	Medium	Large
buttermilk	¾ cup	1 ⅛ cups	1 ½ cups
white or brown sugar	1 tsp.	1 ½ tsp.	2 tsp.
salt	¼ tsp.	⅓ tsp.	½ tsp.
baking soda	¼ tsp.	⅓ tsp.	½ tsp.
bread flour	2 cups	3 cups	4 cups
yeast	1 tsp.	1 ½ tsp.	2 tsp.

Lemon Dough

Use Spinach Filling, page 218, for a delicious meal.

	Small	Medium	Large
water	⅔ cup	1 cup	1 ⅓ cups
lemon juice	1 ½ tsp.	2 ¼ tsp.	1 tbs.
olive oil	1 ½ tsp.	2 ¼ tsp.	1 tbs.
sugar	1 tsp.	1 ½ tsp.	2 tsp.
salt	dash	⅛ tsp.	⅛+ tsp.
bread flour	2 cups	3 cups	4 cups
yeast	1 tsp.	1 ½ tsp.	2 tsp.

Apple Dough

Fill this with Sausage Filling, page 218, for an absolutely unbeatable combination. You must try this one. Watch the dough about 5 minutes into the kneading. If it looks too dry (balls or crumbly), add apple juice 1 tbs. at a time until one nice round ball is formed.

	Small	Medium	Large
apple juice	⅔ cup	1 cup	1 ⅓ cups
olive oil	1 tbs.	1 ½ tbs.	2 tbs.
honey	1 tbs.	1 ½ tbs.	2 tbs.
salt	¼ tsp.	⅓ tsp.	½ tsp.
rosemary, dried	½ tsp.	¾ tsp.	1 tsp.
whole wheat flour	1 cup	1 ½ cups	2 cups
bread flour	1 cup	1 ½ cups	2 cups
yeast	1 tsp.	1 ½ tsp.	2 tsp.

Spinach Dough

Cook and drain the spinach and use all-purpose or bread flour. Suggested fillings: spinach or cheese. This dough can also be used for a different and unique pizza dough with the cheese filling used as a topping instead of the more familiar tomato topping.

	Small	**Medium**	**Large**
water	½ cup	¾ cup	1 cup
spinach	½ cup	¾ cup	1 cup
lemon juice	2 tsp.	1 tbs.	1⅓ tbs.
olive oil	2 tsp.	1 tbs.	1⅓ tbs.
sugar	1 tsp.	1½ tsp.	2 tsp.
salt	¼ tsp.	⅓ tsp.	½ tsp.
bread flour	2 cups	3 cups	4 cups
yeast	1 tsp.	1½ tsp.	2 tsp.

Sweet Yeast Dough

Sandra Farace says she uses this recipe for everything from a stollen to cinnamon or caramel rolls. Sandra has been baking yeast breads for 23 years and does not use a bread machine. I have adapted her recipe for the machines.

	Small	**Medium**	**Large**
heavy cream	½ cup	¾ cup	1 cup
evaporated milk	2 tbs.	3 tbs.	¼ cup
egg yolks	1	2	3
butter or margarine	4 tbs.	6 tbs.	8 tbs.
sugar (white)	2 tbs.	3 tbs.	¼ cup
salt	½ tsp.	¾ tsp.	1 tsp.
cinnamon	½ tsp.	¾ tsp.	1 tsp.
nutmeg	½ tsp.	¾ tsp.	1 tsp.
bread flour	1⅔ cups	2½ cups	3⅓ cups
yeast	1 tsp.	1½ tsp.	2 tsp.

Fructose Cinnamon Rolls

Dough Cycle

Andrea Hebert-Donatelli adapts recipes to use fructose instead of sugar. This is one of her family's favorite recipes. Follow directions for coffeecake rolls, page 198. Pour cream (room temperature) on top before baking to glaze.

	Small	Medium	Large
milk	½ cup	¾ cup	1 cup
egg(s)	1	1½	2
butter or margarine	2 tbs.	3 tbs.	4 tbs.
salt	⅓ tsp.	½ tsp.	¾ tsp.
fructose	2½ tbs.	¼ cup	⅓ cup
all-purpose flour	1¾ cups	2⅔ cups	3½ cups
yeast	1 tsp.	1½ tsp.	2 tsp.
Filling			
butter, softened	2 tbs.	3 tbs.	4 tbs.
raisins	¼ cup	⅓ cup	½ cup
fructose	2 tbs.	3 tbs.	¼ cup
cinnamon	1 tsp.	1½ tsp.	2 tsp.
whipping cream	½, cup	¾ cup	1 cup

Pizza Dough

Dough Cycle

This is our current pizza dough recipe — we are always looking for new ones. Whole wheat or any other flour may be substituted for half or all of the bread flour. If using flours such as amaranth or quinoa for their high nutritional content, start off using only a small portion (¼-⅓ total amount) and adjust to taste. Follow directions for pizza, page 199, or fill following directions for stromboli or jelly roll.

	Small	Medium	Large
water	⅔ cup	1 cup	1⅓ cups
olive oil	2 tbs.	3 tbs.	¼ cup
salt	¼ tsp.	⅓ tsp.	½ tsp.
sugar	½ tsp.	¾ tsp.	1 tsp.
bread flour	2 cups	3 cups	4 cups
yeast	1 tsp.	1½ tsp.	2 tsp.

Butter Crescents

This sweet, buttery dough can be used as a basis for any coffeecake or sweet rolls. This recipe can also be baked in your bread machine for a delicious, sweet bread. Be sure to use the sweet cycle if applicable and not to overfill the size of your machine as it's a high-rising loaf. Follow directions for crescents, page 198.

	Small	Medium	Large
milk	½ cup	¾ cup	1 cup
butter	4 tbs.	6 tbs.	8 tbs.
egg	1	1½	2
sugar	¼ cup	⅓ cup	½ cup
salt	¼ tsp.	⅓ tsp.	½ tsp.
all-purpose flour	2 cups	3 cups	4 cups
yeast	1 tsp.	1½ tsp.	2 tsp.
Filling			
melted butter	1 tbs.	1½ tbs.	2 tbs.

Chocolate Cream Cheese Rolls

A tester of recipes, Debbie Nicholson developed this recipe to cover two of her favorite foods, cream cheese and chocolate. Follow directions for jelly roll or stromboli, page 199. Beat the cream cheese and confectioners' sugar together; spread this on top of dough and layer chocolate chips and nuts on top of that.

	Small	Medium	Large
milk	½ cup	¾ cup	1 cup
cream cheese	¼ cup	⅜ cup	½ cup
sugar	2 tbs.	3 tbs.	¼ cup
eggs	1	1½	2
salt	⅓ tsp.	½ tsp.	⅔ tsp.
bread flour	2 cups	3 cups	4 cups
yeast	1 tsp.	1½ tsp.	2 tsp.
Filling			
cream cheese	4 oz.	6 oz.	8 oz.
confectioners' sugar	½ cup	¾ cup	1 cup
chocolate chips	¼ cup	⅓ cup	½ cup
chopped nuts, optional	½ cup	¾ cup	1 cup

Traditional French Bread

Dough Cycle

Combine the ease of making the dough in the machine with the tradition-al French bread shape for a true winner. For an extra crisp loaf, put a pan of water on the bottom rack of the oven during baking. Another trick is to use a ceramic or clay pizza or baking stone for an extra crisp crust.

	Small	**Medium**	**Large**
water	¾ cup	1 cup	1⅛ cups
sugar	⅓ tsp.	½ tsp.	⅔ tsp.
salt	⅔ tsp.	1 tsp.	1⅓ tsp.
bread flour	⅔ cup	¾ cup	1 cup
cake flour	1⅓ cups	1½ cups	2 cups
yeast	1½ tsp.	2 tsp.	2½ tsp.
cornmeal for shaping			

Allow the dough to rise in the machine for at least 1½ hours — even if the machine has stopped. Punch down the dough while it is still in the pan in the machine and allow it to rise in the turned off but still warm machine or other warm, draft-free location for 30 to 40 minutes. See page 200 for shaping and baking guidelines.

English Muffins 1

Dough Cycle

Perhaps the only purchased bread which I have actually missed (but still refuse to buy) are English muffins. After years of thinking it looked too difficult to figure out, I finally attempted it — to rave reviews. These have now become an easy staple in our household. If farina is not on hand, Cream of Wheat can be used instead. See shaping and baking guidelines, page 199.

	Small (10)	**Medium (15)**	**Large (20)**
milk	¾ cup	1⅛ cups	1½ cups
corn syrup	1 tbs.	1½ tbs.	2 tbs.
salt	⅓ tsp.	½ tsp.	⅔ tsp.
farina	¼ cup	⅓ cup	½ cup
all-purpose flour	1¾ cups	2⅔ cups	3½ cups
yeast	1 tsp.	1½ tsp.	2 tsp.

English Muffins 11

I really like playing around with this recipe, using orange juice with a little orange peel, apple juice with raisins added, using half whole wheat — the variations are unlimited! For instance, use buttermilk in place of the milk or water and add baking soda, 1/4 tsp. 1/3 tsp. 1/2 tsp. See shaping and baking guidelines, page 199.

	Small (10)	Medium (15)	Large (20)
milk or water	3/4 cup	1 1/8 cups	1 1/2 cups
butter or margarine	1 tbs.	1 1/2 tbs.	2 tbs.
sugar	2 tsp.	1 tbs.	1 1/3 tbs.
salt	1/3 tsp.	1/2 tsp.	2/3 tsp.
all-purpose flour	2 cups	3 cups	4 cups
yeast	1 tsp.	1 1/2 tsp.	2 tsp.

Egg Pasta Dough

Andy Hebert-Donatelli became frustrated when her husband no longer had the time to make their pasta dough. Not liking the way it turned out in her Kitchen Aid, she decided to try the bread machine. Low and behold, she says it's perfect.

Servings:	**3-4**	**5-6**	**7-8**
eggs	3	4	6
all-purpose flour	2 1/4 cups	3 cups	4 1/2 cups

Put flour in the pan and crack the eggs into the center of the flour. Start the machine and check to make sure it isn't working too hard. If so, add a tablespoon of cold water at a time until it is kneading without trouble. (She usually does not have to do this.) Remove the dough as soon as the kneading has stopped. Check the dough before rolling by inserting a finger into the center; if it comes out almost dry, then it is ready to use. Take small pieces of dough at a time and roll it to the thickness of the noodle you want and slice it lengthwise. Flour the noodles and set them aside. You can hang them on a drying rack, but Andy uses hers right away. To cook fresh noodles, bring to a boil 2/3 large pan of salted water. Add pasta and bring water back to a boil, cooking uncovered for 5 to 20 seconds after the water returns to a boil. DO NOT OVERCOOK PASTA! If your pasta is more than a day old, it requires longer cooking.

Naan

Dough Cycle

This flatbread from India makes a great alternative to bagels. While the traditional naan has onions, try substituting lemon or orange peel, anise or fennel.

	2	**3**	**4**
water	¼ cup	⅓ cup	½ cup
yogurt (plain)	½ cup	¾ cup	1 cup
butter	1½ tbs.	2 tbs.	3 tbs.
sugar	1 tsp.	1½ tsp.	2 tsp.
salt	⅛ tsp.	⅛+ tsp.	¼ tsp.
all-purpose flour	2 cups	3 cups	4 cups
yeast	1 tsp.	1½ tsp.	2 tsp.
Topping			
melted butter	1 tbs.	1½ tbs.	2 tbs.
onion, finely diced	1-2 tbs.	1½-3 tbs.	3-4 tbs.

Upon removing dough from machine, divide into the appropriate number of pieces. Roll each piece into a small 7- to 8-inch circle and place on a greased pizza or baking pan. Brush tops with melted butter; press onion slivers into the dough. Bake in a preheated 500° oven for 10 to 15 minutes until puffy and brown.

About Toppings and Fillings

Toppings can be served along with individual slices of bread, much as you would butter and/or jelly or jam.

Glazes are used as a type of frosting, covering an entire loaf of bread. Cover the loaf while it is still warm and allow the glaze to dry.

Washes are brushed onto the loaves or rolls just prior to baking as a finishing touch. Any of the following may be used. If using a wash, be sure to cover the entire top — don't miss a section or it will bake a different color.

Butter wash - Use melted butter with or without an extract mixed in. I like using extract (¼ tsp. of extract for every 1 tbs. butter) to pick up the flavor of the bread. For example, if the bread has almonds in it, I'll add ¼ tsp. almond extract to 1 tbs. melted butter.

Egg wash - Many people use a beaten egg, either whole or egg white only.

Cold water wash - A few tablespoons of cold water are effective in achieving a crispy crust. A pinch of salt may be added if desired although I do not feel it necessary.

Seeds and nuts with washes - Once a wash has been used (usually the egg or water), sprinkle a tablespoon or two of any of the following seeds or very finely ground nuts evenly over the top as an additional treat. Try anise, caraway, celery, coriander, dill, fennel, poppy or sesame seeds; or even a coarse sea salt may also be used. Consider the flavor of the bread and make sure that the tastes will blend. Using seeds and nuts with washes for loaves baked in the machine is possible too! Just open the lid towards the end of the second rising and sprinkle the desired seeds or nuts on top of the loaf. Try not to spill them down the side of the pan.

Fillings are used for coffeecake breads. Select your filling to match the dough. For example, make coffeecake rolls with a sweet dough and corresponding sweet filling. Recipes created specifically for fillings are provided in three amounts which correspond to the doughs. Recipes for toppings which may also be used for fillings may be easily doubled if desired. Spread just enough on the dough so the dough is covered; keep any remaining topping on hand to serve later.

Follow directions for filling coffeecakes and breads found on pages 198–200. For sweet coffeecake or dessert-type breads, I prefer using crescents, coffeecake rolls, monkey bread, wreath or jelly roll formations. For sandwich rolls or meals, I prefer using the directions for jelly rolls, stromboli or pizza.

In addition to the few fillings listed here, try your favorite sandwich fillings or leftovers.

Unless otherwise stated, all filling ingredients are mixed together using a mixer, blender or food processor.

Orange Glaze

This can be drizzled on top of any orange bread or rolls while still hot. Allow to cool and then serve.

½ cup confectioners' sugar
1 tbs. butter, melted
1 tbs. orange juice

Mix ingredients together and warm in the microwave or in a saucepan. Makes ½ cup.

Orange Honey Syrup

The thinner (1 tsp. cornstarch) version of this can be used as a glaze and the thicker version (2 tsp. cornstarch) can be served as a topping or filling.

⅔ cup orange juice
½ cup honey
½ tsp. orange peel
1-2 tsp. cornstarch

Mix ingredients together in a saucepan and bring to a boil, stirring constantly. Heat until thickened. Makes 1 ¼ cups.

Confectioners' Sugar Glaze

This familiar topping is good on breads, cakes and buns.

1 cup confectioners' sugar (approximately)
1 tbs. milk
¼ tsp. vanilla extract

Mix ingredients until desired consistency is obtained. Pour over bread while it is still hot. Other extracts such as almond or coconut may be used in place of the vanilla if desired. Makes approximately 1 cup.

Chocolate Sauce

Wonderful is the best word to describe this. Use as a glaze or as a thin topping. For variety, add 2 tbs. coconut flakes — truly decadent!

⅓ cup heavy cream
2 tbs. honey
½ cup semisweet chocolate chips

Heat cream and honey until warm — do not boil. Add chocolate chips and stir until chocolate has melted. Pour over a sweet bread and allow to cool or eat warm. Makes approximately ¾ cup.

Herb Butter

Use this as either a topping or a filling for swirled dinner rolls (follow directions for coffeecake rolls). Pair with a pizza, sourdough or buttermilk dough. 1/4 cup butter, softened, or yogurt cheese or cream cheese

½ tsp. dried chives, or 1½ tsp. diced green onion (scallion)
½ tsp. dried oregano or basil, or 1½ tsp. chopped fresh
½ tsp. dried parsley, or 1½ tsp. chopped fresh

Mix ingredients together. Makes approximately ½ cup.

Orange Honey Butter

This decadent butter or cheese can be used as either a topping or a filling for a coffeecake. If using as a filling, glaze the top with orange glaze and sprinkle with some nuts. Use a sweet dough.

½ cup butter, softened, yogurt cheese or cream cheese
¼ cup honey
2 tbs. orange juice concentrate
¼ tsp. grated orange peel

Mix ingredients together. Makes approximately ¾ cup.

Gingered Peach Spread

The sweet ginger is the perfect combination with peaches.

¼ cup butter or margarine
½-¾ tsp. crystallized ginger
¼ cup peach preserves

Chop ginger in a food processor or blender until finely crumbled and add butter or margarine until both are creamed together. Gently mix in preserves. Orange marmalade can be substituted for the preserves if desired. Chill and use as a topping or use as a filling with a basic sweet yeast or buttermilk dough. Makes approximately ½ cup.

Strawberry Topping

This is absolutely delicious — a sweet, decadent topping to serve with toast for breakfast or brunch. This also makes a great filling with a sweet dough.

4 oz. cream cheese, softened
½ cup confectioners' sugar
1 tbs. pureed strawberries or strawberry preserves

Cream the softened cream cheese, add the sugar until well mixed in and then fold in the strawberries. Serve chilled or warmed from the microwave. Makes approximately ½ cup.

Spicy Butter

This flavored butter is wonderful served with any apple or raisin bread.

¼ cup butter, softened
1 tsp. honey
½ tsp. pumpkin pie spice

Combine ingredients with a mixer or food processor until well blended. Serve at room temperature. Makes approximately ¼ cup.

Cranberry Butter

Here is pure delight for a festive fall treat.

1/2 cup (1 stick) unsalted butter, softened
2 tbs. confectioners' sugar
1/8 tsp. orange peel
3 tbs. chopped fresh cranberries

Mix butter and confectioners' sugar with a food processor or blender until well blended. Add orange peel and cranberries and process or blend until just mixed in. Shape with individual butter molds, cookie cutters or into a ball. This can be served chilled or at room temperature. Butter can be refrigerated for several days. Makes approximately 1/2 cup.

Orange Topping

Serve with any raisin or cranberry bread. Delicious!

4 oz. cream cheese, softened
1/2 cup confectioners' sugar
4-5 Mandarin orange segments
1/8 tsp. orange peel

Cream the softened cream cheese and mix in the remaining ingredients. Serve chilled or warmed from the microwave. Makes approximately 1/2 cup.

Sautéed Apple Topping

This is superb served with any oatmeal, raisin or apple bread. For Maple Apple Topping, omit cinnamon and use 2 tbs. maple syrup.

1 medium apple, peeled and thinly sliced or diced
1/4 tsp. cinnamon
1 tbs. butter or margarine

Melt butter or margarine in pan over low heat. Add apple and cinnamon and sauté until crisp-tender. Makes approximately 3/4 cup.

Buttered Preserves

This is easy, and no additional syrups or butters are required. Serve softened at room temperature. Cream butter and add preserves until well blended. Use the food processor, a mixer or a blender. Makes approximately 1/2 cup.

1/4 cup unsalted butter, softened
1/4 cup favorite preserve: strawberry, apricot, peach, etc.

Fruited Honey

Creamy honey with your favorite fruits makes a terrific topping to bread. Suggested concentrates: orange, apple, grape, strawberry, blueberry, blackberry, raspberry. Keep refrigerated. Makes approximately 1/4 cup.

1/4 cup honey
1 tbs. fruit juice concentrate

Spiced Honey

Spiced honey is a delectable topping for toast of all kinds. Mix ingredients together and serve at room temperature. Keep refrigerated. Makes 1/4 cup.

1/4 cup honey
1/2 tsp. cinnamon
1/8 tsp. nutmeg
1/8 tsp. ground cloves

Peanut Butter and Honey

Children will ask for toast just to eat this. It's good in a sandwich, too, with jelly or a sliced banana.

1/4 cup honey
2 tbs. peanut butter

Mix together and serve at room temperature. Keep refrigerated. Makes approximately 1/3 cup.

Coconut Delight

Serve this topping with any tropical-island type bread which contains coconut. It's also delicious with breads containing macadamia nuts.

1/2 cup coconut cream (canned)
1/4 cup water
1 1/2 tbs. cornstarch
1 tbs. coconut flakes

Heat coconut cream, water and cornstarch over low heat until mixture thickens. Stir in coconut flakes until just mixed in and remove from heat. Serve warm. Can be reheated in the microwave. Makes 3/4 cup.

Papaya Coconut

Here's a tropical delight.

1/4 cup papaya juice
1/4 cup coconut cream (canned)
2 tbs. water
1 tbs. cornstarch
1 tbs. coconut flakes

Heat papaya juice, coconut cream, water and cornstarch over low heat, stirring occasionally, until mixture thickens. Stir in coconut flakes until just mixed in and remove from heat. Serve warm. Can be reheated in microwave. Makes 1/2 cup.

Peach and Orange Topping

This is an astonishingly good topping or filling. It can be made in advance and warmed for serving.

1 can (8 1/4 oz.) peaches, or pears
1/4 cup orange juice
1 tbs. cornstarch
2 tbs. sugar
1/4 tsp. cinnamon
1/8 tsp. grated orange peel

Drain the peaches and process in blender or food processor until smooth. Combine all ingredients in a small saucepan and heat over low heat, stirring often, until sauce has thickened. Simmer until you are ready to serve or allow to cool and refrigerate until needed. Makes approximately 1 cup.

Lemon Cream

This is a must-try with any lemon bread.

4 oz. cream cheese, softened
¼ cup confectioners' sugar
1 tbs. lemon juice
½ tsp. grated lemon peel
1 tsp. poppy seeds, or to taste, optional

Cream the softened cream cheese, add sugar and remaining ingredients until blended. Serve at room temperature or warmed in a microwave. Makes approximately ¾ cup.

Orange Filling

Any fruit concentrate or puree can be used in place of the orange concentrate. To puree fruits such as berries, process with a blender or food processor until the proper consistency is obtained.

	Small	Medium	Large
cream or yogurt cheese	4 oz.	6 oz.	8 oz.
confectioners' sugar	½ cup	¾ cup	1 cup
orange juice concentrate	1-2 tsp.	2-3 tsp.	1-1⅓ tbs.

Cheese Filling

Fill dough jelly roll-style for a quick and easy appetizer or meal.

	Small	Medium	Large
mozzarella cheese	½ cup	¾ cup	1 cup
ricotta cheese	½ cup	¾ cup	1 cup
egg	1	1½	2
garlic powder, optional	pinch	dash	⅛ tsp.
oregano	1 tbs.	1½ tbs.	2 tbs.

Praline Roll Filling

Here's a delicious use for those southern pecans which should be finely ground with a food processor.

	Small	Medium	Large
melted butter	2 tbs.	3 tbs.	4 tbs.
pecans	½ cup	¾ cup	1 cup

Orange Coconut

This is great with the coconut sweet dough or a basic sweet dough. Make as a jelly roll or rolled biscuits.

	Small	Medium	Large
orange or peach preserves	2 tbs.	3 tbs.	¼ cup
coconut flakes	2 tbs.	3 tbs.	¼ cup

Caramel Filling 1

Raisins could be added to this also — to taste.

	Small	Medium	Large
melted butter	2 tbs.	3 tbs.	4 tbs.
brown sugar	2 tbs.	3 tbs.	¼ cup
chopped nuts	¼ cup	⅓ cup	½ cup

Caramel Filling 11

Who can pass up a great caramel filling? Here's another variation.

	Small	Medium	Large
melted butter	2 tbs.	3 tbs.	4 tbs.
brown sugar	¼ cup	6 tbs.	½ cup
light corn syrup	1 tbs.	1½ tbs.	2 tbs.
finely chopped pecans	¼ cup	⅓ cup	½ cup

Spinach Filling

This is delicious paired with Pizza Dough, page 204, or Spinach Dough, page 203. Pair it with a salad or a bowl of soup for a satisfying lunch or supper.

	Small	Medium	Large
chopped spinach	10 oz.	15 oz.	20 oz.
onion	2-3 tbs.	3-4 tbs.	4-6 tbs.
garlic clove, minced	1	1½	2
salt and lemon pepper	to taste	to taste	to taste
feta cheese, crumbled	1 cup	1½ cups	2 cups

Sauté onion and garlic in a little olive oil until soft and slightly golden. Spinach should be thawed and drained if frozen or washed and well drained if fresh. Add spinach, salt and pepper and simmer for about 5 minutes. Drain mixture and then toss in the cheese until well blended. Follow directions for stromboli, page 199.

Note: One package of frozen spinach is 10 oz.

Sausage Filling

Use this filling with Apple Dough, page 202, for an unbeatable combination. If you prefer a really gooey, cheesy filling, the amount of cheese can be increased to taste.

	Small	Medium	Large
sausage, diced	1 cup	1½ cups	2 cups
mozzarella cheese	½ cup	¾ cup	1 cup
rosemary	¼ tsp.	⅓ tsp.	½ tsp.
salt and pepper	to taste	to taste	to taste

To prepare filling, cook sliced or diced sausage and drain well. Mix filling ingredients together. Remove dough from machine and roll into 1 or 2 rectangles. Spread filling mixture on top of middle third of rectangle and fold each side over top of filling so that it is encased. Pinch ends closed and place fold side down on a well greased baking sheet. Rub top with a little olive oil and sprinkle rosemary on top as a garnish. Bake in a preheated 350° oven for 20 to 30 minutes or until golden brown.

The Bread Machine *Cookbook* V

Favorite Recipes from 100 Kitchens

Farmhouse White Bread

Raisin or Basic cycle

Joan Garneau loves making this bread and says it has a surprise taste and crunch because of the sesame seeds. Use an egg yolk, white or 2 tbs. egg substitute for the half egg.

	1 lb.	1½ lb.	1¾ lb.
milk	⅔ cup	1 cup	1¼ cups
egg	½	1	1
butter	1 tbs.	2 tbs.	2 tbs.
salt	⅓ tsp.	½ tsp.	⅔ tsp.
sugar	1 tbs.	1½ tbs.	2 tbs.
bread flour	2 cups	3 cups	3½ cups
yeast	1 tsp.	1½ tsp.	2 tsp.
*sesame seeds	1½ tbs.	2 tbs.	2½ tbs.

*Add seeds at the beep or appropriate time for your machine.

Stollen

Raisin or Sweet cycle

Joanne Bauer and Caryn Gates have adapted this recipe to fit their bread machines. This family recipe has been handed down through the generations since the 1880s. Joanne says that she sometimes substitutes rum or rum extract for the almond and adds a pinch of cardamom to it. If citron or candied red and green cherries are unavailable, use dried fruit mix. Breads with high amounts of fruits and nuts may have difficulty baking through properly in some machines. If that is the case, cut the amount of fruit in half and be sure to use a sweet cycle if available. This is a low-rising bread and is almost cake-like in texture.

	1 lb.	1½ lb.	2 lb.
milk	½ cup	¾ cup	1 cup
eggs	1	1½	2
butter or margarine	2 tbs.	3 tbs.	4 tbs.
almond extract, or rum extract	¼ tsp.	⅓ tsp.	½ tsp.
sugar	¼ cup	⅓ cup	½ cup
salt	¼ tsp.	⅓ tsp.	½ tsp.
cinnamon	⅛ tsp.	¼ tsp.	⅓ tsp.
bread flour	2 cups	3 cups	4 cups
yeast	1 tsp.	1½ tsp.	2 tsp.
*raisins	¼ cup	⅓ cup	½ cup
*citron or dried fruit	¼ cup	⅓ cup	½ cup
*red or green cherries	¼ cup	⅓ cup	½ cup
*almonds, chopped	¼ cup	⅓ cup	½ cup

*Add at the beep or appropriate time for your machine.

Easy Cheese Bread

Lorena Vensel prefers using a Quatro Fromage blend of cheese in this but Swiss or freshly grated Parmesan are also tasty. When using a drier cheese such as Parmesan, liquid may need to be added. Watch the dough and adjust the consistency as required with water or flour. While the recipe calls for a multi-blend flour (found at health food stores), rye or oat flour may also be substituted. If the machine has difficulty kneading the ingredients initially (notorious with cheese breads), scrape the sides of the pan with a rubber spatula to help the ingredients get picked up by the kneading paddle.

	1 lb.	1 ½ lb.	1 ¾ lb.
milk	⅓ cup	½ cup	⅔ cup
water	⅓ cup	½ cup	⅔ cup
freshly grated cheese	⅔ cup	1 cup	1 ⅓ cups
sugar	2 tsp.	1 tbs.	1 ⅓ tbs.
salt	½ tsp.	1 tsp.	1 tsp.
dill weed, dried	½ tsp.	1 tsp.	1 tsp.
multi-blend flour	½ cup	¾ cup	1 cup
bread flour	1 ⅓ cups	2 cups	2 ⅔ cups
vital gluten	2 tbs.	3 tbs.	¼ cup
yeast	1 ½ tsp.	2 tsp.	2 tsp.

Sally Lunn

Maxine Frazier and her friend spent their vacation playing with their bread machines and sent me this recipe for Sally Lunn. I used only milk rather than water and milk. I warm the milk to lukewarm as usual. This is a high-rising, sweet bread with a moist, soft dough which may climb the walls of the pan — like a tornado.

	1 lb.	1 ½ lb.	2 lb.
milk	⅔ cup	1 cup	1 ¼ cups
egg	1	1	2
butter or margarine	2 tbs.	3 tbs.	4 tbs.
salt	½ tsp.	1 tsp.	1 tsp.
sugar	¼ cup	⅓ cup	½ cup
bread flour	2 cups	3 cups	4 cups
yeast	1 tsp.	1 ½ tsp.	2 tsp.

Hawaiian Bread

Sweet or Basic cycle

Carol Sclove finds bread baking to be a great hobby. Her recipe proves she has talent for it! One small can (6 oz.) equals ¾ cup of pineapple juice. One half egg equals 1 yolk or white or 2 tbs. egg substitute. This has been an often requested recipe!

	1 lb.	1½ lb.	1¾ lb.
pineapple juice	⅔ cup	¾ cup	1 cup
egg	½	1	1
vegetable oil	1½ tbs.	2 tbs.	2½ tbs.
honey	2 tbs.	2½ tbs.	3 tbs.
salt	½ tsp.	¾ tsp.	1 tsp.
bread flour	2¼ cups	3 cups	3½ cups
dry milk powder	1½ tbs.	2 tbs.	2½ tbs.
yeast	1½ tsp.	2 tsp.	2 tsp.

Hawaiian Sweet Bread

Sweet or Basic cycle

Penny Grant fell in love with Hawaiian sweet bread while visiting a friend in Hawaii. When she couldn't find a recipe for it for her machine, she developed one herself! She uses Butter Crisco; I tested using margarine. One small can (6 oz.) of pineapple juice equals approximately ¾ cup. Water may be added to that if you don't want to open a second can. Orange juice may be substituted for a slightly different flavor. Use an egg yolk, white or 2 tbs. egg substitute for the half egg. This is a winner. If you have a 1¼ lb. machine (Seiko), make only the 1 lb. size to prevent overflows. This can be a high-rising bread.

	1 lb.	1½ lb.	2 lb. only
pineapple juice	⅔ cup	¾ cup	1 cup
egg	½	1	1
milk	3 tbs.	¼ cup	⅓ cup
butter or margarine	2½ tbs.	4 tbs.	4 tbs.
coconut or vanilla extract	1 tsp.	1 tsp.	1 tsp.
ground ginger	pinch	¼ tsp.	⅓ tsp.
salt	⅓ tsp.	½ tsp.	1 tsp.
sugar	¼ cup	⅓ cup	⅓ cup
potato flakes	⅓ cup	½ cup	½ cup
bread flour	2½ cups	3 cups	3½ cups
vital gluten, optional	2 tsp.	1 tbs.	1 tbs.
yeast	1 tsp.	1½ tsp.	1½ tsp.

Quick Potato Bread

Sweet or Basic cycle

Ruth Lee makes this in her Hitachi on the rapid cycle using quick or rapid rise yeast. She says it lasts about 3 minutes with her two grandsons around! This is a simple bread to make when you use instant potato flakes. I cut back on her butter.

	1 lb.	1½ lb.	1¾ lb.
water	¾ cup	1¼ cups	1⅓ cups
butter	2½ tbs.	3 tbs.	3 tbs.
sugar	2 tbs.	2½ tbs.	2½ tbs.
salt	⅔ tsp.	1 tsp.	1 tsp.
potato flakes	1½ tbs.	2 tbs.	2½ tbs.
bread flour	2 cups	3 cups	3½ cups
yeast	1 tsp.	1½ tsp.	2 tsp.

Potato Bread

Whole Wheat, Sweet or Basic cycle

Pat Hall says this is one of their standby breads and she makes it all the time. Cook the new or small potato in the microwave until soft and cut it into quarters or eighths (the machine will mash it during the kneading). Place the cut potato, peel and all, into the liquid measuring cup and add water up to the level given. She sometimes adds 1-2 tbs. buttermilk dressing mix (dry) for extra flavor.

	1 lb.	1½ lb.	2 lb. only
potato, cooked	4 oz.	6 oz.	7 oz.
water	as needed	as needed	as needed
wet ingredients should equal	1 cup	1½ cups	1¾ cups
butter	1 tbs.	1½ tbs.	2 tbs.
sugar	1½ tbs.	2 tbs.	2½ tbs.
salt	¾ tsp.	1 tsp.	1 tsp.
bread flour	2 cups	3 cups	3½ cups
yeast	1 tsp.	1½ tsp.	2 tsp.

Finnish Pulla (Coffee Bread)

Jo Ulvila adapted this bread from her mother-in-law's recipe. The men in the fields would listen for the whistle of the afternoon train at 3:00, the signal to go home for their coffee and pulla. It is usually made in a straight braid but may be shaped into a wreath for special occasions. Jo says that she sometimes adds a teaspoon of vanilla and some chopped citrus fruit for a slightly different flavor. This was tested as a loaf in the bread machines. If, however, you want to make this on the dough cycle, make the 1 1/2 lb. size. Upon completion, remove the dough, divide it into three sections, braid it and let it rise for about 30 minutes. Bake in a preheated 375° oven for 25 to 30 minutes. Do not overbake as it will dry out.

	1 lb.	1 1/2 lb.	2 lb.
milk	1/2 cup	3/4 cup	3/4 cup
egg	1	1 1/2	2
butter	2 tbs.	3 tbs.	4 tbs.
sugar	1/4 cup	1/3 cup	1/2 cup
salt	2/3 tsp.	1 tsp.	1 tsp.
ground cardamom	2/3 tsp.	1 tsp.	1 1/4 tsp.
bread flour	2 cups	3 cups	3 1/2 cups
yeast	1 1/2 tsp.	2 tsp.	2 tsp.

Glaze: Add 1/4 cup sugar to 1 beaten egg and mix well. Brush on raised bread. Sprinkle sugar and poppy seeds or chopped or sliced almonds on the top and bake. If doing this in the machine, be very careful not to spill into the machine itself.

Houska (Bohemian Sweet Bread)

Jean Allen is not sure if her great grandma is appalled or applauding her efforts for adapting this old family recipe to the bread machine! She says that her mother sometimes adds golden raisins. This bread may appear to have too much liquid, but it is supposed to be very moist. It is traditionally braided.

	1 lb.	1 1/2 lb.	2 lb.
milk	1/2 cup	1 cup	1 cup
eggs	1	1	2
butter	2 tbs.	3 tbs.	1/4 cup
salt	1/2 tsp.	3/4 tsp.	1 tsp.
sugar	3 tbs.	1/4 cup	1/3 cup
mace	1/4 tsp.	1/2 tsp.	1/2 tsp.
bread flour	2 cups	3 cups	3 1/2 cups
yeast	1 tsp.	1 1/2 tsp.	2 tsp.

Blue Cheese Bread

Ramona Schall has made this bread (with the raisins) for years the old-fashioned way, and is now able to do it with the bread machine! Serve with tossed salad or soup. Watch the dough, scrape the pan sides and add flour or water if necessary.

	1 lb.	1 ½ lb.	1 ¾ lb.
milk	¾ cup	1 cup	1 ⅓ cups
butter or margarine	1 tbs.	1 ½ tbs.	2 tbs.
crumbled blue cheese	¼ cup	⅓ cup	½ cup
sugar	1 ⅓ tbs.	1 ½ tbs.	2 tbs.
salt	½ tsp.	½ tsp.	1 tsp.
bread flour	2 ¼ cups	3 cups	3 ½ cups
rapid or quick yeast	1 ½ tsp.	1 ½ tsp.	2 tsp.
*raisins, optional	⅓ cup	½ cup	⅔ cup

*Add raisins at the beep or appropriate time for your machine.

Cheese Wine Bread

Terry Ward says that this is her family's all time favorite bread — it's great with chili. She usually uses a pepper Jack cheese or adds a jalapeño or two to regular Monterey Jack. She likes to use Chardonnay, but has also used flat beer. If you prefer no alcohol, substitute water. Terry says she adds half of the cheese at the beginning and the other half at the beep in her Hitachi. I cut her butter amount in half.

	1 lb.	1 ½ lb.	2 lb.
wine, beer or water	⅓ cup	½ cup	⅔ cup
butter	2 tbs.	4 tbs.	5 tbs.
egg	2	3	3
cheese, shredded	½ cup	1 cup	1 cup
salt	½ tsp.	1 tsp.	1 tsp.
sugar	1 ½ tsp.	2 tsp.	2 ½ tsp.
bread flour	2 cups	3 cups	3 ½ cups
yeast	1 ½ tsp.	2 tsp.	2 tsp.

English Muffin Bread

Whole Wheat, Sweet or Basic cycle

Judy Shroyer scalds the milk and stirs in the instant potato flakes to dissolve them. I am lazy and warm the milk as usual and then put both the milk and potato flakes in together so they mix in the machine.

	1 lb.	1½ lb.	2 lb.
milk	¾ cup	1⅛ cups	1⅓ cups
potato flakes	1½ tbs.	2 tbs.	2½ tbs.
unsalted butter	2½ tbs.	4 tbs.	5 tbs.
sugar	2 tsp.	1 tbs.	1⅓ tbs.
salt	¾ tsp.	1 tsp.	1 tsp.
bread flour	2 cups	3 cups	3½ cups
yeast	1 tsp.	1½ tsp.	1½ tsp.

New Hampshire White Bread

Basic cycle

Loosey Blake says that this is her favorite basic white recipe. Use scant measurements of the water. Loosey sometimes makes this into rolls and also enjoys the bread toasted.

	1 lb.	1½ lb.	1¾ lb.
water	¾ cup	1 cup	1¼ cups
butter or margarine	2 tbs.	2½ tbs.	3 tbs.
sugar	2 tbs.	2½ tbs.	3 tbs.
salt	1 tsp.	1 tsp.	1 tsp.
bread flour	2 cups	3 cups	3½ cups
yeast	1 tsp.	1½ tsp.	2 tsp.

About Fruit and Vegetable Breads

Bread recipes that use fruit or vegetables for some or part of the liquid must be watched carefully for the proper moisture content. The moisture content of the fruit or vegetable which you use may vary from one day to the next depending on the ripeness and freshness of the produce.

Fruit recipes also tend to be higher in sugar due to the fruit itself. If you have a sweet cycle or specific raisin cycle, use it for the lower baking temperature. If the bread has a doughy spot in the middle of the loaf, cut the amount of dried fruit or nuts in half the next time.

Honey Raisin Cinnamon Bread
Raisin or Sweet cycle

Norma Davis Stoyenoff developed this recipe much to the delight of her family. The salt amounts given are half of what she submitted. Norma also uses more water than I found worked in most machines.

	1 lb.	1½ lb.	1¾ lb.
water	⅔ cup	1 cup	1⅛ cups
margarine or vegetable oil	2 tsp.	1 tbs.	1⅓ tbs.
honey	1½ tbs.	2 tbs.	3 tbs.
salt	½ tsp.	¾ tsp.	1 tsp.
cinnamon	1 tsp.	1½ tsp.	1¾ tsp.
whole wheat flour	⅓ cup	½ cup	⅔ cup
bread flour	2 cups	2½ cups	3 cups
yeast	1½ tsp.	2 tsp.	2 tsp.
*raisins	⅓ cup	½ cup	⅔ cup

*Add raisins at the beep or appropriate time for your machine.

Heavenly Raisin Nut Bread

Raisin, Sweet or Basic cycle

Lee Hickney has been very creative in developing recipes for his bread machine. I slightly decreased the amount of butter he uses. This moist dough rises very well.

	1 lb.	1½ lb.	1¾ lb.
water	⅔ cup	1 cup	1⅛ cups
egg, large	1	1½	2
butter or vegetable oil	2 tbs.	3 tbs.	¼ cup
molasses	1 tbs.	1½ tbs.	2 tbs.
sugar	2 tbs.	3 tbs.	3 tbs.
salt	1 tsp.	1½ tsp.	1½ tsp.
cinnamon	1 tsp.	1½ tsp.	1½ tsp.
dry milk powder	2 tbs.	2½ tbs.	3 tbs.
bread flour	2 cups	3 cups	3½ cups
yeast	1 tsp.	1½ tsp.	2 tsp.
*raisins	½ cup	⅔ cup	¾ cup
*chopped walnuts	½ cup	⅔ cup	¾ cup

*Add raisins at the beep or appropriate time for your machine.

Cranberry Cornmeal Bread

Sweet or Basic cycle

Caryn Hart is a veteran bread baker and has adapted many of her favorite recipes for the bread machine. She pours boiling water over the cornmeal before placing it in the machine. I take the lazy way and simply put it all in the machine at once. The cranberries should be coarsely chopped. They will add some liquid to the dough. As usual with any fruit like this, adjust the dough with flour or water if necessary.

	1 lb.	1½ lb.	2 lb.
water	¾ cup	1 cup	1⅛ cups
fresh cranberries	½ cup	¾ cup	1 cup
butter or vegetable oil	1½ tbs.	2½ tbs.	3 tbs.
honey	3 tbs.	¼ cup	⅓ cup
cornmeal	⅔ cup	¾ cup	1 cup
bread flour	2 cups	2½ cups	3 cups
yeast	1 tsp.	1½ tsp.	2 tsp.

Date Bread

Sweet or Basic cycle

Dorothy Thompson requested an adaptation of a sugar-free quick bread using equal amounts of chopped dates and flour. That high amount of fruit would not work with a yeast product, so I came up with this flavorful yeast bread instead. I buy dates already chopped. Walnut meal is very finely ground walnuts. Let the dough knead for about 5 minutes before checking the consistency. Add a tablespoon of liquid if needed — I found slight variations using different dates.

	1 lb.	**1½ lb.**	**2 lb. only**
water	⅔ cup	1 cup	1⅓ cups
apple juice concentrate	2 tbs.	3 tbs.	¼ cup
salt	½ tsp.	⅔ tsp.	¾ tsp.
chopped dates	¼ cup	⅓ cup	½ cup
walnut meal	½ cup	¾ cup	1 cup
bread flour	2 cups	3 cups	4 cups
yeast	1 tsp.	1½ tsp.	2 tsp.

Blueberry Oatmeal Bread

Sweet or Basic cycle

Larry Jochims uses canned blueberries for this recipe (1 cup blueberries equals ½ a 15 oz. can). If using fresh blueberries, they should be mashed tightly into the measuring cup. As with any recipe using fruit for moisture, watch the dough and adjust with water or flour as needed.

	1 lb.	**1½ lb.**	**1¾ lb.**
blueberries and juice	1 cup	1¼ cups	1½ cups
canola oil	1 tbs.	1⅓ tbs.	1½ tbs.
sugar	1 tbs.	1⅓ tbs.	1½ tbs.
salt	¼ tsp.	⅓ tsp.	½ tsp.
oats	½ cup	¾ cup	1 cup
bread flour	2 cups	2½ cups	3 cups
yeast	1½ tsp.	2 tsp.	2 tsp.

Cranberry Walnut Bread

Dorie Meredith developed this delicious bread. Grind the walnuts with a food processor, or place nuts in a locking plastic bag and roll with a rolling pin until coarsely ground. It's well worth the extra effort! You can also use raisins or dried blueberries.

	1 lb.	1 1/2 lb.	2 lb.
water	3/4 cup	1 1/8 cups	1 1/2 cups
applesauce	2 tbs.	3 tbs.	1/4 cup
canola oil	2 1/2 tbs.	1/4 cup	1/3 cup
sugar	1 1/2 tbs.	2 tbs.	3 tbs.
salt	1/2 tsp.	3/4 tsp.	1 tsp.
walnut meal	1/2 cup	3/4 cup	1 cup
bread flour	2 cups	3 cups	4 cups
dry milk powder	1 1/2 tbs.	2 tbs.	3 tbs.
yeast	1 tsp.	1 1/2 tsp.	2 tsp.
*dried cranberries	1/3 cup	1/2 cup	2/3 cup

*Add dried cranberries at the beep or appropriate time for your machine.

Cranberry Bread

Kathy Pawlak uses cranberry liqueur for a little additional cranberry flavor in this bread. You can use frozen cranberry juice concentrate, thawed, or combine the water and cranberry flavoring and use cranberry juice as a substitute if desired.

	1 lb.	1 1/2 lb.	1 3/4 lb.
water	2/3 cup	1 cup	1 1/3 cups
cranberry flavoring	1 1/2 tsp.	2 tsp.	1 tbs.
vegetable oil	1 tbs.	1 1/2 tbs.	2 tbs.
honey	2 tbs.	3 tbs.	1/4 cup
salt	1/3 tsp.	1/2 tsp.	2/3 tsp.
whole wheat flour	1 cup	1 1/2 cups	2 cups
bread flour	1 cup	1 1/2 cups	2 cups
yeast	1 tsp.	1 1/2 tsp.	2 tsp.
*dried cranberries	1/3 cup	1/2 cup	3/4 cup

*Add dried cranberries at the beep or appropriate time for your machine.

Onion Cheese Bread

Sweet or Basic cycle

Joanne MacGregor says to add the cheese slowly as the machine is kneading. She adds it at the beep (raisin cycle) but it could also be added early during the second kneading cycle. If your machine stops kneading when the lid is open, add the cheese 1/4 at a time, close lid until it is kneaded in and repeat until all cheese is added. The onion amounts are approximate and the flour should be adjusted to compensate for more or less liquid. If the machine has difficulty kneading the ingredients into a dough ball, scrape the sides of the pan to help push the ingredients toward the kneading paddle.

	1 lb.	1 1/2 lb.	1 3/4 lb.
diced onion	1/4 cup	1/3 cup	1/2 cup
butter	1 tbs.	1 tbs.	1 1/2 tbs.

Sauté diced onion in butter until soft. Set aside to cool. Place in the bread machine loaf pan and add the following ingredients:

milk	1/2 cup	3/4 cup	1 cup
butter or margarine	1 tsp.	1 1/2 tsp.	2 tsp.
sugar	1 tsp.	1 1/2 tsp.	3/4 tsp.
salt	3/4 tsp.	1 tsp.	1 tsp.
bread flour	2 cups	3 cups	3 1/2 cups
yeast	1 tsp.	1 1/2 tsp.	2 tsp.
*grated cheddar	2/3 cup	1 cup	1 1/4 cups

*Add cheese during kneading.

Apple Cider Bread

Sweet or Basic cycle

Elaine Billets came up with a delicious fall treat! If cider is not available, apple juice can be used. The sunflower seeds can be added at the beginning or at the beep. The 9 (or 7 or 12) grain cereal is found in some large grocery stores or in health food stores.

	1 lb.	1 1/2 lb.	2 lb.
apple cider	2/3 cup	1 cup	1 1/3 cups
vegetable oil	1 1/3 tbs.	2 tbs.	2 2/3 tbs.
honey	1 tbs.	1 1/2 tbs.	2 tbs.
salt	2/3 tsp.	1 tsp.	1 tsp.
sunflower seeds	1/4 cup	1/3 cup	1/2 cup
9 grain cereal	2/3 cup	1 cup	1 1/3 cups
bread flour	1 1/3 cups	2 cups	2 2/3 cups
yeast	1 tsp.	1 1/2 tsp.	2 tsp.

Pecan Raisin Bread

Norma McIntosh uses Great Grains cereal with dates, raisins and pecans. This is a dense loaf.

	1 lb.	1 ½ lb.	2 lb.
water	¾ cup	1 ⅛ cups	1 ½ cups
butter or vegetable oil	1 tbs.	1 ½ tbs.	2 tbs.
honey	2 tbs.	3 tbs.	4 tbs.
salt	½ tsp.	¾ tsp.	1 tsp.
Great Grains cereal	⅓ cup	½ cup	⅔ cup
whole wheat flour	⅔ cup	1 cup	1 ⅓ cups
bread flour	1 ⅓ cups	2 cups	2⅔ cups
dry milk powder	1 ½ tbs.	2 tbs.	2 ½ tbs.
yeast	1 tsp.	1 ½ tsp.	2 tsp.
*raisins	3 tbs.	¼ cup	⅓ cup
*pecans, chopped	3 tbs.	¼ cup	⅓ cup
*oat bran	3 tbs.	¼ cup	⅓ cup

*Add at the beep or appropriate time for your machine.

Banana Raisin Nut Bread

This bread won Janis Bosenko a blue ribbon from the "Machine Made Bread" category at the Marin County Fair. The banana should be very ripe, medium in size, and cut into chunks. Bananas vary in moisture content, so adjust the water or flour as necessary, 1 tablespoon at a time. Use either a yolk or white for the half egg. The cinnamon may be adjusted to taste. This is a low-rising, moist loaf of bread. If your machine is prone to the doughy blues, cut the amount of raisins and nuts in half.

	1 lb.	1 ½ lb.	1 ¾+ lb.
water	⅓ cup	½ cup	⅔ cup
egg	½	½	1
vegetable oil	1 tbs.	1 ½ tbs.	2 tbs.
honey	2 tbs.	3 tbs.	¼ cup
banana	¾	1	1 ½
salt	½ tsp.	¾ tsp.	1 tsp.
cinnamon	½ tsp.	¾ tsp.	1 tsp.
yeast	1 tsp.	1 ½ tsp.	2 tsp.
bread flour	2 cups	3 cups	3 ½ cups
*raisins	½ cup	¾ cup	1 cup
*broken walnuts	¼ cup	⅓ cup	½ cup

*Add raisins and nuts at the beep or appropriate time for your machine.

Mushroom Bread

Whole Wheat or Sweet cycle

Elizabeth Hand requested this adaptation of a favorite conventional recipe. She says the mushrooms disappear and give the bread lots of minerals and moisture. Use fresh mushrooms. Watch the dough carefully and adjust with water or flour as necessary.

	1 lb.	1 ½ lb.	1 ¾ lb.
water	¾ cup	1 ⅛ cups	1 ½ cups
mushrooms, finely chopped	2 tbs.	3 tbs.	¼ cup
vegetable oil	1 ½ tsp.	2 tsp.	1 tbs.
molasses	⅓ cup	½ cup	⅔ cup
salt	½ tsp.	¾ tsp.	1 tsp.
wheat germ	¼ cup	⅓ cup	½ cup
oats	¼ cup	⅓ cup	½ cup
whole wheat flour	½ cup	¾ cup	1 cup
bread flour	1 ½ cup	2 ⅓ cups	3 cups
yeast	1 ½ tsp.	2 tsp.	2 ½ tsp.
*raisins	¼ cup	⅓ cup	½ cup

*Add raisins at the beep or appropriate time for your machine.

Orange Cranberry Bread

Sweet or Basic cycle

Barbara Miller makes her own candied orange peel for this bread. Candied peel can be found in some gourmet shops or you can substitute regular fresh peel or ⅓ the amount with dried peel. The salt can be cut in half if desired. This is really good.

	1 lb.	1 ½ lb.	1 ¾ lb.
water	1 cup	1 ⅓ cups	1 ½ cups
butter or margarine	1 tbs.	1 ⅓ tbs.	1 ½ tbs.
sugar	2 tbs.	3 tbs.	scant ¼ cup
salt	1 tsp.	1 ½ tsp.	1 ½ tsp.
candied orange peel	2 tbs.	3 tbs.	3 ½ tbs.
bread flour	2 ¼ cups	3 cups	3 ½ cups
dry milk powder	1 tbs.	1 ½ tbs.	2 tbs.
yeast	1 ½ tsp.	2 tsp.	2 tsp.
*dried cranberries	⅓ cup	½ cup	⅔ cup

*Add dried cranberries at the beep or appropriate time for your machine.

Tomato Bread

This is an adaptation of a favorite recipe of Ramona Schall's. If using commercially prepared canned tomato juice, omit the salt. Seasonings can be adjusted to taste.

	1 lb.	1 ½ lb.	1 ¾ lb.
tomato juice	¾ cup	1 ⅛ cups	1 ⅓ cups
vegetable oil	1 tbs.	1 tbs.	1 ½ tbs.
salt	½ tsp.	¾ tsp.	1 tsp.
sugar	2 tbs.	3 tbs.	¼ cup
ground ginger	pinch	dash	¼ tsp.
celery seed	1 ½ tsp.	2 tsp.	2 ½ tsp.
Italian seasoning	¼ tsp.	⅓ tsp.	½ tsp.
bread flour	2 cups	3 cups	3 ½ cups
yeast	1 ½ tsp.	2 tsp.	2 tsp.

Tropical Banana Chip Bread

Laurie Coffino says she finds the high amount of gluten is necessary in this moist, tropical bread. It should rise to a medium height with the gluten because of the high amount of sugar. As with any bread that uses a fruit for all or part of the liquid, watch the dough carefully. If you elect to use a medium-sized banana and not measure it precisely, take care to watch the dough. Add water or flour as necessary, one tablespoon at a time. Use very ripe bananas. The banana chips should be crushed. Pineapple extract can be used in place of the coconut if desired.

	1 lb.	1 ½ lb.	1 ¾ lb.
orange juice	⅓ cup	½ cup	⅔ cup
mashed bananas	⅞ cup	1 ¼ cups	1 ½ cups
vegetable oil	1 ⅓ tbs.	2 tbs.	2 tbs.
honey	3 tbs.	¼ cup	¼ cup
coconut extract	1 ½ tsp.	2 tsp.	2 ½ tsp.
salt	⅔ tsp.	1 tsp.	1 tsp.
orange peel	⅔ tsp.	1 tsp.	1 tsp.
coconut flakes	⅔ cup	1 cup	1 ¼ cups
vital gluten	¼ cup	⅓ cup	⅓ cup
bread flour	2 cups	3 cups	3 ½ cups
yeast	1 ½ tsp.	2 tsp.	2 tsp.
*banana chips	½ cup	¾ cup	¾+ cup

*Add banana chips at the beep or appropriate time for your machine.

Sauerkraut Rye

Whole Wheat or Basic cycle

Jean Schenk requested a recipe for a bread that she purchased in the past. With only a name to go on, I hope this compares favorably! Caraway seeds could be added to taste. The instant coffee gives the bread its dark color.

	1 lb.	1 ½ lb.	2 lb.
water	⅔ cup	1 cup	1 ⅓ cups
vegetable oil	1 tbs.	1 ½ tbs.	2 tbs.
molasses	2 tbs.	3 tbs.	¼ cup
sauerkraut	¼ cup	⅓ cup	½ cup
salt	½ tsp.	¾ tsp.	1 tsp.
instant coffee granules	1 tbs.	1 ½ tbs.	2 tbs.
vital gluten	1 tbs.	1 ½ tbs.	2 tbs.
rye flour	½ cup	¾ cup	1 cup
bread flour	1 ¾ cups	2 ½ cups	3 ½ cups
yeast	1 ½ tsp.	2 tsp.	2 ¼ tsp.

Apricot Almond Bread

Sweet or Basic cycle

Carol Ashman uses "slab" apricots for this recipe as they are the sweetest she has found. I tested using dried apricots from a grocery store. She says the real trick to this bread is to mix the additional ingredients together so that the sugar coats the almonds and apricots. Add them at the appropriate time for your machine. This is a "must-try." If your machine is prone to the doughy blues, cut the fruit and nut amounts in half and cover the glass only with a small piece of aluminum foil, but don't block the air vents. I buy almond paste in the grocery store in a 7 oz. roll and use ½ of the roll to equal about ⅔ cup diced and slightly less for the ½ cup and slightly more for the ¾ cup.

	1 lb.	1 ½ lb.	1 ¾ lb.
water	⅔ cup	1 cup	1 cup
egg	1	1 ½	2
almond extract	1 tsp.	1 ½ tsp.	2 tsp.
vegetable oil	2 tbs.	3 tbs.	¼ cup
salt	¼ tsp.	⅓ tsp.	½ tsp.
sugar	¼ cup	⅓ cup	⅓ cup
bread flour	2 cups	3 cups	3 ½ cups
yeast	1 ½ tsp.	1 ½ tsp.	2 tsp.
*almonds, chopped	¼ cup	⅓ cup	½ cup
*dried apricots, diced	½ cup	¾ cup	1 cup
*almond paste, diced	½ cup	⅔ cup	⅔ cup
*sugar	2 tbs.	3 tbs.	¼ cup

*Add at the beep or appropriate time for your machine.

Cherry Almond Bread

Sweet or Basic cycle

Larane Coffino loves cherries and couldn't find a recipe using them so she made one up. She uses the gluten to obtain a tall, moist loaf which has a slightly tart cherry flavor. Larane packs cherries tightly in the measuring cup. She uses twice the amount of yeast — I do not find that much necessary. This is a low-rising, dense loaf.

	1 lb.	1½ lb.	1¾ lb.
canned tart cherries	1 cup	1½ cups	1¾ cups
almond extract	¾ tsp.	1 tsp.	1 tsp.
butter	1½ tbs.	2 tbs.	2½ tbs.
salt	¾ tsp.	1 tsp.	1 tsp.
sugar	¼ cup	⅓ cup	½ cup
bread flour	2 cups	3 cups	3½ cups
vital gluten	1½ tbs.	2 tbs.	2½ tbs.
yeast	1 tsp.	1½ tsp.	2 tsp.
*slivered almonds	⅓ cup	½ cup	⅔ cup

*Add almonds at the beep or appropriate time for your machine.

Bing Cherry Coconut Bread

Sweet or Basic cycle

Trish Boyer says to make sure to use coconut milk, not cream of coconut.

	1 lb.	1½ lb.	2 lb.
coconut milk	⅔ cup	1 cup	1⅓ cups
walnut or vegetable oil	1½ tbs.	2⅓ tbs.	3 tbs.
honey	1½ tbs.	2⅓ tbs.	3 tbs.
egg	½	½	1
salt	⅓ tsp.	½ tsp.	¾ tsp.
whole wheat flour	½ cup	¾ cup	1 cup
rolled oats	½ cup	¾ cup	1 cup
bread flour	1 cup	1½ cups	2 cups
yeast	1 tsp.	1½ tsp.	2 tsp.
*dried Bing cherries	¼ cup	⅓ cup	½ cup
*flaked coconut	¼ cup	⅓ cup	½ cup
*sliced almonds	2 tbs.	3 tbs.	¼ cup

*Add at the beep or appropriate time for your machine.

Sweet Potato Bread

Sweet or Basic cycle

Lillian Ho says that the sweet potato adds a wonderful, moist texture and subtle taste to this bread. Cook and place the approximate amount of sweet potato into a 2-cup measuring cup, add the egg and fill with water up to the given measurement mark. The machine will mash the sweet potato for you. This is a very high-rising bread that is great for turkey sandwiches.

	1 lb.	1 1/2 lb.	2 lb.
sweet potato, cooked (or yam)	2/3 cup	3/4 cup	1 cup
egg	1	1	1
water	as needed	as needed	as needed
wet ingredients should equal	1 cup	1 1/2 cups	2 cups
butter	1 1/2 tbs.	2 tbs.	2 1/2 tbs.
brown sugar	1 1/2 tbs.	2 tbs.	2 1/2 tbs.
salt	3/4 tsp.	1 tsp.	1 tsp.
cinnamon	1/3 tsp.	1/2 tsp.	2/3 tsp.
nutmeg	1/4 tsp.	1/3 tsp.	1/2 tsp.
allspice	1/4 tsp.	1/3 tsp.	1/2 tsp.
whole wheat flour	1/3 cup	1/2 cup	2/3 cup
bread flour	1 2/3 cups	2 1/2 cups	3 1/3 cups
yeast	1 tsp.	1 1/2 tsp.	2 tsp.

Lazy Onion Bread

Basic cycle

The lazy part of this recipe is simply using onion soup mix. Thanks to Wendy Ceracche for sharing this one. There is no salt included in the recipe as there is some in the onion soup.

	1 lb.	1 1/2 lb.	1 3/4 lb.
water or milk	7/8 cup (7 oz.)	1 1/4 cups	1 1/2 cups
sugar	1 1/2 tbs.	2 tbs.	2 1/2 tbs.
onion soup mix	1 1/2 tsp.	2 tsp.	1 tbs.
dry milk powder, optional	1 tbs.	1 tbs.	1 1/2 tbs.
bread flour	2 cups	3 cups	3 1/2 cups
yeast	1 tsp.	1 1/2 tsp.	2 tsp.

Coconut Bread

Beulah Donison says her family frequently requests this bread. Be sure to use unsweetened coconut milk such as A Taste of Thai, not the cream of coconut milk. Use an egg yolk, white or 2 tbs. egg substitute for the half egg.

	1 lb.	1 ½ lb.	2 lb. only
coconut milk	⅔ cup	1 cup	1 ¼ cups
egg	½	½	1
vegetable oil	1 tbs.	1 ½ tbs.	2 tbs.
coconut extract	1 tsp.	1 ½ tsp.	1 tsp.
sugar	2 tbs.	2 ½ tbs.	3 tbs.
salt	½ tsp.	¾ tsp.	1 tsp.
coconut flakes	¼ cup	⅓ cup	½ cup
bread flour	2 cups	3 cups	3¾ cups
yeast	1 tsp.	1 ½ tsp.	2 tsp.

Czechoslovakian Orange Bread

Ruth Morgan requested this recipe adaptation. This bread is traditionally baked in a crescent and is glazed with honey and orange juice mixed together and warmed.

	1 lb.	1 ½ lb.	1 ¾ lb.
milk	½ cup	⅔ cup	¾ cup
butter or margarine	3 tbs.	4 tbs.	5 tbs.
egg	1	1	1
salt	¼ tsp.	⅓ tsp.	½ tsp.
sugar	3 tbs.	¼ cup	⅓ cup
orange peel	1 tsp.	1 ¼ tsp.	1 ½ tsp.
ground mace	dash	¼ tsp.	¼ tsp.
bread flour	2 cups	3 cups	3 ½ cups
yeast	1 tsp.	1 tsp.	1 ½ tsp.

Zahtar Bread

French, Sweet or Basic cycle

Karen Abu-Hamdeh says this bread is wonderful and I agree. Oregano or thyme can be substituted for zahtar. Zahtar is a Middle Eastern spice blend.

	1 lb.	1 ½ lb.	1 ¾ lb.
water	¾ cup	1 ⅛ cups	1 ⅓ cups
olive oil	1 ½ tbs.	2 tbs.	2 ½ tbs.
sugar	¾ tsp.	1 tsp.	1 ¼ tsp.
salt	¾ tsp.	1 tsp.	1 tsp.
zahtar	1 ½ tbs.	2 tbs.	2 ½ tbs.
bread flour	2 cups	3 cups	3 ½ cups
yeast	1 tsp.	1 ½ tsp.	2 tsp.

Garlic Dill Bread

Whole Wheat, Sweet or Basic cycle

Lynn Connor uses the bottled chopped or crushed garlic (salt free) for this bread. The garlic and dill combine nicely. This low- to medium-rising bread has a good, dense texture and is very garlicky!

	1 lb.	1 ½ lb.	2 lb.
water	⅔ cup	1 cup	1 ⅓ cups
chopped garlic	¼ cup	⅓ cup	½ cup
butter	1 tbs.	1 ½ tbs.	2 tbs.
dill weed or seed, dried	½ tsp.	¾ tsp.	1 tsp.
salt	½ tsp.	¾ tsp.	1 tsp.
whole wheat flour	1 ⅛ cups	1 ⅔ cups	2 ¼ cups
bread flour	1 ⅛ cups	1 ⅔ cups	2 ¼ cups
yeast	1 tsp.	1 ½ tsp.	2 tsp.

Italian Herb Bread

French or Basic cycle

Mrs. William Miller serves this with spaghetti and freshly grated Parmesan.

	1 lb.	1 ½ lb.	1 ¾ lb.
water	¾ cup	1 ⅛ cups	1 ⅓ cups
olive oil	2 tsp.	1 tbs.	1 ⅓ tbs.
sugar	2 tsp.	1 tbs.	1 ⅓ tbs.
Parmesan cheese, grated	¼ cup	⅓ cup	½ cup
garlic powder	½ tsp.	1 tsp.	1 tsp.
Italian seasoning	½ tsp.	1 tsp.	1 tsp.
bread flour	2 cups	3 cups	3 ½ cups
yeast	1 tsp.	1 ½ tsp.	2 tsp.

Indian Yogurt Bread

Whole Wheat, Sweet or Basic cycle

Priscilla Ward has fun developing recipes for use in her Maxim machine. Garam masala is a blend of Indian spices and can be found in Indian and Asian grocery stores. Any spice blend can be substituted. Add milk slowly after the machine has been kneading for 3 to 4 minutes. Use only enough for the dough to form a round ball.

	1 lb.	1 ½ lb.	2 lb.
plain yogurt	1 cup	1 ½ cups	1 ¾ cups
olive oil	2 tbs.	3 tbs.	¼ cup
honey	2 tbs.	3 tbs.	¼ cup
garam masala	1 tsp.	1 ½ tsp.	2 tsp.
salt	½ tsp.	¾ tsp.	1 tsp.
bread flour	2 cup	3 cups	3 ½ cups
whole wheat flour	¾ cup	1 ⅛ cups	1 ⅓ cups
yeast	1 ½ tsp.	2 tsp.	2 ½ tsp.
*milk	as needed; add 1-2 tbs. at a time		

Garlic Dill Whole Wheat Bread

Whole Wheat or Basic cycle

Virginia Colson makes this flavorful bread for family and friends. Celery seed or rosemary can be substituted for the dill weed. Use 3 or 4 cloves of minced or pressed garlic for every teaspoon of powder if desired.

	1 lb.	1 ½ lb.	1 ¾ lb.
water	⅞ cup (7 oz.)	1 ¼ cups	1 ¾ cups
butter or margarine	1 tbs.	1 ½ tbs.	2 tbs.
salt	½ tsp.	¾ tsp.	1 tsp.
garlic powder	1 tsp.	1 ½ tsp.	2 tsp.
dill weed, dried	2 tsp.	1 tbs.	1 ⅓ tbs.
dry milk powder	1 tbs.	1 ½ tbs.	2 tbs.
whole wheat flour	1 cup	1 ½ cups	2 cups
bread flour	1 cup	1 ½ cups	2 cups
yeast	1 ½ tsp.	2 tsp.	2 tsp.

Savory Herb Cornbread

Basic cycle

Beth Dash Koruitz uses defatted chicken broth. Chicken bouillon can be substituted, but if it is salty, cut back on or omit salt. She serves this warm with a garlic butter spread or in poultry dressing.

	1 lb.	1½ lb.	2 lb.
chicken broth	½ cup	¾ cup	1 cup
water	⅓ cup	½ cup	⅔ cup
canola oil	2 tbs.	1 tbs.	1⅓ tbs.
molasses	1 tbs.	1½ tbs.	2 tbs.
salt	¾ tsp.	1 tsp.	1 tsp.
sage	1 tsp.	1½ tsp.	2 tsp.
cornmeal	¼ cup	⅓ cup	½ cup
instant potato flakes	¼ cup	⅓ cup	½ cup
dry milk powder	1 tbs.	1½ tbs.	2 tbs.
bread flour	1¾ cup	2⅔ cups	3½ cups
yeast	1 tsp.	1½ tsp.	2 tsp.

Garlic Herb Cheese Bread

Sweet or Basic cycle

Camille B. Henderson adapted this recipe to fit her machine. She recommends using sharp cheddar as it gives the bread more flavor. Some people have said that they have difficulty with breads using garlic — that they don't rise. We have never experienced this in the test kitchen. All of our test loaves on this recipe rose very high. Keep an eye on the dough and adjust as necessary because of the cheese. The cheese should be lightly packed in the measuring cup. The garlic and herbs can be adjusted to taste. Scrape the sides of the pan with a rubber spatula if the ingredients are not mixing.

	1 lb.	1½ lb.	1¾ lb.
milk	½ cup	⅝ cup (5oz.)	¾ cup
eggs	2	2	3
butter or margarine	2 tbs.	2½ tbs.	3 tbs.
grated cheese, lightly packed	¾ cup	1 cup	1 cup
salt	½ tsp.	1 tsp.	1 tsp.
sugar	1½ tsp.	2 tsp.	2½ tsp.
garlic clove, minced	1	1½	1½
cayenne pepper	dash	⅛ tsp.	¼ tsp.
oregano, dried	⅛+ tsp.	¼ tsp.	⅓ tsp.
basil, dried	¼ tsp.	½ tsp.	½ tsp.
caraway seeds	1½ tsp.	2 tsp.	2½ tsp.
bread flour	2 cups	3 cups	3½ cups
yeast	1 tsp.	1½ tsp.	2 tsp.

Norma's Dilly Bread

Norma Herbert's aunt gave her this recipe years ago and Norma request-ed an adaptation for her bread machine. She recommends using creamed cot-tage cheese. The minced instant onion is found with spices in your grocery store. The cottage cheese can throw off the liquid balance — adjust with water or flour 1 tablespoon at a time.

	1 lb.	1½ lb.	1¾ lb.
cottage cheese	¾ cup	1 cup	1⅛ cups
egg	1	2	2
sugar	1½ tbs.	2 tbs.	3 tbs.
salt	½ tsp.	1 tsp.	1 tsp.
onion or onion powder	2 tsp.	1 tbs.	1⅓ tbs.
baking soda	¼ tsp.	½ tsp.	½ tsp.
dill seed	1½ tsp.	2 tsp.	1 tbs.
bread flour	2 cups	3 cups	3½ cups
yeast	1 tsp.	1½ tsp.	2 tsp.

Herb Bread

Marie Ehlers recently bought a bread machine and has already adapted this recipe. The green onions may throw off the moisture content slightly, so watch the dough and adjust with flour or water if needed. I cut her salt amount in half.

	1 lb.	1½ lb.	2 lb.
water	⅞ cup (7 oz.)	1¼ cups	1½ cups
vegetable oil	1 tbs.	1⅓ tbs.	1½ tbs.
salt	½ tsp.	¾ tsp.	1 tsp.
sugar	1 tbs.	1⅓ tbs.	1½ tbs.
green onion tops, chopped	3 tbs.	¼ cup	⅓ cup
fresh parsley, chopped	2 tbs.	2½ tbs.	3 tbs.
or dried parsley	1 tsp.	1¼ tsp.	1½ tsp.
dill seed	1 tsp.	1¼ tsp.	1½ tsp.
caraway seed	1 tsp.	1¼ tsp.	1½ tsp.
bread flour	2⅛ cups	3 cups	3¾ cups
yeast	1 tsp.	1½ tsp.	2 tsp.

Oregano Herb Bread

Basic cycle

Romaine Blount came up with this bread for her husband. If using fresh herbs, triple the amount. Leftovers, if there are any, make flavorful croutons.

	1 lb.	1½ lb.	1¾ lb.
water	1 cup	1½ cups	1⅔ cups
olive oil	2 tbs.	3 tbs.	3 tbs.
sugar	⅓ tsp.	½ tsp.	⅔ tsp.
salt	½ tsp.	¾ tsp.	¾ tsp.
parsley, dried	1 tsp.	1½ tsp.	1¾ tsp.
thyme, dried	1 tsp.	1½ tsp.	1¾ tsp.
oregano, dried	2 tsp.	1 tbs.	1⅓ tbs.
bread flour	2¼ cups	3 cups	3½ cups
dry milk powder	3 tbs.	¼ cup	⅓ cup
yeast	1½ tsp.	2 tsp.	2 tsp.

Sugar-Free Italian Herb Bread

French or Basic cycle

Albert Santoni came up with this sweetener-free bread. He suggests substituting rosemary, garlic powder and/or dill for the oregano. Herb amounts should be tripled if using fresh herbs.

	1 lb.	1½ lb.	1¾ lb.
water	⅔ cup	1 cup	1¼ cups
olive oil	1⅓ tbs.	2 tbs.	2½ tbs.
salt	⅓ tsp.	½ tsp.	½ tsp.
oregano, dried	1 tsp.	1½ tsp.	2 tsp.
bread flour	2 cups	3 cups	3½ cups
yeast	1 tsp.	1½ tsp.	1½ tsp.

Dill Onion Bread

Flarane Wold enjoys making this bread with sour cream, but yogurt could also be used. Adjust the dough consistency with flour or water as necessary. Use an egg yolk, white or 2 tbs. egg substitute for the half egg.

	1 lb.	1 1/2 lb.	1 3/4 lb.
sour cream	1 cup	1 1/2 cups	1 3/4 cups
egg	1	1	1 1/2
salt	1/2 tsp.	1 tsp.	1 tsp.
baking soda	1/4 tsp.	1/3 tsp.	1/2 tsp.
sugar	2 tbs.	3 tbs.	1/4 cup
dried onion flakes	2 tbs.	3 tbs.	3 tbs.
dill weed, dried	1 tbs.	1 1/3 tbs.	1 1/2 tbs.
bread flour	2 cups	3 cups	3 1/2 cups
yeast	1 tsp.	1 1/2 tsp.	1 1/2 tsp.

French Herb Bread

Karen Swanson based this recipe on a bread that was a grand champion winner at the Alaska State Fair a few years ago. Karen normally likes to make whole grain breads but uses white flour for this as the flavors of the herbs carry better. If using the "green can" Parmesan cheese, omit the salt. Use an egg yolk, white or 2 tbs. egg substitute for the half egg. If using fresh herbs, triple the amount given. Herbs can be adjusted to taste.

	1 lb.	1 1/2 lb.	1 3/4 lb.
water	2/3 cup	7/8 cup (7 oz.)	1 cup
vegetable oil	1/2 tbs.	1 tbs.	1 tbs.
egg	1/2	1	1
salt, optional	1/2 tsp.	3/4 tsp.	1 tsp.
sugar	2 1/2 tsp.	1 tbs.	1 1/3 tbs.
garlic powder	dash	1/8 tsp.	1/4 tsp.
Italian seasoning	dash	1/8 tsp.	1/4 tsp.
oregano, dried	1/4 tsp.	1/3 tsp.	1/2 tsp.
basil, dried	1/4 tsp.	1/3 tsp.	1/2 tsp.
thyme, dried	1/4 tsp.	1/3 tsp.	1/2 tsp.
Parmesan cheese, grated	2 tsp.	1 tbs.	1 1/3 tbs.
bread flour	2 1/4 cups	3 cups	3 1/2 cups
dry milk powder	2 tbs.	2 1/2 tbs.	3 tbs.
yeast	1 tsp.	1 1/2 tsp.	2 tsp.

Onion Soup Bread

Basic cycle

Evelyn Fehrmann and a friend make this in their bread machines. The (Lipton's) onion soup mix can be adjusted to taste. After 10 minutes of kneading, adjust the consistency of the dough as needed by adding a tablespoon of water at a time until a dough ball is formed — it may require none or up to 4 tbs., depending on the loaf size.

	I lb.	1 1/2 lb.	1 3/4 lb.
cottage cheese	1/2 cup	2/3 cup	3/4 cup
sour cream	1/2 cup	2/3 cup	3/4 cup
egg	1/2	1	1
butter or margarine	1 tbs.	1 tbs.	1 1/2 tbs.
sugar	2 tbs.	2 1/2 tbs.	3 tbs.
baking soda	1/4 tsp.	1/4 tsp.	1/2 tsp.
onion soup mix	2 tbs.	1 1/2 tbs.	3 tbs.
bread flour	2 1/4 cups	3 cups	3 1/2 cups
yeast	1 tsp.	1 tsp.	1 1/2 tsp.

Pizza Bread

Sweet or Basic cycle

Chris Brakebill says this bread has a marvelous pizza taste and aroma with an earthy color. Her grandchildren love this so much there is frequently none left for the grownups!

	1 lb.	1 1/2 lb.	1 3/4 lb.
tomato or V-8 juice	7/8 cup (7 oz.)	1 1/4 cups	1 1/3 cups
vegetable oil	1 1/2 tbs.	2 tbs.	2 1/2 tbs.
egg (egg yolk or white for 1/2)	1/2	1/2	1
Parmesan cheese, freshly grated	3 tbs.	1/4 cup	1/3 cup
basil, dried	2 tsp.	1 tbs.	1 tbs.
oregano, dried	1/3 tsp.	1/2 tsp.	3/4 tsp.
sugar	1 1/2 tbs.	2 tbs.	2 tbs.
salt	1/2 tsp.	1 tsp.	1 tsp.
garlic powder	1/2 tsp.	1 tsp.	1 tsp.
onion powder	1/2 tsp.	1 tsp.	1 tsp.
bread flour	2 cups	3 cups	3 1/2 cups
yeast	1 tsp.	1 1/2 tsp.	1 1/2 tsp.

Good Seasons Bread

Basic cycle

Lee Hickney uses Good Seasons Garlic Cheese Salad Dressing mix. We preferred either a Good Seasons blend or a Mrs. Dash Dressing Mix (jar). If the dry seasoning mixes contain salt, none needs to be added to the bread. One .65 oz. package of mix equals about 2½ tbs. and can be used for all sizes. I cut Lee's water amount to avoid overflows. The water amount is less for the 1¾ lb. size because of the amount of eggs.

	1 lb.	1½ lb.	1¾ lb.
water	½ cup	¾ cups	⅔ cups
egg	1	1	2
canola oil	1½ tbs.	2 tbs.	2 tbs.
salt, optional	¼ tsp.	½ tsp.	½ tsp.
sugar	1 tbs.	1½ tbs.	1½ tbs.
salad dressing mix	2½ tbs.	2½ tbs.	2½ tbs.
bread flour	2 cups	3 cups	3½ cups
yeast	1 tsp.	1½ tsp.	2 tsp.

Vegetable Herb Bread

Sweet or Basic cycle

Camille Carter says she hopes others enjoy this recipe as much as her family. It is a wonderful, spicy light-textured and colored bread which she calls "Old-Fashioned Stuffing Bread" and uses for leftover turkey sandwiches. Watch dough for moisture.

	1 lb.	1½ lb.	1¾ lb.
water	¾ cup	1⅛ cups	1⅓ cups
butter or margarine	½ tbs.	1 tbs.	1 tbs.
diced onion	¼ cup	⅓ cup	⅓ cup
sugar	1 tsp.	1½ tsp.	2 tsp.
salt	¾ tsp.	1 tsp.	1 tsp.
black pepper	¾ tsp.	1 tsp.	1 tsp.
sage, dried	¾ tsp.	1 tsp.	1 tsp.
thyme, dried	1½ tsp.	2 tsp.	2 tsp.
diced celery including leafy top	¼ cup	⅓ cup	½ cup
bread flour	2 cups	3 cups	3½ cups
yeast	1½ tsp.	2 tsp.	2 tsp.

Carlin's Dilly Bread

This bread has been a favorite of Carlin Nerhus since childhood. Adjust with water or flour as needed only after a full 10 minutes of kneading. This is a high-rising loaf of bread. I cut Carlin's yeast and egg amounts in half. If you have a 1 1/4 lb. machine (Seiko), make only the 1 lb. size to prevent overflows.

	1 lb.	**1 1/2 lb.**	**2 lb.**
water	2 tbs.	3 tbs.	1/4 cup
cottage cheese	3/4 cup	1 cup	1 1/4 cups
eggs	1	2	2
salt	1/2 tsp.	1-1 1/2 tsp.	1-1 1/2 tsp.
dill seed	1 1/2 tbs.	2 tbs.	2 1/2 tbs.
instant onion	1 1/2 tbs.	2 tbs.	2 1/2 tbs.
sugar	2 tbs.	2 1/2 tbs.	3 tbs.
baking soda	1/2 tsp.	1/2 tsp.	1 tsp.
bread flour	2 cups	3 cups	3 1/2 cups
yeast	1 tsp.	1 1/2 tsp.	1 1/2 tsp.

So Many Grains Bread

Whole Wheat, Sweet or Basic cycle

Rona Waltzer developed this recipe, and you will enjoy its texture and unique, flavorful taste.

	1 lb.	1½ lb.	2 lb.
water	¾ cup.	1⅛ cups	1½ cups
vegetable oil	1 tbs.	1½ tbs.	2 tbs.
molasses or honey	2 tbs.	3 tbs.	4 tbs.
salt	½ tsp.	¾ tsp.	1 tsp.
vital gluten, optional	1 tbs.	1½ tbs.	2 tbs.
rye flour	2 tbs.	3 tbs.	¼ cup
buckwheat flour	2 tbs.	3 tbs.	¼ cup
soy flour	2 tbs.	3 tbs.	¼ cup
yellow cornmeal	2 tbs.	3 tbs.	¼ cup
rolled oats	¼ cup	⅓ cup	½ cup
whole wheat flour	¾ cup	1⅛ cups	1½ cups
bread flour	¾ cup	1⅛ cups	1½ cups
yeast	1 tsp.	1½ tsp.	2 tsp.

Kashi Rye Bread

Whole Wheat, Sweet or Basic cycle

Howard has adapted this recipe and is having trouble supplying all the requests for samples. Kashi (uncooked breakfast pilaf) is usually found with cereals in grocery stores. This recipe calls for cooked kashi.

	1 lb.	1½ lb.	1¾ lb.
water	½ cup	¾ cup	1 cup
margarine or vegetable oil	1 tbs.	1 tbs.	2 tbs.
cooked kashi	⅓ cup	½ cup	⅔ cup
sugar	1 tbs.	1½ tbs.	2 tbs.
salt	⅔ tsp.	1 tsp.	1 tsp.
caraway seeds	1 tsp.	1½ tsp.	2 tsp.
light rye flour	⅓ cup	½ cup	⅔ cup
bread flour	1⅓ cups	2 cups	2⅔ cups
yeast	1 tsp.	1½ tsp.	2 tsp.

Orange Bran Bread

I decreased the amount of bran in Mrs. M. Morrison's recipe, as it cuts the gluten's elastic network, which reduces the bread's rising. This has a nice flavor and rises nicely.

	1 lb.	1 1/2 lb.	1 3/4 lb.
orange juice	7/8 cup (7 oz.)	1 1/4 cups	1 3/4 cups
butter or margarine	1 tbs.	1 1/2 tbs.	2 tbs.
sugar	2 tbs.	3 tbs.	1/4 cup
salt	3/4 tsp.	1 tsp.	1 tsp.
orange peel	1/2 tsp.	3/4 tsp.	1 tsp.
wheat bran	1/4 cup	1/3 cup	1/2 cup
dry milk powder, optional	1 tbs.	1 1/2 tbs.	2 tbs.
bread flour	1 3/4 cups	2 3/4 cups	3 1/2 cups
vital gluten	1 tbs.	1 1/2 tbs.	2 tbs.
yeast	1 1/2 tsp.	2 tsp.	2 tsp.
*raisins	1/3 cup	1/2 cup	2/3 cup

*Add raisins at the beep or appropriate time for your machine.

Shingletown Rye

Betty Hermida came up with this bread quite by accident. It was not quite what she was looking for (gingerbread), but one of the best-tasting and best-looking loaves of bread she has made. Use a yolk or white for the half egg. The ginger and cinnamon can be adjusted to taste.

	1 lb.	1 1/2 lb.	2 lb.
water	2/3 cup	1 cup	1 1/3 cups
egg	1	1 1/2	2
vegetable oil	1 tbs.	2 tbs.	2 1/2 tbs.
molasses	2 tbs.	3 tbs.	1/4 cup
unsweetened cocoa	1 tbs.	1 1/2 tbs.	2 tbs.
brown sugar	2 tsp.	1 tbs.	1 1/2 tbs.
instant coffee granules	1 tsp.	1 tsp.	1 1/2 tsp.
salt	3/4 tsp.	1 tsp.	1 tsp.
ground ginger	3/4 tsp.	1 tsp.	1 1/4 tsp.
cinnamon	3/4 tsp.	1 tsp.	1 1/4 tsp.
vital gluten, optional	1 tbs.	1 1/2 tbs.	2 tbs.
rye flour	1/2 cup	3/4 cup	1 cup
whole wheat flour	1/2 cup	3/4 cup	1 cup
bread flour	1 cup	1 1/2 cups	2 cups
yeast	1 tsp.	1 1/2 tsp.	2 tsp.

Old World Rye

Rae Rubin has adapted this old-world rye recipe. Add the lemon juice 10 minutes after starting the machine — in all machines. If fresh buttermilk is on hand, substitute it for the water (cup for cup) and omit the buttermilk powder.

	1 lb.	1 ½ lb.	1 ¾ lb.
water	⅞ cup (7 oz.)	1 cup	1 ¼ cups
vegetable oil	2 tsp.	1 tbs.	1 tbs.
honey	2 tsp.	1 tbs.	1 tbs.
salt	½ tsp.	¾ tsp.	1 tsp.
baking soda	¼ tsp.	⅓ tsp.	½ tsp.
dried onion flakes	2 tsp.	2 ½ tsp.	1 tbs.
caraway seeds	2 tsp.	1 tbs.	1 tbs.
buttermilk powder	2 ½ tbs.	3 tbs.	¼ cup
wheat germ	1 tbs.	1 ½ tbs.	2 tbs.
vital gluten, optional	1 tbs.	1 ½ tbs.	2 tbs.
soy flour	1 tbs.	1 ½ tbs.	2 tbs.
whole wheat flour	⅔ cup	¾ cup	1 cup
rye flour	¼ cup	⅓ cup	½ cup
bread flour	1 cup	1 ½ cups	2 cups
yeast	1 ½ tsp.	1 ½ tsp.	2 tsp.
*lemon juice	2 tsp.	2 ½ tsp.	1 tbs.

*Add 10 minutes after starting machine.

Here's To Your Health

This is a recipe adaptation made for Martha Babcock. It results in a low-rising, moist, open grain loaf with lots of flavor. Watch the dough for moisture.

	1 lb.	1 ½ lb.	2 lb.
water	½ cup	¾ cup	1 cup
cottage cheese	⅓ cup	½ cup	⅔ cup
vegetable oil	1 tbs.	1 ½ tbs.	2 tbs.
honey	2 tbs.	3 tbs.	¼ cup
salt	⅓ tsp.	½ tsp.	⅔ tsp.
wheat germ	2 tbs.	3 tbs.	¼ cup
oats	¼ cup	⅓ cup	½ cup
whole wheat flour	¾ cup	1 ⅛ cups	1 ½ cups
bread flour	1 ⅛ cups	1 ⅔ cups	2 ¼ cups
yeast	1 tsp.	1 ½ tsp.	2 tsp.
*raisins	¼ cup	⅓ cup	½ cup

*Add raisins at the beep or appropriate time for your machine.

Rye Bread

The allspice really adds a unique, flavorful twist to this recipe developed by Peter Dahl. All of Peter's recipes are very low-rising, dense breads with tremendous flavor. If you judge successful bread based on how high it rises in your pan, don't even try this. If you judge successful bread based on flavor and texture, you must try this. There is a lot of flour in this recipe, so watch the kneading and scrape the sides of the pan if necessary.

	1 lb.	1 ½ lb.	2 lb.
water	1 ⅛ cups	1 ½ cups	1 ¾ cups
vegetable oil	1 tbs.	1 ⅓ tbs.	2 tbs.
honey	1 ½ tbs.	2 tbs.	2 ½ tbs.
salt	¾ tsp.	1 tsp.	1 tsp.
ground allspice	¾ tsp.	1 tsp.	1 tsp.
caraway seed	2 tsp.	1 tbs.	1 ½ tbs.
dry milk powder	1 ½ tbs.	2 tbs.	2 tbs.
vital gluten	2 tsp.	1 tbs.	1 ½ tbs.
rye flour	1 ½ cups	2 cups	2 ½ cups
bread flour	1 ½ cups	2 cups	2 ½ cups
yeast	2 tsp.	2 ½ tsp.	2 ½ tsp.

Grape Nuts Bread

Jodi Kresel developed this one. If your machine has difficulty baking properly with the large amount of raisins, cut them in half. I have received calls or letters from two people who have said that using Grape Nuts has scratched their machine pans. Neither I nor any testers have had this problem, but I mention it anyway. Remember that these pans are designed for nuts and other hard foods. Add the Grape Nuts in the order given, or for DAK/Welbilt owners, put the flour in and then the Grape Nuts. Adjust water or flour if necessary.

	1 lb.	1 ½ lb.	2 lb.
water	⅔ cup	1 cup	1 ⅓ cups
butter or margarine	1 tbs.	1 ½ tbs.	2 tbs.
sugar	1 ½ tbs.	2 tbs.	3 tbs.
salt	½ tsp.	¾ tsp.	1 tsp.
cinnamon	¾ tsp.	1 tsp.	1 ½ tsp.
dry milk powder	1 tbs.	1 ½ tbs.	2 tbs.
Grape Nuts cereal	½ cup	¾ cup	1 cup
bread flour	1 ¾ cups	2 ¾ cups	3 ½ cups
yeast	1 tsp.	1 ½ tsp.	2 tsp.
*raisins	½ cup	¾ cup	1 cup

*Add raisins at the beep or appropriate time for your machine.

Swedish Rye

Whole Wheat, Sweet or Basic cycle

Jack Hiller says that he prefers using powdered fennel seeds for this recipe which he adapted from a recipe of his mother, Myrtle. The fennel can be adjusted to taste. He heaps the sugar and adds water but I tested using the given amounts.

	1 lb.	**1 ½ lb.**	**1 ¾ lb.**
water	⅔ cup	1 cup	1 ⅓ cups
butter or margarine	3 tbs.	4 tbs.	5 tbs.
salt	½ tsp.	½ tsp.	1 tsp.
fennel seed	1 ½ tbs.	2 tbs.	2 ½ tbs.
sugar	3 tbs.	¼ cup	⅓ cup
rye flour	1 cup	1 ½ cups	2 cups
bread flour	1 cup	1 ½ cups	2 cups
vital gluten	1 ½ tbs.	2 tbs.	2 ½ tbs.
yeast	1 ½ tsp.	2 tsp.	2 tsp.
*candied or dried mixed fruit	¼ cup	⅓ cup	½ cup

*Add fruit at the beep or appropriate time for your machine

Whole Wheat
Irish Soda Bread

Whole Wheat, Sweet or Basic cycle

Frank puts the raisins in the water, microwaves them for 2 minutes and then lets them soak for at least 2 hours before straining them. The swollen, soft raisins spread into small particles throughout the loaf. Add the raisins with the liquids. I am lazy and add unplumped raisins at the beginning.

	1 lb.	**1 ½ lb.**	**1 ¾ lb.**
buttermilk	⅞ cup (7 oz.)	1 ⅛ cups	1 ½ cups
margarine or oil	1 tbs.	1 ½ tbs.	2 tbs.
honey	1 tbs.	1 ½ tbs.	2 tbs.
raisins	½ cup	¾ cup	1 cup
sugar	1 tbs.	1 ½ tbs.	2 tbs.
salt	½ tsp.	½ tsp.	1 tsp.
baking soda	½ tsp.	½ tsp.	1 tsp.
vital gluten, optional	1 tbs.	1 ½ tbs.	2 tbs.
whole wheat flour	½ cup	¾ cup	1 cup
bread flour	1 ½ cups	2 ¼ cups	3 cups
yeast	1 ½ tsp.	2 tsp.	2 tsp.

Multi-Grain Bread

Whole Wheat, Sweet or Basic cycle

Punki Gehring uses a 10-grain cereal for this flavorful loaf. As not all stores carry it, use either a 7-, 9-, 10- or 12-grain cereal as available. Apple juice concentrate can be used instead of the applesauce. Punki adds a tablespoon or two of water to adjust the texture of the dough. She uses the higher amount of salt, but I prefer less.

	1 lb.	1½ lb.	1¾ lb.
buttermilk	⅞ cup (7 oz.)	1¼ cups	1½ cups
applesauce	1½ tbs.	2 tbs.	3 tbs.
sugar	1½ tbs.	2 tbs.	2½ tbs.
salt	½-¾ tsp.	¾-1 tsp.	1 tsp.
vital gluten	2 tbs.	3 tbs.	¼ cup
10-grain cereal	½ cup	⅔ cup	¾ cup
whole wheat flour	¾ cup	1 cup	1⅛ cups
bread flour	1½ cups	2 cups	2½ cups
yeast	1½ tsp.	2 tsp.	2 tsp.
water	as needed	as needed	as needed

Seeded Wheat Bread

Whole Wheat, Sweet or Basic cycle

Margaret Curtin used to make this by hand. She uses honey crunch wheat germ. Amaranth and teff give it lots of nutrition and a special nutty flavor. I reduced the amount of salt.

	1 lb.	1½ lb.	1¾ lb.
milk	3 tbs.	¼ cup	⅓ cup
water	⅝ cup (5 oz.)	⅞ cup (7 oz.)	1¼ cups
butter or margarine	1 tbs.	1½ tbs.	2 tbs.
sugar	2 tbs.	3 tbs.	¼ cup
salt	½ tsp.	¾ tsp.	1-1½ tsp.
wheat germ	1½ tbs.	2 tbs.	2½ tbs.
teff grains or seeds	1½ tbs.	2 tbs.	2½ tbs.
amaranth grains	2 tsp.	1 tbs.	1⅓ tbs.
vital gluten	2 tsp.	1 tbs.	1⅓ tbs.
whole wheat flour	⅓ cup	½ cup	⅔ cup
bread flour	1⅔ cups	2½ cups	3⅓ cups
yeast	1 tsp.	1½ tsp.	2 tsp.

Sunflower Bran Bread

Whole Wheat, Sweet or Basic cycle

R.M. Olmstead developed this tasty treat. The recipe states fine bran flakes, but I use bran, not bran cereal. I cut the salt amount in half.

	1 lb.	1 1/2 lb.	1 3/4 lb.
water	3/4 cup	1 1/4 cups	1 1/2 cups
butter or oil	1 tbs.	1 1/2 tbs.	1 1/2 tbs.
molasses	1 1/2 tbs.	2 tbs.	2 1/2 tbs.
salt	1/2 tsp.	3/4 tsp.	1 tsp.
bran (wheat or oat)	1/2 cup	3/4 cup	1 cup
sunflower kernels	1/4 cup	1/3 cup	1/3 cup
bread flour	2 cups	3 cups	3 1/2 cups
yeast	2 tsp.	2 tsp.	2 1/2 tsp.

Whole Wheat Sandwich Bread

Whole Wheat, Sweet or Basic cycle

Erma Autenrieth says that she has finally perfected a dense whole wheat bread which holds up to her meat and lettuce sandwiches.

	1 lb.	1 1/2 lb.	1 3/4 lb.
water	3/4 cup	1 1/8 cups	1 1/2 cups
corn oil	2 tbs.	3 tbs.	1/4 cup
sugar	2 tsp.	1 tbs.	1 1/3 tbs.
salt	1/2 tsp.	1 tsp.	1 tsp.
dry milk powder	1 1/2 tbs.	2 tbs.	2 1/2 tbs.
whole wheat flour	1 cup	1 1/4 cups	1 3/4 cups
bread flour	1 1/4 cups	1 3/4 cups	2 1/3 cups
yeast	1 1/2 tsp.	2 tsp.	2 tsp.

German Rye Bread

Whole Wheat, Sweet or Basic cycle

Sherry Libsack has adapted her mother-in-law's light rye recipe for her bread machine. The gluten is vital: it can be found in most health food stores.

	1 lb.	1 1/2 lb.	2 lb.
water	7/8 cup	1 1/3 cups	1 2/3 cups
sugar	1 1/2 tbs.	2 tbs.	2 1/2 tbs.
salt	1/3 tsp.	1/2 tsp.	2/3 tsp.
vital gluten	2 tsp.	1 tbs.	1 tbs.
rye flour	1/3 cup	1/2 cup	1/2 cup
bread flour	2 cups	3 cups	3 1/2 cups
yeast	1 1/2 tsp.	2 tsp.	2 tsp.

Chocolate Cream of Wheat Bread

Raisin, Sweet or Basic cycle

Martha Punches has several blue ribbons from the Pennsylvania State Fair for breads made in her premachine days. If your machine is prone to the doughy blues, cut the amount of sugar to 3 tbs., ¼ cup or ⅓ cup. The dough starts out looking very wet but it does form a ball after about 10 minutes of kneading.

	1 lb.	1½ lb.	2 lb.
milk	⅔ cup	1 cup	1⅓ cups
butter or margarine	2 tbs.	3 tbs.	4 tbs.
eggs	1	1½	2
salt	1 tsp.	1-1½ tsp.	1-2 tsp.
sugar	¼ cup	⅓ cup	½ cup
unsweetened cocoa	1 tbs.	1½ tbs.	2 tbs.
Cream of Wheat, uncooked	⅔ cup	1 cup	1⅓ cups
bread flour	1⅓ cups	2 cups	2⅔ cups
yeast	1 tsp.	1½ tsp.	2 tsp.
*chocolate chips, optional	¼ cup	⅓ cup	½ cup

*Add chocolate chips at the beep or appropriate time for your machine.

Jerry's Daily Bread

Whole Wheat, Sweet or Basic cycle

Jerry Snelling says this is truly his daily bread — reliable, basic and so very good! The sunflower kernels could also be added at the appropriate time for raisins. He uses gluten flour but I used vital gluten for testing. The loaf rises moderately well.

	1 lb.	1½ lb.	1¾ lb.
water	⅔ cup	1⅛ cups	1¼ cups
vegetable oil	1 tbs.	1½ tbs.	2 tbs.
honey	1 tbs.	1½ tbs.	2 tbs.
molasses	1 tbs.	1½ tbs.	2 tbs.
salt	½ tsp.	¾ tsp.	1 tsp.
dry milk powder	1½ tbs.	2 tbs.	3 tbs.
sunflower kernels	3 tbs.	¼ cup	⅓ cup
vital gluten	1 tbs.	1½ tbs.	2 tbs.
whole wheat flour	⅔ cup	1 cup	1¼ cups
bread flour	1⅓ cups	2 cups	2¼ cups
yeast	1 tsp.	1½ tsp.	2 tsp.

Multi-Grain Raisin Bread

Whole Wheat, Sweet or Basic cycle

I cut Carol Ann Johnson's amount of oil in half to avoid the doughy blues. The cinnamon can be adjusted to taste. This has a moderate rise and may be somewhat dense.

	1 lb.	1½ lb.	1¾ lb.
water	1 cup	1⅓ cups	1½ cups
vegetable oil	1½ tbs.	2 tbs.	3 tbs.
honey	3 tbs.	¼ cup	⅓ cup
salt	¾ tsp.	1 tsp.	1 tsp.
cinnamon	1½ tsp.	2 tsp.	1 tbs.
oat bran	¼ cup	⅓ cup	½ cup
vital gluten, optional	1½ tbs.	2 tbs.	2½ tbs.
whole wheat flour	¾ cup	1 cup	1¼ cups
bread flour	1½ cups	2 cups	2½ cups
yeast	1½ tsp.	2 tsp.	2 tsp.
*raisins	½ cup	⅔ cup	¾ cup

*Add raisins at the beep or appropriate time for your machine.

Porcupine Bread

Sweet or Basic cycle

Flarane Wold says that her husband makes this but says that sometimes it's difficult to find a porcupine!

	1 lb.	1½ lb.	2 lb.
water	⅞ cup (7 oz.)	1⅛ cups	1⅓ cups
vegetable oil	2 tsp.	1 tbs.	1 tbs.
salt	½ tsp.	¾ tsp.	1 tsp.
sugar	1 tbs.	1½ tbs.	2 tbs.
sesame seeds	1½ tbs.	2 tbs.	3 tbs.
sunflower seeds	2 tbs.	3 tbs.	¼ cup
rolled oats	⅓ cup	½ cup	½ cup
bread flour	2 cups	3 cups	3½ cups
yeast	1½ tsp.	2 tsp.	2 tsp.
*raisins, optional	¼ cup	⅓ cup	½ cup

*Add raisins at the beep or appropriate time for your machine.

Catskill Rye

Donna Celeiro developed this high-rising, light and fluffy rye bread. I cut her salt and yeast in half and slightly decreased the dry milk powder. One trick to achieve a high-rising rye is increasing the amount of flour. If necessary, scrape the sides of the pan with a rubber spatula, pushing the ingredients into the middle.

	1 lb.	**1 ½ lb.**	**2 lb.**
water	1 cup	1 ¼ cups	1 ⅔ cups
vegetable oil	1 tbs.	1 ⅓ tbs.	1 ½ tbs.
honey	2 tbs.	2 ½ tbs.	3 tbs.
salt	½ tsp.	⅔ tsp.	1 tsp.
caraway seeds	1 tbs.	1 ⅓ tbs.	1 ½ tbs.
dry milk powder	2 tbs.	2 ½ tbs.	3 tbs.
vital gluten	¼ cup	5 tbs.	⅓ cup
rye flour	1 cup	1 ¼ cups	1 ½ cups
bread flour	1 ¾ cups	2 ¼ cups	3 ⅔ cups
yeast	1 ½ tsp.	2 tsp.	2 ½ tsp.

Golden Honey Cornbread

Beth Dash Koruitz developed a winner with this delicious cornbread. The potato flakes and the cornmeal make a great combination.

	1 lb.	**1 ½ lb.**	**2 lb.**
water	⅞ cup (7 oz.)	1 ¼ cups	1 ½ cups
canola oil	1 tbs.	1 ⅓ tbs.	1 ½ tbs.
honey	1 tbs.	1 ½ tbs.	2 tbs.
salt	¾ tsp.	1 tsp.	1 tsp.
instant potato flakes	¼ cup	⅓ cup	½ cup
dry milk powder	1 tbs.	1 ½ tbs.	2 tbs.
cornmeal	¼ cup	⅓ cup	½ cup
bread flour	2 cups	3 cups	3 ½ cups
yeast	1 tsp.	1 ½ tsp.	2 tsp.

Cottage Cheese Wheat Bread

Whole Wheat, Sweet or Basic cycle

Margaret Nelson uses small curd cottage cheese in this bread which has much body and moisture. Cottage cheese can be finicky as a main liquid contributor to dough — watch the dough and adjust with water or flour as necessary. If you have a 1 1/4 lb. machine manufactured by Seiko, use the 1 lb. recipe to prevent overflows.

	1 lb.	1 1/2 lb.	2 lb. only
cottage cheese	1 cup	1 1/2 cups	1 2/3 cups
egg	1	1	2
butter or margarine	1 tbs.	1 1/2 tbs.	1 1/2 tbs.
dill weed, dried	1 tsp.	1 1/2 tsp.	1 1/2 tsp.
baking soda	1/4 tsp.	1/2 tsp.	1/2 tsp.
salt	1/2 tsp.	1 tsp.	1 tsp.
sugar	1 tbs.	1 tbs.	2 tbs.
whole wheat flour	1/4 cup	1/3 cup	1/2 cup
bread flour	2 cups	3 cups	3 1/2 cups
yeast	1 tsp.	1 1/2 tsp.	2 tsp.

Oat Sunflower Millet Bread

Whole Wheat, Sweet or Basic cycle

Carl Kielmann, a retired banker, first had similar rolls from a bakery in Jackson Hole, Wyoming. He has figured out the recipe for his bread machine. This moist, flavorful bread was a real hit with many tasters. I cut back on the amount of salt to soften the crust a little bit. Carl generally adds walnuts but any nut could be used. This moist dough may be prone to the doughy blues in the glass domed machines — make the 1 1/2 lb. size and not the 2 lb.

	1 lb.	1 1/2 lb.	2 lb. only
water	3/4 cup	1 1/8 cups	1 1/2 cups
canola oil	1/4 cup	1/3 cup	1/2 cup
honey	3 tbs.	1/4 cup	1/3 cup
sugar	3 tbs.	1/4 cup	1/3 cup
salt	1/2 tsp.	3/4 tsp.	1 tsp.
millet	2 tbs.	3 tbs.	1/4 cup
sunflower kernels	1 tbs.	1 1/2 tbs.	2 tbs.
chopped nuts	2 tbs.	3 tbs.	1/4 cup
dry milk powder	1 tbs.	1 1/2 tbs.	2 tbs.
rolled oats	2 1/2 tbs.	1/4 cup	1/3 cup
whole wheat flour	1/2 cup	3/4 cup	1 cup
bread flour	1 1/2 cups	2 1/3 cups	3 cups
yeast	1 tsp.	1 1/2 tsp.	1 1/2 tsp.

Molasses Wheat Bread

Whole Wheat, Sweet or Basic cycle

Quentin Stanton says he sometimes adds raisins and/or walnuts for variety.

	1 lb.	1½ lb.	2 lb.
water	¾ cup	1 cup	1½ cups
vegetable oil	½ tbs.	1 tbs.	1½ tbs.
molasses, or maple or corn syrup	1½ tbs.	2 tbs.	2½ tbs.
honey	1½ tbs.	2 tbs.	2½ tbs.
egg	½	1	1
salt	¾ tsp.	1 tsp.	1 tsp.
dry milk powder	3 tbs.	¼ cup	⅓ cup
wheat germ	3 tbs.	¼ cup	⅓ cup
whole bran cereal	3 tbs.	¼ cup	⅓ cup
vital gluten, optional	1½ tbs.	2 tbs.	2 tbs.
rolled oats	3 tbs.	¼ cup	⅓ cup
whole wheat flour	1⅛ cups	1½ cups	2 cups
bread flour	1⅛ cups	1½ cups	2 cups
yeast	1½ tsp.	2 tsp.	2 tsp.

Oatmeal Bread

Sweet or Basic cycle

Martha Punches makes the large recipe in her machine on the dough cycle and then bakes two loaves in her oven. Use an egg white or yolk for the half egg. I cut the amount of milk, salt and yeast.

	1 lb.	1½ lb.	2 lb.
milk	⅔ cup	¾ cup	1 cup
applesauce	2½ tbs.	¼ cup	⅓ cup
egg	½	1	1½
sugar	1½ tbs.	2 tbs.	2½ tbs.
salt	½ tsp.	1 tsp.	1 tsp.
vital gluten	1 tbs.	1½ tbs.	2 tbs.
oats	1 cup	1½ cups	2 cups
bread flour	1¾ cups	2 cups	2⅔ cups
yeast	1 tsp.	1½ tsp.	2 tsp.

Cracked Wheat Bread

Whole Wheat, Sweet or Basic cycle

Camille Carter says that this is her very favorite all-purpose bread and she bakes it at least once a week. She has also used the recipe for dinner rolls and has received rave reviews. Soak the cracked wheat for at least 1 hour before adding to the pan with remaining ingredients. Adjust dough as necessary with milk or flour.

	1 lb.	1½ lb.	1¾ lb.
boiling water	½ cup	⅔ cup	1 cup
cracked wheat	½ cup	⅔ cup	1 cup
soak at least 1 hour			
milk	½ cup	½ cup	⅔ cup
vegetable or canola oil	1 tbs.	1½ tbs.	2 tbs.
honey	1 tbs.	1½ tbs.	2 tbs.
salt	½ tsp.	¾ tsp.	1 tsp.
bread flour	2 cups	2½ cups	3 cups
yeast	1½ tsp.	2 tsp.	2½ tsp.

About the Dough Cycle

Recipes in this chapter are given in one size only. All machines, whether 1 lb. or 2 lb., will successfully knead (but not bake) this amount of dough. If you have a 1 lb. machine, you may want to watch the dough and puncture it with a bamboo skewer if it starts to rise over the top of the machine pan (I only had this happen one time out of all the testing done).

If you have a Welbilt ABM 100 or DAK machine, these recipes were tested using the basic (white) manual setting with one kneading and rising only. The first kneading is about 20 minutes and the rising is about 1 hour. The machine was then turned off and the dough removed. Testing indicated that allowing the machine to go through the full second kneading made the dough too airy and difficult to roll or shape. Testing was done on all other machines on the regular dough cycle.

Once the dough is removed from the machine, it is helpful to lightly flour both your hands and the counter (or board). I find it helpful to have a little flour in my hand when I reach into the machine pan and pull the dough from the bottom. The extra flour at this point makes the dough less sticky and allows me to remove all the dough easily. Use only enough flour to allow you to shape it. The softer the dough, the lighter and fluffier the texture of the finished product. It is not necessary to knead the dough after removing it from the machine. The dough is only punched down during the shaping process.

You probably know of several ways to shape rolls. Here are two simple ideas. First, you can break off a given number of pieces and roll them into balls. Or, you can roll the dough into a rectangle, roll it up starting at the wide end and then cut the dough into a given number of pieces. Rolls can be placed either on a lightly greased baking sheet or in muffin cups and baked according to directions.

Walnut Sticky Buns

Dough cycle

Caryn Hart shares a favorite recipe adapted to the machines. How deliciously decadent! Caryn uses kosher salt in this, but sea salt or regular salt can be used also. Makes 12.

Dough

¾ cup milk
2 tbs. butter or margarine
1 egg
½ tsp. salt

½ cup sugar
2½ cups bread flour
1½ tsp. yeast

Put dough ingredients in machine and start the dough cycle. Mix filling ingredients together and divide in half. Distribute half of the filling among 12 muffin pan cups which have been sprayed with nonstick vegetable spray and set aside. Remove dough from machine and roll into a large rectangle. Flour the work surface and/or the dough if necessary to prevent sticking. Spread remaining filling over dough and roll as if a jelly roll starting with the wide end. Cut roll into 12 equal pieces and place in muffin cups on top of first half of filling. Let rise in a warm, draft-free location for 35 to 45 minutes. Bake in a preheated 375° oven for 20 minutes. Turn pan over to release buns while still hot.

Filling

6 tbs. butter or margarine
2½ tbs. honey
1 cup brown sugar, packed

½ tsp. cinnamon
1 tsp. all-purpose or bread flour
2 cups chopped walnuts

Melt butter, add remaining ingredients and mix together.

Poppy Seed Rolls

Dough cycle

Woody Higgins makes these delicious rolls and shares the recipe with us. Woody does not use the sugar, but I like it. The choice is yours!

1⅓ cups water
3 tbs. olive oil
1 tsp. salt
1 tbs. poppy seeds

1½ tsp. sugar, optional
3½ cups bread flour
¼ cup dry milk powder
2 tsp. yeast

At the end of the dough cycle, remove dough, form into rolls (see page 261) and place on a greased baking sheet. Cover and allow to rise in a warm, draft-free location for 1 hour. Bake in a preheated 375° oven for 12 to 15 minutes or until lightly browned.

Baked Portzelka

Bill Ashman adapted this recipe from a deep fried recipe handed down from his grandmother. He remembers them as a special treat and hopes that his grandmother would approve of his changes to make them with less fat. Bill uses less flour but then adds more by hand after the machine has stopped. I added some at the beginning. I added some orange peel (½-1 tsp.) to one test group and used dried cranberries instead of the raisins — Mmmmm.

5 oz. evaporated milk
2 eggs
2 tbs. butter or margarine
¼ cup sugar

½ tsp. salt
2-2⅓ cups bread flour
1 tsp. yeast
½ cup raisins

Glaze
1 egg, beaten with 1 tbs. water

The raisins should be added to all machines 10 minutes after the dough cycle is started. Remove dough from the machine at the completion of the dough cycle. Break and shape dough into small, ping-pong-sized balls and place on a greased baking sheet. Cover and let rise for 1½ hours. Brush tops with glaze and bake in a preheated 350° oven for 12 to 15 minutes.

Zahtar Pita

Gloria Sanceda uses zahtar, a Middle Eastern spice blend which consists of the dried, ground berries of the sumac bush, roasted sesame seeds and thyme. Pita bread is usually cut into small triangles and the cut end of the pita is dipped in olive oil and then in the zahtar blend. Zahtar is available from Middle Eastern stores, or simply substitute thyme or oregano. The secret to good pitas is a really hot oven.

1⅛ cups water
1 tbs. olive oil
1 tbs. zahtar, or oregano or thyme
1 tbs. sugar

1 tsp. salt
3 cups bread flour
1½ tsp. yeast

Remove dough from the machine at the completion of the dough cycle and divide into about 8 pieces. Flatten each piece by hand into a small circle about 6 inches in diameter and place on a greased baking sheet. Cover and let rise for 30 minutes. Brush top with a little olive oil and bake in a preheated 500° oven for 8 to 10 minutes.

Taco Pita Pockets

Dough cycle

Denise Bradshaw says the key to pitas puffing is a very hot oven, so pre-heat it for at least 30 minutes. Stuff the pockets with your favorite taco fixings or serve as a side bread with chili.

¾ cup water
¼ cup taco sauce, or salsa
2 tbs. vegetable oil
1 tbs. sugar
½ tsp. salt

1 ½ tbs. taco seasoning
1 ½ cups bread flour
1 cup whole wheat flour
1 ½ tsp. yeast

Remove dough from the machine at the completion of the dough cycle. Divide into 6 or 8 balls, and flatten each ball with a rolling pin to make a 6-inch circle. Place on a cornmeal-covered baking sheet, cover and let rise for 30 minutes. Slide pitas off baking sheet onto a pizza stone, bake directly on oven rack or bake on baking sheet. Bake at 500° for about 8 minutes or until golden brown. Remove and place in a closed paper bag until cool.

Hot Cross Buns

Dough cycle

Debbie Woodard loves this recipe. Hot cross buns are traditionally served during the week preceding Easter, especially on Good Friday. Golden raisins, dried currants, dried cranberries or dried blueberries can be substituted for the raisins.

1 cup milk
2 eggs
1 tsp. vanilla extract
2 tbs. butter or margarine
¾ cup raisins

½-1 tsp. cinnamon
½ cup sugar
1 tsp. salt
4 cups bread flour or all-purpose flour
1 ½ tsp. yeast

Glaze
1 egg yolk, beaten with 1 tbs. water

Remove dough from the machine at the completion of the dough cycle. Break into pieces of dough about the size of an egg. Roll each piece into a ball and place on a greased baking sheet. Cover with a towel and place in a warm, draft-free location for about ½ hour. Brush tops with glaze. Bake in a preheated 375° oven for about 25 minutes or until golden brown. Allow to cool and then drizzle frosting over tops in the form of a cross.

Frosting
¼-½ cup confectioners' sugar
¼-½ tsp. vanilla or lemon extract

1-2 tbs. milk

Mix ingredients together, using enough milk to achieve a good consistency.

Cranberry Buns

Larry Bennett gave us this flavorful recipe. There is no substitute for piping hot buns right out of the oven. Apple juice or cranapple juice can be used in place of the cranberry juice. Idea: Place the buns around the outer edge of a pizza pan and make an edible wreath for holiday entertaining.

1 1/2 cups cranberry juice
2 tbs. butter or margarine
2 tbs. brown sugar
1/2-1 tsp. cinnamon

1/4 tsp. nutmeg
1/2-1 tsp. salt
4 cups bread flour
2 tsp. yeast

Remove dough from the machine and roll into a large rectangle. Spread filling ingredients on top and roll in a jelly roll fashion starting at the wide end. Cut roll into 1-inch-wide segments and lay on a greased baking sheet. Brush top with melted butter if desired. Bake in a preheated 350° oven for 20 to 30 minutes or until golden brown.

Filling

1/2 cup brown sugar, packed
2 tbs. cinnamon
2/3 cup dried cranberries, or raisins

1/2 cup chopped nuts (walnuts or pecans)
1/4 cup butter, melted

Mix ingredients together.

Doughnuts

Penny Lucas loves making these doughnuts, and her daughters (and my girls as well) have become addicted to them. Makes 12 to 15.

3/4 cup milk or water
2 eggs
1/4 cup butter
1 tsp. salt

1/3 cup sugar
3-3 1/4 cups all-purpose flour
4 tsp. yeast

Upon completion of the dough cycle, punch down dough, remove it from the pan and let it rest for 10 minutes. On a lightly floured counter or board, roll dough out to about 1/2-inch thick and cut out rings with a floured dough-nut cutter or with the open end of two glasses, one smaller than the other. Place on a greased baking sheet, cover and let rise for about an hour or until very light. Heat 4 cups of cooking oil in a deep fryer (375° if you have a temperature control). Add 2 or 3 doughnuts at a time and fry each side about 1 minute. Remove from oil and drain on paper towels. Glaze with confectioners' sugar mixed with a little water or milk, or dust with confectioners' sugar.

Dinner Rolls

Dough cycle

Karen Swanson won a blue ribbon at the state fair for this recipe! She makes her own multi-grain flour blend, but there are blends available in health food stores or mail order catalogs. Makes 12 rolls.

1 cup warm water
1 egg
3 tbs. vegetable oil
3 tbs. sugar
1 tsp. salt

⅓ cup dry milk powder
1 cup multi-grain flour
2 cups bread flour
2 tsp. yeast

Upon completion of the dough cycle, remove dough and form rolls, place on a greased baking sheet, cover with a towel and let rise in a warm, draft-free location for 30 to 40 minutes. Bake in a preheated 400° oven for 15 to 18 minutes.

Vegetarian-Stuffed Pizza

Dough cycle

Mrs. Edwin T. Wright makes the dough for this great pizza in her bread machine. She makes a pizza sauce from tomato sauce simmered for just a few minutes with some basil. Prepared pizza sauces could also be used. If using frozen vegetables, thaw and drain. I confess that I used a full 16 oz. bag of frozen broccoli and cauliflower (3 cups) and 2 cups of cheese.

1½ cups warm water
2 tbs. vegetable or olive oil
1 tsp. salt
1 tsp. sugar

1 cup whole wheat flour
2⅓-2½ cups bread flour
1 pkg. (2¼ tsp.) yeast

Glaze
beaten egg or pizza sauce

Preheat oven to 375°. Sprinkle a greased 12-inch pizza pan with 1 tbs. cornmeal. Remove dough from the machine. Roll ⅔ dough into 14-inch circle and place on a 12-inch pan. Mix together filling ingredients and spoon over dough, leaving a 2-inch border. Roll remaining dough into a 14-inch circle and place on top. Fold edges over and crimp, sealing shut. Slit top with fork or sharp knife in 4 or 5 places. Brush with beaten egg or pizza sauce and bake for 25 to 35 minutes or until top is golden. If you did not bake pizza sauce on pizza, warm it and pour over baked pizza when serving.

Filling
2-3 cups shredded mozzarella cheese
1 cup broccoli florets

1 cup cauliflower florets
½-1 tsp. dried oregano, to taste

Cinnamon Monkey Bread

Dough cycle

Lorraine Petrasek now uses her Panasonic machine to make this old family favorite. She either uses her dough cycle and makes the monkey bread or she removes the dough, rolls it as a jelly-roll, fills it with cottage and cream cheeses and returns it to her machine for further baking. This variety cycle is only on the National and Panasonic machines. The dried cranberries are a variation which is fun for fall or winter entertaining.

Dough

¼ cup water	1 tsp. salt
1 cup milk	2 eggs
⅓ cup butter	3½-3¾ cups bread flour
⅓ cup sugar	2 tsp. yeast

Upon completion of dough cycle, divide dough into small balls (just smaller than an egg) and dip into melted butter and then into sugar mixture. Put in a greased tube or loaf pan, cover with a towel and let rise in a warm, draft-free location for 30 to 40 minutes. Bake in a preheated 375° oven for about 45 minutes.

Coating

½ cup butter	1 cup finely chopped nuts
1 cup sugar	½ cup raisins or dried cranberries
1½ tsp. cinnamon	

Melt butter. Mix remaining ingredients together in a small bowl.

Scallion Herb Rolls

Dough cycle

Mary Vollendorf came up with these rolls for hamburgers or hot dogs. This can also be baked in either a 1½ lb. or 2 lb. machine. Makes 12.

1 cup milk or water	1 tsp. dried basil
1 tbs. butter or margarine	1 clove garlic, minced
1 egg	2 scallions, diced
½-1 tsp. salt	3 cups bread flour
1½ tsp. sugar	1½ tsp. yeast

After the dough cycle, remove dough from the machine and roll into a rectangle. Roll as a jelly roll from wide end to wide end, cut into 12 equal pieces and shape as desired. Place on a cornmeal-covered baking sheet, cover and allow to rise in a warm, draft-free location for 1 hour. Bake in a preheated 375° oven for 12 minutes.

Banana Orange Nut Bread

Betty Hermida makes both breads on the dough cycle (put the first in the refrigerator after it is done and while the other one is in the machine.) Use fully ripe bananas for best moisture. Adjust moisture consistency if necessary. If your dough cycle has a raisin beep, add the nuts then. If not, add the nuts about 10 minutes after starting the machine. If desired, a glaze of confectioners' sugar, vanilla extract and milk can be drizzled on top while still warm.

Dough I

1/3 cup water
1 medium-sized fully ripe banana
1 tbs. vegetable oil
1 tbs. honey
1 1/2 tsp. vanilla extract
1/2 tsp. salt

1/8 tsp. nutmeg, or to taste
2/3 cup oats (quick or old-fashioned)
1 tsp. vital gluten, optional
1 1/2 cups bread flour
1 tsp. yeast
*1/2 cup chopped walnuts

Dough II

2/3 cup orange juice
1 tbs. vegetable oil
1 tbs. honey
1/2 tsp. salt

1/2 tsp. dried orange peel
1/2 cup coconut flakes
1 cup oats (quick or old-fashioned)
1 1/4-1 1/2 cups bread flour
1 tsp. yeast

After both doughs are finished, remove the first from the refrigerator and the second from the machine. Roll both into equal, thin rectangles, the width equal to the length of the loaf pan. Sprinkle one of the doughs with cinnamon and place the other dough on top. Roll the two rectangles together in a jelly roll fashion. Place in a medium to large loaf pan and let rise for about 30 minutes. Bake in a preheated 350° oven for 35 minutes or until golden brown.

Hard Rolls

Karen Swanson won <u>another</u> blue ribbon at the state fair for these hard rolls. Makes 12 delicious rolls.

1 1/4 cups warm water
1 egg white
1 tbs. vegetable oil
1 tbs. sugar

1 1/2 tsp. salt
3-3 1/4 cups bread flour
2 tsp. yeast

Upon completion of the dough cycle, remove dough. Form rolls, place on a greased baking sheet, cover with a towel and let rise in a warm, draft-free location for 30 to 40 minutes. Bake in a preheated 400° oven for 12 to 15 minutes.

The Bread Machine *Cookbook* VI

Hand-Shaped Breads from the Dough Cycle

About the Dough Cycle

Using the dough cycle on your bread machine gives you the opportunity to be as creative as you wish, and allows you to use almost any bread recipe in your bread machine to produce hand-shaped bread or bread baked in a container in your regular oven.

The great joy of using a bread machine's dough cycle is that you do not struggle with the first kneading of the dough, which is the most difficult (and messy!). Once the machine has kneaded the dough and allowed it to rise, it is ready for you to shape according to tradition or to what suits your mood. Whether making rolls or a loaf, there are hundreds of variations of shapes. This book is a compilation of traditional breads, ethnic breads and some new variations on older themes. All recipes are made using the dough cycle of your bread machine.

Any yeast-raised bread recipe that contains approximately 4 cups of flour or less may be made using the dough cycle of your machine. Use your favorite family recipe for traditionally made bread, or any of the recipes in my previous books. Add the ingredients to your machine in the manner suggested by your manufacturer and let the machine take the dough through the first rising. If a soft dough is being used, you will need to use a pan to hold the shape. Firm doughs can be baked in pans or formed into round or oblong loaves, rolls or other shapes.

It may be necessary to adjust baking time and temperature, depending on the recipe and form of the dough. In general, breads with high sugar and/or fat content should be baked at 350°F or lower. Recipes for breads with crisp, crusty exteriors should be baked at higher temperatures, from 400° to as much as 500°. Small rolls will take less time than large forms.

Bread Machine Dough Cycle: General Directions

The dough cycle kneads the dough and lets it rise once, for a long period. Upon completion of the cycle, the dough is removed from the machine, shaped by hand, generally allowed to rise again and baked in a conventional oven.

All machines, even a 1 lb. machine, are capable of kneading up to 4 cups of flour. *Please do not try to bake these recipes in your machine.* If you have a 1 lb. machine and the dough is rising too high, you may either deflate the dough (by puncturing it) and allow it to continue with the cycle, or you may remove the dough and proceed to shape it, as it is probably only a few minutes from completion of the cycle.

Many machines have a double kneading on the dough cycle with a short rest of 5 to 10 minutes in between. The dough is then left to rise in the warm machine for 30 minutes to 1 hour. When testing recipes, I allow the machine to complete the entire cycle. In some cases, however, when making something for my family or when I am not testing, I have been known to shorten the dough cycle. For example, if your dough cycle takes 1½ hours, you probably have a kneading period of about 15 minutes, a short rest and then about 10 more minutes of kneading before about 1 hour of rising. If you are really in a time crunch, it is possible to allow the machine to knead the first time (for the 10 or 15 minutes) and then, during the rest period, turn off the machine and let the dough sit for 45 to 60 minutes. I emphasize that I tested these recipes using the complete dough cycle. I have, however, received enough phone calls and letters asking about shortening the cycle that, yes, I acknowledge you can experiment.

If you own a DAK, Welbilt 100 or Citizen machine, allow the manual cycle to knead once, and the dough to rise for about 1 hour. Then turn off the machine and remove the dough before it goes into the second full kneading. If you allow the machine to knead a full cycle after a 1-hour rising, the dough often becomes so airy and light that it is difficult to work with.

While most bread machines have timer features on the regular bake cycle, very few have a dough cycle which works on a timer. If you want to make a dough for a specific time, you can figure out the math for your machine and set it on the regular timer. The concern when doing this is that you must be home in time to stop the machine so that it does not go into a bake cycle — this is extremely important if you are using a dough recipe with a higher amount of flour than your machine calls for. Also, remember not to use any recipe with eggs, milk or cheese (which could spoil) on the timer.

Some machines have a stir-down feature which rotates the kneading paddle for 20 to 30 seconds just before the buzzer sounds to indicate that the dough cycle is complete. The purpose of this is to allow air in the dough to escape. A traditional bread recipe often indicates that you should punch down the dough or knead it a second time. When using the machine's dough cycle, merely taking the dough out of the machine punches it down and it is not necessary for you to do so.

You may find it helpful to place the dough on a lightly floured work surface and to dust it with a little flour to prevent it from sticking (to your hands or to the work surface). You should take care not to add too much flour as it can make the final product hard and tough. Some recipes such as brioche or challah are naturally sticky and you may be tempted to add flour to work with it. In this case, it is better to grease your hands and the work surface instead of using flour. I simply spray the work surface and my hands with a nonstick vegetable spray.

When dividing dough into a given number of equal sizes, roll the dough into a log. Divide the log in half and then divide each half in half (quarters). Divide each quarter into the appropriate number necessary.

If at any time during the rolling or shaping the dough becomes difficult to work, let it rest for 5 to 10 minutes to relax. It will then be easier to shape.

Spray all pans with a nonstick vegetable spray, or grease them with butter.

Preparing Dough to Bake Later

Refrigerating dough: Dough can be made, shaped, placed on a greased baking sheet and completely, but loosely, covered with plastic wrap. Place it in the refrigerator for 2 to 10 hours. When ready to bake, remove the dough from the refrigerator to a warm, draft-free location to bring it to room temperature while you preheat the oven. Bake according to directions in the recipe. The dough will rise in the refrigerator, but the cold temperature makes the dough rise more slowly.

Freezing dough: Dough can be made, shaped, placed on a greased baking sheet, covered with plastic wrap and then placed in the freezer until firm. At that point, it can be placed in a plastic bag and frozen for up to 2 weeks. When ready to bake, remove dough from the freezer and place on a greased baking sheet in a warm, draft-free location to thaw and rise for about 4 hours. Bake according to directions.

Shaping Dough

Each recipe in this book includes directions for a simple shape, but this section will give you ideas to try with any recipe as you desire. You should watch the baking times when experimenting with different shapes. Larger rolls may take longer to bake and vice versa.

Crescent rolls: Roll the dough into 1 or 2 large rounds on a lightly floured work surface. A 4-cup recipe will easily make 2 rounds. A 3-cup recipe will make a large round and very large crescents, or 2 rounds and smaller crescents. Using a knife or pizza wheel, cut each round into 8 equal pieces (as you would a pie). Roll each piece firmly from the wide end to the narrow end. Place the pointed side down on a greased baking sheet and bend the outer ends down to form a curve. Cover, let rise and bake according to directions.

Flower (knot) rolls: Divide the dough into 8 to 12 equal pieces. Roll each piece into an 8- to 10-inch rope, about ½ inch in diameter. Tie into a loose knot with long ends. Bring one end over and under the roll and the other end up and over, and tuck it into the center of the knot. Cover, let rise and bake according to directions.

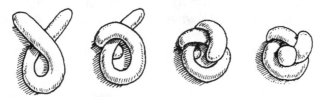

Coil rolls: Divide the dough into 8 to 12 equal pieces. Roll each piece into an 8- to 10-inch rope, about ½ inch in diameter. Coil the rope around on itself and tuck the end underneath. Cover, let rise and bake according to directions.

Cloverleaf rolls: Divide the dough into 36 equal pieces (about 1 inch in size). Dip each piece in melted butter and place 3 in each lightly greased muffin cup. Cover, let rise and bake according to directions.

Parker House rolls: Roll the dough on a lightly floured work surface into a large, ¼-inch-thick rectangle. Using a 2½- to 3-inch biscuit cutter (or similar tool), cut into rounds. Brush each round with melted butter and then fold each round almost in half (with the buttered side in), pressing on the fold. Cover, let rise and bake according to directions.

Fan rolls: Roll the dough into a large, thin rectangle. Using your fingers or a pastry brush, brush the top of the rectangle with about 1 tbs. melted butter. With a sharp knife, pastry or pizza wheel, cut the dough into small rectangles (about 1½ x 2 inches). Place 5 rectangles on top of each other and place short side down in a greased muffin cup. As the dough rises and bakes, the rolls will fan out. Cover, let rise and bake according to directions.

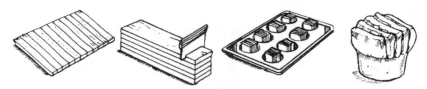

Twisted breadsticks: Form the dough into 20 or 24 equal balls. Roll each ball to form a rope 8 to 10 inches long. Starting with the first rope made (this rest allows the dough to relax and makes it easier to work with), take one end in one hand and hold it in place as you twist with the other hand. Either leave the dough in a long rope or pinch the ends together to make a twisted ring. Cover, let rise and bake according to directions.

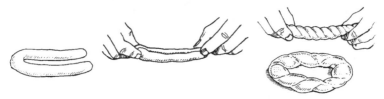

Jelly-roll (and slices): Roll the dough into a large, thin rectangle. If a filling is to be used, the filling should be spread evenly over the rectangle, leaving a ½-inch border around the edge. Starting with the wide edge closest to you, roll the dough tightly, encasing the filling. Pinch to seal. For rolls, slice into about 12 equal slices. Cover, let rise and bake according to directions.

Kaiser rolls: Divide dough into 8 to 10 equal pieces and roll each piece into a 6- or 7-inch round. Fold one edge toward the middle. Starting about halfway along that fold, fold another piece toward the middle. Continue around the edge until you have 5 folds. Tuck the last half of the last fold under the first fold and press firmly to seal. Place folded side up on a greased baking sheet. Cover, let rise and bake according to directions.

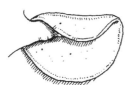  

Braid: Divide the dough into 3 equal pieces and roll each piece into a long rope. The three strands should be braided together as you would hair. If you have difficulty starting the braid, begin in the center and work toward the ends. Seal and tuck the ends underneath and place the braid on a greased baking sheet. Cover, let rise and bake according to directions.

Mock braid: Roll the dough into a large rectangle. Using scissors, a sharp sknife, pastry or pizza wheel, cut 1-inch strips down each side, from the center third to the edge. Fold strips over the center, alternating side, and angling each folded strip toward you. Tuck the ends inside to give the appearance of a braid. Place on a greased baking sheet. Cover, let rise and bake according to directions.

Filled rolls: Form the dough into equal balls a little bigger than an egg. Flatten each ball into a thick round and place the filling in the middle. Pull the edges of the dough over the filling and press tightly together to seal the filling inside. Place seam side down in greased muffin cups, or on a baking sheet. Cover, let rise and bake according to directions.

Pretzels: Form the dough into 10 equal balls. Roll each ball into a long rope, about 15 to 20 inches long, and shape into a wide U. Cross one end over the other and press together gently. Pick up the ends that are crossed and cross a second time. Fold the twisted portion over the bottom of the U following the illustration. Cover, let rise and bake according to directions.

Daisy wheel: Divide the dough into 9 equal pieces. Roll one piece into a ball and place it in the center of a greased pizza pan or round baking sheet. Shape remaining 8 pieces into long ovals and place them around the center ball, radiating out from the center like petals. Cover, let rise and bake according to directions. After baking, remove in one piece to cool on a wire rack.

Cookie cutter wreaths: One of my favorite (and so very easy) gifts is a bread wreath. Over the years, I have made orange pumpkin wreaths for Halloween, green tree wreaths for Christmas, red heart wreaths for Valentine's Day, or other shaped wreaths for any time of the year.

Add a few drops of appropriate food coloring to the liquid. Roll the dough into a large, 1/2-inch-thick rectangle on a lightly floured surface. Using a 2 1/2- to 3-inch cookie cutter (pumpkin, heart, star, etc.), cut the dough into as many rolls as possible. Place each roll on the outer rim of a lightly greased (disposable if you're giving them away) pizza pan so that the rolls touch each other slightly. If you have rolls left, place 2 or 3 in the center or use another pan. Cover, let rise and bake according to directions.

Crust Treatments

Washes: A wash is brushed on the bread dough just before it goes into the oven. Use a pastry brush (or your fingers) to gently "paint" the top of the dough — be careful not to push down and deflate the risen dough.

- An egg white beaten with 1 tbs. water will give the bread a shiny, crisp crust. Milk may be used instead of water for a softer but still shiny crust.
- A complete egg or just the yolk mixed with 1 to 2 tbs. milk or water is used for a shiny, richer and darker-colored crust.
- Milk or cream (alone) gives a shiny finish (not quite as dark as an egg) to the bread.
- Any kind of oil or melted butter can be brushed on to give the bread a soft crust.
- A honey wash gives bread a sweet, glossy finish. Use 1 to 2 tbs. each honey and water.
- Cold water can be brushed or sprayed (use a plant mister or similar device) on the bread for a crisp, chewy crust for French or Italian breads.
- Lemon juice mixed with 2 to 3 tbs. sugar gives a fruity, sweet flavor.

Embellishments: Seeds, herbs, nuts and similar toppings are added to the tops of breads after the dough has been lightly washed, just before it is baked. The wash acts as "glue."

- Seeds such as poppy, sesame, fennel, anise, caraway, celery, or sunflower add flavor to breads and give them a professional-looking finish.
- Similar in size to seeds, small grains such as teff or amaranth can also be used.
- Rolled grains such as oats or wheat add an interesting appearance and texture.
- Herbs can be sprinkled on top of bread which has been washed with water or oil.
- Finely chopped nuts can be used either before baking with a wash or after baking on top of a glaze.

"Crusty" Crusts: Baguettes and many other breads require a crispy, crunchy crust which is aided by adding steam to the baking process. This can be done in one of several ways or in combination.

- Use a clean mister (such as a plant mister) to spray the dough just before you put it in the oven and then mist it again two more times during the first half of the baking. Simply open the oven door and briefly spray the mist into the oven, but be careful not to spray any electrical elements.
- Use a pastry brush and brush the bread with COLD water just before you put the bread into the oven.
- Place a shallow pan of an inch or so of water on the bottom shelf or bottom of the preheated oven about 5 minutes before putting the bread in the oven.
- Place a shallow, empty pan on the bottom shelf or bottom of the oven when you start to preheat it. Just before you place the dough in the oven, put 4 or 5 ice cubes into the empty, hot pan. Be very careful not to spill the ice on an electrical element!
- Clay baking tiles (or pizza or baking stones) give breads an extra crispy crust. If you preheat tiles or a stone in the oven (for the best crust), the dough should be placed on a cornmeal-covered pizza peel or a rimless baking sheet to rise so that it can be easily slipped directly onto the stone. The dough may also be placed on parchment paper and the dough and paper together placed directly on the stone.
- Clay ovens (la cloche) have both a top and a bottom. The top can be turned upside down and placed in a large pan in the sink and filled with water to soak while the dough is rising and the oven is preheating. The clay bottom could be preheated (place the dough on parchment paper so that you can get it into the bottom easily) or the dough can be placed in the clay bottom to rise. Once the dough is ready to put in the oven, empty the water from the top and place it on top of the clay bottom. It may take a little longer to bake this way; I remove the lid during the last minute or two.

- A perforated pizza pan is perfect for crisp, crusty breads or breadsticks.
- I tested several different types of baguette pans for this book and prefer a perforated baguette pan, much like the pizza pans. Spray it with a nonstick vegetable spray such as PAM. If you do not have a baguette pan, use a perforated pizza pan or a plain baking sheet. These pans generally hold 2 or 3 baguettes.
- Cast-iron breadstick pans make wonderful, thick breadsticks, or as my girls call them, mini-baguettes. Cast-iron corn stick pans in the shape of corn, cactus, etc., can also be used for breadsticks. If you do not have one, use a perforated pizza pan or a plain baking sheet.

Parker House Rolls

The Parker House in historic Boston made these uniquely shaped rolls famous. This basic dinner roll recipe can also be made in other shapes (see pages 272–277). Why not serve with a flavored butter from Finishing Touches, beginning on page 342?

Dough

1 1/4 cups milk
2 tbs. butter or margarine
1 tbs. sugar

1/2 tsp. salt
3 cups all-purpose flour
1 1/2 tsp. yeast

Wash

1/2-1 tbs. butter, melted

Remove dough from the machine upon completion of the dough cycle. Roll dough on a lightly floured work surface into a large, 1/4-inch-thick rectangle. With a 2 1/2- or 3-inch biscuit cutter (or similar tool), cut into rounds. Brush each round with melted butter and then fold each round almost in half (with buttered side in), pressing on the fold (see page 274). Place on a greased baking sheet or in muffin cups, cover and let rise for 30 to 45 minutes. Bake in a preheated 350° oven for 12 to 15 minutes.

Herbed Monkey Bread

Turn a simple spaghetti meal into a feast with the addition of this bread. Serve whole and allow guests to help themselves by pulling off a portion.

Dough

1 1/8 cups water
2 tbs. olive oil
1 tsp. sugar
1/2 tsp. salt

1 tbs. dried oregano, or 3 tbs. fresh
3 cups bread flour
2 tsp. yeast

Additional Ingredients

1/3 cup olive oil
1 cup freshly grated Parmesan cheese

Remove dough from the machine upon completion of the dough cycle. Break off pieces of dough to form as many 1-inch balls as possible. Roll balls in olive oil and then in cheese. Place balls in a greased Bundt baking pan. If there is any remaining oil, pour it on top of balls and sprinkle with remaining cheese. Cover and let rise for about 1 hour. Bake in a preheated 350° oven for 30 to 35 minutes.

Brioche

Yield: 12 rolls

Fill rich brioche dough with just a little cheese, meat or preserves for a special delicious treat (don't use too much or it will leak out). This recipe makes wonderful, rich rolls without filling. Just follow the directions and omit it. Start with 3 cups flour and add more if you need it to make the dough the right consistency.

Brioche Dough

½ cup milk
¼ cup butter
3 eggs
2 tbs. sugar

1 tsp. salt
3-3¼ cups all-purpose flour
2 tsp. yeast

Filling

4-5 oz. Brie cheese, cut into 1-inch cubes, or your favorite preserve, marmalade or apple butter, about 1 tsp. per roll, or your favorite filling, about 1 tsp. per roll

Wash

1 egg beaten with 1-2 tbs. milk or cream

Remove dough from the machine upon completion of the dough cycle. If dough is sticky, grease your hands and the work surface, or knead in only enough flour so that it is easily handled, and divide into 12 equal pieces. Form each piece into a ball and stuff each one with about a 1-inch cheese cube or 1 tsp. filling (see page 276). Pinch ends together to seal. Place rolls in greased muffin cups. Cover and let rise in a warm, draft-free location for about 30 minutes. Brush with egg wash. Bake in a preheated 350° oven for about 15 to 20 minutes.

Hawaiian Pineapple Rolls

Yield: 8-10 rolls

While one would assume that these are delicious as breakfast rolls (and they are), they also make fabulous ham sandwiches! Use your favorite shaping technique on pages 272–277. If you are serving these as sweet buns, glaze them while warm.

1 1/8 cups pineapple juice	2 tbs. brown sugar
2 tbs. butter	1/2 tsp. salt
1 tsp. grated fresh ginger, or to taste, or 1/4 tsp. ground ginger	3 cups all-purpose flour
	2 tsp. yeast

Remove dough from the machine upon completion of the dough cycle and place on a lightly floured work surface. Form dough into 8 to 10 balls and place on a lightly greased baking sheet. Cover with a kitchen towel and let rise for about 1 hour in a warm, draft-free location. Bake in a preheated 350° oven for 15 to 20 minutes.

Cheese Scallion Bread

Yield: 2 loaves

The combination of fresh green onions and sharp cheddar cheese rolled into this bread makes it an all-time winner.

Dough

1 1/8 cups milk	1/2 tsp. salt
2 tbs. butter or margarine	3 cups all-purpose flour
1 tbs. sugar	1 1/2 tsp. yeast

Filling
1 cup grated sharp cheddar cheese
2-4 green onions, diced

Remove dough from the machine upon completion of the dough cycle and divide in half. On a lightly floured work surface, roll each half into a large rectangle. Spread 1/2 cup grated cheddar cheese and 1/2 of the diced green onions on dough. Roll jelly-roll fashion (see page 275) and pinch tightly to seal closed. Place seam side down on a greased baking sheet, cover and let rise for about 45 minutes. Bake in a preheated 350° oven for 15 to 18 minutes.

Herb-Filled Loaf

This recipe uses a very easy, basic dough that has an herb filling rolled into it for flavor. Vary the herb according to the meal with which it is served — perhaps oregano and/or basil with Italian entrées, cilantro with Mexican or Oriental flavors.

Dough

1 cup water
1 tsp. sugar
1/2 tsp. salt

3 cups all-purpose flour
1 1/2 tsp. yeast

Filling

1 tbs. dried herbs, or 3 tbs. chopped fresh
1/3 cup nonfat *Yogurt Cheese*, follows

Mix herbs into *Yogurt Cheese* and set aside. Remove dough from the bread machine upon completion of the dough cycle. Roll dough into a large rectangle on a lightly floured work surface. Spread filling on top of dough and roll jelly-roll fashion, starting on the wide side (see page 275). Cut into 12 equal pieces and place in greased muffin cups. Cover with a kitchen towel and let rise in a warm, draft-free location for 30 minutes. Bake in a preheated 350° oven for 15 minutes or until golden brown.

Yogurt Cheese

Coffee filters and a small colander work just as well as the yogurt cheese makers available in some stores. Place two or three layers of coffee filters in a small colander and place the colander on top of a small bowl. Put nonfat yogurt (without gelatin — check the label) into the colander and refrigerate for 2 to 10 hours. The whey will separate from the yogurt and drain into the bowl beneath it. The remaining yogurt will be very thick and can be used as a substitute for cream cheese in many recipes. The whey can be disposed of or may be refrigerated and included in 1 to 2 teaspoon portions with the liquid for bread baking as a dough enhancer. The yield from yogurt is usually about half: 4 cups yogurt yields about 2 cups *Yogurt Cheese*.

Potato Rye Cheese Rolls

Yield: 12 rolls

   Because rye grows so well in the northern climes of Europe, it is a staple in their bread making. Many ryes, like Dutch Roggerbrood or some German ryes, use potatoes; this recipe uses potato flakes for ease. Because of the high percentage of rye flour, it is necessary to allow the rolls to rise longer than normal. This dough should be moist and will be slightly sticky. Take care not to add too much flour, which produces a heavier roll. Instead, spray your hands and the work surface with a nonstick vegetable spray. These rolls can be made with or without the cheese filling. The cocoa and coffee are used to give the bread a darker color. Start with 1½ cups flour and add more if necessary to obtain the right consistency.

Dough

1 cup water	1-2 tbs. caraway or other seeds
2 tbs. vegetable oil	½ cup rye flour
3 tbs. molasses or honey	½ cup whole wheat flour
2 tbs. brown sugar	½ cup instant potato flakes
1 tsp. salt	1½-1¾ cups bread flour
1 tbs. unsweetened cocoa	2 tsp. yeast
1 tbs. instant coffee granules	

Filling
twelve ½- or 1-inch cubes very sharp cheddar cheese

Wash
cold water

Topping
caraway seeds or favorite seeds

   Grease hands and work surface (rather than flouring) and remove dough from the machine upon completion of the dough cycle. Divide dough into 12 equal pieces. Form dough into balls and stuff each one with cheese cube (see page 276). Pinch ends together to seal in cheese and place on a greased baking sheet, or perforated pizza pan for a crustier roll. Cover and let rise in a warm, draft-free location for 1 to 1½ hours. Brush or spray rolls with a cold water wash and sprinkle with seeds. Bake in a preheated 350° oven for 15 to 20 minutes. Cool slightly in pans and remove to a rack to finish cooling.

Cheese-Filled Herb Rolls

Yield: 12 rolls

These simple-to-make rolls make a great accompaniment to soup or salad for a light meal. While the recipe calls for basil, use mint, oregano or cilantro (or any favorite herb) as a variation. I particularly like basil with mozzarella and mint with feta. Of course, there is also cheddar with cilantro...

Dough

1 cup water
2 tbs. olive oil
1 clove or 1 tsp. minced garlic
1 tbs. sugar
1/2 tsp. salt

1/4 cup chopped fresh basil, or 1 tbs. dried
3 cups bread flour
1 1/2 tsp. yeast

Filling
2 cups (8 oz.) grated mozzarella or crumbled feta cheese

Wash
cold water or olive oil

Remove dough from the machine upon completion of the dough cycle and divide into 12 equal pieces. On a lightly floured work surface, roll each piece into a 6- or 7-inch round. Place about 2 tbs. cheese in the center of each round. Fold sides over to center, encasing cheese, and press firmly to seal closed (see page 276). Place seam side down on a greased baking sheet, cover and let rise for about 1 hour. Just before baking, pierce top of dough with the tines of a fork and brush with water for a crusty exterior, or olive oil for a softer crust. Bake in a preheated 350° oven for about 15 minutes.

Herb Rolls

Yield: 12-15 rolls

These herb rolls make great sandwich or dinner rolls. Experiment with some of the flavored olive oils (garlic, jalapeño, etc.), found in grocery stores, for added flavor. Use any shape described on pages 272–277.

1 1/3 cups water
2 tbs. olive oil
1 tbs. sugar
1 tsp. salt
1 clove or 1 tsp. minced garlic

1 tsp. black pepper
1 tbs. dried basil, or 1/4 cup chopped fresh
4 cups bread flour
2 tsp. yeast

Remove dough from the machine upon completion of the dough cycle and place on a lightly floured work surface. Divide dough into 12 to 15 equal pieces, shape into small balls and place on a lightly greased baking sheet. Cover with a kitchen towel and let rise for about 1 hour in a warm, draft-free location. Bake in a preheated 350° oven for 15 to 20 minutes.

Olive Walnut Bread

Yield: 1 loaf

Carol Neel serves this festive bread at holiday meals. Begin with 1 1/4 cups water and add more as needed.

Dough
1 1/4-1 1/3 cups water
3 tbs. olive oil
1 tsp. sugar
1 tsp. salt

1/2 tsp. black pepper
4 cups all-purpose flour
2 tsp. yeast

Filling
1 can (3.8 oz.) sliced black olives
1/2 cup chopped walnuts

Remove dough from the machine upon completion of the dough cycle. On a lightly floured work surface, roll dough into a large rectangle. Sprinkle dough with olives and walnuts. Roll jelly-roll fashion, beginning on the short side (see page 275). Pinch seams to seal and place seam side down on a greased baking sheet, tucking ends under. With a sharp knife or razor, cut several 1/8-inch-deep slashes in top of loaf. Cover with a kitchen towel and let rise in a warm, draft-free location for about 20 minutes. Bake in a preheated 400° oven for 20 to 25 minutes or until bread sounds hollow when tapped. Cool on a wire rack and cut into thin slices to serve.

Simple Baguettes

Yield: 2 large or 3 medium baguettes

Because there is no oil, baguettes are best eaten when very fresh. Generate steam for a crisp crust (see pages 272–277).

Dough
1 1/2 cups water
1 tbs. sugar
1 tsp. salt
4 cups bread flour
2 tsp. yeast

Wash
cold water

Topping
sesame seeds, poppy seeds or other favorite seeds, optional

Remove dough from the machine upon completion of the dough cycle and divide in half. On a cornmeal-covered work surface (to prevent sticking), roll each portion of dough into a large rectangle. Roll dough jelly-roll fashion, beginning on the wide side (see page 275). Place on a greased, cornmeal-covered baguette pan or baking sheet to rise for 1 to 1 1/2 hours. Just before baking, slash top of bread with a razor blade or very sharp knife. Wash with cold water and top with seeds if desired. Bake in a preheated 400° oven for about 15 minutes until bread is brown and sounds hollow when tapped.

Sponge Baguettes

Yield: 2 medium baguettes

The flavor of bread is developed as the dough rises and rests. The sponge allows the bread to develop a more distinct flavor as it rests for several hours or, better still, overnight. Use any of the techniques for developing a crisp crust found on pages 272–277.

Sponge*
1 cup water
2 cups bread flour
1 tsp. yeast

Dough
*sponge
1 tbs. sugar
1 tsp. salt
1 cup bread flour
1 tsp. yeast
1-2 tbs. water if necessary

Wash
cold water

Topping
poppy seeds, sesame seeds or other
  favorite seeds, optional

Add sponge ingredients to the machine pan, start machine and allow it to knead for 5 to 10 minutes. Turn off machine and allow sponge to sit undisturbed in pan for 6 to 10 hours. If you have a Welbilt, DAK or Citizen machine or if your machine is otherwise occupied, mix sponge in a large bowl, cover with plastic wrap and allow to sit undisturbed in a warm, draft-free location for 6 to 10 hours.

After 6 to 10 hours, add remaining ingredients, except water, to sponge and start the dough cycle. Allow dough to knead for a few minutes and then add 1 to 2 tbs. water to soften dough if necessary. Remove dough from machine upon completion of the dough cycle. Divide dough in half and roll each half into a large rectangle. Beginning on the wide side, roll jelly-roll fashion (see page 275) into baguette shapes. Place on a greased, cornmeal-covered baguette pan or baking sheet to rise for 1 to 1½ hours. Just before baking, wash or spray bread with cold water, slash top with a razor blade or very sharp knife and sprinkle with seeds if desired. Bake in a preheated 400° oven for 20 to 25 minutes until bread is brown and sounds hollow when tapped.

Mexican-Flavored Baguettes or Breadsticks

Yield: 2 baguettes or 24 breadsticks

Use these delightful breads to scoop up your favorite salsa. Masa harina may be found in Mexican groceries, through mail order companies or in some large grocery stores. It may be found under the name "maseca." Generate steam for a crisp crust with techniques from pages 272–277.

Dough

1 ⅓ cups water
2 tbs. olive oil
1-2 tsp. diced jalapeños, or to taste
2-4 tbs. chopped fresh cilantro
1 tbs. sugar

1 tsp. salt
½ cup masa harina
3 cups bread flour
1 ½ tsp. yeast

Wash
cold water

Topping
coarse salt, optional

For baguettes: Remove dough from the machine upon completion of the dough cycle and divide in half. Roll dough into 2 large rectangles on a cornmeal-covered work surface to prevent sticking. Roll dough jelly-roll fashion, beginning on the wide side (see page 275). Place on a greased, cornmeal-covered baguette pan or baking sheet to rise for 45 to 60 minutes. Just before baking, slash top of bread with a razor blade or very sharp knife. Wash or spray with cold water and bake in a preheated 400° oven for about 15 minutes until bread is brown and sounds hollow when tapped.

For breadsticks: Remove dough from the machine upon completion of the dough cycle. Divide into 24 equal pieces. Roll each piece into a thin rope about 6 to 8 inches long. Place on a lightly greased baking sheet (or perforated pizza pan for a crisper stick), cover and let rise in a warm, draft-free location for about 15 minutes. Brush or spray with cold water and sprinkle with coarse salt if desired. Bake in a preheated 400° oven for 10 to 15 minutes. The longer they bake, the crisper they will be. Do not store in plastic wrap, as they will soften.

Jalapeño Cheese Cornmeal Baguettes or Breadsticks

Yield: 2 baguettes or 24 breadsticks

Dip these breadsticks into salsa instead of using tortilla chips. These are similar to Mexican-flavored baguettes or breadsticks, but use easy-to-find cornmeal instead of the masa harina. Generate steam for a crisp crust (see pages 272–277).

Dough

1 ¼ cups water
2 tbs. olive oil
½ cup shredded cheddar cheese
1-2 jalapeños, diced, or to taste
1 tsp. sugar

½ tsp. salt
¼ tsp. cayenne pepper
½ cup cornmeal
3 cups bread flour
1 ½ tsp. yeast

Wash
cold water

Topping
coarse salt, optional

See instructions for *Mexican-flavored Baguettes and Breadsticks,* page 288.

Orange Ginger Baguettes or Breadsticks

Yield: 2 baguettes or 24 breadsticks

Serve these Oriental-flavored breadsticks with soups or salads. Fresh, finely chopped ginger is best, but ginger packed in jars, sold in the produce section of large grocery stores, is an acceptable substitute. See pages 272–277 for methods of steaming to form a crisp crust.

Dough

1 ⅛ cups orange juice
2 tbs. olive oil
1 clove or 1 tsp. minced garlic
1 tsp. grated fresh ginger, or to taste
1 tbs. sugar

1 tsp. salt
1 tsp. coarsely ground black pepper
3 cups bread flour
1 ½ tsp. yeast

Wash
cold water

Topping
coarse salt, optional

See instructions for *Mexican-flavored Baguettes and Breadsticks,* page 288.

Tomato Herb Baguettes or Breadsticks

Yield: 2 baguettes or 24 breadsticks

Dried tomatoes should be cut into tiny pieces for this, or use tomato sprinkles if your grocery store carries them. The basil can be increased to taste if desired. Generate steam (pages 272–277) for a crisp crust.

Dough

1 1/8 cups water
2 tbs. olive oil
1 clove or 1 tsp. minced garlic
1 tbs. sugar
1 tsp. salt

1/4 cup coarsely chopped dried
  tomatoes
1-2 tbs. chopped fresh basil, or
  1-2 tsp. dried
3 cups bread flour
1 1/2 tsp. yeast

Wash

cold water

Topping

coarse salt, optional

See instructions for *Mexican-flavored Baguettes and Breadsticks*, page 288.

Parmesan Pepper Baguettes or Breadsticks

Yield: 2 baguettes or 24 breadsticks

A twist on an Italian herb bread, this bread uses freshly grated Parmesan cheese. In a pinch, the grated Parmesan cheese found in the refrigerated cheese section can be used, but do not use the "green can" cheese. Use either freshly ground pepper or the coarse grind as found in the grocery store. Generate steam (see pages 272–277) for a crisp crust.

Dough

1 1/8 cups water
1 tbs. olive oil
1/2 cup grated Parmesan cheese
1 tbs. sugar

1 tsp. salt
1 tsp. coarsely ground black pepper
3 cups bread flour
2 tsp. yeast

Wash

cold water

Topping

coarse salt, optional

See instructions for *Mexican-flavored Baguettes and Breadsticks*, page 288.

Italian Breadsticks (Grissini)

Enjoy these rustic variations of plain breadsticks with a hearty bottle of wine and chunks of cheese.

Dough
1 cup milk
2 tbs. butter or margarine
1 tsp. sugar
½ tsp. salt
3 cups all-purpose flour
1½ tsp. yeast

Additional Ingredients
about ½ cup milk
about ¼ cup sesame seeds

Remove dough from the machine upon completion of the dough cycle. Divide dough into about 24 pieces. Roll each piece into a thin rope 6 to 8 inches long. Dip each one into milk (in a bowl) and then roll in seeds on a plate or piece of waxed paper. Place about 1 inch apart on a greased baking sheet and immediately bake in a preheated 450° oven for 10 to 12 minutes or until golden brown. Do not store in plastic wrap, as they will soften.

Pretzels

These soft pretzels are best eaten warm or reheated. As a variation, sprinkle the pretzels with any favorite seed instead of the salt.

Dough
1⅛ cups water
2 tsp. sugar
½ tsp. salt
3 cups all-purpose flour
1½ tsp. yeast

Additional Ingredients
2 qt. water, plus 2 tbs. baking soda

Wash
1 egg beaten with 1 tbs. water

Topping
coarse salt or seeds

Remove dough from the machine upon completion of the dough cycle. Divide it into 10 equal pieces and roll each one into a long rope, 15 to 20 inches. If you have trouble rolling ropes that long, let them rest for about 5 or 10 minutes and then roll out again. After ropes are formed, shape them into pretzels (see page 276), place on a lightly greased baking sheet, cover and let rise for 20 to 30 minutes. Meanwhile, bring 2 quarts water to a boil in a large, nonaluminum pan and stir in baking soda. Reduce heat slightly so that water is just below a boil. With a large slotted spoon, gently place 2 or 3 pretzels at a time into water and cook for about 30 seconds on each side. Remove from water and return to greased baking sheet. Brush with egg wash, sprinkle with salt or seeds and bake in a preheated 450° oven for 10 to 12 minutes or until golden and crusty.

Beer Breadsticks

The beer does not have to be flat, but should be warmed in the microwave for 30 to 60 seconds. Add water if you don't have quite enough beer.

Dough
1 1/8 cups beer
1 tbs. vegetable oil
1 tsp. sugar
1/2 tsp. salt
3 cups all-purpose flour
1 1/2 tsp. yeast

Wash
cold water

Topping
coarse salt or seeds of choice

Remove dough from the machine upon completion of the dough cycle. Divide dough into 20 to 24 pieces. Roll each piece into a rope about 6 to 8 inches long. Place about 1 inch apart on a greased baking sheet, brush or spray with cold water, sprinkle with coarse salt or seeds, and immediately bake in a preheated 450° oven for 10 to 12 minutes or until golden brown. Do not store in plastic wrap, as they will soften.

Sweet Rolls

These sweet rolls are a delightful treat for breakfast, sandwiches or dinner. Make ordinary shapes (below) or use any of the fancy variations on pages 273–277. Add food coloring to the liquids for a decorative touch. For a sweeter treat, glaze rolls (see Finishing Touches, page 342–346) while still warm instead of washing with the egg.

Dough

1 ⅛ cups milk
2 tbs. butter or margarine
1 egg, large
¼ cup sugar

1 tsp. salt
4 cups all-purpose flour
2 tsp. yeast

Wash

1 egg beaten with 1-2 tbs. milk or cream

Remove dough from the machine upon completion of the dough cycle and place on a lightly floured work surface. Divide dough into 12 equal pieces, shape into desired roll shape or small balls, and place on a lightly greased baking sheet. Cover with a kitchen towel and let rise for about 1 hour in a warm, draft-free location. Brush with egg-milk wash. Bake in a preheated 350° oven for 15 to 20 minutes.

Sweet Monkey Bread

There are hundreds of variations on monkey breads, or "pull-aparts," but this is one of my favorites. Serve whole and pull off a portion to eat. Great fun!

Dough

1 ⅛ cups milk
2 tbs. butter or margarine
1 egg, large
1 tsp. vanilla extract

¼ cup sugar
1 tsp. salt
4 cups all-purpose flour
2 tsp. yeast

Additional Ingredients

6 tbs. butter, melted
1 cup very finely chopped nuts

Remove dough from the machine upon completion of the dough cycle. Form as many 1-inch balls as possible. Roll balls in melted butter and then in chopped nuts. Place balls in a greased tube pan or Bundt pan. If there is any remaining melted butter, pour it on top of balls and sprinkle with any remaining nuts. Cover and let rise for about 1 hour. Bake in a preheated 350° oven for 30 to 35 minutes.

Cinnamon Buns

Yield: 12 buns

This traditional recipe for a simple cinnamon bun is always a winner.

Dough
¾ cup milk
2 tbs. butter or margarine
1 egg, large
2 tbs. sugar

1 tsp. salt
3 cups all-purpose flour
2 tsp. yeast

Filling
1 tbs. butter, melted
¼ cup sugar
1 tbs. cinnamon

½ cup raisins
¼ cup chopped walnuts

Glaze
Confectioners' Sugar Glaze, page 342, optional

Remove dough from the machine upon completion of the dough cycle and roll into a rectangle on a floured work surface. Add only enough flour to prevent sticking. Brush dough with melted butter. Mix sugar and cinnamon together and spread evenly over dough. Sprinkle with raisins and nuts. Roll dough jelly-roll fashion (see page 275), beginning on the wide side. Cut into 12 equal slices and place in greased muffin cups. Cover and let rise in a warm, draft-free location for 30 to 45 minutes. Bake in a preheated 350° oven for 20 to 30 minutes or until golden brown. Glaze while warm if desired.

Walnut Raisin Cinnamon Rolls

Yield: 12 rolls

Enjoy these for breakfast or a mid-afternoon snack. Vary shaping with ideas on pages 272–277.

Dough
1⅓ cups milk
¼ cup sugar
2 tbs. walnut or vegetable oil
1 tsp. vanilla extract
1 tsp. salt

1 tsp. cinnamon
4 cups all-purpose flour
2 tsp. yeast
Add: ½ cup raisins
Add: ¼ cup chopped walnuts

Wash
1 egg beaten with 1-2 tbs. milk or cream

Add raisins and nuts after the machine kneads for about 5 minutes regardless of what machine you have. Remove dough from machine upon completion of the dough cycle and place on a lightly floured work surface. Form dough into 12 small balls and place in lightly greased muffin cups. Cover and let rise for about 1 hour in a warm, draft-free location. Brush with wash. Bake in a preheated 350° oven for 15 to 20 minutes.

Orange Cranberry Buns

For variety, use any favorite dried fruit (apricots, cherries, etc.).

Dough
1 ⅛ cups orange juice
2 tbs. butter or margarine
1 egg, large
1 tbs. sugar
1 tsp. salt
1 tsp. dried orange peel, or freshly grated to taste
3 cups all-purpose flour
2 tsp. yeast

Filling
1 tbs. butter, melted
¼ cup sugar
1-2 tsp. dried orange peel, or freshly grated to taste
½ cup dried cranberries
¼ cup finely chopped almonds

Glaze
Orange Glaze, page 343, optional

Remove dough from the machine upon completion of the dough cycle and roll into a rectangle on a floured work surface. Add only enough flour to prevent sticking. Brush dough with melted butter. Mix sugar and orange peel together and spread evenly over dough. Sprinkle with dried cranberries and nuts. Roll dough jelly-roll fashion, beginning on the wide side (see page 275). Cut into 12 equal slices and place in greased muffin cups. Cover and let rise in a warm, draft-free location for 30 to 45 minutes. Bake in a preheated 350° oven for 20 to 30 minutes or until golden brown. Glaze while warm if desired.

Caramel Almond Buns

Yield: 12 buns

These are sinfully rich and are a definite "must-try."

Dough
¾ cup milk
2 tbs. butter or margarine
1 egg, large
1 tsp. almond extract
2 tbs. sugar
1 tsp. salt
3 cups all-purpose flour
2 tsp. yeast

Filling
2 tbs. butter, melted
¼ cup brown sugar, packed
1 tsp. almond extract
½ cup finely chopped almonds

Glaze
Confectioners' Sugar Glaze with
almond extract, page 342, optional

Remove dough from the machine upon completion of the dough cycle and roll into a rectangle on a floured work surface. Add only enough flour to prevent sticking. Mix together melted butter, brown sugar and almond extract and spread evenly over dough. Sprinkle with almonds. Roll dough jelly-roll fashion, beginning on the wide side (see page 275). Cut into 12 equal slices and place in greased muffin cups. Cover and let rise in a warm, draft-free location for 30 to 45 minutes. Bake in a preheated 350° oven for 20 to 30 minutes or until golden brown. Glaze while warm if desired.

Potato Cinnamon Rolls

Yield: 12 rolls

Use regular baking or sweet potatoes for this delightful cinnamon roll variation.

Dough
½ cup mashed potatoes
½ cup milk
1 egg
2 tbs. butter or margarine
1 tsp. vanilla extract
¼ cup sugar
½ tsp. salt
3-3½ cups all-purpose flour
1½ tsp. yeast

Filling
2 tbs. butter, melted
1 tbs. cinnamon
½ cup raisins, or dried fruit of choice
⅓ cup chopped walnuts or pecans

Glaze
Confectioners' Sugar Glaze, page 342,
optional

Remove dough from the machine upon completion of the dough cycle. On a lightly floured work surface, roll dough into a large rectangle. Brush with melted butter and sprinkle with cinnamon. Spread raisins and nuts on top and roll tightly, jelly-roll fashion, beginning on the wide side (see page 275). Cut into 12 equal slices and place in lightly greased muffin cups. Cover and let rise for about 1 hour in a warm, draft-free location. Bake in a preheated 350° oven for 15 to 20 minutes. Glaze while warm if desired.

Sticky Buns

You can also make this recipe in greased muffin cups.

Dough
1 cup milk
1 egg
¼ cup brown sugar, packed
½ tsp. salt
1 tsp. cinnamon
3 cups all-purpose flour
1½ tsp. yeast

Filling and Topping
6 tbs. butter or margarine, melted
¾ cup brown sugar, packed
½-1 tsp. cinnamon
¼ cup raisins, dried cranberries or
    other favorite dried fruit
½ cup chopped pecans

Make filling while dough is rising in the machine. Mix together butter, brown sugar and cinnamon; divide in half and set aside. Remove dough from machine upon completion of the dough cycle. Roll dough into a large rectangle. Spread half of the filling on top of dough, sprinkle evenly with raisins and nuts and roll tightly, jelly-roll fashion, beginning on the wide side (see page 275). Spread remaining filling on the bottom of an 8- or 9-inch round cake pan. Cut dough into 12 equal slices and place on top of mixture. Cover with a kitchen towel and let rise for about 1 hour in a warm, draft-free location. Bake in a preheated 350° oven for 15 to 20 minutes. Cool for about 5 minutes in pan and then turn pan upside down on a large plate or platter. Serve sticky side up.

Honey Buns

This is a combination of a sticky bun and a cinnamon bun.

Dough
1 cup milk
1 egg, large
2 tbs. vegetable oil
2 tbs. honey
1 tsp. salt
4 cups all-purpose flour
2 tsp. yeast

Filling
2 tbs. butter, melted
½ cup finely chopped nuts

Topping
¼ cup honey mixed with ¼ cup soft
    butter

Remove dough from the machine upon completion of the dough cycle and roll into a rectangle on a floured work surface. Add only enough flour to prevent sticking. Brush dough with melted butter and sprinkle nuts evenly over dough. Roll dough jelly-roll fashion, beginning on the wide side (see page 275). Cut into 12 equal slices and place on a lightly greased baking sheet. Cover and let rise in a warm, draft-free location for 30 to 45 minutes. Bake in a preheated 350° oven for 20 to 30 minutes or until golden brown. Immediately spread rolls with honey butter mixture.

Double Chocolate Rolls

Yield: 12 rolls

Karen Hubachek says that this recipe was inspired by the "pain au choco-lat" eaten after school by children in France. These will disappear quickly.

Dough

¾ cup warm milk
1 egg
¼ cup butter or margarine
¼ cup sugar
¾ tsp. salt

½ tsp. cinnamon, or to taste, optional
2 tbs. Dutch-process cocoa
2½ cups bread flour
1 heaping tsp. yeast

Filling

Hershey Kisses, chocolate chips or any favorite chocolate candy bar

Glaze

Confectioners Sugar Glaze, page 342, optional

Remove dough from the machine upon completion of the dough cycle. If dough is sticky, knead in only enough flour so that it is easily handled. Form dough into 12 equal balls and stuff each one with a piece of chocolate (see page 276). Pinch ends together to seal in chocolate and place in greased muffin cups. Cover and let rise in a warm, draft-free location for 45 to 60 minutes. Bake in a preheated 350° oven for about 15 minutes. Glaze while warm.

Coconut Chocolate Rolls

Yield: 12 rolls

The combination of coconut and chocolate is delicious. Top with Coconut Glaze, *page 343, for an even richer roll.*

Dough

⅞ cup (7 oz.) milk
2 tbs. butter or margarine
1 egg, large
1 tsp. coconut extract
2 tbs. sugar

1 tsp. salt
¾ cup coconut flakes
3 cups all-purpose or bread flour
2 tsp. yeast

Filling

12 Hershey Kisses, or 1 oz. pieces chocolate

Remove dough from the machine upon completion of the dough cycle. If the dough is sticky, knead in only enough flour so that it is easily handled and divide into 12 equal pieces. Form into 12 balls and stuff each one with a Hershey Kiss or similar size piece of chocolate. Pinch ends together to seal in chocolate (see page 276) and place on a greased baking sheet or in greased muffin cups. Cover and let rise in a warm, draft-free location for 45 to 60 minutes. Bake in a preheated 350° oven for about 15 minutes. Cool slightly in pans and then remove to cool on a rack.

Swedish Chocolate Bread

Yield: 1 loaf

Nutella chocolate hazelnut filling is found in larger grocery stores.

Dough
1 cup warm milk
½ cup butter or margarine
¼ cup sugar
½ tsp. salt
3 cups bread flour
1½ tsp. yeast

Filling
⅓-½ cup Nutella or similar chocolate spread

Wash
1 egg beaten with 1-2 tbs. milk or cream

Remove dough from the machine upon completion of the dough cycle. Roll on a lightly floured work surface into a large rectangle. Spread Nutella filling on middle third of dough. With scissors, a sharp knife, pastry or pizza wheel, cut 1-inch strips down both sides of dough from filling to edge. Fold the top of filled center over dough and then alternate fold side strips over filling, angling each folded strip down (see mock braid, page 276). Place on a greased baking sheet, cover and let rise for about 1 hour. Brush with egg wash and bake in a preheated 350° oven for 20 to 25 minutes.

Mexican Chocolate Rolls

Yield: 12 rolls

This roll boasts the traditional Mexican combination of chocolate and cinnamon.

Dough
¾ cup milk
2 tbs. butter or margarine
1 egg, large
2 tbs. sugar
1 tsp. salt
1 tbs. unsweetened cocoa
1 tsp. cinnamon
3 cups all-purpose flour
2 tsp. yeast

Filling
1 tbs. butter, melted
¼ cup sugar
1 tbs. unsweetened cocoa
1 tsp. cinnamon
½ cup chopped toasted hazelnuts or walnuts

Glaze
Confectioners' Sugar Glaze, page 342, optional, or dust with confectioners' sugar

Remove dough from the machine upon completion of the dough cycle and roll into a rectangle on a floured work surface. Add only enough flour to prevent sticking. Brush dough with melted butter. Mix sugar, cocoa and cinnamon together. Sprinkle dough with sugar mixture and nuts. Roll dough jelly-roll fashion, beginning on the wide side (see page 275). Cut into 12 equal slices and place in greased muffin cups. Cover and let rise in a warm, draft-free location for 30 to 45 minutes. Bake in a preheated 350° oven for 15 to 20 minutes.

Pumpkin Rolls

These rolls are a rich autumn treat to enjoy any time of the year.

Dough
1 cup milk
1 tbs. butter or margarine
1/4 cup sugar
1/2 tsp. salt
1/2-1 tsp. cinnamon
1/2 cup oats
2 1/2 cups bread flour
1 1/2 tsp. yeast

Filling
1 cup canned pumpkin
1/2 cup brown sugar, packed
1/2 cup raisins, dried cranberries or dried cherries
1/2 cup chopped walnuts or pecans

Glaze
Confectioners' Sugar Glaze with a pinch of cinnamon, page 342, optional

Remove dough from the machine upon completion of the dough cycle and roll into a rectangle on a lightly floured work surface. Add only enough flour to prevent sticking. Mix all filling ingredients together and spread evenly over dough. Roll dough jelly-roll fashion, beginning on the wide side (see page 275). Cut into 12 equal slices and place in greased muffin cups. Cover and let rise in a warm, draft-free location for 30 to 45 minutes. Bake in a pre-heated 350° oven for 20 to 30 minutes or until golden brown.

Hawaiian Nut Crescents

These tropical-flavored rolls are delicious served with coffee. Use macadamia nuts for the fullest Hawaiian flavor, but walnuts, pecans or Brazil nuts may be substituted as a less expensive alternative. I have a real sweet tooth and love the optional combination of chocolate and coconut — the only problem is that I can't eat just one (or two)! If you don't want to use a glaze, you can wash with an egg beaten with a little milk just before baking.

Dough
¾ cup milk
½ cup butter or margarine
1 egg, large
2 tbs. sugar
1 tsp. salt
½ cup coconut flakes
3 cups all-purpose flour
2 tsp. yeast

Filling
1 tbs. butter
1 tsp. coconut extract
½ cup coarsely chopped macadamia nuts
½ cup chocolate chips, optional

Glaze
Confectioners' Sugar Glaze with with coconut extract, page 342, or *Coconut Glaze*, page 343

Remove dough from the machine upon completion of the dough cycle and roll into a large round on a floured work surface. Add only enough flour to prevent sticking. Melt butter and allow to cool slightly; mix in coconut extract. Brush dough with butter mixture and sprinkle evenly with nuts. With a knife or a pizza wheel, cut round into 8 pieces as you would a pie. If using chocolate chips, divide them evenly among pieces sprinkled around outside (thicker) edge of triangle; this is so the chocolate is firmly rolled inside each crescent to avoid a chocolate leak. Roll each piece from wide end to point, pressing tightly together as you roll, to form a crescent shape (see page 273). Place rolls on a lightly greased baking sheet. Cover and let rise in a warm, draft-free location for 30 to 45 minutes. Bake in a preheated 350° oven for 15 to 20 minutes or until golden brown.

Lemon Crescents

Fresh lemon juice and peel is preferred for the best flavor, but commercially bottled lemon juice and dried peel may be used. You will release more juice from the lemon if you first roll it on the kitchen counter, pushing down on it with the palm of your hand. You can grate the lemon peel (zest) directly into the bread machine pan to taste. Use the higher amount of sugar in the filling for a sweeter crescent.

Dough
1 cup water
2 tbs. lemon juice
2 tbs. butter or margarine
1 egg
1/4 cup sugar
1 tsp. salt
1 tsp. dried lemon peel, or freshly grated to taste
4 cups all-purpose flour
2 tsp. yeast

Filling
4 oz. cream cheese, softened
1/4-1/2 cup confectioners' sugar
1 tsp. dried lemon peel, or freshly grated to taste

Glaze
Lemon Glaze, page 344

Remove dough from the machine upon completion of the dough cycle and roll into a large round on a floured work surface. Add only enough flour to prevent sticking. Mix filling ingredients together and spread evenly over the outside half of the dough. (By spreading it on the outside, the filling is better encased in the dough to prevent leaking during baking.) With a knife or a pizza wheel, cut the round into 8 pieces as you would a pie. Roll each piece from the wide end to the point of the triangle, pressing tightly together as you roll, to form a crescent shape (see page 273). Place rolls on a lightly greased baking pan. Cover and let rise in a warm, draft-free location for 30 to 45 minutes. Bake in a preheated 350° oven for 20 to 25 minutes or until golden brown. Glaze while crescents are still hot.

Poppy Seed-Filled Rolls

Based on a Hungarian stuffed roll, these make great coffee rolls. Begin with 3 cups flour and add more if necessary to form the right consistency.

Dough
¾ cup milk
¼ cup butter
2 eggs
2 tbs. sugar
1 tsp. salt
1 tsp. dried lemon peel, or freshly grated to taste
3-3¼ cups all-purpose flour
2 tsp. yeast

Filling
2 tbs. poppy seeds
¼ cup finely ground almonds
1½ tbs. honey

Wash
1 egg beaten with 1 tbs. milk

While dough is rising in the machine, make filling. In a medium bowl, combine poppy seeds and almonds. Add honey; using your hands, mix until all ingredients are moistened and form a doughy consistency; set aside.

Remove dough from machine upon completion of the dough cycle. If dough is sticky, knead in only enough flour so that it is easily handled and divide into 12 equal pieces. Form each piece into a ball and stuff each with a large spoonful of filling (see page 276). Pinch dough together to seal. Place rolls in greased muffin cups or on a baking sheet. Cover and let rise in a warm, draft-free location for about 30 minutes. Brush with egg wash. Bake in a preheated 350° oven for 15 to 20 minutes.

German Coffee Crescents

Yield: 8 rolls

These coffee crescents are a combination of a filled crescent and a croissant. Bet you can't eat just one! While margarine could be used, butter is preferred.

Dough
¾ cup milk
1 egg
2 tbs. butter
¼ cup sugar
1 tsp. salt
3 cups all-purpose flour
2 tsp. yeast

Additional Ingredients
¼ cup butter, softened
2 tbs. sugar

Filling
½ cup raisins or chopped dried fruits of choice
½ cup chopped walnuts
¼ cup sugar
2 tbs. butter, melted

While dough is rising in the machine, make filling. With a food processor, process dried fruits and nuts until coarsely ground. Add sugar and butter and process until mixture forms a paste. Set aside.

Remove dough from machine upon completion of the dough cycle. Roll dough into a large rectangle on a lightly floured work surface. Spread 2 tbs. of the butter on top of dough and sprinkle with 1 tbs. of the sugar. Fold rectangle into thirds, as you would a letter, and roll into another large rectangle. Spread remaining 2 tbs. butter on top, sprinkle with remaining sugar and fold into thirds again. Fold corners into center to form a ball, turn over and roll dough into a large circle. With a knife, pastry or pizza wheel, cut circle into 8 equal pieces. Place an equal amount of filling mixture on the wide end of each triangle and roll dough from wide end to narrow end to form a crescent (see page 273), tightly pressing and sealing filling inside. Place crescents on a greased baking sheet, cover and let rise for about 30 minutes. Bake in a preheated 350° oven for 20 to 25 minutes or until puffed and golden.

German Sour Cream Sweet Rolls

Yield: 12-16 rolls

These delightful sweet breads are rolled in sugar and are shaped into small twists or crescents. Keep an eye on the dough and add water if necessary, ½ tbs. at a time, while dough is kneading. Sour cream sometimes makes it necessary to adjust moisture to get the right consistency. This dough should be very soft. Scrape the sides of the pan with a rubber spatula if necessary to help push ingredients towards the kneading paddle.

Dough

¾ cup sour cream
2 tbs. butter or margarine
1 egg
1 tsp. vanilla extract
¼ cup sugar
1 tsp. salt
3 cups all-purpose flour
2 tsp. yeast

Additional Ingredient

½ cup sugar

Warm sour cream in the microwave for 30 to 60 seconds before adding to the machine pan.

Upon completion of the dough cycle, liberally sprinkle sugar on the work surface. Remove dough from machine and press into a large rectangle. Flip dough over several times, coating with sugar to prevent sticking. The dough is so soft that it is easier to press by hand than it is to roll it with a rolling pin. With a knife or a pizza wheel, cut dough into small rectangles. Twist each rectangle into a long spiral and curl into a round, pinching sides closed to seal. Place twisted rounds on a slightly greased baking sheet, cover with a kitchen towel and place in a warm, draft-free location to rise for about 1 hour. Bake in a preheated 350° oven for 20 to 25 minutes or until lightly browned. The twists will be sticky because of the sugar. If they are browning too quickly, cover with a tent made with aluminum foil.

Moravian Coffeecake

Yield: one 9-x-13-inch cake

Variations of this popular sweet coffeecake are enjoyed all over the world.

Dough
1 1/4 cups milk
2 tbs. butter or margarine
1/4 cup sugar
1 tsp. salt
1/4 cup instant potato flakes
3 cups all-purpose flour
1 1/2 tsp. yeast

Topping
1/2 cup brown sugar, packed
1 tbs. cinnamon
1/4 cup butter, melted

Remove dough from the machine upon completion of the dough cycle and press into a lightly greased 9-x-13-inch baking pan. Make small indentations in dough with your finger, randomly or in a pattern. Mix sugar and cinnamon together and press sugar mixture into indentations. Sprinkle any remaining sugar over the top. Drizzle with melted butter. Cover and let rise in a warm, draft-free location for 45 to 60 minutes, or until almost to top of pan. Bake in a preheated 350° oven until bread is brown and crust is hard, about 25 to 30 minutes. Cool on a wire rack.

German Coffeecake

Yield: one 9-x-13-inch cake

This coffeecake variation uses sour cream in the topping.

Dough
3/4 cup milk
1 egg
3 tbs. butter or margarine
1 tsp. salt
2 tbs. sugar
3 cups all-purpose flour
1 1/2 tsp. yeast

Topping
1/2 cup sour cream
1/4 cup sugar
1 tsp. cinnamon

Remove dough from the machine upon completion of the dough cycle. Press into a lightly greased 9-x-13-inch baking pan, cover and let rise in a warm, draft-free location for 45 to 60 minutes, until almost to top of pan. After dough has risen, make small indentations in dough with your finger, randomly or in a pattern. Spread a thin layer of sour cream over dough — there will be slightly more sour cream in indentations. Mix sugar with cinnamon and sprinkle on top. Bake in a preheated 350° oven until bread is brown and crust is hard, about 25 to 30 minutes. Cool on a wire rack.

Streusel-Topped Coffeecake

Yield: one 9-x-13-inch cake

Similar to a Moravian Coffeecake, this has a topping that can't be beat!

Dough
1 cup milk
1/4 cup butter or margarine
1 tsp. vanilla extract
1/4 cup sugar
1 tsp. salt
3 cups all-purpose flour
1 1/2 tsp. yeast
Add: 1/2 cup chopped nuts of choice

Topping
1/2 cup all-purpose flour
1/4 cup brown sugar, packed
1/4 cup sugar
1 tsp. cinnamon
1/4 cup butter, cold, cut into small pieces

Add nuts to the machine after dough ball has formed, about 5 to 8 minutes after kneading starts. To make streusel topping, place all topping ingredients in a medium bowl. With your fingers or a pastry blender, rub or blend ingredients together until well mixed and crumbly; set aside.

Upon completion of the dough cycle, remove dough from machine and press into a lightly greased 9-x-13-inch baking pan. Make small indentations in dough with your finger, randomly or in a pattern. Press topping ingredients into indentations. Sprinkle any remaining topping over dough. Cover with a kitchen towel and place in a warm, draft-free location to rise for 45 to 60 minutes, or until almost to top of pan. Bake in a preheated 350° oven until bread is brown and crust is hard, about 25 to 30 minutes. Cool on a wire rack.

Directions for Bagels

Upon completion of the first kneading, turn off the machine and allow dough to sit undisturbed in the machine for about 45 minutes. Because bagels do not rise after shaping, preheat the oven to 450° and boil 2 quarts water in a large, nonaluminum pan before removing the dough from the machine. Once the water has come to a boil, stir in 1 tbs. sugar and lower the temperature so that the water maintains a steady, gentle boil.

Remove dough from the machine and form into 8 equal balls. Shape dough into bagels using any of the following methods:

- Roll each piece of dough into a rope and then shape into a circle, pressing the ends together. If dough does not seal, moisten dough lightly with a few drops of water.
- Roll each piece into a ball and slightly flatten between the heels of your palms. Push your thumb through the center to form a hole and twist dough to enlarge the hole.
- Remove dough from the machine and roll into a 1/2- to 3/4-inch-thick rectangle on a lightly floured work surface. Cut bagels with a bagel or doughnut cutter.

Gently place 2 or 3 bagels at a time in the water. Cook the first side for 1 1/2 to 2 minutes and then turn them over and cook the other side for another 1 to 1 1/2 minutes (3 minutes total). Remove bagels with a slotted spoon and place on a well-greased perforated pizza pan (for crisp bottoms) or baking sheet.

Using a pastry brush, lightly brush bagels with beaten egg white and sprinkle with seeds if desired. Bake for 15 to 18 minutes or until golden brown.

Plain Bagels

Yield: 8 bagels

Sprinkle with sesame, poppy, anise, fennel or caraway seeds, or instant onion flakes if desired.

1 1/8 cups water	3 cups all-purpose flour
2 tbs. sugar	2 tsp. yeast
1/2 tsp. salt	

Follow directions for making bagels.

Egg Bagels

Sprinkle with poppy seeds if desired.

¾ cup water
2 eggs
2 tbs. sugar

½ tsp. salt
3 cups all-purpose flour
2 tsp. yeast

Follow directions for making bagels on page 308.

Pumpernickel Bagels

Sprinkle with caraway seeds as a finishing touch.

1 ¼ cups water
2 tbs. brown sugar
½ tsp. salt
1 tbs. unsweetened cocoa
½ cup rye flour

½ cup whole wheat flour
2 cups all-purpose flour
2 tsp. yeast
Add: ⅓ cup raisins, optional

Follow directions for making bagels on page 308.

Whole Wheat Bagels

Sprinkle with sesame, poppy, anise, fennel or caraway seeds, or instant onion flakes if desired.

1 ⅛ cups water
2 tbs. brown sugar
½ tsp. salt

1 cup whole wheat flour
2 cups all-purpose flour
2 tsp. yeast

Follow directions for making bagels on page 308.

Onion Bagels

Watch the dough; add water or flour a teaspoon at a time to obtain a smooth dough ball. Sprinkle with your favorite seeds or onion flakes if desired.

1 ⅛ cups water
¼ cup grated cheddar cheese, lightly
   packed
2 tbs. sugar

½ tsp. salt
2 tbs. instant onion flakes
3 cups all-purpose flour
2 tsp. yeast

Follow directions for making bagels on page 308.

Orange Raisin Bagels

Yield: 8 bagels

1 ¼ cups orange juice
2 tbs. sugar
½ tsp. salt
1 tsp. dried orange peel, or freshly grated to taste

3 cups all-purpose flour
2 tsp. yeast
Add: ⅓ cup raisins, dried cranberries or other dried fruit

Follow directions for making bagels on page 308. Add raisins to the machine with dry ingredients at the beginning of the cycle.

Cinnamon Raisin Bagels

Yield: 8 bagels

These are good sprinkled with poppy seeds.

1 ¼ cups water
2 tbs. sugar
½ tsp. salt
1 tsp. cinnamon, or to taste

3 cups all-purpose flour
2 tsp. yeast
Add: ⅓ cup raisins or favorite dried fruit

Follow directions for making bagels on page 308. Add raisins to the machine with dry ingredients at the beginning of the cycle.

Apple Cinnamon Raisin Bagels

Yield: 8 bagels

1 ⅓ cups apple juice
2 tbs. sugar
½ tsp. salt
1 tsp. cinnamon, or to taste
½ cup oats

3 cups all-purpose flour
2 tsp. yeast
Add: ¼ cup raisins
Add: ¼ cup chopped dried apples

Follow directions for making bagels on page 308. Add raisins and dried apples to the machine with dry ingredients at the beginning of the cycle.

Directions for English Muffins

Remove dough from the machine upon completion of the dough cycle. Press dough by hand into a ½-inch-thick rectangle on a cornmeal-covered work surface. Turn dough over several times so that both sides are coated with cornmeal to prevent sticking. Cut muffins with a biscuit or cookie cutter, or use the top of a drinking glass. Place on a baking sheet, cover and let rise for 45 to 60 minutes.

Cook on an ungreased griddle (or cast-iron skillet) over low to medium heat for 5 to 7 minutes on each side or until golden. Cook muffins fairly close together — leave only about ½ inch between them. Split open with a fork and serve warm or toasted.

Basic English Muffins

Yield: 12-15 muffins

The softer the dough, the lighter the muffin will be.

1 cup milk
3 tbs. butter or margarine
1 egg
2 tsp. sugar
½ tsp. salt
3 cups all-purpose flour
1 ½ tsp. yeast
Add: cornmeal for rolling dough

Follow directions for English Muffins.

Whole Wheat English Muffins

Yield: 12-15 muffins

Whole wheat adds a nutty flavor as well as nutrients.

1 cup milk
3 tbs. butter or margarine
1 egg
1 tbs. sugar
½ tsp. salt
1 cup whole wheat flour
2 cups all-purpose flour
1 ½ tsp. rapid or quick yeast
Add: ½ cup raisins, optional
Add: cornmeal for rolling dough

Follow directions for English Muffins. Add raisins 5 minutes after dough has formed a ball.

Orange Raisin English Muffins

Yield: 12-15 muffins

1 cup orange juice
2 tbs. butter or margarine
1 egg
¼-½ tsp. dried orange peel, or
    freshly grated to taste
2 tsp. sugar

½ tsp. salt
3-3¼ cups all-purpose flour
1½ tsp. yeast
Add: ½ cup raisins or dried
    cranberries
Add: cornmeal for rolling dough

    Follow directions on page 311. Add raisins 5 minutes after dough has formed a ball.

Cinnamon Raisin English Muffins

Yield: 12-15 muffins

1 cup milk
3 tbs. butter or margarine
1 egg
1 tbs. sugar
½ tsp. salt

1 tsp. cinnamon, or to taste
3-3¼ cups all-purpose flour
1½ tsp. yeast
Add: ½ cup raisins
Add: cornmeal for rolling dough

    Follow directions on page 311. Add raisins 5 minutes after dough has formed a ball.

Almond Apricot English Muffins

Yield: 12-15 muffins

1 cup orange juice
1 egg
2 tbs. butter or margarine
2 tsp. almond extract
1 tbs. sugar
½ tsp. salt

3-3¼ cups all-purpose flour
1½ tsp. yeast
Add: ¼ cup finely diced apricots
Add: ¼ cup finely chopped almonds
Add: cornmeal for rolling dough

    Follow directions on page 311. Add apricots and nuts 5 minutes after dough has formed a ball.

Hawaiian-Style English Muffins

Yield: 12-15 muffins

These muffins are really special. The recipe calls for macadamia nuts for a tropical flavor, but almonds could be used as a less expensive alternative.

1 cup pineapple juice
2 tbs. butter or margarine
1 egg
2 tsp. coconut extract
1 tbs. sugar
½ tsp. salt

½ cup coconut flakes
3 cups all-purpose flour
1½ tsp. yeast
Add: ¼ cup finely chopped
   macadamia nuts
Add: cornmeal for rolling dough

Follow directions on page 311. Add macadamia nuts about 5 minutes after dough has formed a ball.

Crumpets

Yield: 24 crumpets

The dough for crumpets is really more like a batter and will have to be poured into crumpet rings on a hot griddle or (cast iron) frying pan. Do not make this recipe in a Welbilt, DAK or Citizen machine because of the hole in the bottom of the pan. Crumpets are best eaten warm or toasted, with lots of butter.

1¼ cups milk
2 tbs. butter
1 egg
1 tbs. sugar

1 tsp. salt
2 cups all-purpose flour
2 tsp. yeast

Use the dough cycle to knead batter. Once the machine has completed kneading, allow dough (batter) to rise for 45 to 50 minutes. About 30 minutes into the rising phase, start preheating a cast-iron skillet or griddle over low heat. Lightly grease crumpet rings (you can use clean, empty tuna fish cans or similar cans with both ends removed). Place ring(s) on the griddle and spoon about 2 tbs. batter into each ring. Cook batter for about 3 minutes until it is bubbly, firm and lightly browned on the bottom. Slide a spatula underneath ring to pick up ring and crumpet. Remove hot ring and cook second side of crumpet until it is lightly browned on the bottom. Repeat the process until batter is used.

Fried Mexican Sweet Rolls (Sopaipillas) *Yield: 12-15 rolls*

This favorite Mexican sweet roll can be enjoyed with a meal or for dessert. Sprinkle with cinnamon sugar or confectioners' sugar or eat with honey. The softer the dough, the lighter the sopaipilla, so take care when adding flour.

1 cup milk	1 tsp. salt
2 tbs. butter	3-3¼ cups all-purpose flour
1 egg	2 tsp. yeast
2 tbs. sugar	oil for deep frying

Remove dough from the machine upon completion of the dough cycle. Roll dough into large rectangle on a lightly floured work surface to prevent sticking. Fold dough in half and roll out into another large rectangle. With a sharp knife or a pizza wheel, cut dough into small rectangles and then in half to make 2 triangles (or other desired shape). Fry 2 at a time for 1 to 2 minutes on each side in a full (4-cup) deep fat fryer. They should puff up and are done when lightly golden in color.

Basic Doughnuts

Yield: 12-15 doughnuts

This dough is made the evening before and rises in the refrigerator overnight. The dough should be slightly sticky. The overnight refrigeration makes the sticky dough easier to roll and handle — and it allows you to have fresh doughnuts early in the morning! With the exception of Welbilt, DAK and Citizen machines (because of the hole in the bottom of the pan), the dough can be loosely covered with plastic wrap right in the bread machine pan and placed in the refrigerator. Otherwise, place the dough in a lightly greased glass or plastic bowl, cover with plastic wrap and refrigerate.

1 cup milk	1 tsp. salt
2 tbs. butter or margarine	3 cups all-purpose flour
1 egg	1½ tsp. yeast
½ cup sugar	oil for deep frying

Upon completion of the kneading (before the rising phase), remove the pan containing dough, cover lightly with plastic wrap and place in the refrigerator to rise overnight. In the morning, remove dough, place on a lightly floured work surface and roll into a ½-inch thickness. The softer the dough, the lighter the doughnut, so take care when adding flour. It may be helpful to grease your hands when handling dough to prevent sticking. Cut doughnut shapes with a greased or floured doughnut cutter and place on a well-greased baking sheet. Cover with a kitchen towel and let rise until light and airy (1 to 1½ hours). Fry 2 at a time in a full (4-cup) deep fat fryer.

Beignets

No visit to New Orleans would be complete without enjoying these for breakfast. Serve with confectioners' or cinnamon sugar. Do not add too much flour.

⅞ cup (7 oz.) milk
2 tbs. butter
1 egg
¼ cup sugar
1 tsp. salt

1 tsp. cinnamon, optional
3 cups all-purpose flour
1½ tsp. yeast
oil for deep frying

Upon completion of the kneading, cover dough lightly with plastic wrap and place in the refrigerator to rise overnight. In the morning, remove dough, place on a lightly floured work surface and roll into a ½-inch thickness. With a sharp knife or pizza wheel, cut dough into 2- or 3-inch squares and place on a well-greased baking sheet. Cover with a kitchen towel and let rise for about 1 hour. Fry 2 at a time in a full (4-cup) deep fat fryer.

Chocolate Doughnuts

If you like the combination of chocolate and coconut as much as I do, try glazing these doughnuts with Coconut Glaze, page 343.

1 cup milk
2 tbs. butter or margarine
1 egg
½ cup sugar
1 tsp. salt

2 tbs. unsweetened cocoa
3 cups all-purpose flour
1½ tsp. yeast
oil for deep frying

Upon completion of the kneading, remove dough, cover lightly with plastic wrap and place in the refrigerator to rise overnight. In the morning, remove dough, place on a lightly floured work surface and roll into a ½-inch thickness. The softer the dough, the lighter the doughnut, so take care when adding flour. It may be helpful to grease your hands when handling dough to prevent sticking. Cut doughnut shapes with a greased or floured doughnut cutter and place on a well-greased baking sheet. Cover with a kitchen towel and let rise until light and airy (1 to 1½ hours). Fry 2 at a time in a full (4-cup) deep fat fryer.

Coconut Doughnuts

Yield: 12-15 doughnuts

You'll think you're in the tropics when you eat these breakfast doughnuts! The softer the dough, the lighter the doughnut, so take care when adding flour. It may be helpful to grease your hands when handling the dough to prevent sticking.

1 1/4 cups canned, unsweetened coconut milk
2 tbs. butter or margarine
1 egg
1/4 cup sugar

1 tsp. salt
1/2 cup coconut flakes
3 cups all-purpose flour
1 1/2 tsp. yeast
oil for deep frying

Upon completion of the kneading, remove dough, cover lightly with plastic wrap and place in the refrigerator to rise overnight. In the morning, remove dough, place on a lightly floured work surface and roll into a 1/2-inch thickness. Cut doughnut shapes with a greased or floured doughnut cutter and place on a well-greased baking sheet. Cover with a kitchen towel and let rise until light and airy (1 to 1 1/2 hours). Fry 2 at a time in a full (4-cup) deep fat fryer.

West Indian Floats

Yield: 12 fried breads

These fried breads are usually served with fish, but can also be eaten alone any time of the day. Unlike many of the other fried breads, these are not sweet.

1 cup water
2 tbs. shortening or butter
1 tsp. salt

3 cups all-purpose flour
1 1/2 tsp. yeast
oil for frying

Remove dough from the machine upon completion of the dough cycle. Divide dough into 12 equal pieces and shape into balls. Place on a greased baking sheet, cover and let rise for about 30 minutes. Fry for about 2 minutes on each side in a full (4-cup) deep fat fryer or in a few inches of vegetable oil until golden brown.

Fastnachts

These German "doughnuts" are eaten just before Lent and the name means, literally, "night before fasting." They are enjoyed by the Pennsylvania Dutch as well. While they can be eaten just as they are, we like to sprinkle them with confectioners' sugar or cinnamon sugar. The softer the dough, the lighter the results, so take care when adding flour.

1 cup milk
2 tbs. butter
1 egg
1 tsp. vanilla extract
¼ cup sugar
1 tsp. salt

1 tsp. dried lemon peel, or freshly
  grated to taste
½ cup instant potato flakes
3 cups all-purpose flour
1½ tsp. yeast
oil for deep frying

Upon completion of the dough cycle, remove dough, place on a lightly floured work surface and roll into a ½-inch thickness. With a sharp knife or pizza wheel, cut dough into 2- or 3-inch diamond shapes and place on a well-greased baking sheet. Cover with a kitchen towel and let rise for about 30 minutes. Fry 2 at a time in a full, (4-cup) deep fat fryer.

Crusty Mexican Rolls (Bolillos and Teleras) *Yield: 12 rolls*

These two crusty Mexican rolls are made from the same basic dough, but are shaped differently. The flavor develops while the sponge sits overnight or during the day. Mr. and Mrs. Polk say that they make these rolls all the time in their machine. Use your favorite method(s) for generating steam for a crisp crust (see pages 277–279).

Sponge*
⅓ cup water
1 tsp. sugar
¼ tsp. salt
¾ cup all-purpose flour
1 tsp. yeast

Add sponge ingredients to the machine pan, start the machine and allow it to knead sponge for 5 to 10 minutes. Turn off machine and allow sponge to sit undisturbed in the pan for 6 to 10 hours. If you have a Welbilt, DAK or Citizen machine or if your machine is otherwise occupied, mix sponge in a large bowl, cover with plastic wrap and allow to sit undisturbed in a warm, draft-free location for 6 to 10 hours.

After 6 to 10 hours, add remaining dough ingredients, except water, to sponge and start the dough cycle. Allow dough to knead for a few minutes and then add 1 to 2 tbs. water to soften dough if necessary. Upon completion of dough cycle, remove dough from machine and roll it into a long rope about 2 inches thick. Divide dough into 12 equal pieces and flatten each into an oval between your hands.

For bolillos: Fold one third (lengthwise) of the oval over towards the center and flatten with your hands. Fold the other third over on top of the previous fold and flatten it again with your hands. Roll dough slightly to tighten; round the ends. Place dough seam side up on greased baking sheets.

For teleras: With a small rolling pin or the handle of a wooden spoon, press down in the center of the oval (lengthwise) so that dough is almost cut in half. Turn each piece upside down and place on a greased baking sheet. Cover bolillos and/or teleras with a towel and place in a warm, draft-free location for 1 hour. Bake in a preheated 400° oven until golden brown, about 15 to 20 minutes.

Greek Psomi

Who can resist this light and airy bread with a crisp crust?

Dough

1 cup water
1 tbs. olive oil
2 tbs. honey

1 tsp. salt
3 cups bread flour
1 1/2 tsp. yeast

Wash

cold water

Remove dough from the machine upon completion of the dough cycle. Roll into a long rope about 2 inches thick. Divide dough into 4 equal pieces and flatten each one into an oval between your hands. Fold one third (length-wise) of the dough towards the center and flatten with your hands. Fold the other third on top of the previous fold and flatten it again with your hands. Roll dough slightly to tighten; round the ends. Place dough seam side up on greased baking sheets. Cover and let rise in a warm, draft-free location for 45 minutes to 1 hour. While bread is rising, preheat oven to 400°. About 5 minutes before putting bread in oven, place a shallow pan with 1 or 2 inches of water on bottom shelf of oven or use another method to obtain a crisp crust (see pages 277–279). Slash top of each mini-loaf with a sharp knife or razor blade, spray or wash with cold water and bake for 10 to 15 minutes.

French Flatbread (Fougasse)

This crusty flatbread is enjoyed in Southern France. Use your favorite method to obtain a crisp crust (see pages 277–279).

Dough

1 cup water
2 tbs. olive oil
1 tsp. salt

3 cups bread flour
1 1/2 tsp. yeast

Wash

cold water

Remove dough from the machine upon completion of the dough cycle. Divide dough into 6 equal pieces and let rest for about 10 minutes. Roll each piece into an oval or triangle and place on a lightly greased baking sheet. Cover with a towel and let rise in a warm, draft-free location for 45 minutes to 1 hour. While bread is rising, preheat oven to 400°. About 5 minutes before putting bread in oven, place a shallow pan with 1 or 2 inches of water on bottom shelf of oven. With your fingertips, press several indentations into dough and then slash an X into top with a very sharp knife or a razor blade. Spray or brush with cold water. Bake for 10 to 12 minutes or until golden.

Pita Bread

Yield: 8 pitas

The secrets to getting pitas to puff are a very hot oven and a preheated baking sheet, pizza stone or pizza tiles. Let the pitas rise on a flat, cornmeal-covered surface (a rimless baking sheet or pizza peel) and slide them onto the heated pan or stone. If for some reason the pitas don't puff, wrap them around your filling.

Dough
1¼ cups water
3 tbs. olive oil
2 tbs. sugar

1 tsp. salt
3 cups bread flour
2 tsp. yeast

Wash
olive oil, optional

Remove dough from the machine upon completion of the dough cycle. Form dough into 8 equal balls and flatten each ball into a round with a rolling pin or your hands. Place on a cornmeal-covered pizza peel or other flat surface, cover with a towel and let rise in a warm, draft-free location for 20 to 30 minutes. Brush with olive oil, if desired. Slide pita rounds onto a preheated baking sheet or pizza stone in a preheated 500° oven for 8 to 12 minutes.

Persian Flatbread (Barbari)

Yield: 4 flatbreads

These traditional Iranian breads are used to scoop up foods or to soak up sauces. Unlike pita breads, these are scored to prevent pockets from forming. Various seeds (sesame, anise or fennel) can be sprinkled onto the dough just before baking.

Dough
1 cup water
2 tbs. olive oil
1 tsp. salt
3 cups all-purpose flour
2 tsp. yeast

Wash
olive oil

Topping
sesame, anise or fennel seeds, optional

Remove dough from the machine upon completion of the dough cycle and form into 4 equal balls. Brush each ball lightly with olive oil and roll or press each into a round or rectangle. Brush with additional oil if necessary to prevent sticking. Place on a lightly greased baking sheet, cover and let rise for 20 to 30 minutes. Brush tops with more olive oil. With a sharp knife or razor blade, score 4 or 5 parallel lines across the length and width of bread so that bread is covered with little squares. Top with seeds, if desired. Bake in a preheated 425° oven for 12 to 15 minutes.

Greek Psomi

Yield: 4 small loaves

Who can resist this light and airy bread with a crisp crust?

Dough
1 cup water
1 tbs. olive oil
2 tbs. honey

1 tsp. salt
3 cups bread flour
1 ½ tsp. yeast

Wash
cold water

Remove dough from the machine upon completion of the dough cycle. Roll into a long rope about 2 inches thick. Divide dough into 4 equal pieces and flatten each one into an oval between your hands. Fold one third (lengthwise) of the dough towards the center and flatten with your hands. Fold the other third on top of the previous fold and flatten it again with your hands. Roll dough slightly to tighten; round the ends. Place dough seam side up on greased baking sheets. Cover and let rise in a warm, draft-free location for 45 minutes to 1 hour. While bread is rising, preheat oven to 400°. About 5 minutes before putting bread in oven, place a shallow pan with 1 or 2 inches of water on bottom shelf of oven or use another method to obtain a crisp crust (see pages 277–279). Slash top of each mini-loaf with a sharp knife or razor blade, spray or wash with cold water and bake for 10 to 15 minutes.

French Flatbread (Fougasse)

Yield: 6 flatbreads

This crusty flatbread is enjoyed in Southern France. Use your favorite method to obtain a crisp crust (see pages 277–279).

Dough
1 cup water
2 tbs. olive oil
1 tsp. salt

3 cups bread flour
1 ½ tsp. yeast

Wash
cold water

Remove dough from the machine upon completion of the dough cycle. Divide dough into 6 equal pieces and let rest for about 10 minutes. Roll each piece into an oval or triangle and place on a lightly greased baking sheet. Cover with a towel and let rise in a warm, draft-free location for 45 minutes to 1 hour. While bread is rising, preheat oven to 400°. About 5 minutes before putting bread in oven, place a shallow pan with 1 or 2 inches of water on bottom shelf of oven. With your fingertips, press several indentations into dough and then slash an X into top with a very sharp knife or a razor blade. Spray or brush with cold water. Bake for 10 to 12 minutes or until golden.

Pita Bread

The secrets to getting pitas to puff are a very hot oven and a preheated baking sheet, pizza stone or pizza tiles. Let the pitas rise on a flat, cornmeal-covered surface (a rimless baking sheet or pizza peel) and slide them onto the heated pan or stone. If for some reason the pitas don't puff, wrap them around your filling.

Dough

1 ¼ cups water
3 tbs. olive oil
2 tbs. sugar

1 tsp. salt
3 cups bread flour
2 tsp. yeast

Wash
olive oil, optional

Remove dough from the machine upon completion of the dough cycle. Form dough into 8 equal balls and flatten each ball into a round with a rolling pin or your hands. Place on a cornmeal-covered pizza peel or other flat surface, cover with a towel and let rise in a warm, draft-free location for 20 to 30 minutes. Brush with olive oil, if desired. Slide pita rounds onto a preheated baking sheet or pizza stone in a preheated 500° oven for 8 to 12 minutes.

Persian Flatbread (Barbari)

Yield: 4 flatbreads

These traditional Iranian breads are used to scoop up foods or to soak up sauces. Unlike pita breads, these are scored to prevent pockets from forming. Various seeds (sesame, anise or fennel) can be sprinkled onto the dough just before baking.

Dough

1 cup water
2 tbs. olive oil
1 tsp. salt
3 cups all-purpose flour
2 tsp. yeast

Wash
olive oil

Topping
sesame, anise or fennel seeds,
    optional

Remove dough from the machine upon completion of the dough cycle and form into 4 equal balls. Brush each ball lightly with olive oil and roll or press each into a round or rectangle. Brush with additional oil if necessary to prevent sticking. Place on a lightly greased baking sheet, cover and let rise for 20 to 30 minutes. Brush tops with more olive oil. With a sharp knife or razor blade, score 4 or 5 parallel lines across the length and width of bread so that bread is covered with little squares. Top with seeds, if desired. Bake in a preheated 425° oven for 12 to 15 minutes.

Armenian Rolls

These delicious coffee rolls are based on an Armenian recipe that uses sesame seed paste (tahini) instead of peanut butter. Use tahini if you have it.

Dough
¾ cup milk
¼ cup butter or margarine
1 egg
2 tbs. sugar

½ tsp. salt
3½ cups all-purpose flour
1½ tsp. yeast

Filling
⅓-½ cup peanut butter
3-4 tbs. brown sugar

Wash
1 egg beaten with 1 scant tbs. milk

Upon completion of the dough cycle, divide dough into 8 equal pieces and roll into small 6- to 8-inch rectangles. Spread each one with a large spoonful of peanut butter and sprinkle with about 1 tsp. brown sugar. Roll each rectangle jelly-roll fashion, beginning on the wide side (see page 275), and pull into a long, twisted rope. Coil each rope (see page 273) and tuck the end underneath. Place on a greased baking sheet, cover and let rise in a warm, draft-free location for about 30 minutes. Brush tops with egg wash and bake in a preheated 350° oven for 15 to 20 minutes.

Mahlab Rings

This is a yeasted adaptation of a Middle Eastern pastry ring. Mahlab, from black cherry seeds, must be crushed with a mortar and pestle.

Dough
¾ cup milk
2 tbs. corn or vegetable oil
1 egg
2 tbs. sugar

1 tsp. salt
1 tsp. ground mahlab or allspice
3 cups all-purpose flour
1½ tsp. yeast

Filling
2 tbs. lemon juice
2 tbs. sugar

⅓-½ cup sesame seeds

Upon completion of the dough cycle, remove dough from the machine and roll into a large rectangle. Mix together lemon juice and sugar; coat dough with lemon mixture with a brush. Sprinkle with sesame seeds. Cut dough into small rectangles 6 inches x ½ inch. Twist each rectangle into a long spiral and curl into a ring, pinching ends closed to seal. Place twisted rings on a lightly greased baking sheet, cover with a towel and place in a warm, draft-free location to rise for about 1 hour. Bake in a preheated 350° oven for 20 to 25 minutes or until lightly browned.

Rosemary Raisin Bread

Yield: 4 rounds

This Italian bread is unique because the raisins are first sautéed in olive oil. The mashed raisins will impart flavor throughout the loaf. Use fresh rosemary if you can.

Dough

2 tbs. golden raisins sautéed in
   1 tbs. olive oil
1 cup water
1 tbs. honey
1 tsp. salt

1 tbs. chopped fresh rosemary,
   or 1 tsp. dried
3 cups bread flour
2 tsp. yeast

Remove raisins from heat and cool to lukewarm. Add raisins and olive oil to the bread machine with other liquid ingredients. Upon completion of the dough cycle, divide dough into 4 equal pieces. With your hands, flatten each piece into a 1-inch-thick round and place on a greased baking sheet. Cover and let rise in a warm, draft-free location for 20 to 30 minutes. Just before baking, slash an X in top of each round, wash or spray with cold water and bake in a preheated 350° oven for about 30 minutes or until golden brown.

Anise Sesame Rolls

Yield: 8-10 rolls

Not only is the combination of anise and sesame seeds a favorite in the Mediterranean countries and Middle East, but it is in Mexico too! Crush the anise seeds lightly with a mortar and pestle or between two spoons to bring out their flavor.

Dough

¾ cup milk
2 tbs. butter or margarine
1 egg
¼ cup sugar

1 tsp. salt
1 tsp. anise seed, lightly crushed
3 cups all-purpose flour
1½ tsp. yeast

Wash

1 egg white beaten
   with 1 tbs. water

Topping

sesame seeds

Upon completion of the dough cycle, remove dough from the machine and divide into 8 to 10 equal pieces. Place on a lightly greased baking sheet, cover and let rise for about 1 hour. With a sharp knife or razor blade, slash an X in the top of each roll. Brush with egg wash and liberally sprinkle with sesame seeds. Bake in a 350° oven for 15 to 20 minutes or until golden brown.

Mediterranean Cheese Flatbreads

Yield: 6 rounds

Substitute walnuts for pine nuts if desired.

Dough

1 cup water
2 tbs. olive oil
2 oz. (½ cup) grated mozzarella
   or feta cheese
1 tbs. chopped fresh basil,
   or 1 tsp. dried

1 tbs. sugar
1 tsp. salt
¼ cup ground pine nuts or walnuts
3 cups bread flour
1½ tsp. yeast

Wash

olive oil

Add ground pine nuts or walnuts to the machine 5 minutes after machine starts kneading, regardless of the type of machine. Upon completion of the dough cycle, remove dough and divide into 6 equal pieces. Roll each piece into a round and place on a lightly greased baking sheet. Cover with a towel and let rise in a warm, draft-free location for 45 minutes to 1 hour. With your fingertips, press several indentations into dough and then brush with olive oil. Bake in a preheated 500° oven for 5 to 8 minutes or until golden.

French Walnut Rolls

Yield: 6 rolls

These rustic French country breads are often served with nothing more than cheese. The walnuts add both flavor and color. Walnut oil, available in large grocery stores, imparts additional flavor. Vegetable oil can be substituted.

Dough

1 cup water
1 tbs. walnut or vegetable oil
1 tsp. sugar
½ tsp. salt

3 cups bread flour
1½ tsp. yeast
Add: ¼-⅓ cup chopped walnuts

Wash

cold water

Add walnuts to dough about 5 minutes after dough ball has formed. Upon completion of the dough cycle, remove dough from the machine, divide into 6 equal pieces and shape into balls. Place on a greased baking sheet, cover and let rise for 45 minutes to 1 hour. With a sharp razor blade or knife, cut an X or a tic-tac-toe pattern on top of each roll, brush or spray with cold water and bake in a preheated 350° oven until rolls are brown and sound hollow when tapped, about 15 to 20 minutes.

Golden Valencian Rolls

Yield: 8 rolls

The beaten egg white makes a meringue-like topping. The dough and the rolls are very heavy and dense in nature. Scrape the sides of the pan with a rubber spatula if necessary to help form a dough ball — and add a tiny bit of milk to soften the dough if the machine seems to struggle.

Dough

⅔ cup milk
⅓ cup vegetable oil
2 eggs

½ cup sugar
1 tsp. salt
4 cups all-purpose flour
2 tsp. yeast

Topping

1 egg white beaten until stiff

Additional Ingredient

sugar

Remove dough from the machine upon completion of the dough cycle. Divide dough into 8 equal pieces and shape each into a ball. Place on a greased baking sheet, cover and let rise in a warm, draft-free location for about 2 hours. After rising, gently spread 1 tsp. stiffly beaten egg white onto each ball. Sprinkle each with a pinch of sugar and bake in a preheated 350° oven for 30 to 35 minutes or until the bread is a deep golden color.

Spanish Sugar Rolls

Yield: 12 rolls

The secret to these sweet rolls is filling the slashed top with sugar. A few drops of yellow food coloring can be added to the dough for a richer color.

Dough

⅞ cup (7 oz.) water
2 tbs. butter or margarine
1 egg
¼ cup sugar

½ tsp. salt
3 cups all-purpose flour
2 tsp. yeast

Additional Ingredient

2 tbs. sugar

Wash

1 whole egg beaten with 2 tbs. milk

Remove dough from the machine upon completion of the dough cycle. Form dough into 12 equal balls or ovals. With a very sharp knife or razor blade, make a deep slash going about halfway through the middle of each ball. Place on a greased baking sheet, cover and let rise in a warm, draft-free location for about 1 hour. After rising, fill each slashed opening with ½ tsp. sugar. Brush tops of rolls with egg wash, avoiding sugared slashes, and bake in a preheated 350° oven for 15 to 20 minutes or until golden.

Kugelhopf

Serve this with fruit preserves for a festive treat. Special kugelhopf molds are available by mail order catalog or at kitchen specialty shops. I use a Bundt pan.

Dough
¾ cup milk
2 tbs. butter or margarine
3 eggs
½ cup sugar
1 tsp. salt
3½ cups all-purpose flour
2 tsp. yeast
Add: ½ cup golden raisins or chopped favorite dried fruit (or combination)
Add: ¼ cup chopped or sliced almonds

Additional Ingredient
¼ cup coarsely chopped or sliced almonds
confectioners' sugar

Add raisins and ¼ cup almonds to the machine about 5 minutes after the dough ball has been formed. Heavily grease a Bundt pan or kugelhopf mold and sprinkle additional ¼ cup almonds on the bottom. Upon completion of the dough cycle, scrape dough into prepared pan. Cover with a kitchen towel and let rise for 1½ to 2 hours in a warm, draft-free location. Bake in a preheated 350° oven for about 30 minutes until nicely browned. Cool on a wire rack. Dust with confectioners' sugar.

Croissants

Yield: about 12 medium croissants

The key to flaky, light croissants is folding butter into the dough repeatedly. The soft dough is easier to work if it has been refrigerated before each folding. Making croissants is not a difficult process, but it is somewhat time-consuming because of the need to work the dough every half hour or so. If at any time the dough becomes too sticky or the butter starts to break through, place it in the refrigerator for 10 to 15 minutes. The dough is a bit on the wet side, which contributes to the lightness of the final product, so add flour only if necessary. Croissants can be frozen and then heated in a medium (350° to 375°) oven for about 5 minutes.

Dough
1 ¼ cups milk
1 tbs. sugar
½ tsp. salt
3 cups all-purpose flour
2 tsp. yeast

Additional Ingredients
¾ cup butter, softened
1 tbs. butter, melted

Remove dough pan with dough from the machine upon completion of the dough cycle. If you have a Welbilt, DAK or Citizen machine with a hole in the pan, remove dough from pan and put it in a greased bowl. Seal bread machine pan or bowl with plastic wrap and refrigerate for about 30 minutes.

On a very lightly floured work surface, roll dough into a large rectangle. Spread softened butter evenly over dough, leaving a ½-inch border. Fold dough into thirds, as you would a business letter. Wrap dough in plastic wrap (or use a large plastic bag) and return to refrigerator for 30 minutes. Repeat this process 3 more times (4 foldings total; 2 hours total in the refrigerator).

After the final fold and the final 30-minute refrigeration, roll dough back into a large rectangle. With a sharp knife, pastry or pizza wheel, cut dough into squares of about 5 inches. Slice each square in half to form 2 triangles. Starting at the wide end, tightly roll dough so that the small, pointed end is on top and place on a lightly greased baking sheet. Cover and let rise in a warm, draft-free location for about 30 minutes. If baking the croissants in the morning, wrap baking sheet loosely in plastic and put it in the refrigerator. In the morning, remove croissants on baking sheet and let them come up to room temperature while you preheat the oven, about 20 minutes. Brush croissants with melted butter and bake in a preheated 350° oven for about 20 minutes or until golden.

Scottish Rowies

Yield: 10-12 rolls

These buttery breads are a cross between croissants and rolls and are truly decadent! Use butter and not margarine, as the margarine tends to leak out the sides too much during rolling.

Dough

1 ⅛ cups milk
2 tbs. butter
1 tbs. sugar

1 tsp. salt
3 cups all-purpose flour
1 ½ tsp. yeast

Filling
½ cup butter, softened

Remove dough from the machine upon completion of the dough cycle and loosely wrap in a plastic bag or plastic wrap. Place in the refrigerator for 15 to 20 minutes — cold dough will be easier to handle.

Roll dough into a large rectangle on a lightly floured work surface. Spread butter evenly on top of dough and fold dough into thirds, as you would a business letter. Wrap folded dough in plastic wrap again and return to the refrigerator for 20 to 30 more minutes. Roll dough again into a large rectangle and fold into thirds. Wrap folded dough in plastic wrap and return to the refrigerator for 20 to 30 more minutes. Repeat this process one more time.

After the final refrigerated rise, roll dough into a large rectangle. With a knife, pastry or pizza wheel, cut dough into 2- to 3-inch squares. Place squares on a lightly greased baking sheet, cover and let rise for about 1 hour. Bake in a preheated 350° oven for 25 to 30 minutes or until puffed and golden.

German Farm Bread

This bread rises in a banneton or a muslin-lined basket, which leaves traditional ridges. Bannetons are available at large gourmet shops or through mail order catalogs. If you do not have one, use a medium-sized round woven basket or a large glass bowl. Place a 12- to 14-inch square piece of muslin in the basket or bowl and sprinkle it with 2 or 3 tbs. flour. Place the dough in the muslin-covered basket to rise and then turn onto a baking sheet or stone for baking. The dough will have indentations from the basket ridges.

Dough
1 1/4 cups water
2 tbs. butter or margarine
2 tbs. brown sugar
1 tsp. salt

1/2 cup whole wheat flour
1/2 cup rye flour
1/2 cup oats
2 cups bread flour
2 tsp. yeast

Wash
cold water

Topping
caraway seeds or other favorite seeds

For a loaf: Remove dough from the machine upon completion of the dough cycle. Place in a prepared banneton or basket to rise in a warm, draft-free location for about 2 hours or until double in bulk. Carefully turn loaf onto a greased baking sheet or stone so that the patterned side is up. Bake in a preheated 375° oven for about 30 minutes or until loaf is well browned and sounds hollow when tapped.

For rolls: Remove dough from the machine upon completion of the dough cycle and divide into 12 equal pieces. Shape each piece into a roll, place on a lightly greased baking sheet, cover and let rise for about 1 hour. Brush or spray rolls with cold water and sprinkle with caraway or other seeds if desired. Bake in a preheated 375° oven for about 20 minutes.

Middle Eastern Flatbread (Churek)

Yield: 6 flatbreads

These Middle Eastern flatbreads are best eaten warm, right out of the oven. They do not rise for very long and are quick and easy to make. Eat warm with a meal or with cheese as a snack.

Dough
1 1/8 cups water
2 tbs. olive oil
1/2 tsp. salt
3 cups bread flour
2 tsp. yeast

Wash
cold water

Topping
sesame seeds or other favorite seeds

Remove dough from the machine upon completion of the dough cycle and divide into 6 equal pieces. Roll each piece into a small, thin round and place on a lightly greased baking sheet. Cover and let rest for 10 to 15 minutes. Brush or spray with cold water and sprinkle with sesame seeds if desired. Bake in a preheated 350° oven for about 15 minutes.

Challah

Yield: 1 braided loaf

This Jewish egg bread is enjoyed by people of all religions any day of the year. If you want a really deep yellow color, use 2 yolks instead of 1 of the eggs, or just cheat a little and add some yellow food coloring.

Dough
3/4 cup milk
2 tbs. butter or margarine
2 eggs
1/4 cup sugar
1 tsp. salt
3 cups all-purpose flour
1 1/2 tsp. yeast

Wash
1 egg mixed with 2 tbs. milk or cream

Topping
poppy seeds

Remove dough from the machine upon completion of the dough cycle. Divide dough into 3 equal pieces. On a lightly floured work surface, roll each piece into a long, slender rope. Braid the 3 ropes together (see page 275), place on a lightly greased baking sheet, cover and let rise in a warm, draft-free location for 1 to 1 1/2 hours. Brush with egg wash, sprinkle with poppy seeds and bake in a preheated 350° oven until golden, about 25 to 30 minutes.

Butterflake Rounds

These Middle Eastern breads remind me of a combination of croissants and pita breads! Eat warm with fruit preserves or cheese (or all by themselves!).

Dough
1 cup milk
2 tbs. butter
1 egg
1 tbs. sugar
½ tsp. salt
3 cups all-purpose flour
1½ tsp. yeast

Filling
2 tbs. butter, melted

Wash
1 egg beaten with 2 tbs. milk or cream

Topping
sesame seeds

Remove dough from the machine upon completion of the dough cycle. Divide dough into 8 equal pieces and roll each into a large, thin round. Spread rounds with melted butter and roll each up tightly in jelly-roll fashion (see page 275). Coil each roll and flatten into a small round. Place flattened round on a greased baking sheet, cover and let rise for about 45 minutes. Wash with egg wash and sprinkle with sesame seeds. Bake in a preheated 350° oven for about 12 minutes or until golden.

Chinese Steamed Buns

Steam these buns in a bamboo basket set in a covered wok (in traditional Chinese fashion), or in a vegetable steamer, and serve hot with meat.

1⅛ cups water
1 tbs. brown sugar

3 cups all-purpose flour
1½ tsp. yeast

Remove dough from the machine upon completion of the dough cycle. Form dough into about 24 equal balls, place on a lightly greased baking sheet or waxed paper, cover and let rest for about 20 minutes. Meanwhile, bring water to a boil in the bottom of the steamer. Place rolls in steamer basket, leaving at least 1 inch between rolls. Steam rolls for about 10 minutes or until firm and cooked through. The rolls can be resteamed if necessary. Serve hot.

Italian Sweet Wreath

Yield: 1 loaf

This recipe is based on a recipe for an Italian Corona Dolce, or a sweet wreath, which is served at holiday times. The flavorful topping makes this bread stand apart.

Dough
1 1/3 cups water
2 tbs. butter or margarine
2 tbs. sugar
1 tsp. salt
4 cups all-purpose flour
2 tsp. yeast

Topping
1/4 cup sugar
1 tsp. cinnamon
1 tsp. anise seed
1/8 tsp. nutmeg

Wash
1 egg beaten with 2 tbs. water

Remove dough from the machine upon completion of the dough cycle and place on a lightly floured work surface. Divide dough into 3 equal pieces, roll each piece into a long, slender rope and braid ropes together (see page 275). Shape braid into a wreath-shaped circle and pinch ends together to seal. Place on a lightly greased baking sheet. Cover and let rise for 30 to 40 minutes in a warm, draft-free location. Mix topping ingredients together. Brush top with egg wash and sprinkle with topping. Bake in a preheated 350° oven for about 20 minutes or until golden brown.

Greek Holiday Bread

Yield: 1 loaf

This holiday bread is either braided or made into a simple round loaf and stamped with a floured church seal before rising. Mahlab is part of the seed of the black cherry and must be crushed with a mortar and pestle.

Dough
2/3 cup milk
2 tbs. butter or margarine
2 eggs
1/2 cup sugar
1 tsp. salt

1/2 tsp. cinnamon
1 tsp. ground mahlab or allspice
3 cups all-purpose flour
2 tsp. yeast

Wash
1 egg yolk beaten with 1-2 tbs. milk

Topping
almond meal (finely ground almonds)

Remove dough from the machine upon completion of the dough cycle and divide into 3 equal pieces. Roll each piece on a lightly floured work surface into a long, slender rope. Braid ropes together (see page 275), place on a lightly greased baking sheet, cover and let rise in a warm, draft-free location for about 1 hour. Brush with egg wash and sprinkle liberally with almond meal. Bake in a preheated 350° oven until golden, about 25 to 30 minutes.

Middle Eastern Filled Holiday Buns

Yield: 12-15 buns

These sweet rolls are traditional for both Easter and Christmas. Mahlab is part of the seed of the black cherry and must be crushed with a mortar and pestle. It is possible that you can find it at a Middle Eastern restaurant, but the easiest way to find it is by mail order. Allspice can be used as a substitute. Start with 3 cups flour and add more if necessary to obtain the right consistency.

Dough
½ cup water
¼ cup vegetable oil
3 eggs
2 tbs. sugar
1 tsp. salt
1-2 tsp. ground mahlab or allspice
3-3¼ cups all-purpose flour
2 tsp. yeast

Filling
½ cup finely chopped dates
½ cup finely ground almonds
1 tsp. cinnamon
½ tsp. nutmeg
about 2 tbs. honey

Wash
1 egg beaten with 1 tbs. milk

While dough is rising in the machine, make filling. In a medium bowl, combine dates, almonds, cinnamon and nutmeg. Add honey. With your hands, mix until filling is well blended; set aside.

Upon completion of the dough cycle, remove dough from machine. If dough is sticky, knead in only enough flour so that it is easily handled. Divide into 12 to 15 equal pieces. Form each piece into a ball and stuff each one with a large spoonful of filling (see page 276). Pinch ends together to seal. Place rolls in greased muffin cups. Cover and let rise in a warm, draft-free location for about 30 minutes. Brush with egg wash. Bake in a preheated 350° oven for 15 to 20 minutes.

Hot Cross Buns

Traditionally eaten all over the world on Good Friday, these buns have a cross made with confectioners' sugar glaze on top. This variation uses dried fruits.

⅞ cup (7 oz.) milk
2 tbs. butter or margarine
1 egg
¼ cup sugar
1 tsp. salt

1 tsp. lemon or orange peel or 1 tsp. cinnamon
3 cups all-purpose flour
1½ tsp. yeast
Add: ½ cup dried fruits of choice

Glaze
Confectioners' Sugar Glaze with vanilla, almond or orange extract, page 342

Add fruit to the machine pan after dough ball has been formed, about 5 to 8 minutes into the kneading phase. Remove dough from machine upon completion of the dough cycle. Divide dough into 12 equal pieces, shape into small balls and place in lightly greased muffin cups. Cover and let rise for about 1 hour in a warm, draft-free location. Just before baking, score a cross into the top of each bun with a sharp razor blade or knife. Bake in a preheated 350° oven for 15 to 20 minutes. While buns are still warm, drizzle glaze in a cross on top of each bun.

Easter Bagels (Tadale)

Donna Harrington always made her grandmother's recipe by hand for Easter to give to friends. She can now make it by machine. The original recipe calls for shortening instead of butter. These are really rich and delicious!

¾ cup milk
5 tbs. butter or shortening
1 egg
½ cup sugar

½ tsp. salt
1½ tsp. anise seed, or to taste
3½ cups all-purpose flour
2 tsp. yeast

Remove dough from the machine upon completion of the dough cycle and divide into 12 equal balls. Shape dough like bagels by forming a bun, pushing a hole in the middle with your thumb and stretching it a little. Drop bagels into gently boiling water a few at a time. When they come to the top, they are ready to bake. Place on the bottom rack of the oven or directly on a pizza stone. Bake in a preheated 350° oven for 30 to 35 minutes or until golden brown.

Greek Easter Bread (Tsoureki)

Yield: 1 braided loaf

This version of tsoureki is made with crushed anise seeds (use a mortar and a pestle) although mahlab is also frequently used. For a deeper yellow color, use food coloring or two egg yolks instead of one egg.

Dough
¾ cup milk
¼ cup butter or margarine
1 egg
¼ cup sugar
1 tsp. salt

1 tsp. dried lemon peel, or freshly
  grated to taste
1 tsp. ground anise seeds
3 cups all-purpose flour
2 tsp. yeast

Wash
1 egg yolk beaten with 1-2 tbs. milk

Remove dough from the machine upon completion of the dough cycle. Divide dough into 3 equal pieces and roll each piece on a lightly floured work surface into a long, slender rope. Braid ropes together, place on a lightly greased baking sheet, cover and let rise in a warm, draft-free location for about 1 hour. Brush with egg yolk wash and bake in a preheated 350° oven until golden, about 25 to 30 minutes.

Turkish Easter Bread

Yield: 1 loaf

The mahlab can be replaced with allspice. Add yellow food coloring to the milk for a deeper color if desired.

Dough
1 cup milk
2 tbs. butter or margarine
1 egg yolk
¼ cup sugar

1 tsp. salt
1 tsp. ground mahlab or allspice
3 cups all-purpose flour
2 tsp. yeast

Wash
1 egg yolk beaten with 1-2 tbs.
  milk or cream

Topping
finely chopped almonds or hazelnuts

Upon completion of the dough cycle, remove dough from the machine. Divide dough into 3 equal pieces and roll each piece on a lightly floured work surface into a long, slender rope. Braid ropes together (see page 275), place on a lightly greased baking sheet, cover and let rise in a warm, draft-free location for 1 to 1½ hours. Brush with egg yolk wash, sprinkle with nuts and bake in a preheated 350° oven until golden, about 25 to 30 minutes.

Danish Christmas Bread (Julkage)

This Christmas bread is similar to Pulla, but with dried fruits and nuts.

Dough

1 cup milk
1 egg
2 tbs. butter or margarine
1 tsp. vanilla extract
1/4 cup sugar
1 tsp. salt
1/2 tsp. cinnamon
1/2 tsp. dried lemon peel, or freshly grated to taste
1/2 tsp. ground cardamom
3 cups all-purpose flour
2 tsp. yeast
Add: 1/2 cup dried fruits (raisins, cherries)
Add: 1/4-1/2 cup chopped almonds

Wash

1 egg beaten with 2 tbs. milk or cream

Add dried fruits and nuts to the machine pan about 5 minutes after kneading has started. Remove dough from the machine upon completion of the dough cycle and divide into 3 equal pieces. Roll each piece into a long rope and braid ropes together (see page 275). Place braid on a lightly greased baking pan, cover and let rise for about 1 1/2 hours. Brush dough with egg wash and bake in a preheated 350° oven for 25 to 30 minutes or until golden.

German Stollen

A traditional Christmas bread, stollen is often packed with candied orange peels, citron or dried fruits. This adaptation uses dried fruits. Because of the high amount of sugar, this bread is a heavy, dense loaf that does not rise very high, even with a long rising time.

Dough

1/4 cup orange juice
3/4 cup milk
2 tbs. butter or margarine
1 tsp. rum extract
1 tsp. almond extract
1/4 cup sugar
1/2 tsp. salt
1 tsp. dried orange peel, or freshly grated to taste

1/2 tsp. cinnamon
3 cups all-purpose flour
2 tsp. yeast
Add: 1/4 cup golden raisins
Add: 1/4-1/3 cup dried cherries, blueberries, dried cranberries or a combination
Add: 1/4-1/3 cup chopped almonds

Glaze

Orange Glaze or *Confectioners' Sugar Glaze*, pages 343 or 342

Add fruits and nuts to the machine pan after dough has formed a ball, about 5 minutes into the first kneading. Allow dough to sit in the machine undisturbed for about 2 hours after completion of the dough cycle. If you have a 1 lb. machine, place dough in a large, greased bowl, cover it and place it in a warm draft-free location. Because dough is so heavy, it will not rise very high. Remove dough from machine upon completion of the dough cycle and roll it into a thick 8-x-12-inch oval on a lightly floured work surface. Fold dough in half lengthwise with the top half folding over about 3/4 of the bottom, and press to seal seams together. Place on a lightly greased baking sheet, cover and let rise in a warm, draft-free location for about 2 hours. Bake in a preheated 350° oven until golden, about 35 to 40 minutes.

Scandinavian Sweet Bread (Pulla)

Yield: 1 loaf

This Scandinavian sweet bread is often served at Christmastime and is either braided or made into animal shapes.

Dough

1 cup milk	1 tsp. salt
2 tbs. butter or margarine	1/2-1 tsp. ground cardamom
1 egg	3 cups all-purpose flour
1 tsp. vanilla or almond extract	2 tsp. yeast
1/4 cup sugar	

Wash

1 egg beaten with 2 tbs. milk or cream

Remove dough from the machine upon completion of the dough cycle and divide into 3 equal pieces. Roll each piece into a long rope and braid ropes together (see page 275). Place braid on a lightly greased baking pan, cover and let rise for about 1 1/2 hours. Brush dough with egg wash and bake in a preheated 350° oven for 25 to 30 minutes or until golden.

St. Lucia Buns

Yield: 12 buns

These buns are traditionally served to Swedish families by the eldest daughter at dawn on December 13th. They can be enjoyed on any day.

Dough

pinch saffron, or 1-2 drops yellow food coloring	1/3 cup sugar
1 cup milk	1/2 tsp. salt
1/4 cup butter	3 cups all-purpose flour
1 tsp. vanilla extract	2 tsp. yeast

Wash

1 egg beaten with 1-2 tbs. cream or milk

Topping

a few raisins

Remove dough from the machine upon completion of the dough cycle. Divide into 24 equal pieces and roll into long, slender ropes. Using 2 ropes for each bun, make an X and then coil dough. Place on a greased baking sheet, cover and let rise for about 40 to 50 minutes. Brush with egg wash and place a few raisins decoratively in center of coils. Bake in a preheated 350° oven until golden, about 20 to 25 minutes.

Bread of the Kings

This bread is traditionally eaten in both Spain and Mexico on Epiphany (January 6). There is a cake-like version that is also eaten in New Orleans but it is not a yeast-leavened product. Hidden in the bread (or cake) is a small trinket or coin (I use a nut), which brings good luck to the person who finds it. I use either fruit bits (from the grocery store) or a combination of dried cherries, blueberries and golden raisins.

Dough
1 cup milk
1 egg
3 tbs. butter or margarine
1 tsp. vanilla or almond extract
1 tsp. salt
¼ cup sugar
1 tsp. dried lemon peel, or freshly grated to taste
3½ cups all-purpose flour
2 tsp. yeast
Add: ½ cup mixed dried fruits

Additional Ingredient
1 small nut (½ almond or pecan or ¼ walnut)

Wash
1 egg beaten with 1-2 tbs. milk

Add fruits to the machine pan after the dough ball has formed, about 5 to 8 minutes after the kneading starts. Heavily grease a Bundt or angel food cake pan. Upon completion of the dough cycle, remove dough from machine and push nut into dough. Shape and place dough in prepared pan. Cover with a kitchen towel and let rise for 1½ to 2 hours in a warm, draft-free location. Bake in a preheated 350° oven for about 30 minutes or until nicely browned. Cool on a wire rack.

Greek New Year Bread (Vasilopita)

Yield: 1 loaf

Like Bread of the Kings, a coin (in years past a gold one) is hidden inside this loaf of bread, which is eaten at midnight on New Year's Eve. The one who finds the coin, according to tradition, is blessed with luck during the New Year.

Dough
⅞ cup (7 oz.) milk
1 egg
2 tbs. butter or margarine
2 tsp. almond extract
½ cup sugar
1 tsp. salt
1 tsp. ground mahlab or allspice
1 tsp. cinnamon
1 tsp. dried orange peel, or freshly grated to taste
3 cups all-purpose flour
2 tsp. yeast

Additional Ingredient
1 small nut (½ almond or pecan or ¼ walnut)

Wash
1 egg yolk beaten with 1-2 tbs. milk or cream

Topping
sliced or chopped almonds

Remove dough from the machine upon completion of the dough cycle. Roll dough into a large rectangle on a floured work surface. Add only enough flour to prevent sticking. Place a small nut somewhere on the dough. With scissors, a sharp knife or a pastry or pizza wheel, cut 1-inch strips down both sides of the dough from the center third to the side. Fold down a 1-inch piece of dough over the center third and then alternately fold side strips over, angling each folded strip down. Tuck ends inside to give the appearance of a braid (see mock braid, page 276). Place on a greased baking sheet, cover and let rise in a warm, draft-free location for about 1 hour. Brush with egg yolk wash, sprinkle with nuts and bake in a preheated 350° oven until golden, about 30 to 35 minutes.

About Glazes and Butters

A glaze is spread over the cooked bread while it is still warm. While glazes may be applied with a pastry brush, it is very common to simply pour the glaze over an entire loaf of bread or to spoon the glaze on top of rolls or shaped breads. Glazes are typically sweet and used on rich and/or sweet breads.

Butters and spreads are very easy to make and can be that special finishing touch for bread. For gifts or for special meals, chill the butters in fancy little shapes or fill small ramekins or decorative jars. Flavored butters can be wrapped tightly in plastic or wrapped paper and frozen for 6 weeks or refrigerated for about 1 week.

Butter logs or rolls are easily made by placing the butter on a piece of plastic wrap and rolling it up into a roll. Twist the ends and tie closed. Chill until firm, about 1 hour.

Butters molded with cookie cutters are extremely easy to make for a great presentation. Select a (holiday-shaped) cookie cutter that is open on both top and bottom. Spray it with nonstick vegetable spray and place on a piece of waxed paper. Fill with butter and refrigerate for several hours. When firm, carefully push the butter out of the cutter onto a small plate to serve.

Butter molds can be found in gourmet shops or mail order catalogs. Follow the directions that come with the molds.

Confectioners' Sugar Glaze

This is the basis for literally hundreds of variations of glazes. While the common extract used is vanilla, try almond, lemon, coconut or rum to complement the flavor of the bread. The thicker the glaze, the heavier it will be. A light glaze will pour easily.

½ cup confectioners' sugar
1-2 tbs. milk
½ tsp. extract

Mix ingredients together in a small bowl. Adjust consistency with milk as desired.

Orange Glaze

Orange juice can be substituted for the concentrate, but it will have less orange flavor.

½ cup confectioners' sugar
1-2 tbs. frozen orange juice concentrate
1 tsp. orange extract
½ tsp. orange peel

Mix ingredients together in a small bowl. Adjust consistency with juice concentrate as desired.

Coconut Glaze

Try this glaze with any chocolate or coconut breads.

½ cup confectioners' sugar
¼ cup coconut flakes
2-3 tbs. milk
1 tsp. coconut extract

Mix ingredients together in a small bowl. Adjust consistency with milk as desired.

Walnut Butter

This is really delicious spread on top of Walnut Raisin Cinnamon Rolls, page 294. I use walnuts, but any other nut can be used as a variation. The light toasting enhances the flavor of the nuts.

½ cup walnut pieces
½ cup unsalted butter, softened
1 tbs. honey

Spread nuts on a greased baking sheet and bake in a preheated 350° oven for about 10 minutes. Cool. Process cooled nuts with a food processor until finely chopped. Add softened butter and honey; process until blended.

Rum Glaze

If you prefer, you can use ½ tbs. rum extract and a little water as a substitute for the rum.

½ cup confectioners' sugar
1 tbs. rum
1 tbs. butter, melted

Mix ingredients together in a small bowl. Adjust consistency with rum or water as desired.

Fruit Glaze

This simple glaze gives breads a festive, holiday presentation — great for gifts.

½ cup fruit preserves or jam (apricot, orange, etc.)
1 tbs. brandy

Melt preserves or jam in the top of a double boiler over low heat. Remove from heat, stir in brandy and strain through cheesecloth into a small bowl. Apply strained glaze while bread is still warm.

Lemon Glaze

Use this as a special finishing touch for any bread that contains lemon peel.

½ cup confectioners' sugar
1-2 tbs. lemon juice
1 tsp. almond extract
dried lemon peel, or freshly grated to taste

Mix ingredients together in a small bowl. Adjust consistency with lemon juice as desired.

Orange Ginger Butter

This can be eaten on just about any bread, and could also be served with vegetables.

½ cup butter, softened
¼ cup orange marmalade
½-1 tsp. chopped fresh ginger

Cream butter in a mixer or food processor. Add remaining ingredients and process until well blended. Chill for at least 1 hour to set. Serve chilled or at room temperature.

Basil Butter

This is a great accompaniment to any herb roll or bread. Any fresh herb (such as mint, parsley or cilantro) can be used instead of the basil.

½ cup butter, softened
¼ cup basil leaves, lightly packed
½ tsp. coarsely ground pepper

Cream butter in a mixer or food processor. Add remaining ingredients and process until well blended. Chill for at least 1 hour to set. Serve chilled or at room temperature.

Cranbutter

This is a sweet butter spread for a fall breakfast treat or with sweet rolls for Thanksgiving dinner.

½ cup butter, softened
¼ cup confectioners' sugar
3-4 mandarin orange segments
½ tsp. orange peel
¼ cup fresh cranberries

Cream butter in a mixer or food processor. Add remaining ingredients and process until well blended. Chill for at least 1 hour to set. Serve chilled or at room temperature.

Spicy Honey Butter

Apple pie or pumpkin pie spice adds pizzazz to ordinary honey butter.

½ cup butter, softened
2 tbs. honey
1 tsp. apple or pumpkin pie spice

Cream butter in a mixer or food processor. Add remaining ingredients and process until well blended. Chill for at least 1 hour to set. Serve chilled or at room temperature.

Orange Cheese Spread

This dresses up any sweet roll.

4 oz. cream cheese, softened
½ cup confectioners' sugar
1 tsp. orange peel
1-2 tbs. frozen orange juice concentrate, thawed

Put cream cheese in a mixer or food processor. Add remaining ingredients and mix or process until well blended. Chill for at least 1 hour to set. Serve chilled or at room temperature.

Herbed Yogurt Cheese Spread

You can add flavored extracts and fruits to yogurt cheese for sweet spreads and dessert toppings. Yogurt cheese makers are available through kitchen or gourmet shops, but a colander can also be used. The whey can be used in bread making as a dough enhancer and conditioner. Add 1-2 tsp. to the bottom of the measuring cup before adding the liquid.

½ cup yogurt cheese*
1 tsp. or 1 clove minced garlic
½ tsp. coarse black pepper
¼ cup chopped fresh herbs

Stir finely chopped herbs into yogurt cheese and chill.

*To make yogurt cheese: Line a small colander with several thicknesses of coffee filters and rest the colander over a small bowl. Place nonfat yogurt without gelatin in the colander and refrigerate for several hours. The whey will drain into the bowl, leaving a thick yogurt with a consistency similar to softened cream cheese. Yield is about half, or 1 cup yogurt cheese from 2 cups yogurt.

Index